An Ordinary Life?

Ohio University Press Polish and Polish-American Studies Series

Series Editor: John J. Bukowczyk, Wayne State University

Framing the Polish Home: Postwar Cultural Constructions of Hearth, Nation, and Self, edited by Bozena Shallcross
Traitors and True Poles: Narrating a Polish-American Identity, 1880–1939, by Karen Majewski
Auschwitz, Poland, and the Politics of Commemoration, 1945–1979, by Jonathan Huener
The Exile Mission: The Polish Political Diaspora and Polish Americans, 1939–1956, by Anna D. Jaroszyńska-Kirchmann
The Grasinski Girls: The Choices They Had and the Choices They Made, by Mary Patrice Erdmans
Testaments: Two Novellas of Emigration and Exile, by Danuta Mostwin
The Clash of Moral Nations: Cultural Politics in Piłsudski's Poland, 1926–1935, by Eva Plach
Holy Week: A Novel of the Warsaw Ghetto Uprising, by Jerzy Andrzejewski
The Law of the Looking Glass: Cinema in Poland, 1896–1939, by Sheila Skaff
Rome's Most Faithful Daughter: The Catholic Church and Independent Poland, 1914–1939, by Neal Pease
The Origins of Modern Polish Democracy, edited by M. B. B. Biskupski, James S. Pula, and Piotr J. Wróbel
The Borders of Integration: Polish Migrants in Germany and the United States, 1870–1924, by Brian McCook
Between the Brown and the Red: Nationalism, Catholicism, and Communism in Twentieth-Century Poland—The Politics of Bolesław Piasecki, by Mikołaj Stanisław Kunicki
Taking Liberties: Gender, Transgressive Patriotism, and Polish Drama, 1786–1989, by Halina Filipowicz
The Politics of Morality: The Church, the State, and Reproductive Rights in Postsocialist Poland, by Joanna Mishtal
Marta, by Eliza Orzeszkowa, translated by Anna Gąsienica Byrcyn and Stephanie Kraft, with an introduction by Grażyna J. Kozaczka
Writing the Polish American Woman in Postwar Ethnic Fiction, by Grażyna J. Kozaczka
Colonial Fantasies, Imperial Realities: Race Science and the Making of Polishness on the Fringes of the German Empire, 1840–1920, by Lenny A. Ureña Valerio
An Ordinary Life? The Journeys of Tonia Lechtman, 1918–1996, by Anna Müller

Series Advisory Board

M. B. B. Biskupski, Central Connecticut State University
Robert E. Blobaum, West Virginia University
Anthony Bukoski, University of Wisconsin-Superior
Bogdana Carpenter, University of Michigan
Mary Patrice Erdmans, Case Western University
Thomas S. Gladsky, Central Missouri State University (ret.)
Padraic Kenney, Indiana University
John J. Kulczycki, University of Illinois at Chicago (ret.)
Ewa Morawska, University of Essex
Antony Polonsky, Brandeis University
Brian Porter-Szűcs, University of Michigan
James S. Pula, Purdue University Northwest
Daniel Stone, University of Winnipeg
Adam Walaszek, Jagiellonian University
Theodore R. Weeks, Southern Illinois University

An Ordinary Life?

The Journeys of Tonia Lechtman, 1918–1996

Anna Müller

OHIO UNIVERSITY PRESS
ATHENS

Ohio University Press, Athens, Ohio 45701
ohioswallow.com
© 2023 by Ohio University Press
All rights reserved

To obtain permission to quote, reprint, or otherwise reproduce or distribute material from Ohio University Press publications, please contact our rights and permissions department at (740) 593-1154 or (740) 593-4536 (fax).

Printed in the United States of America
Ohio University Press books are printed on acid-free paper ∞ ™

Cover photo: Tonia working for the Unitarian Service Committee.
From the private collection of Vera and Marcel Lechtman)

Author photograph by Amy Kimball

Library of Congress Cataloging-in-Publication Data
Names: Müller, Anna, 1975– author.
Title: An ordinary life? : the journeys of Tonia Lechtman, 1918–1996 / Anna Müller.
Other titles: Journeys of Tonia Lechtman, 1918–1996
Description: Athens : Ohio University Press, [2023] | Series: Polish and Polish-American studies series | Includes bibliographical references and index.
Identifiers: LCCN 2022036331 (print) | LCCN 2022036332 (ebook) | ISBN 9780821424971 (hardcover) | ISBN 9780821447826 (pdf)
Subjects: LCSH: Lechtman, Tonia, 1918–1996. | Jews, Polish—Europe—Biography. | Jewish communists—Poland—Biography. | Jewish women—Biography. | Jewish refugees—Biography. | Holocaust survivors—Biography. | Jews, Polish—Israel—Biography.
Classification: LCC DS134.72.L399 M85 2023 (print) | LCC DS134.72.L399 (ebook) | DDC 940.53/18092 [B]—dc23/eng/20220815
LC record available at https://lccn.loc.gov/2022036331
LC ebook record available at https://lccn.loc.gov/2022036332

The Polish and Polish-American Studies Series is made possible by:

The Polish American Historical Association and the Stanley Kulczycki Publication Fund of the Polish American Historical Association, New Britain, Connecticut,

The Stanislaus A. Blejwas Endowed Chair in Polish and Polish American Studies, Central Connecticut State University, New Britain, Connecticut,

The Frank and Mary Padzieski Endowed Professorship in Polish/Polish American/Eastern European Studies at the University of Michigan, Dearborn,

The Kosciuszko Foundation,

The Piast Institute, and

The Polish Institute of Arts and Sciences of America.

Support is also provided by the following individuals:

Thomas Duszak (Benefactor)
George Bobinski (Contributor)
Alfred Bialobrzeski (Friend)
William Galush (Friend)
Col. John A. and Pauline A. Garstka (Friend)
Jonathan Huener (Friend)
Grażyna Kozaczka (Friend)
Neal Pease (Friend)
Mary Jane Urbanowicz (Friend)
Maria Swiecicka-Ziemianek (Friend)

I expected this to be an easy book to write.

To portray the life story of one woman—

why should that pose any serious writing problems?

I also expected this to be a short book.

The life story of one woman—why should that require a very long book?

—Ruth Behar, *Translated Woman*

Contents

List of Illustrations	xi
Series Editor's Preface	xiii
Acknowledgments	xv
Guide to Pronunciation	xix
Introduction	1
1. Bobbin Lace and Assimilation *The Life of a Jewish Family in Łódź, 1918–1935*	19
2. A Dream of New Life *Communism and Palestine, 1935–1938*	43
3. "Flies in Amber" *Paris, Spain, and the World of Letters, 1937–1942*	70
4. Life on the Run *War and Uncertainty in France, 1939–1942*	109
5. Mother, Refugee, and Social Worker *Life in Switzerland, 1942–1945*	149
6. The Return *Building Communism in Poland, 1945–1954*	189
7. "Life Is So Knotty" *The Final Return, 1954–1996*	235
Conclusion	277
Notes	287
Index	343

Illustrations

Maps

4.1	Tonia's travels through France, 1937–42	110
5.1	Tonia's travels in Switzerland, 1942–44	148
5.2	France-Switzerland border, indicating where Tonia most likely crossed into Switzerland in 1942	150
5.3	Tonia's travels in Germany and Poland, 1946–48	187
6.1	Sioma's lifetime travels	199

Figures

1.1	Tonia with her mother, Róża Bialer, and siblings during a vacation, Rytro, Poland, 1933	34
1.2	Aaron Bialer with his son Julek, Łódź, late 1920s	38
2.1	Tonia's school class on a trip to Kraków, 1934 or 1935	47
2.2	Tonia and Sioma before they left Palestine in 1937	63
2.3	Dinner with Sioma's family, 1936 or 1937	67
2.4	A gathering of friends and family just before Tonia and Sioma's departure from Palestine	68
4.1	Tonia with Sioma and Vera, Gurs, France, 1937	113
4.2	Tonia with Marcel and Vera, Oloron, 1940	129

4.3	Sioma and three other prisoners in Le Vernet, ca. 1941	134
6.1	Vera at Itschnach, ca. 1943–45	203
6.2	Marcel at Itschnach, ca. 1943–45	203
6.3	Tonia working for the Ukrainian Service Committee	207
6.4	Tonia and her children, Switzerland, 1944 or 1945	211
7.1	Dorothea Jones and Tonia at Tonia's apartment in Warsaw, 1957	238
7.2	Tonia, her children, and Noel Field	251

Series Editor's Preface

With *An Ordinary Life? The Journeys of Tonia Lechtman, 1918–1996,* historian Anna Müller presents a unique wartime and postwar biography of an actually not-so-ordinary young Polish Jewish woman who lived through both the Holocaust in Europe and the postwar Stalinist era in communist Poland.

The daughter of a Jewish lacemaker, Tonia Lechtman began her life and spent her teenage years in Łódź in prewar Poland. Growing estranged from both her conservative Jewish parents and a society where conditions for Jews were darkening, Tonia joined the Polish Communist Party, as many young Jews did in those years, considering it, in part, a means of resistance to the antisemitic strains in Polish society and, particularly, in the rising Polish Right. Reading the handwriting on the wall, Tonia and her family left Poland for Palestine a few years before the Nazi invasion, which began for her a most exciting and unusual odyssey. Tonia's husband joined the antifascist Republican forces fighting in Spain, and Tonia hid out in France for much of the war under the protection of French communist comrades but later escaped Vichy France and made her way into Switzerland. After the war, Tonia returned to Poland, but there ran into the no less antisemitic (and Stalinist) Polish Communist Party, which accused her of espionage and clapped her in prison for several years. Once released, Tonia returned to Palestine, now the newborn State of Israel, where she lived out the rest of her life. Throughout this time, Tonia, and hence also Müller's biography, wrestled with questions of personal, ethnic, and religious identity—Pole, Jew, woman, wife, mother—questions facing many young Polish Jews who managed to survive the war.

Despite her rough years in Poland, Tonia never lost her affective attachments to that country, her homeland, and to a Polish identity, but in the end it was only Israel that could offer her shelter, safety, and sustenance after traumatic years on the run during the early years of her life. Tonia died several years ago, but Müller enjoyed the kind cooperation of Tonia's two grown children, who provided her with full access to family photographs, letters, diaries, and documents, yielding a manuscript that is richly sourced. Readers, I think, will find it captivating and be enthralled by the personal voice of the author's prose.

Anna Müller, the Frank and Mary Padzieski Endowed Professor in Polish / Polish American / Eastern European Studies at the University of Michigan–Dearborn, is a well-trained and widely published scholar, with an undergraduate degree from the University of Gdańsk and a PhD from Indiana University. Her previous book is *If the Walls Could Speak: Inside a Women's Prison in Communist Poland* (Oxford University Press, 2017).

Publication by the Ohio University Press in its Polish and Polish-American Studies Series marks a milestone in the maturation of the Polish studies field and stands as a fitting tribute to the scholars and organizations whose efforts have brought it to fruition. Supported by a series advisory board of accomplished Polonists and Polish-Americanists, the Polish and Polish-American Studies Series has been made possible through generous financial assistance from the Polish American Historical Association and that organization's Stanley Kulczycki Publication Fund, the Stanislaus A. Blejwas Endowed Chair in Polish and Polish American Studies at Central Connecticut State University, the Kosciuszko Foundation, the Polish Institute of Arts and Sciences of America, the Piast Institute, and the Frank and Mary Padzieski Endowed Professorship in Polish / Polish American / Eastern European Studies at the University of Michigan–Dearborn and through institutional support from Wayne State University and Ohio University Press. The series meanwhile has benefited from the warm encouragement of a number of other persons, including Gillian Berchowitz, M. B. B. Biskupski, the late Stanislaus A. Blejwas, Thomas Duszak, Mary Erdmans, Martin Hershock, Rick Huard, Anna Jaroszyńska-Kirchmann, Grażyna Kozaczka, Anna Mazurkiewicz, Brian McCook, Anna Müller, Thomas Napierkowski, Neal Pease, Beth Pratt, James S. Pula, and Thaddeus Radzilowski, and from the able assistance of the staff of Ohio University Press. The series also has received generous assistance from a growing list of series supporters, including benefactor Thomas Duszak, contributor George Bobinski, and additional friends of the series, including Alfred Bialobrzeski, William Galush, John A. and Pauline A. Garstka, Jonathan Huener, Grażyna Kozaczka, Neal Pease, Maria Swiecicka-Ziemianek, and Mary Jane Urbanowicz. The moral and material support from all of these institutions and individuals is gratefully acknowledged.

—*John J. Bukowczyk*

Acknowledgments

The idea to write Tonia's story was born after my first visit with Vera Lechtman, Tonia's daughter. The first thank-you should thus go to the late Teresa Torańska, who shared with me Vera's email address, and then to Vera, who welcomed a stranger with open arms, good food, and hours of time for entertaining all my questions. It was consequently her brother, Marcel Lechtman, and his wife, Henia Lechtman, who opened their hearts and home to share with me stories, memories, reflections, and a vast archive of Tonia's documents. They are the backbone of the project.

It was then John Bukowczyk, a Polish American historian, a mentor, and I hope a friend, who after hearing me talk about Tonia suggested that her story is worth documenting and that the Polish American series at Ohio University Press (OUP) may be a good place for that. John, by believing in this project, kept pushing me to make it better. Rick Huard, Tyler Balli, and Don McKeon, my OUP editors, were the kindest, most thoughtful editors I could imagine. Thank you all for helping me turn this love project into something tangible—a book. Equally amazing was the entire staff working at OUP. Additionally, the financial support of my dean, Marty Hershock, the Fulbright Commission and the Office of Research and Sponsored Programs at the University of Michigan–Dearborn allowed me to embark on research trips that helped me find answers to many of my questions. I am enormously grateful to Andrzej Kamiński and Lilka Łazarska for inviting me to participate in the Recovering Forgotten History conference, during which I had a chance to present parts of the manuscript. The comments I received from Bożena Szaynok, Kamil Kijek, and Marek Wierzbicki are impossible to overestimate. Similar words of appreciation go to Natalia Aleksiun and to the anonymous reviewers of the full manuscript who provided thoughtful and sometimes provocative commentary. Anna Mazurkiewicz, Natalia Jarska, and Katarzyna Sierakowska invited me to give lectures and created a space where I could receive comments on the early stages of the project. Basia Nowak kept reading versions of chapters without judgment or frustration for my still complete lack of understanding of the use of articles in the English language and with empathy for my linguistic shortcoming. Thank you, Basia.

The majority of this book was written in 2020 during COVID-19 isolation in my parents' home, located in one of the most remote corners of Gdańsk, Poland, and surrounded by fields and trees and more fields. It was in many regards a difficult year, but it was also a year of rekindling many relationships. Suddenly, when the hustle and bustle of our lives was forcibly slowed down, conversations with friends and loved ones became the best medium to feel less atomized and more grounded and connected.

And it was these relationships with the most extraordinary women that carried me through this project. Even though a number of male friends, colleagues, and family members supported me throughout this project (Bartłomiej Garba, Pierre Goetschel, Andy Hinnant, Padraic Kenney, Jack Hutchens, Steven Seegel, John Swanson, Michał Wilczewski, Nathaniel Wood, Michael Uhl, Tomek Zerek, Adrian Zdrada), it was the women who stood by me, wiped tears from my eyes, listened to my frustrations, and complained, cried, and laughed with me. So much happened during these past two years—regret and grief, some pain—and yet there was even more understanding and appreciation and countless (even if sometimes virtual) cups of coffee and tea. Similarly to the way Tonia was carried by women—close and distant—I, too, felt carried by women. Thank you from the bottom of my heart to a student turned research assistant turned friend (not necessarily in that order). This is about you, Taylorann Lenze. Thank you, Meryl Lavenant, Anna Topolska, and Ruth Fivaz-Silbermann, for making it possible to continue doing research under COVID. Thank you to Alicja Kusiak for talking with me about this project in its initial stage and to Maria Kapajeva for always being there for me and for your wise advice, for listening, for tears and laughter and silence, and for providing me with a sense of being heard. We both had our share of difficulties these past years, and yet it feels as if we walked through some of them together. Jadzia Biskupska, Muriel Blaive, Marta Cieślak, Patrice Dabrowski, Mayhill Fowler, Yedia Kanfer, Colleen More, Anna Mazurkiewicz, Katie Wróblewski, Milena Wicepolska—you all provided invaluable comments and suggestions, but you also helped me build my confidence and taught me to believe that I have a voice. Tawana Banks, Magda Canvillo, Iza Koperska, Maja Kosińska, Lou Ann Plewa, and Cecilia Woloch—you either were or have become part of my universe in the years when I was writing this book. We shared meals, concerns over loved ones, moments of feeling proud, and moments of incredible sadness. You were part of my women's *khruzok* that made me a better person and a more sensitive researcher. Mira Rosenthal and I created our own little khruzok. While looking for Zuzanna Ginczanka, we found each other again. I am grateful that COVID somehow helped us rekindle this friendship. It was my dissertation adviser, Marci Shore, who years ago taught me the value of a khruzok for our intellectual and emotional lives. Staying in your khruzok, Marci, is one of the best things that happened to me in America.

I am indebted to my Detroit/Dearborn community: their comments on the chapters they read, their enthusiasm and commitment to their students and projects, and their drive for making this world a better place not only helped me grow but also showed me that Dearborn is home. Like Tonia, I made home with and through people in a place that I had a hard time recognizing as home at first. For that I would like to thank my Dearborn restless women: Francine Banner, Maya Barak, Suzanne Bergeron, Audrea Dakho, Georgina Hickey, Kristin Palm, Pam Pennock, Kristin Poling, Sue Steiner, and Belinda Soliz. There is also a group of fierce students, Women in Learning and Leadership (WILL) who made me believe that a better world is in the making. WILL students, thank you!

My family has long suffered from my unhealthy schedule and my constant absence. I have no words to apologize enough—the moments I lost are lost forever. But looking at my sweet and smart son, Allen, and independent daughter, Zoey, I trust that not everything got lost. Teenage Zoey is just about to enter the world of adulthood. Seeing how confident and committed she is, I like to think that that is who Tonia was when she first embarked on changing the world. Zoey is also supported by a close circle of women, hopefully learning that relying on others makes us better, that asking for help does not mean imposing, and that vulnerability is a strength. So, maybe not everything got lost and she learned a thing or two from me. And my final thank-yous go to my mom, Halina Müller, and to Henia Lechtman—two women I admire and love deeply for their strength to hold up others, for their bravery to live in the shadow of someone else's story, and for their wisdom and breathtaking selflessness. Thank you for giving me a chance to learn from you.

Guide to Pronunciation

The following key provides a guide to the pronunciation of Polish words and names.

    a is pronounced as in *father*
    c as ts, as in *cats*
    ch as guttural h, as in German BACH
    cz as hard ch, as in *church*
    g (always hard), as in *get*
    i as ee, as in *meet*
    j as y, as in *yellow*
    rz as hard zh, as in French *jardin*
    sz as hard sh, as in *ship*
    szcz as hard shch, as in *fresh cheese*
    u as oo, as in *boot*
    w as v, as in *vat*
    ć as soft ch, as in *cheap*
    ś as soft sh, as in *sheep*
    ż as hard zh, as in French *jardin*
    ź as soft zh, as in *seizure*
    ó as oo, as in *boot*
    ą as a nasal, as in French *bon*
    ę as a nasal, as in French *vin* or *fin*
    ł as w, as in *way*
    ń as ny, as in *canyon*

The accent in Polish words almost always falls on the penultimate syllable.

Introduction

> Każdy przecież początek
> To tylko ciąg dalszy,
> a księga zdarzeń
> zawsze otwarta w połowie.
>
> —Wisława Szymborska, *Miłość od pierwszego wejrzenia*
>
> Every beginning
> is only a sequel, after all,
> and the book of events
> is always open halfway through.
>
> —Translated by Stanisław Barańczak and Clare Cavanagh

A Jew, Pole, daughter, mother, wife, widow, communist, migrant, refugee, Holocaust survivor driven to fight for a better world. Ordinary or anything but? In Tonia Lechtman's life, the lofty and the quotidian intertwined, making everything she did both monumental and mundane. Who was she?

Tonia Lechtman (née Bialer) was born in 1918 into a Jewish industrialist family in Łódź, Poland. Early in her life, at the threshold of her teenage years, she embraced communism. Through communism she articulated principles that would define her public stance and her private life. Her ideals strengthened in Palestine, where she met and married fellow communist Sioma Lechtman, a Russian Jew raised in Vienna. In 1937 Tonia and Sioma immigrated to France to build a new life. In 1943 she fled France as a single mother of two young children and spent the rest of the war, 1943–45, as a refugee in Switzerland. In 1946 she returned to Poland. That return was supposed to end her wandering; Poland in 1946 promised a new, better communist world committed to eliminating hatred and injustices. Three years after her return, in 1949, Tonia was arrested as an "enemy of the state" and imprisoned for five years. She returned to Palestine (now Israel) in 1971 and died in 1996, surrounded by a loving family bewildered by the role communism had occupied in her life.

A couple of decades after Tonia's death, a photo of Rosa Luxemburg still hangs in her old living room. For years communism—the way she understood and lived it—was everything to her. It freed her from the limitations of the class structures of interwar Polish and Polish Jewish society; promised a world free from antisemitism; framed her social relationships, allowing her to define herself on her own terms; and, later in life, helped her deal with loss and trauma. Tonia's life encompassed many roles and identities: the liminal life of a person belonging to a national minority; the contingent life of a woman; the hopeful life of a communist; the desperate life of a mother, wife, and widow; and the contingent life of traumatic choices and few opportunities. Over and over again, some of her most consequential choices were driven by her convictions: to remain a communist, to define herself as a Jew in the middle of the war in France, to choose Poland and Polishness after the war. I imagine her as a restless and relentless woman, determined to live by her principles. Love is an essential element of this image, as are growing disillusionment and trauma of loss and fear. Toward the end of her life, she did not appear bitter or disappointed, but the pain that accumulated in her found ways to resurface.

An Ordinary Life?

I frame Tonia's life as ordinary. She was a migrant and a refugee searching for a place to settle and longing to be useful in making the world a better place—an urge that appears to be the best evidence of belonging for someone from the margins. Tonia was aware of the scale of the historical forces she faced. I see her life as a way to investigate how "human beings understand the world and their place in it," make sense of their available choices, and try to retrieve agency even if it appears to be unavailable.[1] Isn't this constant juggling of identities and a search for belonging ordinary, perhaps now, in our contemporary world, more than ever?

For her and members of her generation—Polish Jews born on the threshold of an independent Poland—choices appeared limitless. They lived in a moment of "historical optimism and faith in national self-determination."[2] Tonia represented a generation born and educated during the interwar years that believed it lived in an exceptional time that gave hope for inclusion. Yet this generation had its dreams crushed. In the name of these dreams and the impudence of acting upon them, Tonia was imprisoned four times by three states (Poland, Palestine, France, and Poland again). She was also interned in France and Switzerland for being a communist, a Jew, a refugee, or a Jewish communist. Her identities were sometimes advantageous and sometimes disadvantageous. The modern state providing her with choices was simultaneously categorizing, defining, and limiting these choices. Is that not an ordinary story of modernity, however brazen that statement and cruel that reality appears to be?

At the beginning of her journey, she was a young woman who unexpectedly became a widowed mother of two children. She had to face the responsibility of raising them alone under circumstances of war, chaos, and political and social transformations. The threatening world most likely made her question many life decisions. The documents she left behind portray a woman constantly attempting to balance her life with the lives of her children. Is this not the most ordinary of life trajectories?

Communism, fascism, the Spanish Civil War, World War II, the Holocaust, and Stalinism were all part of her life experience. She certainly lived in interesting times, as the Chinese proverb that sounds like a curse has it. History with a capital *H* rolled through her life, shaping her and affecting her life intensely and intimately. At the same time, she resisted these forces as if she did not realize the scope of the unfolding events. She struggled to understand what the changing social and political horizons meant for her and her family and how she could remain faithful to the world she believed had shaped her and the world she hoped to (re)build. How could her life be anything but extraordinary? But a brief look at our last few decades reveals similarly powerful events and forces that have dominated our lives—for example, the Arab Spring, refugee crises, the European Community's decline, the Black Lives Matter movement, climate change, COVID-19. Aren't we all living through decades dominated by forces that are beyond imagination? Aren't we living and experiencing history, sometimes in the most terribly intimate ways?

Larger historical context hung over Tonia's life like a cloud, suggesting the next chapters of her story before we even begin reading them. Her story is one of relationships between ethnic Poles and Polish Jews, the struggle of Jewish communists, "choiceless choices" and tragedies, acceptance and adaptation, rejection and trauma.[3] Careful investigation shows the scope of her various possible choices, decisions she made, and efforts she undertook to avoid the disasters toward which she was constantly heading. It also unveils the incidental nature of many of her decisions. Tonia encountered many misfortunes, but she also had luck and people willing to help her. Each of us can decide whether the presence of good people in our lives is ordinary.

"Then, how unique or representative was her life?" is another typical question historians ask. Did history produce her? And if so, how?[4] On one hand, social, political, and cultural factors defined her life: conditions circumscribed her responses. "'No man is an island, entire of itself; every man is a piece of the Continent, a part of the main.' . . . To paint a man's life is to present these things," says biographer Hermione Lee, quoting poet John Donne in her book on the development of the biography as a genre in the Western world, suggesting that we all are part of a larger story.[5] On the other, this larger story does not fully explain who we are, nor does it exhaust the possibilities of how an individual can develop. Historian Marci Shore, in an interview inspired by her book on the choices of people who participated in the Maidan Uprising, the 2014 revolution of dignity in Ukraine, maintains that "any historical situation contains elements of both the particular and the universal. . . . No moment is ever *exactly* the same as any other, just like no human being is exactly the same as any other." Shore insists that each particular situation teaches us something about the human condition: our strengths, weaknesses, and tendencies to normalize the abnormal.[6] To recognize that is to exercise one's historical imagination and see individual behaviors as historically contingent yet developing in surprising ways.

Biography: The Stream and the Fish

In her 1939 autobiographical essay "Sketch of the Past," Virginia Woolf wrote, "I see myself as a fish in a stream; deflected; held in place but cannot describe the stream."[7] Lee sees Woolf's comment as representing a conflict within personal writing, such as a diary or autobiography, but also illustrating Woolf's awareness "that one of biography's tasks is to place its subject in its 'age': the question is how best to do it." Biography "has a duty to the stream as well as to the fish."[8]

While pondering big historical questions, historians usually play with the "how" and "why." As historian Christopher Clark emphasizes in his breakthrough work on how the great powers went to war in 1914, the "why" invites us to search for categorical causes, while the "how" invites us to look at the sequence of interactions between the larger context and individuals. The "'why' approach offers analytical clarity, but it also has a distorting effect because it causes the illusion of steadily building pressure" that leads to inevitable consequences.⁹ Similar questions appear in works on individual lives. "How" creates space for individual intricacies: choices made, actions undertaken, or interpretations of one's life. The "why" helps us define Woolf's stream and reveals itself as epistemological impossibility for historians. History is always both overdetermined and underdetermined in that multiple outcomes were possible and multiple factors simultaneously played a role in those outcomes.¹⁰

The themes that flow through Tonia's life are rich. The most apparent is the complex and dynamic intersection between Polishness and Jewishness, which helps us understand some of the intricacies of her life choices. Historian Katrin Steffen uses the term "Jewish Polishness" to reveal the close interconnectedness of both identities.¹¹ Tonia identified as Polish, but that Polishness was deeply and inseparably linked with her Jewishness. Polishness and Jewishness played parallel roles in her life: her understanding of Polishness and Jewishness, as well as the relationship between the two, kept changing yet remained dependent on each other.¹² In terms of citizenship, all inhabitants of the Second Polish Republic, the state where Tonia first learned what it meant to be Jewish and Polish, were Polish. Tonia's experiences give space to question the experience of ethnic Poles as normative and suggest making a distinction between non-Jewish Poles and Jewish Poles rather than Poles and Jews.¹³

Her place in both communities was complicated by her gender: a Polish Jewish daughter, wife, widow, mother, and female communist. Communism and the various roles it played in her life—from providing a space to mature to giving her purpose and helping her deal with trauma—are indispensable elements of that story. Is communism a framework—perhaps a stream—for the identities within which she defined her other roles? I avoid the word "emancipation" to describe the role communism played, as emancipation implies a preceding subjugation. Her identity as a young Polish Jewish woman did not hold her back but propelled her forward; she embraced communism in this context. She did not try to escape the world she came from but tried to build a new one from its depths.[14]

The fluidity of her identities underscored her mobility—a physical mobility of moving between places and a mental mobility of shifting among various social contexts and self-definitions. The moments when she traveled physically imbued her with the strength to reshape her life and restart her personal narrative. In other words, she consciously chose the life of a migrant as if physical mobility drove her mental capabilities for acceptance and adaptation. But she was forced to cease to be a voluntary migrant, and her status shifted to that of refugee. Her life became part of a larger story of modern prisons and camps that in many respects overshadowed the twentieth century. The Holocaust affected her, but her Jewishness was not the only reason why she was persecuted; her vulnerability was intensified by being a communist, a woman, a mother. Her life is a chapter in the study of one of the most barbarous moments in European history. It is also part of the modern story of ordering and categorization that came with the fluidity the twentieth century offered her as a promise of unlimited opportunities.

Tonia's life is a story of imagining a perfect home, searching for that home, and reinventing it over and over again. As a woman and homemaker, she reimagined home for her children: the small, more intimate home, the place in which they lived their everyday lives, and the larger home, the country in which they chose to live. A communist utopian vision of the end of history and the promise of the end of all suffering drove her efforts to fight for this home. Even if utopian, it defined her motherhood and also forced her children to share their mother's love with ideals that undermined their well-being. Her life is about reconciling the love of humanity with love for people close to her, neither of which were a given but which she had to constantly refuel.

Her story is about women. It is about the importance and physical presence of women in her life: her mother, her aunt, her female friends who encouraged her to join a communist youth organization, and many other women who helped her survive. In a literary sense, it is a story about social workers or women who felt compelled to help, modern angels who repeatedly came to her rescue. Their stories are largely unknown and forgotten. These women fed Tonia and her children, found shelter for them, took them in, and provided her with false documents. Beyond survival, they also enabled her children to feel safe and even thrive under conditions of war. Their efforts transcended the boundaries of the various countries Tonia lived in and were international but delineated by languages—mostly German and French—that made connections possible. The form that remembrance takes is another aspect of her story. Women often remember through the presence of others in their lives. Tonia's story is certainly not unique in this respect. She constructed a life story centered on others, mostly women, who made her survival and growth possible.

Life writing and memory are certainly crucial for Tonia's story. Tonia never wrote an autobiography or a memoir, but the lengthy interviews she left behind and the effort her family put into maintaining contact via correspondence and then preserving that correspondence reminds me of the importance of life writing and individual self-construction.[15] How Tonia remembered, what she forgot, and even what she represented differently in various sources are also crucial. Oral history historian Alessandro Portelli has explained that how and what we remember, what we forget, and what we distort in our memory tells a tremendous amount about our individual experiences—much more than the story itself.[16] What Tonia and her children remembered or chose to remember was conditioned by the trauma they experienced. Her children have struggled throughout their lives with how to think about their own past and the place they occupied in their mother's life, a place they see as having been limited by her activism, her communism, and her urge to treat the outer world as a necessary prerequisite for the safety of her private home. The dilemma of Vera and Marcel, Tonia's children, of what to think of the heritage their Polish Jewish communist mother left behind does not belong only to them. The reflections and anxieties of her children speak to the experiences of many people like themselves, people affected by dislocation and loss. Her story and their stories show the diverse directions that "fish" can take in a "stream."

History as "Purgatorio": The Challenges

My interest in writing Tonia's biography, a woman only few know about, grew out of my fascination with her complex story and my sympathy, even admiration, for her and her strength. While acknowledging my emotional involvement in her story, I still act as a historian, following Tonia's life trajectory while simultaneously juxtaposing my understanding of particular historical moments with larger dynamics of history. Writing her story meant creating a plot and imposing a linear narrative on her life, with a beginning and an end. Ordering stories—organizing facts, finding references in the context of a master narrative, providing a story with necessary historical explanations—is what historians do because our trade and skills require that of us. But it is also what we do to make sense of the material we work with, to understand the avalanche of facts before they overwhelm us, and to respond to our internal drive and motivation. I can only echo the words of Daniel Mendelsohn, the author of *The Lost: A Search for Six of Six Million*, when he admits that putting facts in order is calming: he felt pain and anxiety when confronted with mass amounts of information that resisted being organized.[17] Likewise, at multiple moments in Tonia's story, imposing a narrative felt like an artificial impulse to control her life when chaos was the main principle. Consequently, at times including longer quotations from Tonia, rather than analyzing her story, felt more appropriate, allowing her to narrate her experiences in her own voice.

The question of how to organize a story and at the same time maintain the voice of the person being written about is crucial in any project centered on individual stories, the danger being that larger historical forces could easily dominate the individual's life.[18] Perhaps equally important is the question of what pushes historians to investigate individual lives. What are they searching for, what motivations drive them, and how do they situate themselves in relation to the story and people they write about? In other words, what is behind our curiosity and voyeurism, both essential factors in the process of reconstructing an individual's past?

The books that have inspired me while researching and reflecting on Tonia's life combine the stories of small groups of largely unknown individuals with transparency regarding the historian's own process and motivation, at least to the extent possible and bearable for readers. One such book is *The Lost*, in which Mendelsohn discusses his research on, or perhaps search for, six members of his family lost in the Holocaust, people whose presence despite absence has dominated his life. In family memory, they were not so much dead as lost because nobody ever spoke about them. From the fragmentary bits and pieces of information still available, he tries to establish what is unknown to somehow tame what is unknowable.

Ivan Jablonka's book *A History of the Grandparents I Never Had* is similar to Mendelsohn's in that it focuses on recovering his own family's past. He conveys his motivation with an existential urgency: "These anonymous souls belong not to me but to us all. Before they are erased forever, I felt it urgent to recover their traces, the footprints they left on life, the involuntary evidence of their time on earth."[19] Both books promote a romantic concept of history as imbuing historians with skills and the ability to return past experiences to the present, but the voices of both authors are also mediated by an awareness of their roles and positionality in the process of retrieving the past and making it available to readers. Mendelsohn's work, with dense references to antiquity, reflections on available sources, and the nature of witnessing the Holocaust, implies shifts in interest from a desire to recover the voices of the past to the fundamental significance of historical knowledge for us all, an imperative that is as powerfully illuminating as it is paralyzing. "For those who are compelled by their natures always to be looking back at what has been, rather than forward into the future," he states, "the great danger is tears, the unstoppable weeping that the Greeks, if not the author of Genesis, knew was not only a pain but a narcotic pleasure, too: a mournful contemplation so flawless, so crystalline, that it can, in the end, immobilize you."[20]

In that reading, history as a desire to immerse oneself in someone's past is about the present and the urge not so much to understand as to bring order and meaning to chaos. Historian Ewa Domańska, although in a more theory-driven context, writes about historians' attraction to tragedy in history as providing catharsis: writing about people and facts from the past is a process that conjures a new world. She notes that "the most important moments of becoming of the world, the moments when reality (and the past) reveals its true face, are moments of trauma, which is a wound inflicted on the world and people." Domańska implies something palpable in our attraction to tragedy and the people who experienced it. "The tragedy contains mourning over the history of a man (humanity), and history—the tragic nature of human purgatory. In both cases it is about cleansing. History (historical writing) is like a *purgatorio*. In history, unlike life, however, people get another chance when their deeds are brought to justice."[21] This comment clearly refers to Dante's *Divine Comedy*, which perceived purgatory as a relatively creative space, not necessarily a space of eternal waiting between heaven and hell. Rather than being an unnavigated space, it is liminal space that we cross to search and receive "expiatory purification" or, to put it in less threatening terms, to search for catharsis, for self-enlightenment.[22]

Another element in the trope of searching for and retrieving stories of those lost in the past is the lives of ordinary people whose existence is somehow inseparably linked with that of the writers. For Mendelsohn, his search begins with his physical resemblance to one of his lost family members, suggesting a search for his own identity, "his face in the face of the Loss."[23] For Jablonka, it is a search for the grandparents he never knew but whose life choices determined his own life in Paris. In another book, *East West Street*, international law specialist Philippe Sands explores the life of his maternal grandparents while arriving at a different understanding of his own past.[24] Finally, Katja Petrowskaja, in her part memoir, part family history *Maybe Esther*, poses an important half-statement and half-question: "maybe," as an adverb that permanently describes the scope of silences around her family but also evocatively describes the twenty-first-century condition of people whose past is buried in history yet whose lives are closely intertwined with history.[25] An important caveat is appropriate here: none of the above-mentioned authors are professional historians, which may give them courage to stretch the disciplinary boundaries to use history as a tool for a deeply existential and personal search. They walk the fine line between existential urgency, their own lives, and the lives they write about, but they do it with caution in reading the sources, academic honesty for the claims and comparisons they bring forward, and a commendable sense of responsibility for the representations of the various lives they have taken upon themselves.

The strong presence of autobiography, even if indirect, in many history texts, especially biographies, has been noted by scholars for years. For example, Lee states:

> It has been argued—especially in the modernist period . . .—that all biography is a form of autobiography. Even biographers who resist the notion that the story they are telling has anything to do with them, and put themselves in the narrative as little as possible, have to admit that their choice of subject has been made for a reason. . . . We write from a certain position, constructed by our history, nationality, race, gender, class, education, beliefs. More specifically, there is likely to be some shared experience between the writer and the subject.[26]

Sociologist Aneta Ostaszewska writes evocatively about the place of subjectivity in academic writing. In her view, the road of writing and researching is a road to (self-)discovery. She argues that objectivity means "situated knowledge," resulting from looking from a particular social perspective. Furthermore, she maintains that reflexivity on individual experience and all the factors that condition it are elements of our feminist—and I would argue also academic—imagination and therefore should become part of our methodology.[27] Thinking about a woman who struggled most of her life with fragmentation, mobility, and choices brings me to reflect on the affinity between us and the heroes of our stories, the people we find fascinating, who teach us with their lives about our own lives.

Only toward the end of the research did I gain the courage to admit that my autobiography had played a role in this project.[28] My own experiences as a feminist, scholar, migrant, and mother who daily struggles with solitude and a desire to make the world around me "home" were elements of the story I had set out to tell. Some moments made this crystal clear. One was that people involved in this project kept calling me Tonia. At one point, two of my research assistants—Meryl Lavenant and Taylorann Lenze—emailed me saying that they needed to be careful not to call me Tonia. Ruth Fivaz-Silbermann, a researcher from the University of Geneva, did this as well. Taylorann is a friend who knows me well; Meryl and Ruth do not. They were getting to know me through Tonia's life, and in their minds I became associated with Tonia. For some reason, this association was pleasing. Does it mean that I identify with Tonia? No, but the intensity with which certain moments of her life lived in my mind somehow transpired in my relationships with the people who helped make this book possible.

Willingly or not, I read some moments of Tonia's experiences through my own experience. One such moment was particularly salient. It was December 2019, and I was traveling to Dearborn, Michigan, where I work as a participant in the Inside-Out Prison Exchange Theory Group. On the morning of a scheduled visit, I was enjoying coffee in my favorite café in Dearborn, waiting for the time to pass. I was looking forward to wishing a good holiday season to the group. There is nothing like the holidays to remind us of the importance of various communities that sustain us through life. While waiting, I noticed an email from Amicale de Vernet, an organization located at the site of one of the camps where Sioma, Tonia's husband, was confined during the war, a place

Tonia had attempted to visit. The email contained her denied application to visit. Almost precisely at the same moment, my visit to Macomb was canceled due to some circumstances that had decreased the number of guards. The reasoning seemed trivial, but my opinion was of course irrelevant. Here I held both Tonia's and my thwarted attempts to visit the imprisoned. Of course, the situations differed, but there was something in that moment that made me think of my own investment in stories replete with individual vulnerabilities and negotiations between individual needs and institutional barriers. Tonia's story was uniquely intense yet ordinary in the way it also evoked an anger at the coldness of state institutions. At this particular moment, the story was also very personal: it reminded me of my own painful limited ability to protest circumstances I disagree with. Is writing about injustice akin to activism?

There is always a moment when a story begins speaking to a historian on a personal level. In a conversation with a curator at the United States Holocaust Memorial Museum about his book *East West Street,* Sands evocatively explains that the title refers to a street where many walked. Hersch Lauterpacht, a human rights advocate, had lived in Lwów near Sands's grandmother, Malka.[29] The last street she walked on toward Treblinka, where she died, was the same street on which Bella and Joseph Lemkin walked. Bella and Joseph were the parents of Raphael Lemkin, another man Sands studies. They all died in the same place. Sands's grandmother's life is thus "bookended" by the men he studies. Reflecting on this bizarre coincidence, Sands comments, "You could not invent that. You would not believe it. I discover these points of connections . . . that situate you in that place."[30] Was it a coincidence? Of course. But the questions remain: How do we make sense of these coincidences, and how do they guide us through our research and seemingly voyeuristic attempt to uncover certain lives?

The "points of connections" that Sands mentions increase our affinity to the researched people/topics and push us to think about what initially led us to a given topic. Tonia's story is the story of a woman who constantly negotiated various roles and vulnerabilities but also insisted on the need for morality and values in the public world. Toward the end of her life, Tonia began doubting her belief in communism, but her insistence on the necessity to fight for the collective good beyond pure individualism remained steady. Along these lines, for me personally, her unwavering belief means returning to the reasons for her engagement in communism, which at a particular moment in history was life-sustaining for many. For people of my generation, who grew up at the beginning of so-called postcommunism, at a time when the Western world blamed communism for all the evil in the world, unraveling the complex motivations of people who supported ideologies aimed at healing the world is important. It carries redemptive qualities.

My decision to call Tonia by her first name also requires editorial commentary. The argument goes that a man would never be called by his first name in a biography because that is not how we would address him. Despite their life trajectory, most men create an air of seriousness that pushes one to think about them more formally. Yet in my mind Tonia Lechtman was "Tonia"— that is how I think about her. She organized her life around friends and intimate relationships. Reading her letters, I felt like one of her friends, one who tries to understand her choices and empathize with her in her struggles. To me, she is Tonia, and that is how I have presented her to you—intimately, personally, ordinarily.[31]

"Maybe" and the Illusion of Sources

Multiple sources are available to tell Tonia's story. I first encountered a 1994 interview with Dorota Dowgiałło, the daughter of the first ambassador from postcommunist Poland to Israel. The available version lacks the questions that were posed, so we know little about the process and intentions of the person who collected the interview. Since the conversation took place two years before Tonia's death, it certainly created a space for Tonia to reflect on her life. While reading it one cannot help wondering if Tonia ever considered writing an autobiography. Interviews "suggest a strong, consistent, unitary voice looking back in time, in control of a narrative."[32] Her interview with Dowgiałło hence plays the role of an autobiography that Tonia dictated, perhaps curated by Dowgiałło.

In my attempt to understand the story, long conversations with Tonia's daughter, Vera Lechtman, and Tonia's son and his wife, Marcel and Henryka (Henia) Lechtman, followed. Our conversations began and still continue in kitchens in Tel Aviv, where Vera lives, and in Stockholm, where Marcel and Henia reside. Tonia's children's input into this book is significant; this special kind of cooperation is deeply linked to the intuition that comes with children's intimacy to their mother.

The biggest draw was Tonia's private documents and letters, in the possession of her children. I call it "Tonia's closet," almost a living being with a heart, mind, and guts. The richness of this collection is one of the most convincing arguments for writing this book. The cache of photos and letters seems to be never-ending. Some of the documents are as distant as the medical certificate of her grandfather, Tobiasz Bialer, stating that her father, Aron, had chickenpox when he was nine years old. The touch and smell of these old documents help us practically feel the family's presence. This feeling reminds me of the romantic absorption with which Natalie Zemon Davis wrote about historians' fetish for archives: "Absorbed as we are, we experience the wonder of the register when it finally comes, its look, the touch of its binding, and the feel of its paper or parchment. We struggle with handwriting difficult to decipher and are relieved when the reading is easy. We turn the pages, hoping for discovery, not just for what we planned ahead of time, but . . . for the unexpected, the surprise."[33]

Most of the sources in Tonia's closet are letters. The first letters go back to the 1920s. The most intense correspondence begins in 1937 and continues for four decades. Her friends were becoming her family's friends, who had no choice but to be pulled into a conversation about Tonia's life. The letters mention mysterious friends, family members, events, and trips, which show the richness of her life. Life continues uninterrupted in the bliss of the present, awareness of the past, and uncertainty of the future. The letters are mostly in Polish and German, with multiple fragments of Yiddish and Hebrew. Over time, German disappears, and Polish becomes dominant, while Hebrew and Yiddish remain.[34] Over time, Tonia's closet became the depository of other memories. For many of Tonia's friends, her house became the best place to store their letters, writing, and deathbed memoirs. Was she a person seen as able to keep secrets?

Besides letters, her closet includes collections of photos in beautiful albums documenting the pre-Holocaust Jewish world of prewar Poland. Many carry images of people impossible to identify. In the 1970s and in accordance with the Israeli school curriculum, her granddaughter, Anna Rajf-Ligęza, wrote down her grandmother's story; her project helps to return from oblivion the oldest family members whose faces are documented in these old photos. Historian Anna Landau-Czajka asserts that surviving sources from the war usually push us to idolize the past.[35] Looking at the photos of a world that disappeared with the Holocaust makes for an easy idolization. People lived normal lives. Vacation photos depict smiling faces rather than locations the family visited. The 1920s was a time of increasing leisure, and that leisure is well documented in Tonia's closet. The photos do not end in the 1920s: through the war and postwar years, Tonia kept getting photos taken of her and her children. Many of these photos made it to her family back in Tel Aviv and ultimately became part of the rich depository of Tonia's closet.

But there is more in her closet: family porcelain from Łódź, Rosenthal porcelain from postwar Poland, a collection of graphics Sioma collected in one of the camps and Tonia smuggled out. The depth and richness of its contents took my breath away. The photos as well as material witnesses to Tonia's story work as Barthesian punctum, inviting a special relationship with the owner. Her closet is evidence of historical self-awareness, first developed by Tonia's parents, perhaps even grandparents, and curated by Tonia in the last decades of her life. It was then passed on to Vera, who held it under lock and key while turning it into a depository of Tonia's past. In recent years, the collection was organized by Marcel, who used it to replace his lack of memory. Eventually, he decided to give most of this collection to Polin: The Museum of the Polish Jewry, located in Warsaw, where it is left to researchers' and curators' imaginations.[36] Family decisions about what to keep and what to share showcase how memory of the past evolves through time within one family. Whenever possible, I tried to comment on these particular struggles with family memory throughout the text.

The family archive provides a sense of wholeness. This contrast between personal and official is most visible when these family documents are juxtaposed with state-produced sources—for example, police documents that appear especially fragmentary, as if cutting people out of their daily lives. The family archives do not necessarily tell the truth, but as Michel Foucault would say, they tell of the truth as they expose an individual wedged between relationships of power and herself.[37] There is no way to access "truth," but the juxtaposition of various sources helps to confirm that sources are impossible to understand outside of their audience and that the confusion or tensions we recognize as emerging between various voices speak to the complexity of an individual life.

The extent to which various states interfered in Tonia's life is impressive or perhaps intimidating. With the help of friends and research assistants, I found traces of Tonia in the state archives of Poland, Israel, France, and Switzerland—in each country in which she lived. French archives presented me with bits and pieces, appropriate to her presence in this country as, first, an illegal immigrant.

Absolutely fascinating for me, as a Polish historian accustomed to sources gone missing—due to war, chaos, shifting borders, communism, neglect, and displacement—were the Swiss archives and the scrupulous tendency of the administration of different levels to note her whereabouts. It reminds me of historian Arlette Farge's poetic words: "The judicial archive . . . makes it harder to grasp. It is excessive and overwhelming, like a spring tide, and avalanche, or a flood. When working in the archive you will often find yourself thinking of this exploration as a dive, a submersion, perhaps even a drowning."[38] In reality, the experience was overwhelming. I often got lost switching back and forth between three languages, unfamiliar administrative levels, and stamps and signatures of various importance, which I was unable to recognize and whose meanings, outside the absurd Kafkaesque bureaucracies, would have been lost on me if it were not for Ruth Fivaz-Silbermann, whose help in deciphering, explaining, and keeping me sane was invaluable.

Finally, the biggest collection comes from the Polish Institute of National Remembrance (Instytut Pamięci Narodowej, IPN), which houses thousands of pages of minutes of numerous interrogations of Tonia by Polish security personnel after they arrested her in 1949. The questions she was asked often seem deprived of logic, yet in the context of her life story they serve double functions: to help us to understand the confusion and cruelty of her imprisonment in postwar Poland and also to establish some elements of her life. There is nothing like judicial archives to make real the harsh reality of police repression—archives that document the rough traces of lives never expected to be told in the way they were.[39] Paradoxically that harshness brings a level of detail that would otherwise have been lost. These documents helped me reconstruct events and also hear Tonia's voice, especially when she asserted something surprising in light of other sources.

All sources are partial. There's a translucence, not transparency; they present only a fragment of a reality. How I present them here may seem based on the dualism between personal and state-produced—secrets revealed and secrets forced to be revealed and documented. Being drawn to the sensuality of the documents, I tend to recognize myself in the words of Tomasz Kietliński, a political philosopher and cultural and social analyst, who, in a book of stories and photos that evoke a little-known face of a Polish woman, writes, "Archives are the secrets of existence enchanted in the secrets of images and texts. . . . Archives are senses and sensuality of wardrobes, drawers—real and virtual, visual and written, thought and written, spoken and concealed. . . . The archive is a multivoiced, open, process, infinity."[40] Our emotion-hungry and voyeuristic nature should always be in check when in contact with the bottomless potential archives open. Archives do not provide ready answers but rather suggestions or insights into an individual experience, the process of creating an individual as a family being, a lover, a state subject, an individual sometimes lost in the overproduction of the documents but ultimately also saved thanks to the same overproduction. I would like to end my reflection on sources with the words of Farge:

> The allure of the archives entails a roaming voyage through the words of others, and a search for a language that can rescue their relevance. It may entail a voyage through the words today, with the perhaps somewhat unreasonable conviction that we write history not just to tell it, but to anchor a departed past to our words and bring about an "exchange among the living." We write to enter into an unending conversation about humanity and forgetting, origins and death.[41]

To continue with a metaphor of fish in a stream, archives tell something about the currents in the water cycle, instruments in groundwater replenishment, and corridors for fish and wildlife migration: they help us understand the stream of Tonia's life. They also say something about history itself, the urgency with which historians peruse archives, as if in search of meaning and potential redemption. My experience reflects a specific modern experience, when much is delegated to online searches that deprive us of the touch, the sensuality that archives offer. In this particular case, it also reflects the reality of COVID-19, which turned my research year into a shutdown in my parent's house with a view of the walnut trees I climbed as a child. The internet and the good will of many people made finishing this book possible but also made for a unique—or perhaps modern—research experience.

Traveling with Tonia

Tonia's life was amazingly mobile. Hers was the life of a woman who continued crossing various real and imaginary boundaries, and from the beginning I felt that the internal structure of this book would need to reflect that road. As a result, chapters are organized chronologically, or, I should say, her travels created a compulsion to organize the chapters that way.

The first chapter, covering her life in Łódź, provides background on a young Polish Jewish woman. The second is devoted to her maturing as a communist, which coincided with her first major move, to Palestine. The third chapter accompanies Tonia in Paris, where she migrated before the war. The fourth chapter is about her life in France outside of Paris, when, in contrast to her Parisian life as a refugee, her life was dominated by the condition of being an unwanted Jewish refugee. The fifth chapter turns to Tonia's life in Switzerland, to which she fled from the Nazis in France. The sixth chapter is set in Poland after the war. Her return was physical and mental, to a world she hoped would reconcile her private and public lives, giving her a chance to create a home for her children. The last chapter briefly reconstructs her life after she left prison and focuses on her communism as viewed by her children.

In the book's conclusion, I return to Tonia's life historiographically, engaging in the question I skipped here—namely, the meaning her life has for the various historiographic topics that emerge. I end with a return to the question about ordinariness versus extraordinariness. The conclusion hence ends with another larger historiographical question about what we lose (or gain) when we give up the urge to insist on someone's uniqueness yet read that experience through myriad, chaotic, and revealing choices and opportunities.

1 ||| Bobbin Lace and Assimilation

The Life of a Jewish Family in Łódź, 1918–1935

IT IS February 2018. I have repeatedly tried to arrange a Skype conversation with Tonia Lechtman's daughter, Vera Lechtman, but every time we meet virtually, somebody from her family drops by to check on her, interrupting our conversation. After another failed attempt to talk, I remember reading in an extensive interview with Tonia: "We were very family oriented. The end of the week was devoted to family visits. We continue doing this to today."[1]

The first time Vera and I met was in May 2012, when I was finishing a book on women imprisoned in postwar Poland. I flew from Warsaw to Tel Aviv and took a taxi in the middle of the night from Ben Gurion Airport to her apartment. I expected to find a key under the doormat. Except for exchanging a few emails, we were perfect strangers. From the very first email exchange, Vera's openness surprised me, but I welcomed this character trait and looked forward to meeting her. But the key was not there. I decided not to knock at four in the morning and instead sat at the door, at the risk of frightening neighbors who would soon be rushing to work. The night was slowly getting lighter as daylight began creeping into the staircase. Suddenly, half-asleep Vera opened the door with a loud reproach, pronouncing Polish syllables in her characteristic melodious way: "Why? I did say the door would be open." She had not, and I had not tried turning the handle. But she took me in, showed me to my room, and informed me we would talk more over breakfast. When I got up at ten, Vera had already worked out. She was planning a trek in the Himalayas, so she exercised daily. Just like that, Vera openly invited me into her home, family, and life. That is how my journey with this family commenced. When I began to write this book, while trying to connect with Vera her family was always present: argumentative, loving, and convinced that this is how things have been for generations.

The Family Cradle

Tonia Bialer was born in Łódź on January 18, 1918. She was the second child of Róża (Ruchla) (née Wojdysławska) and Aron Bialer. Tonia's brother Romek (Roman/Abram) was almost five years old when Tonia was born. Within the next six years, the Bialers had two more children, Joel and Noemi.[2]

At the time, toward the end of World War I, Łódź, previously part of the Russian partition of Poland, was in its fourth year of German occupation. It was ruled, as other parts of central Poland, by a Regents Board consisting of Polish conservative elites set up by the German occupational authorities. The political situation, however, boded major changes: the old European empires were crumbling, new ideas of how to reorganize the world were emerging, and amid all that change, after 123 years of political nonexistence, Poland anticipated regaining its independence. Questions about the ethnic and religious identities of groups and individuals who inhabited Poland suddenly rose to primary importance. What was this new Poland going to be? And what place would the Jews play in it?

Documents in the Łódź archives suggest at least one change the Bialer family had to contend with: the succession of official languages. The first documents I found were in Russian.[3] The birth certificate of Aron Bialer (b. 1893), Tonia's father, written in beautiful Cyrillic, notes the presence of a local rabbi as a witness to the act of registering the child. His date of birth is recorded according to both the Julian and Gregorian calendars. As if in response to a silent rebuke, it also explains why the child was not registered immediately after birth but a little over a year later. Late registrations were a common practice, and the passage of time between birth and registration sometimes resulted in inaccurate recordation of birth dates.[4] The contrast between Aron's verbose certificate and those of his children is striking. Tonia's succinct, impersonal, and hence modern birth certificate from 1918 states, in both German and Polish, only the place and date of her birth. Joel's birth certificate from 1919 almost mirrors Tonia's but is written only in Polish and is signed by an official civil registry officer, an indication of the restoration of Polish sovereignty.[5]

Tonia's birth certificate carries the Yiddish name Tauba, derived from the word for dove (*toyb*), but her family called her Tonia. The use of two names was not unusual at the time for Ashkenazi Jews. Since the nineteenth century, Jews in Poland frequently used two names: a Polish Christian name on the official certificate and a traditional Hebrew name for religious practices. But women who did not have a place in the public religious realm did not need to have Hebrew names; in fact, they had names in the vernacular, such as Yiddish, as in the case of Tauba.[6] Anyone researching official and private documents of many Jewish families encounters a constant struggle due to the fluidity of first names—their various versions as well as various spellings. For example, in official state documents from Polish and later Mandatory Palestinian (or British) archives, some of Tonia's family members appear as Tuvi, Tovi, or Tobiasz, Ruchla or Rachel, and Basia or Batia. At the same time, personal correspondence reveals the richness of various diminutive and Polonized forms of their names: Tauba/Tonia was often Tonieńka; her mother Ruchla was Róża but also Rózina and Różuchna.

The family cradle was not in Łódź but in Warsaw, where Tonia's entrepreneurial ancestors struggled for financial stability while regularly facing challenges common to Jewish life in a predominantly Christian society. Her great-grandfathers, Zyskind Bialer (1842–1916) and Joel Wegmeister (1837–1919), are cherished as the family's founders: Zyskind represented hard work and wealth; Wegmeister, Hassidic traditions. In the late 1970s, Tonia's granddaughter, Anna Rajf-Ligęza, wrote a family history about her roots (called in Hebrew a *shorashim*), a school project every schoolchild in Israel continues to do. She spent long afternoons both perusing local libraries and talking about her ancestors with her aging grandmother and her great-uncle Joel. The story that resulted from these conversations may not be historically accurate, but it provides insight into the place Zyskind Bialer and Joel Wegmeister occupied in the family imagination. The story speaks to the values that built the family—work ethic, persistence, and a commitment to the local community—and the pride of the positions they occupied in their Jewish and non-Jewish societies.[7]

History records both men as civic leaders who intervened on behalf of the rapidly growing and often impoverished Jewish community through their philanthropic activities and contacts among state and secular authorities. Warsaw changed dramatically over their lifespans. In 1837, when Wegmeister was born, it "had approximately one hundred forty thousand inhabitants, a quarter of whom, around thirty-six thousand, were Jews. When he died in 1919, the Polish capital had almost one million inhabitants, with a third of its population being Jewish. Wegmeister thus saw Warsaw grow from the largest Jewish community in the Kingdom of Poland to one of the most important in the world."[8] The Kingdom of Poland, an entity with a degree of autonomy carved out of the Russian partition of Poland, was an embodiment of Poland in the nineteenth century. But it was also a place that mixed some liberalizing decrees with severe restrictions on Jewish communities.[9] In this context, Wegmeister represents a unique blend of traditional charitable values of Jewish elites with Polish positivism that demanded responsibility for one's own community.[10]

The Bialers became connected with the Wegmeisters when Tonia's grandfather Tobiasz (b. 1864) married Joel Wegmeister's daughter, Basia or Batia (b. 1865), in what most likely was an arranged union.[11] It is impossible to determine what convinced Wegmeister to give Bialer his daughter, but it is possible that Bialer's independence and entrepreneurial nature reminded Wegmeister of his own ambitions.[12] Soon after the wedding, the couple moved to Łódź, a city becoming increasingly attractive for people with ambition. Jechiel Jeszaja Trunk, a Jewish historian and storyteller, views turn-of-the-century Łódź as a place that suited the Jewish character: "In their imagination, Polish Jews identified Łódź with their own fantastic temperament. In contrast to the idyll of Jewish towns on Polish soil, Łódź symbolized gambling with the world and its spaces," he writes.[13] Trunk clearly uses some poetic license, but it is plausible that the possibilities industrial Łódź offered attracted people who searched for opportunities. Łódź was growing extremely quickly, its population increasing more than eighteenfold between 1865 and 1914. According to the 1887 census, Poles constituted the largest ethnic group (46.6 percent), followed by Jews (29.4 percent) and Germans (21.4 percent).[14]

The rapid development of industrial Łódź started around the beginning of the nineteenth century, with a considerable migration of Jews and other immigrants from Bohemia, Saxony, and Germany.[15] Cheap cotton textiles were greatly demanded by the poor. In turn, mass production led to a transition from artisan workshops to factories. Cotton factories, in particular, used huge amounts of water, so Łódź's favorable natural conditions, especially its location on the Jasień River, promoted the development of that industry.[16]

Some important legal changes added to Łódź's rapid development. In 1862 Jews in the Kingdom of Poland were granted legal emancipation and equal rights, ending all restrictions on the right of settlement (abolishing segregated Jewish residential districts) and of purchasing property.[17] In 1864 the emancipation of peasants, who offered cheap labor, contributed greatly to the city's growth spurt. These changes coincided with an introduction of tariffs on the import of Russian grain to stop the expansion of the sale of Russian agricultural goods to Germany. As a result, Łódź received a steady influx of agricultural goods that Russia was otherwise unable to sell. Favorable natural conditions combined with a high birthrate, migration from other towns and cities, and the initiative of people determined to achieve economic success transformed the city from a small provincial town to an industrial metropolis at the threshold of modernity and an El Dorado for creative and success-hungry men.[18]

Łódź was a perfect place for people who, while grounded in traditions, were eager to reach out beyond their old settings in search of new challenges. And Tobiasz Bialer was one of the risk-taking and resourceful individuals to whom Łódź appealed. But Łódź had more meaning for the Bialer family. While it perhaps intoxicated them at first with new possibilities, over the next two generations it also brought doubts regarding the place of traditions in an individual's life and the scope of individual responsibility for one's community.

Lodzermenschen

Even though information about various initiatives of Tobiasz Bialer are scattered, he appears to have been an energetic businessman who took out bank loans to build workshops and factories, which he then resold to build bigger ones. In 1877, at the age of only twenty-three, he established his first business, a workshop that wove ribbon, shoelaces, and elastic fabric.[19] In 1894, together with a partner, Chaim Bromberg, he built a mechanized factory producing ribbon and string from angora wool, a factory he then sold in 1896 to another Łódź entrepreneur.[20] Two years later, he sold his original workshop and built a factory that produced bobbin lace.[21]

Other than the addresses and dates of operation of Bialer's factories, we know only isolated facts about them. Local amateur Łódź historians who, with a detective's magnifying glass, follow the remains of factory buildings still present in Łódź, as well as press and archival documents, helped me reconstruct some of this history as part of the urban development of the city, where fragments of previous factories and workshops remain tucked behind apartment buildings. Today they function as a shadow of their own past, but back then new locations and size meant a commitment to modernization. Bialer's bobbin lace factory employed 150 people.[22] According to a survey published in Poland in 1923 based on the efforts of the American Jewish Joint Distribution Committee, a factory employing that many employees was considered large.[23]

Tobiasz Bialer appeared to be skilled enough to benefit from the opportunities Łódź created. But the story of his success that documents provide is one-sided. This "Polish Manchester," as Łódź was called in the 1920s, was a place where progress and luxury lived alongside backwardness and poverty.[24] Łódź became a site of mass worker protests. The first general strike in the Kingdom of Poland took place in Łódź in 1892. This was followed by the establishment of Polish and internationalist socialist movements.[25] The unrest continued as the city was turning into a platform of growing economic nationalism for Jews, non-Jewish Poles, and Germans, where, as historian Yedida Kanfer shows, "ethno-religious groups defined a national identity through a particularistic economic future."[26] The first decade of the twentieth century saw street violence and an increase in national sentiments that eventually led to attempts at nationalizing industry, which meant open and organized antisemitism, clearly visible in the 1912 boycott of Jewish industries.[27]

The aggressive world of Łódź's industrial growth is well represented in the novel *Promised Land* by Władysław Stanisław Reymont, a well-known literary representation of Łódź, where absurd richness accompanies horrifying poverty and cutthroat competition with imminent bankruptcy. Fires appear often on the pages of the book: fires that destroyed but also rescued owners from financial jeopardy by providing them with insurance money; fires that destroyed the old while paving the road for the new. "The conflagration shouted its triumphant anthem, and yelled and shrieked, and danced, and bit at the walls with glory fangs, tearing the machinery to pieces, licking up the molten iron, consuming everything, destroying everything, and trampling over the ruins it had made," writes Reymont.[28] This time period was full of loss, cruelty, greed, and disregard for human life but also, as portrayed by Reymont, of the epic struggle between a persistent individual and their environment.

There was a term to describe this new Łódź man—*Lodzermensch*—first introduced at the end of the nineteenth century by the writer Wincenty Kosiakiewicz in his novel *Bawełna* (Cotton) and later explored by Reymont in *Promised Land*.[29] In the Polish literary canon, the term is synonymous with the brutal egoism appropriate to the nouveau riche in a land of competition: a man devoted completely to financial success regardless of the consequences. He was a morally degraded figure. But there is another side to the Lodzermensch. Art historian Dariusz Kacprzak underlines that "in workers' stories, [a Lodzermensch] is always a person who is, above all, hard-working and resourceful, but also takes care of the little ones; he tries to embrace working-class districts, schools, nurseries, and pharmacies, etc. with his paternalism."[30] He may, therefore, become a patron or a patriarchal figure who combines personal success with care for others.

Where was Tobiasz Bialer situated on this spectrum? How did he view the aggressive ethnocompetition? How did he treat his rivals? Was he concerned with the well-being of his workers? Unfortunately, these questions must remain unanswered, but Bialer was certainly actively engaged in the Jewish community. In the microfilms of the Gmina Żydowska (Jewish Community) documents left in Łódź, Bialer's name appears in a number of documents and local newspaper articles as early as 1910, which confirm the philanthropy of wealthy Jewish businessmen like him. Local newspapers mentioned him as someone involved in the communal effort to fight the cholera plague among the Jewish poor.[31] Bialer participated in Jewish community school committees that hired teachers and ensured that Jewish history and culture were being taught. He also worked with a Zionist committee in Łódź distributing money from Russia to the poor.[32] He was part of a committee responsible for opening a hospital for mentally ill Jews and a member of the Committee for Assistance to Victims of Pogroms in the Empire.[33] In addition to participating in the Jewish community, he remained active in the Łódź City Council and was part of a group that in 1910 established the Third Łódź Mutual Credit Association. His wife, introduced as Bialerowa Tobiaszowa, with her husband's name and surname, is mentioned in a report from 1916 that summarizes the activity of the Łódź Jewish community in extending care to orphans.[34] Bialer and his wife belonged to the generation of Jews who remained engaged on behalf of the Jewish community as well as the city as a whole and later the Polish state.[35]

Trunk provides yet another spin on the Bialers: regardless of their success, the family did not fit in the Łódź environment well. In a slightly exaggerated tone, Trunk writes of the Bialers as a family that combined wealth with cultural tastes that reminded him more of Warsaw elites than of typical Łódź businessmen. Trunk goes as far as stating that Bialer was a Warsaw man in Łódź, whose delicate and feminine business of lace production did not fit the masculine roughness of the majority of businesses in Łódź.[36] Trunk certainly has a tendency to idealize the past and nostalgically embellish his stories. He himself grew up in Łódź, where, as a young boy he attended a cheder, a traditional Jewish elementary school. He left war-torn Europe through Vilnius and Japan in 1941 and hence escaped the fate of many Jews. After the war, he settled in New York City, where he decided to re-create the lost world of Eastern European Jewry. The final product of his research is a nine-volume history consisting mostly of nostalgic ruminations on a world that is no longer—a morality drama full of commotion but also fortunate coincidences. He wrote in Yiddish, which, at the time was known mostly by those who escaped Eastern Europe. His anticipated audience was hence relatively small; his editors assumed that Trunk was committed to telling only stories his readers knew from their experiences.[37]

Trunk says little about Bialer, but his commentary on his fragility may suggest Trunk's awareness of how cruel and selective Łódź business was. A legal file in Russian from 1909 accuses Bialer of building a mechanized factory, even though according to its plan he was supposed to build a traditional manual workshop. His mechanized factory caused the walls of the neighboring factory to shake, endangering workers on both sides. The file contains complaints and reports written by various city committees that checked the quality of the wall. The documents are inconclusive: while one committee testified that the wall was indeed cracked, the other underlined that the cracks were not dangerous. In the end, Bialer did not fix anything.[38] The story seems to be straight from Reymont, but in the end it indicates that Bialer was a modern man and a Lodzermensch: on one hand, refined and of high culture, engaged in the building of his own community, but on the other, a scheming businessman who experimented with the bureaucracy of the modernizing state.

New Challenges

In November 1918 Poland regained its independence. Throughout the nineteenth century, Polish and Jewish communities had lived in relatively peaceful coexistence, although this past was not devoid of tragic moments, such as a pogrom in Łódź in 1892. Nineteenth-century Polish history is replete with various patriotic upheavals that tried to appeal to a sense of national unity by proclaiming programs of future assimilation and promises of equality that usually led to an increase in antisemitism in the aftermath of a defeat.[39] The early years of the twentieth century, with a shift toward aggressive nationalism, also marked an increase in antisemitic sentiments. On November 11—the day independent Poland was born—a pogrom took place in Kielce.[40] Polish independence made the Jews more vulnerable and dependent on the goodwill of Polish administrators of the new state, while non-Jewish Poles grew stronger and more self-assured. As Eva Hoffman, a Jewish Polish American writer, emphasizes:

> There is no doubt, that in the interwar period Polish politics became increasingly obsessed with the "Jewish question." The nature of that question was perceived differently than before; the imaginary, the very formulation of Jewishness changed in fundamental ways. Jews were still the main Other, the Polish alter ego, but this Otherness was no longer primary religious or caste-based or even cultural. Instead, it had become political and ideological. In the new Polish nation, the Jews began to be seen as another nation, one whose character was utterly distinct from Polish identity. Jews were becoming, then, not so much a part—no matter how loved or denigrated—of the symbolic and social entity that was Poland, but an entity unto themselves, which was experienced as somehow foreign, and which could be mentally detached or expelled from the symbolic universe of a self-contained Polish state.[41]

Łódź and other major Polish cities became the stages for antisemitic outbursts as early as the summer of 1919. Documents from the Gmina Żydowska contain many letters written by the shaken community to the new city authorities. In September 1919, less than a year after Poland regained independence, a group of alienated Jewish citizens wrote a letter that spoke of the pain, shock, and also confusion they were experiencing, albeit in a convoluted and metaphorical way: "Continuous subversive pogrom news poisons the national soul with an unhealthy flattery that lulls society to sleep and brings out the worst—this became the place of yesterday's incidents at Nowy Rynek and Nowomiejska, where Jews were attacked."[42] Antisemitic attacks continued for the next few months. In July 1919 other letters pointed to the actions of the so-called Hallerczycy, the soldiers of General Józef Haller, the Blue Army that had helped win Polish independence. For example, the Hallerczycy humiliated traditional Jews by cutting their beards, public acts that inspired others to engage in physical violence against Jews. Tension between the non-Jewish Polish and Jewish communities was growing.[43]

Questions of national allegiance and growing antisemitism were not the only problems city industrialists experienced. Industries did not grow as fast and as freely (or perhaps chaotically) as they had before. The change was partially caused by the fact that the reestablishment of the independent Polish state ended almost unhindered access to Russian markets. The first years of the 1930s brought the international financial crisis and the global Great Depression that affected many businesses. The difference in the conditions for business development between the end of the nineteenth century and the first decades after independence is symbolically represented at the Łódź cemetery. This is interestingly reflected in the mausoleum of Izrael Poznański, the most successful Łódź industrialist, who died in 1900 and was buried next to the main pathway of the Jewish cemetery in an enormous tomb designed when Poznański was still alive. Everything reflected his success: the size of the tomb built on a circular plane with a diameter of 9.5 meters as well as the materials—marble, granite, and glass. The shape was inspired by the grave of a medieval soldier. It is impressive and excessive—a testimony to the power and money that people like him had a chance to collect at the peak of Łódź's industrial development. Behind Poznański's mausoleum, at times barely visible in the weeds, is a small grave for his son and his son's wife—Maurycy Poznański and Sala Silberstein—who died in 1935. Its small plaque is barely visible in the shadow of Poznański's tomb.[44]

Economic hardships affected the Bialer family as well. In January 1925 the local Łódź newspaper *Głos Polski* announced that the Office of Taxes and Luxury Fees intended to confiscate some of the Bialers' property—machines, chairs, and tables as well as a horse and carriage—to cover taxes and stamp duties.[45] Aron Bialer's entrance to the world of commerce certainly was not easy.

It is difficult to say at what point he was introduced into his father's business, but at the beginning of 1925, soon after the attempted confiscation, the two made an investment together.[46] In October that year, in a faded and barely legible letter, Aron wrote to his wife, Róża (whom he addressed in various diminutive versions of her name), in an enthusiastic tone:

> Rózichno, yesterday we received the first installment of the construction loan. . . . By Monday, we will get two more . . . , so you see my arrival paid off. In general, it seems that our [illegible] . . . , Różyczko, begins to lighten up. Father felt that we cannot go on like this, and on Thursday he sold our shares in a home in Warsaw . . . , in the coming days a serious sum will flow, with which our financial relations can be completely healed. At the factory, I have already paid everyone. . . . I will work only in this new factory, and I hope we will be able to live modestly but completely calmly. After this wandering life, we will not have to experience so much of Łódź either, so I think we have every chance of being happy together.[47]

The letter signals that at least some of the financial worries had passed, but it is interesting for other reasons as well. This intimate note was written in Polish, indicating the family's advanced cultural acculturation, which stands in contrast to what Trunk, an idealistic chronicler of this world, tells us about young Aron, whom he describes as a "quiet . . . man, refined and spirited. Like all the other Bialers, he was not tall. He had large, beautiful black eyes."[48] While explaining that Hasidic leaders worried about the influence of revolutionary movements on youth, Trunk recounts their efforts to turn some Hasidic young men toward religious life. The young grew their side curls and "began to look in appearance more like their old Hasidic grandfathers. . . . Tobiasz Bialer's son also fell under the influence of these circles. He began to grow out his side curls, traveled to Ger [Góra Kalwaria], and observed Hasidism in the way it once was observed."[49] If we believe Trunk that Aron was indeed a Hasid in his youth, then there was a significant sociocultural change between his youth and adult life.[50]

While narrating further Aron's life, Trunk spends considerable time on him meeting his future wife. A chapter titled "Romeo and Juliet" forecasts their story, which is eventually scattered in other chapters. In the family archives, there is also an undated, small pink note, written in pencil that is barely visible today, that testifies to this great love, in which Róża wrote to Aron:

> I have never understood music like I did yesterday. It was as if I was enchanted. I did not see anything in front of me. It was as if I was in the woods with you, and the birds were singing about our happiness. And I felt so, so good. I hoped that upon returning, I would be able to share my impressions with you, and here a sad reality forbade me. I wanted all people after [illegible] that they spoiled this beloved moment. Well, it is hard, but in the meantime, we have to submit to fate. Your Rose. Where is the promised letter?[51]

Trunk and family legend illuminate how they met and also provide insight into how Aron changed from a Hasidic and religious man into an assimilated Jew. "It was a great love," according to Vera. "It was not an arranged marriage," added Marcel.[52] The majority of Jewish weddings during that time were arranged. Tobiasz and Basia's marriage was certainly arranged. The story of Aron and Róża, a story of a love by choice, aims to surprise but also suggests how that tradition gave way to modernity by creating space for new ways to think about love, relationships, and individual identity.

In lyricism full of exaggerations typical for him, Trunk narrates the story of Aron spotting Róża Wojdysławska at the home of his sister, Lotta Bialer. But as gender conventions and their social upbringing prescribed, they were not even allowed to speak to each other. Trunk says, "When Ruchla used to visit her friend Lotta, she often saw the Hasidic young man Aron, Lotta's brother, the young man with the long side curls and with a young fervor for Hasidism. Hasidic young men do not speak with young women. But Ruchla and Aron's glances met despite all barriers and biases."[53] Trunk then speculates that because Róża was emotional and straightforward, she fell very hard and very quickly for Aron: "He was a Hasidic young man with side curls, submerged in the biases of religious observance. . . . He shied from emotion like the Bialers tended to do. He was scared of it. And so it came much more slowly for him."[54]

Tobiasz Bialer opposed the marriage between Aron and Róża and continued to try to arrange a different spouse for his son.[55] But the young couple, who managed to meet in the presence of Lotta, shared their feelings and promised to be faithful to one another. Based on the family tale Rajf-Ligęza re-created, they confirmed their commitment to each other with a *tkias kaf,* or handshake—a legal and ethical binding agreement between two people—which the couple treated as a promise to each other.[56] Finally, Lotta revealed her brother's secret to her mother, explaining that Róża and Aron were already engaged. Initially, their mother was shocked and in disbelief. "'How is it possible that the daughter of Yosef Wojdysławski would do such a thing to her son?!' 'All of Poland will become crazy from such behavior. This is nonsense!,'" recounts Trunk.[57] In the Wojdysławski household the situation developed similarly, except that it was Róża who revealed the truth and declared that she was already a bride.[58] Eventually, after being pressured by some other family members, even Tobiasz acceded to the marriage.

The story resembles a fable, while the details of what happened in reality may be lost to history forever. The narrative underlines the strong character of Róża, about whose coming-of-age we know little but whose life probably mirrored the lives of many women in less religious but Orthodox families who struggled for independence, often resulting in estrangement from their families.[59] It is, for example, unclear what level of education she had. Trunk describes her in the following way: "She couldn't suffer having any darkness in her soul. She wanted everything to be open, clear, rational—and, most importantly, that every feeling should be turned quickly into an action item."[60] But how Róża is remembered as fighting for the right to make her own decisions, even if it meant a rejection of parental authority and traditions, foreshadows the central role she played in Aron's financial decisions. For the rest of her life, she remained Aron's business as well as life partner. It is also likely that her decisiveness was one of the most important factors in Aron's evolution from Hasidism to more secular Polish Jewish bourgeoise, combining Polish patriotism with Zionism, which the Bialer family showcased in the next decade.[61]

Life on Piotrkowska Street

In 1919, when Tonia was only one year old, her grandfather and father bought a beautiful, terraced art nouveau townhouse at 85 Piotrkowska Street for 450,000 Polish marks. (Tobiasz was the owner of four-fifths of the house, while Aron owned the other fifth.)[62] Built in 1897, the building had two richly ornamented bay windows dominating its facade, which featured putti, flower garlands, and shells.[63] The main part of the building had at least six apartments, and in the big courtyard, there were fourteen apartments and utility rooms. Tobiasz, his wife, and Aron's family lived there. Two of Aron's sisters, Lotta and Fajga, resided in the building as well.

For the Bialers, moving into a new house meant entering into various arrangements with the newly independent Polish state. The thick folder from the Polish National Development Bank (Bank Gospodarstwa Krajowego) shows the meticulously noted history of the property from the years 1919 through 1939. The bank's presence in the Bialers' life illustrates the growing place of the Polish state in its citizens' lives. The folder includes documentation about the moment when the house changed ownership, the various investment loans the Bialers as its owners took, and their fire insurance policy. The descriptions of the house as well as the obligations of people taking a loan or paying the insurance premium include various provisions that ultimately underscore that the house was an excellent investment for both the Bialers and the state providing them with loans.[64]

Tonia began narrating her life story to Dorota Dowgiałło, the daughter of the first Polish ambassador in Israel, in 1994 with a description of her home on 85 Piotrkowska. The family occupied six rooms so spacious that her brothers could ride a *drezyna*—a type of balance bicycle—across the house from the front to the back.[65] Tonia's and Romek's rooms were so distant that she rarely knew what her brother was doing.[66] It was a modern house with modern amenities, including electricity, water, toilet, elevators, and a phone. The family had a cook and a live-in maid.

The family was close. Vera's vast closet contains what seems to be a never-ending supply of documents and letters that reveal bits and pieces of the family's story. As photography was becoming more popular at the time, there are a significant number of snapshots showing the family on vacation in the mountains, enjoying city streets, celebrating holidays. They traveled extensively both outside and within Poland. Abroad, they went to Switzerland and Germany. In Poland, they were frequent visitors to Sopot on the Baltic Sea and occasionally the mountains in the south. They corresponded with each other while separated during the summer months. In the 1930s the children spent parts of their summer vacations in Worochta, a resort in the Hutsul region of the eastern Carpathian Mountains, a popular skiing and summer destination, mostly for bourgeois to upper-middle-class Varsovians and people from Eastern Galicia. According to historian Patrice Dabrowski, the village Worochta (or other destinations, such as Jaremcze that one could reach with ease, by train or other means of conveyance) had all the makings of a resort. It had the requisite post office, telegraph, and telephone bureaus; several restaurants and "breakfast rooms," a hairdresser/barber shop, several cobblers (always a necessity in heavily hiked regions) and a watchmaker. There was a radio in one of the villas—at a time when radios were still rare in Poland. Conditions within the boarding houses and villas, although primitive (oil lamps instead of electricity), were sanitary and satisfactorily comfortable.[67]

Postcards and letters from the children testify to the deep bond they had with their parents. "I am very sad without you. If there was a cousin I could at least confide in someone. I am miserable. You told me that you will keep the door and windows open at night so I could come. And according to me, windows and doors are open, and I cannot come," wrote Noemi to her parents.[68] Tonia told Dowgiałło that she was very "anti-Mama" in those years, but a different image emerges from the letters. They show a loving family with a deep mutual attachment. Tonia was warm, open, and friendly with her parents, occasionally even intimate: "Mamusiu, I am doing great, the only thing that exhausted me was my period that I got two weeks after arriving with terrible pains," wrote the fifteen-year-old.[69]

Tonia's memories and family documents from this time revolve around family life. An absence of non-Jewish Poles in the Bialers' social circles stands out in these stories. Tonia's brother claimed that apart from their maid (the cook had to be Jewish), he did not know any non-Jewish Poles. Tonia had a few non-Jewish Polish friends, but they were not close enough to visit her at home. Her mother had some non-Jewish Polish friends from her youth, but the majority of her close friends were Jews who eventually immigrated to Palestine. This world was a reality for many. The Bialers lived in respect for but nevertheless in separation from the non-Jewish Polish communities. What Eva Hoffman wrote about the Jewish and non-Jewish Polish communities she studied applies in this case as well: "They knew each other through proximity and familiarity, but not exchanges or intimacy."[70]

In her conversation with Dowgiałło, Tonia expressed that she viewed her parents as fervent Polish patriots who were deeply entrenched in Polish

FIGURE 1.1. Tonia (left) with her mother, Róża Bialer, and siblings during a vacation, Rytro, Poland, 1933. *(Private collection of Vera and Marcel Lechtman)*

culture and society and committed to Jewish traditions at the same time. While she noticed her parents' sympathies for Zionism, she emphasized that they did not seem to be interested in leaving Poland. In a joke Tonia recollected, a Zionist was a person who took money from one person to send to a third person in Palestine. He himself did not want to leave. Her mother had studied Polish literature at clandestine Polish history and literature courses in Łódź when the city was part of the Russian partition and Russian was the legal language.[71]

Tonia's parents spoke at least a couple of languages and pushed their children to learn them as well. Following her mother, Tonia believed that books had to be read in the language in which they were written and not in translation. Romek was learning French, German, Hebrew, and Latin in Switzerland. Tonia completed first grade in Switzerland and later was often sent for summer vacation to either Germany or Switzerland to practice her German. The children always had a German nanny.[72] Polish, however, remained the primary language of daily conversations and letters exchanged with the children and was the intimate language between Aron and Róża.

While the lack of Polish fluency in Jewish families often inhibited assimilation, mastery of the Polish language did not necessarily lead to adaptation or assimilation.[73] What we know about the Bialers suggests that they were assimilated rather than merely adapted to Polish culture. They felt responsible for the well-being of the country and were culturally embedded in the majority Polish society and culture. From Tonia we know that both of her parents cherished the cultural life offered in Warsaw, where they traveled often. Years later in Palestine, Róża missed the fashion, the streets, and the urban life that Warsaw and to a lesser extent Łódź offered. The family was also politically committed to Poland. Tonia explained straightforwardly her parents' political engagement: her father followed Polish politics and supported certain political strands, which Tonia rationalized by saying that in a democratic country everybody needed to participate in state politics.[74] They were and considered themselves part of Polish society.

Parents' educational choices for their children usually directly correlated to their financial capacity and political and social views. Interwar Poland opened new educational opportunities for children and youth, and the new government mandated that children attend school for at least seven grades.[75]

For Jewish youth, this meant participation in a state-driven mass education campaign that valorized the state at the expense of local, ethnic, and religious communities.[76] The percentage of children enrolled in public schools grew. Until the outbreak of World War II, at least 90 percent of children aged thirteen and below attended school.[77] The process of re-creating what it meant to be Polish was in full swing.

In her conversation with Dowgiałło, Tonia shared a bit about the education she and her siblings received, revealing how her parents' view of their children's education vacillated through the interwar period. Romek, who was born in 1913, started off in a Polish public elementary school (*szkoła powszechna*), from which he was moved to a boarding school—a yeshiva in Switzerland—only to return later to a public school again, most likely due to some financial problems the Bialers encountered at that time. From 1927 to 1933, Tonia attended the private gymnasium—a school of secondary education—of Madame Maria Hochstein for Jewish girls from affluent families. There, in Tonia's words, the students followed the program of the Polish public schools, with Polish being the main language, and she received a "patriotic, fully Polish education."[78] The two youngest children were sent to private schools, where Hebrew and Polish were the two main languages taught. Most Jewish students in interwar Poland attended private school rather than public school, despite the steady impoverishment of the Jewish middle class that limited the number of parents who could pay for a private education.[79] The Bialers started with public schooling and switched to private relatively expensive schools, even as their financial difficulties grew. This shift may reflect their desire to deal with the problems they had with their older son Romek and Tonia, who had become communists early in life. The change may also suggest a consideration of a potential move to Palestine.

The term "assimilation" holds a complex place in Polish historiography.[80] Assimilation was a political program and a process of sociocultural integration. In interwar Poland, official plans for assimilation failed, and it was only by individual decision that minorities integrated with mainstream society.[81] Polish Jews had been living in Poland for centuries and were deeply knitted into the cultural, political, and social fabric of the country. "They lived, quite simply, at home," says historian Michael Steinlauf.[82] This was their land, and many Jews, assimilated and nonassimilated alike, felt at home where they lived. They did not have memories from a life somewhere else that they could compare with their present life. Hence, "it was possible to love Poland, not because they were Poles, but because they were Jews who considered Poland their land," argues historian and sociologist Anna Landau-Czajka. Reflecting on the work of sociologist Anna Kłoskowska, Landau-Czajka insists that in the case of Jewish assimilation we speak of national ambivalence, which signifies that assimilation was not a transfer over generations from one identity to another but rather a condition of suspension in which neither of the cultures (or even neither of the identities) was fully ours nor fully theirs.[83] Interestingly, this theory indicates that full assimilation—the complete melting of one community into another—happened rarely in interwar Poland.[84] Recent research takes this thought a step further, suggesting that what we usually perceive as assimilation is really a form of integration of both cultures, which nevertheless leads to the creation of Polish Jewish subcultures that allow for emotional identification with mainstream Polish symbols and history while maintaining a sense of belonging to a separate ethnic and religious group.[85]

Further complicating the issue of assimilation, Landau-Czajka emphasizes that the desire to assimilate was parallel to modernization, which was one way to emancipate oneself from one's community or to join the mainstream Polish community.[86] For centuries, Jews had constituted a closed community with its own social and religious rules. Toward the end of the nineteenth century, new social, political, and cultural movements—such as a push for girls' education in Austro-Hungary—created new challenges to traditional Jewish life.[87] These challenges continued to be visible in the interwar period, but the departure from tradition could be traumatic. It often implied a rebellion against or at least a rejection of Jewish religion or culture and a socially predetermined path, and the process included Jewish intelligentsia as well as Jews from Orthodox circles.[88] Joanna Wiszniewicz, a second-generation Holocaust survivor, said of her mother's generation growing up in interwar Poland: "This was the entire society: non-Polish, non-Jewish, but assimilated Jews.... What did they have in common? That they were departing from traditional religious Jewry and were marching toward modernity. It was an incredibly traumatic road. Moving to modernity is difficult for every nation, but for Jews it was particularly traumatic. Jews wishing for secularism had to give up their rich culture."[89] Once they decided to follow this path, the level of urbanization and participation in public culture and schools grew quickly. Some Jews were leaving their own structures while hoping to enter

FIGURE 1.2. Aron Bialer with his son Julek, Łódź, late 1920s. *(Private collection of Vera and Marcel Lechtman)*

mainstream Polish ones, but in general they were not accepted by non-Jewish Poles.[90] Non-Jewish Poles were more willing to accept traditional Jews who lived separately, whereas modern and assimilated Jews constituted a threat.[91]

What did that situation mean for Tonia? She grew up in a relatively sheltered life of an affluent assimilated Jewish family.[92] The family was isolated from traditional religious Jewish communities and from mainstream Polish society. The family was isolated due to its wealth and the lifestyle that came with it but also due to the presence of cultural antisemitism that made it almost impossible even for the richest and best educated Polish-speaking Jews to be accepted or considered "Poles," belonging to Poland and its space in the way that non-Jewish Poles belong. Tonia was alienated from both the dominant Jewish and Polish worlds, which pushed many people from milieus similar to hers to take radical steps toward movements, such as communism, that contested almost everything they came from.

Traditions and Beyond

Tonia's recollections of her home on Piotrkowska Street revolved around stories of traditional Jewish holidays celebrated in her household. Tonia was not religious. She was not particularly traditional either, at least for most of her life. But toward the end of her life, when she was narrating her life story to Dowgiałło in Israel, she was rediscovering the importance of meals and traditions. She was also responding to the new life roles she took upon herself in the last phase of her life and was searching for links between her old life and the new one she had embarked on in Israel, and religious traditions certainly provided that link. Decades earlier—at another turning point in her life—she did something similar. Vera remembered that in the 1950s, when her mother was trying to rebuild her family life after her release from prison, she went to a Jewish committee in Warsaw for Passover matzo to show her children what it was and introduce them to at least some aspects of Jewish religious life.[93]

Tonia's childhood home was a traditional kosher home, run by Tonia's grandmother, who chose the cooks, kept a kosher kitchen, and decided details regarding major religious holidays. It was also a household with a generational split: while the grandparents kept traditions alive, the second generation already filtered what they considered important from what they valued less. The children even secretly received money from their mother to buy ham sandwiches. Tonia remembered that her father visited the synagogue twice a year: at Yom Kippur, the holiest day in the Jewish calendar, the day of atonement and repentance, and Rosh Hashanah, the Jewish New Year.[94] But the day they celebrated the most was Passover:

> It was a beautiful rite. Moses's journey was mentioned. The father who read the Hagada loudly had to sit on a throne or a very comfortable chair. We had to sit on a settee with many pillows. He sat all night, dressed in a mortal shirt [*śmiertelna koszula*], in which every Jew gets married, always wears on Pesach, and is buried in. This is basically a normal shirt. But because this night it covers the body of a symbolic king, it has a very beautiful collar embroidered with gold thread. . . . The table also had to be beautifully dressed. Mom used to send me to a Dutch flower shop, where I picked up flowers. And there were always two hyacinth flowerpots on the table. I liked it very much.[95]

The "mortal shirt" from Tonia's description is better known as a *kittel,* a lightweight robe usually tied with a white belt of same material, a garment in which Jewish *men* get married, wear on Pesach, and are buried in.[96] Tonia does not seem to have the precise vocabulary, and even decades later she looked back at these rituals from the perspective of a child: noticing the aesthetic and theatrical value of the rite, with objects that on that special day lost their quotidian features and became sacred. They did not have to be understood by a child, but they were part of the world children understood.[97] She resumed:

> The youngest asked the father about the journey through the desert. There always had to be a goy. In any case—there should be. And an open door. So, I was very scared that a thief or thug would come in. And yet the prophet Elijah would come and wait for the largest cup. We sat for a long time—until twelve o'clock—and adults even longer. The whole ceremony made a great impression on me. The food was not, in my opinion, especially good. Broth with dumplings. And, of course, fish. Then some meat and hard-boiled eggs in salt water that was supposed to symbolize seawater. Then there was a terribly bitter paste at the mention of bad and sad days. At the end, very good apples with nuts, as a memory of later joy.[98]

Tonia most likely misremembered elements of the celebrations as there is no obligation for a non-Jewish person to participate in them. She especially remembered food as an important element of the spectacle. And the memory of food is mixed with Tonia's childlike surprise at other elements that she could not understand or that terrified her:

> Yom Kippur was celebrated very tragically. There was a fast, and Mama said she would not survive any fasting....[99] And she lay in bed all day.... We had to walk on tiptoe, although we lived at the other end of the house. You could not drink water or brush your teeth. In the evening before dinner, my mother received some black coffee to revive her. My father went to the synagogue. In fact, he should have gone barefoot, but he usually put on his shoes.... Two days before Yom Kippur, a live rooster was bought and tied on the balcony. During the feast, my father would say some prayer by raising this bird over my brother's head. The rooster would squawk; I was terrified.[100]

Especially interesting in this story is Aron's insistence on certain traditional celebrations and Róża's resistance or even defiance (in fact, Tonia also recalled Róża locking herself in a room with a headache). Tonia remembered these prayers as half-terrifying and half-amusing.[101]

Then there was Sukkot, the feast of huts. Józef Hen, a Polish author who grew up in Jewish Warsaw on Nowolipie Street before the war, mentions it in his memoirs as the most pleasant of the Jewish holidays and a moment that marked the mixing of the private celebration with the public.[102] Sukkot celebrates the end of harvest time and, thus, of the agricultural year, as well as the Jews' exodus from slavery in Egypt, and is consequently one of the most joyous occasions. The Hebrew word *sukkah* means a temporary dwelling in which farmers lived during the harvest; *sukkot* evolved as walled structures, often covered with fabric. It is also intended as a reminiscence of the type of fragile dwellings the Israelites inhabited during their forty years in the desert after the exodus. Tonia remembered:

> And I still remember the feast of huts. We had a small balcony at the back. Wooden walls were put in there, which had very nice, colorful glass. And this was what it was like—a hut. Palm leaves and special benches were brought from the attic. In theory, for a week, you could eat only there. But, naturally, we ate in the apartment, and pro forma

once a day went for lunch or for dinner on the balcony. Most of those who did not have balconies built shacks in the yard. Now you can buy very cheap plastic shacks with various fabrics for the cover. From that time, I remember the October weather—cold, wet, and windy. My parents showed piety and behaved only for grandparents. . . . but really, I do not know much.[103]

The bits and pieces about religious traditions that Tonia provides suggest a lot about the internal family dynamics, but retrospectively the possibility of narrating that story provided Tonia with a possibility to relive and idealize her early youth in the bosom of her family: things they agreed on, things they quarreled about, and ways they negotiated their contact with the outside world.

|||

Tonia's early life was full of warmth, security, and wealth. Not surprisingly, years later she idealized these years significantly. From the perspective of the end of her life, she chose to speak about the sense of safety and being grounded that her early years and the family home provided. The reality, however, is that despite the inroads that increasing assimilation created for the inclusion of Jews into mainstream Polish society, the sense of belonging to its margins was shared by many Jewish youth, including Tonia. In the 1930s antisemitism in public life was becoming increasingly visible and detrimental to Jewish communities, breaking the fabric of various communities and affecting family and personal life. As a matter of fact, Tonia was most likely experiencing double alienation: from mainstream Polish society and from the more traditional Jewish world from which she felt increasingly withdrawn.

2 ||| A Dream of New Life

Communism and Palestine, 1935–1938

VERA AND Marcel knew that their mother was a communist. Her commitment to communism characterized the fabric of her life and determined her life choices. Toward the end of her life, Tonia began sharing her life story with journalists and historians. Perhaps then, while reflecting on the entirety of her life, she grew increasingly critical of communism. Even then, however, she remained deeply disturbed by the social injustice around her. Yet her children, especially Marcel, misjudged the depth to which her life was intertwined with twentieth-century communist Europe.

In 2011 Marcel Łoziński, a filmmaker and longtime family friend of the Lechtmans, made a movie, *Tonia i jej dzieci* (Tonia and her children), about the complex relationship between Tonia, Vera, and Marcel.[1] In the movie, Vera and Marcel, as well as Łoziński, read various documents from Tonia's life. While reading a fragment of the minutes of one of her Polish security service interrogations, Marcel breaks down in tears, while Vera, aware of their mother's life challenges, is more composed. Marcel, two years younger than Vera, remembers nothing. Vera is familiar with Tonia's intimacy with communism and is hence less inclined to question some of their mother's decisions, but Marcel finds most of them utterly incomprehensible. He needs time to fully comprehend what he is hearing and reading, but the merciless camera catches him off guard. Vera's broader understanding of her mother's past makes her less vulnerable to the stories that unfold during the making of the film. In contrast, the realization of how all-encompassing Tonia's communist engagement was and how little he knew affects Marcel's sense of self. At one point, he reads his mother's statement from interrogation minutes: "I thought that communism is the best solution for the world. And I was not hiding it." "Yes, this is our mama," then, looking straight at the camera, he nods with a weak smile. It is the look of a person who finds consolation in signs that confirm a familiar aspect of the past. He still needs to digest that statement's complexity; nonetheless, the declaration of her straightforward commitment to social justice is reassuring.

Only later, in early spring 2019, during a phone conversation with Tonia's granddaughter, Anna, did I understood Marcel's smile. For Anna, her grandmother's communism was like a dream that had defined Tonia. Despite multiple adversities, her commitment to communism remained youthful and strangely idealistic, even uncontaminated with the doubts caused by her suffering. Marcel and Anna knew a different Tonia, yet both recognized the idealistic communist Tonia. The recognition of this idealism helped Marcel build a bridge between the mother he did not know, the mother he briefly lived with as a teenager, and the mother he occasionally met later in life.[2]

Radical Choices and Communism

During her July 1949 and January 1950 interrogations, Tonia reflected on her initiation into the world of communism.[3] Her early youth constituted only a fragment of the testimonies she deposited back then—under duress, in fear for her children's safety, and confused about why she was being interrogated. In her 1994 interview with Dorota Dowgiałło, she also spoke about her commitment, this time of her own free will. During the interrogations, she desperately tried to prove her communist commitment, but the circumstances did not offer space for reflection. In contrast, the retrospective nature of her meeting with Dowgiałło meant that the conversation turned into a reflective, and relatively safe, space. Tonia, however, offered significantly less detail and told some anecdotes differently. Much time had passed, and the details in her memory were fading in favor of a coherent story that spanned various aspects of her identity: communist, Polish, Jewish.

Communism was not the only radical cultural and political movement that attracted Jews during the interwar. There was a spectrum of responses to questions of Jewish identity and strategies of emancipation, such as Bund, Zionism, and Yiddishism. Jewish propensity for radical solutions should be seen within the context of specific historical contingencies: Jews' cultural and historical heritage and their social marginalization. Jaff Schatz, one of the first scholars to reflect on the sociological and historical nature of interwar Jewish radicalism, argues that in the cleavage created by modernization and secularization—which pushed people to abandon the safety of traditional life for uncertainties of modernity and widened the generational gap—a vision of the future emerged: "utopian, restorative, nationalist, or universalist."[4] This drive for change is visible in a youth memoir collection from the 1930s written for a competition organized by the Yiddish Scientific Institute (YIVO) in Vilnius. One of the authors, Esther from Grójec, wrote, "Why do I have to suffer like this, when I have such a drive to learn? . . . Why must I content myself with conforming, when I know that, given the opportunity, I can accomplish great things."[5] Historian Kamil Kijek argues that the Jewish youth of interwar Poland created their own form of generational weltanschauung—a complex worldview, with a cognitive orientation to the future that demanded a critical overview of the past, including traditions, values, and daily habits.[6] The chasm between their and their parents' expectations pushed Jewish youth to political engagement in the hope that their actions would transform Jewish lives on many levels, from their position within Jewish families to the position they occupied in (or outside) of Polish society.

Young people's attraction to communism, Zionism, or some other form of activism depended on their cultural capital, social status, and place of origin. Social closeness to a given group mattered more than political inclinations. At least until the 1930s, while communism—the most antisystem of the options—incited the poorest families, Zionism was a middle-class movement. Geography also played an important role. Bund sympathizers were in central Poland, whereas communist followers were recruited mostly from big cities. However, participation in a given group was often incidental and dependent on which political group was active nearby.[7] The majority of young people, rather than changing their social environment, often joined the same organization as their siblings or friends.

Communism as the most revolutionary choice was a rather marginal one. As a radical threat to the existing order, communism was officially banned in Poland in 1919 due to its ideological closeness to the Community Party of the Soviet Union and claims against Polish independence. Due to the communist movement's illegality, available statistics are not precise. Some historians suggest that Jews constituted between one-fourth and one-third of the movement. Based on some knowledge on how Jews voted in the 1928 Sejm election, Schatz concludes that "Communist ideals were sympathetic to only about 5 percent of all Jewish voters."[8] And yet Jews were visible in communist activism and leftist parties.[9] For young people who identified as communist, it meant engaging in an outlawed activity, requiring conspiratorial and often militant behavior. Communist activists fought for inclusion in Polish society, while situating themselves outside the legal bounds of that society.

As an idea, communism offered millenarian hope in the inevitability of changes that would transform a hierarchical society into one free from exploitation, misery, oppression, religion, antisemitism, war, and nationalism. This universal alternative to the world they knew presented itself as a historical certainty offering young people a chance to become part of history.[10] Stories of many young communist activists convey their hope to build "out of the ruins of the old order."[11] Historical determinism can be found in the writing of Jewish youth from those years as well. In 1934 A. Greyno wrote in his memoir for the youth memoir competition, "My life entered a new period. I was proud of the knowledge I had acquired, in contrast with the philistine who is absorbed with his personal life and is unfamiliar with the historical development of the society to which he belongs."[12] Finally, as Schatz underlines, communism, regardless of how radical and challenging its past was, drew inspiration from cultural heritage partially defined by "moralism connected to a yearning for justice, a belief in rationality, a respect for learning and study, and a messianic core that was to facilitate the transformation, conservative ballast of tradition into fuel for radicalism."[13]

For Tonia, her communist journey began in 1933 when she was only fifteen years old.[14] Tonia's older brother, Romek, was a member of the Communist Party of Poland (Komunistyczna Partia Polski, KPP), but it was not he who introduced her to communism.[15] As she revealed in an interrogation, that happened through her school. The private gymnasium for Jewish girls she attended left almost no records, so it is impossible to definitively determine which social and political groups were represented in the school.[16] But Tonia claimed that many communists and some Bund followers attended the school. Her first contact with what she described as communism occurred in 1932 when an older school friend asked her to bring food to a prison.[17] During another interrogation, her story changed slightly as she revealed that a schoolmate with whom she shared a room during summer camp in 1933 showed her the value of sharing, by pointing out that the money Tonia had found on the street could be given to political prisoners. During the 1933–34 school year, the same school friend asked her to bring her breakfast to a prison for women political prisoners in Łódź.[18] What she was describing as communism were gestures of compassion extended to the more vulnerable and ultimately people the state punished for their political views. Her introduction to communism illustrates that even before the most infamous prison for communists was established in Bereza Kartuska in 1934, young people were acquiring lessons on political injustice from their peers and observing the world around them. It also suggests that she understood communism as a teenager (and perhaps also decades later when she was under interrogation in communist Poland) as a commitment to brotherhood, justice, and freedom. When talking about her youthful activism, Tonia told Dowgiałło that she wanted to become a scout but her local scout branch informed her that they did not accept Jews, which led her to search for an organization that would accept her, a story that differed from her earlier focus on school friends.[19] Perhaps

FIGURE 2.1. Tonia's school class on a trip to Kraków, 1934 or 1935. *(Private collection of Vera and Marcel Lechtman)*

reflecting forty years later on her past, while living an isolated life in Israel, a sense of rejection and the need for community resonated more with her.

Tonia did join the International Organization of Help to the Revolutionaries (Międzynarodowa Organizacja Pomocy Rewolucjonistom, MOPR), which collected money for "all captives of capitalism in prison."[20] The MOPR was established in 1922 in the Soviet Union during the Fourth Congress of the Communist International (Comintern).[21] In Germany the organization took the name Rote Hilfe, and the Polish section adopted the Polish translation of that name, Red Help (Czerwona Pomoc). Red Help, actively present in Polish public life in the 1930s, was popular among Jews. In 1932 about 90 percent of its six thousand members were Jews.[22] MOPR members collected food for prisoners at prison entry points, but we do not have any information about Tonia's possible involvement.

In her interrogations, Tonia repeated that the first organization she joined was the illegal Union of School Youth (Związek Młodzieży Szkolnej). "The word 'communism' was not even part of its name," she emphasized decades later.[23] Born in 1921, Irena Wojdysławska, three years younger than Tonia, attended the same school. She grew up in a family of assimilated Jews in Łódź and came from a similar social background. Their time at the school likely overlapped.[24] Similarly to Tonia, Wojdysławska remembered the active presence of young communists in school, but in contrast to Tonia, she recalled participating in the meetings of the Union of Communist School Youth (Komunistyczny Związek Młodzieży Szkolnej), a division of the Communist Union of Polish Youth (Komunistyczny Związek Młodzieży Polskiej, KZMP), an organization that certainly carried the adjective "communist" in its name. It was a branch of an illegal youth organization operating from 1922 to 1938 and led by the KPP.

The files of the KZMP, which was active in Łódź in the mid-1930s when Tonia was learning what it meant to be a communist, provide some insight into the organization's life. Typed reports from various meetings are barely legible due to poor paper and ink quality, but they reveal that it mostly organized various strikes and mobilized youth, especially working-class youth, to spark communist activism in Łódź's factories. The future of communism lay in the strike committees germinating in various parts of the city. The organization's work for more advanced activists was based on constant negotiations regarding short- and long-term goals, promotion of strikes among workers who were unwilling to risk their jobs, and organization of mass strikes focused on pressuring various factories' authorities to yield to workers' demands. The work also involved negotiations between socialist groups from various city districts. Meetings often resembled social events during which different youth groups discussed their goals and exchanged opinions in an atmosphere marked with genuine solemnity and commitment to the cause.[25]

Like the KZMP and KPP, the Union of Communist School Youth was a clandestine organization. It played a supportive role to the KZMP by publicly supporting communism and self-education. "A speaker would come to each of the meetings. There were all kinds of propaganda brochures. We'd collect money for political prisoners," remembered Wojdysławska.[26] In 1950 Tonia described her first communist meeting: "Two months after I entered the Union, there was a general meeting which was attended by several people. It took place in a basement and lasted all day. I remember that 'Wacka' gave a lecture. But I don't remember on what."[27] The meetings were educational: they inspired young people to expand their political horizons by reading literature on social injustice and the world's future progress. By creating a space for intellectual exchanges, the meetings also allowed for emotional and social growth, giving young activists a chance to escape from the often-confining atmosphere of their households and to figure out their priorities and values.[28] Tonia was not overly active, but she did paint communist slogans on walls in various parts of the city.[29] At some point, she and her school friends received instructions from the KZMP to participate in *masówki*, meetings that communists organized in connection with strikes or near factories when workers went to or from their jobs. On May 1, 1934, International Workers' Day, she received a beating from a mounted policeman. The KZMP's reports from the May 1 celebration in Łódź confirm that violence usually unfolded on the streets during those days. Participating youth were often dispersed with the use of rifle butts.[30]

Tonia read the *Communist Manifesto*, which she described as "beautiful." Polish intellectual Stanisław Brzozowski's *Płomienie* (Flames), however, registered deepest with her.[31] What resonated most with young people was his romantic (and Polish) version of communism as a world-saving ideology that called them to become "the people of the future—conscious witnesses of history."[32] Communism's connection to Polishness, on one hand, and its visionary and future-oriented character that positioned youth as agents of future transformation, on the other, likely most appealed to Tonia.

The circumstances of how she received the book suggest another possible influence. In her work on Brzozowski, literary specialist Lena Magnone underscores the importance of his reflection in *Płomienie* on women, the body, and sexuality and the links between individual growth and gender identity development.[33] Tonia received her first copy of *Płomienie* from her aunt, an independent and free-thinking woman, whom Tonia saw as a role model. The sources do not reveal Tonia's reflections on women's role in society, but her recognition of this gift as significant in her life and the gift giver—an independent and intellectually stimulating woman—as a role model may signify her views on the importance of women's education and independence.[34]

From all the bits and pieces about Tonia's early experience with communism emerges an image of a young woman committed to social justice. Emerging even more strongly is the place her activism played in her own path to figuring out life priorities, challenging and then growing independent from her own family:

> One day I was working on a banner . . . with a friend. At dinner my sister, six years my junior, who kept watching us, out of nowhere said, "Why is Tonia writing 'Let May 1st Live' instead of May 3rd?"[35] This was terrible. How I beat her then. Mama naturally took everything away from me. In addition, we [communists] had to write different slogans on walls. There were many arrests while doing that. Besides, I always belonged to some athletic group. I loved sports. At school, on the athletic track, I even performed in Spała [the summer residence of the Polish presidents, in western Poland]. And President [Ignacy] Mościcki kissed me. I treated my participation in the communist movement most seriously. I had school friends. In class, I was friends with a girl who was killed in the Soviet Union. She had been angry at me for my contact with communists.[36]

While narrating her life, she mentioned almost in the same breath communism, school sports competitions, and a gesture of recognition she received from the Polish president. Various memory layers are interwoven: adolescent exploration is mixed with ongoing conflict with her parents and a growing chasm between her and her friends. The gesture of sharing encouraged by a friend or the desire to be part of a group were elements of a common thread in her communist recollections: Tonia remembered her communist activism through the prism of others, rather than through its ideological dimension.

Her parents figure predominantly in her recollections. "My parents had a lot of problems with me," she repeated often throughout her conversation with Dowgiałło. When her parents realized that she participated in strikes on May 1, her mother reacted with anger. "My mom wanted to spank me, so out of spite, I told my dad that she hit me. My father yelled at her terribly." Interestingly, she positioned her parents as representing the punishing authorities who refused to accept either her fascination with communism or her participation in an illegal activity. Communism exposed her to ideas that put her in direct conflict with her parents' beliefs and their world. She began questioning their lifestyle by asking about and criticizing the working conditions in her father's factory. In another recollection, she mentioned that in 1935, when Józef Piłsudski died, she started calling out happily, "'Oh, great! The fascist!' Then my father slapped me across my face for the first and only time in my life. He said, 'How dare you talk about Poland's greatest man!' I thought that Dad was an opportunist and respected Piłsudski only for class reasons."[37] Her parents supported Piłsudski, a soft authoritarian, who in the 1930s ran the Non-Party Bloc for Cooperation with the Government (Bezpartyjny Blok Współpracy z Rządem, BBWR), which favored accommodation for minorities. Piłsudski was certainly not an antisemite, and he believed that ethnic groups could join or assimilate into the Polish nation without giving up their communal ties or, within reason, their mother tongue.[38]

Communism was Tonia's stepping-stone in the process of figuring out her life priorities and determining her multiple identities. She was a woman, a Polish Jew, a member of a relatively traditional and affluent Jewish family, and a maturing citizen who needed to reconcile her obligations toward the Polish state with her uneasiness toward it.

First Arrest

In her conversation with Dowgiałło, Tonia did not discuss her perceptions of Łódź, its poverty, or its difficult social relations. Probably shielded by her parents, Tonia had limited opportunities to notice the misery in some parts of the city. Maria Kamińska (b. 1897) was significantly older than Tonia, and in the 1930s she was already a mature activist. She likewise recollected that her childhood was shielded from life outside of her household. Kamińska, a woman from a well-off family of Łódź Jewish industrialists who early in her life became an activist of local communist groups, however, did write about the misery of interwar Łódź and especially Bałuty, an impoverished Jewish district:

> Łódź. Strange city. An ugly, sad, cruel city. When one goes out into the street at dusk, there are lines of hunched, leaning people walking by you. Their step is heavy, exhausted. Raw faces, furrowed with care. Hands, hungry for rest, hang down inertly. Clothing, almost rags: ... frayed jackets, ugly trousers crumpled to the bottom wrapping the tibiae of emaciated legs. ... There is another shift coming out of the factories. They go and they go, and this procession seems to have no end. ... This is living in Łódź—unprotected exploitation.

This injustice pushed Kamińska to activism—visits to Łódź's poor districts and organization of talks and strikes in front of factories—eventually leading to her arrest.[39]

Even though Tonia was shielded, her participation in discussions organized by the KZMP must have made her aware of the city's problems. She also participated in a *masówka*, a mass gathering, at which she eventually got arrested. At the end of May 1934, on the Jewish holiday of Shavuot, she and a couple of friends received an order to participate in a masówka in Bałuty:

> When we arrived, the masówka was already taking place. ... We started chanting slogans we were told to. Toward the end, policemen began coming. People started running. My friend and I began running as well, but at some point we noticed that our third friend was behind us limping. We waited for her and slowly walked together. A policeman was walking a few yards behind us. Walking, we were turned toward the policeman all the time. This probably drew his attention, as he increased his walking speed and, after catching up with us, stopped us and escorted us to the police station.[40]

An interrogation followed, attempting to establish the women's connection to the communists. It is not clear how long Tonia was jailed. In her 1949 interrogation, she revealed that she was confined for eight days.[41] The next year, in 1950, she said she was jailed for two weeks before her parents posted bail.[42]

While talking with Dowgiałło, she remembered being jailed for four or five days. Her lawyer—and a friend of Tonia's parents—suggested she not come to her trial as he feared she would shout communist slogans. During the trial that proceeded without Tonia's presence, she was found not guilty. She told Dowgiałło that she regretted the harm her confinement had caused others. But she also felt humiliated because her family's wealth and social standing made it easier: her mother had brought her more comfortable bedding, and her parents paid to bail her and her friend out of jail.[43]

The Łódź archives do not contain any material related to Tonia's trial, but consequences of communist engagement in Łódź are evident from other early 1930s trials of people imprisoned for communist agitation.[44] The archival files contain names and brief physical descriptions of the people who received sentences of a few years and who lost their civil rights for publicly expressing their support for communism. Most were in their late teens, only slightly older than Tonia at the time of her arrest.[45] The illegality of communism meant that supporting communism came with significant risk, and the number of imprisoned was growing.[46]

The consequences for Tonia were less dire. She was expelled from school without a diploma and with just a certificate. Her mother must have believed in the power of teaching her daughter a lesson, as she sent Tonia to tailoring school. After she returned from jail, her grandfather asked her if it was true that she was a communist. When she answered in the affirmative, he slapped her face. Symbolically, decades later that slap signified the chasm that had grown between her and her family. What she felt was mostly regret and remorse: regret for missing the opportunity to finish high school and the loss of her school friends and remorse for hurting the people close to her—her family and the friend who was jailed with her. The arrest "was tragic, because my friend came from a very poor household; she did not have a mother. She was able to attend a school only because someone paid her tuition. She was very talented. I liked her a lot. I introduced her to the party, took her for her first demonstration. Later I left for Palestine, and my friend was left alone," Tonia told Dowgiałło.[47]

Tonia's experience with communism differs slightly from more familiar ones. There is little of what Ivan Jablonka reconstructs about the life of the communist grandfather he never met as a conviction of being "modern-day Prometheans . . . seeking to break with the status quo and unleash the blessing of freedom in all its forms."[48] Tonia's recollections from decades later tempered her enthusiasm for communism. With the benefit of hindsight, she framed her story with an acute awareness of the harm caused by the Soviet version of communism. She read her past through the consequent decades, and her experiences over the years deeply affected her interpretations at that particular moment; toward the end of her life, she grew increasingly critical of communism. She had received warnings from people around her, though she refused to listen. Her mother tried to discourage her from participating. Also, a close school friend tried to convince her of the more hostile nature of communism. "And she died in the Soviet Union," Tonia concluded.[49] Both her mother and her friend implied that something in the movement was beyond Tonia's understanding, a warning Tonia could not have comprehended in the early 1930s. In the 1990s, looking back at her life, Tonia perceived herself as young and naive. She also exhibited a lingering sense of guilt and disconnect between the hopes she felt in the 1930s and the bitterness communism left her with.

Immigration to and Life in Palestine

In 1935, when the family decided to move to Palestine, Tonia was seventeen. In the online Israeli government archive, I found an application for Palestinian citizenship from 1940 denoting that in November 1934 Aron Bialer had traveled for the first time to Mandatory Palestine for a quick visit to prepare a shipment of factory machines. Róża Bialer and three of her younger children, including Tonia, received a family passport in March 1935. They left Poland soon afterward. In 1950 Tonia testified that ten days prior to their departure, her parents, fearing she might be arrested for her continued communist activism, sent her to her grandparents in Warsaw.[50] In her conversation with Dowgiałło, Tonia emphasized that she did not want to leave Poland. In another interview recorded in 1998 with Polish radio journalist Anna Sekudewicz shortly before Tonia's death, she stressed that she regretted leaving Poland.[51] Poland appeared to be the only place of relative safety in her stormy life. Back then, in 1935, while desperately trying to avoid moving, she ran away at the train station and hid in her aunt's apartment, the aunt who had given her a copy of Brzozowski's *Płomienie*. Her father eventually found her, so she, her mother, and her two siblings left.

Tonia's older brother, Romek, had to wait for a passport. Tonia recollected that his political involvement slowed down the process, but the available sources do not provide details of the delay or the level of intervention required from his parents. Their father had to stay in Łódź to arrange for the transport of more factory machines and the travel of three workers and the foreman to Tel Aviv. While searching for a sign of their departure in city administration documents, I discovered countless applications for passports to Palestine but none for the Bialers. Their paper trail ends with a note in a record book in Łódź, kept to control the movement of permanent Łódź residents, of the immigration of the Bialer family (three women and two men). Two dates accompany the note: their departure was registered on May 21, 1935, and on June 8, 1935, information about their departure was sent to the Ministry of Internal Affairs. That second date likely also signified that the Bialers ceased being Łódź residents.[52]

Since the end of the nineteenth century, the typical route to the Palestine port of Jaffa from Eastern and Central Europe, especially from Austro-Hungary, was through Trieste, in what is now northeastern Italy.[53] With the onset of an independent Polish state came attempts to establish more routes. Eventually, in the 1930s, the Polish government created the Polish Transatlantic Ship Society (Polskie Transatlantyckie Towarzystwo Okrętowe), which over the years acquired three ships on regular routes to North America and Palestine. The route to Palestine from Poland was through Romania; ships traveled from Constanţa, a port in southeastern Romania on the Black Sea. In 1933 the *Polonia* and later the *Kościuszko* began routes from Constanţa to Jaffa. Tonia remembered that the family traveled to Bucharest, where Róża had a niece and where they stayed a couple of days to see the city. From Bucharest, the family traveled to Constanţa, where on May 1 they boarded the *Puławski*, as Tonia recalled, and traveled to Jaffa. It is unlikely, however, that they traveled on the *Puławski* since it sailed mostly to New York and then, starting in 1936, to Buenos Aires.[54] Only the *Kościuszko* and the *Polonia* traveled to Palestine.[55]

It is not clear which argument spoke the loudest in the family's decision to move. Tonia mentioned that it was her and her brother's political activity that pushed the family to look for a different place to live, where their communist involvement would be less problematic. "My parents got scared," recollected Tonia. "They said they did not want to have children in jail, and they started packing their belongings." Political instability and the rise of fascism, however, most likely pushed them to leave. As Tonia recollected, her extended family supported Zionism, but only her immediate family moved to Palestine. Other relatives apparently never considered it. "They were very much against emigration because that meant they would have to leave their possessions behind, and they were very rich," she said.[56] In the 1920s Zionists were committed in principle to the idea of establishing a Jewish homeland, but in practice they protected Jewish interests in Poland and promoted Hebrew education, which meant joining "the nation-building project" without leaving. In the 1930s, however, due to various circumstances, such as growing radical antisemitism all over Europe and systemic discrimination in Poland, Zionist politics reconsidered aliya (immigration to Palestine) and education preparing for it.[57] The years 1931–36 witnessed the biggest wave of Polish Jews leaving for Palestine, including families that previously had not seriously considered immigration. "The political situation in Europe had intensified due to Hitler's rise to power," recalled Tonia. "People began talking about leaving. My father took this seriously." The rest of the family did not consider leaving "because they couldn't believe in the consequences of what was going on."[58]

The international situation did not provide many reasons for optimism. In the 1920s and the second half of the 1930s, both the British and Polish governments encouraged Jewish emigration. But in the middle of the 1930s, conflict between Jews and Arabs in Palestine intensified, and the British authorities limited Jewish immigration to the country.[59] Dvora Hacohen, a historian of modern Jewish history, explains the turn: "The idea was to avoid immigration beyond the country's economic absorption capacity and to prevent the immigrants from becoming a burden on the country's inhabitants and displacing them from their sources of work. Up to 1936, there were no limitations on immigrants with financial resources, on professionals and on students. The group on which immigration limitations were imposed was the workers, people who had a chance of integrating into the labour market in the country."[60]

The Bialers left in 1935, the peak year for immigration to Palestine from Poland, when thirty thousand people moved and just before British policy toward immigration to Palestine became more restrictive.

There is possibly one more reason why the family decided to leave. The 1930s, marked by the global Great Depression, brought Łódź and many Łódź industrialists to the brink of financial crisis, resulting in massive bankruptcies of textile factories. In 1931, when the crisis was at its worst, the number of unemployed reached fifty-five thousand. The situation began to slowly change in 1933, but it took another three years for the textile industry to recover. To show the scale of the crisis, Wiesław Puś, a historian of Łódź, stresses that only one large business, that of the Jewish Eitington family, was formed during this period.[61] Perhaps this financial crisis affected Aron Bialer's factory.

In 1937, soon after their move to Palestine, Róża Bialer embarked on a journey from Palestine back to Poland for two equally important matters: the family's financial troubles and the fate of Romek, who in July 1937 most likely was released from Bereza Kartuska.[62] In the depths of Vera's closet, I found a thick folder with letters Róża sent to Palestine from her time in Poland. The letters are disorganized, some of them missing pages; it is not clear whether these missing links are due to the merciless passing of time or family secrets. The majority of the letters lack dates, and only through the grueling effort of reconstructing the sequence of facts that the letters mention can we begin to understand Róża's struggles. Her handwriting is barely legible, as if stress marked her writing. Marcel, who helped me transcribe them, cried over the family's troubles and Róża's growing profound anxiety. They reveal the scope of the impending crisis, the family's struggles, and their efforts to keep the family afloat.

Possibly a combination of debt in Poland and complications from starting a new life and business in Palestine led to the family's financial struggles. The conversations Róża had with family members, Polish friends, and business partners that she conveyed to her husband in the letters show her deep engagement in the business. For example, she often wondered about the effectiveness of new textile machines for their transplanted factories.[63] In some letters, she gave Aron advice on how to make baleen fabric in the time of crisis or criticized him for not making calculations correctly.[64] In the majority of the letters, she wrote about how to handle the crisis, in both Poland and Palestine—whom to borrow money from and how to deal with debtors. She often referred to a father—most likely her own—as someone who could potentially help them financially, but it is unclear if they received any financial assistance from him.

The letters show her deep preoccupation with the family business and the scale of the family's financial troubles. The factory was temporarily shut down, perhaps while Aron was preparing for some business from Syria, as Róża asked repeatedly about potential orders from there.[65] She even wrote to her youngest son, Julek, imploring him to provide her with more information in light of a lack of response from her husband: "Dear Juleczek. How is the factory? Please tell me precisely, because father forgets. Do we have any orders and how big? What is the situation with the workers' salaries?" Wavering between desperation and hope, she wrote in the same letter, "I am afraid. Terrible crisis (*krach*)." And a couple of lines further, she added, "Try to do something more for the factory. It is more beneficial than this despair and apathy."[66] In light of all these concerns, she still asked and worried about mundane aspects of everyday life, such as picking up clothes from the tailor.[67] Although she was in Poland, busy with trying to avoid the impending crisis, she also attempted to be present in Palestine, reminding the family about the day-to-day responsibilities she was probably engaged with back home.

Despite her effort, she was unable to help much. In the 1930s their house on 85 Piotrkowska Street was nearly auctioned at least four times because of extensive debt on the property. Around 1938 the debt reached over twenty-two thousand Polish zlotys, part of which was the loan Tobiasz and Aron had taken for the house. The debt included mortgage payments that had not been paid since the beginning of 1933, insurance payments for the workers who lived at 85 Piotrkowska, and emergency insurance. The first public auction was supposed to take place on October 7, 1938, shortly after Róża left Poland to return to Palestine. City authorities attempted to auction the house three more times in 1939: January 21, May 10, and September 30, a day before war broke out. Each time, Aron was able to come up with enough money to temporarily save it. During the last auction, the Bialers' lawyer convinced the bankers to account for the financial crisis and respond with more rational loan payments.[68] There is no information about whether or not Aron attempted to pay them at all.

Why did Aron try so hard to save the house? The last Bialer living in the house was Basia Bialer, Aron's mother. Was Aron trying to save the house so she could stay in it? Perhaps he tried to save it since it was the family's most valuable possession. Did the family consider returning to Poland if life in Palestine turned out to be unbearable? None of these questions can be answered definitively. Most likely the answer includes them all, such as the impossibility of knowing what the near future would bring, the uncertainty of life in Tel Aviv—a new home, where the odds of growing a successful business were as unpredictable as in Poland—and a desire to provide the Bialer elders with the comfort they were accustomed to.

The beginning of their lives in Tel Aviv was difficult, not only financially. The only source available to understand this period is Tonia's interviews from later decades. The family settled in Petach Tikva, a settlement on the outskirts of Tel Aviv established by religious pioneers, which soon became the center of industry for incoming immigrants. Here on Olifant Street, Aron Bialer rented space in a building that already housed several shops and opened his new company.[69] The family lived a couple of blocks away. Tonia was sent to a workshop to become a seamstress, but she disliked what she was supposed to be learning there and soon joined her family in their factory.[70]

Her parents did not fit into the world they were trying to adapt to. Like many of the pioneers arriving in Palestine, Tonia's parents were nonreligious (her mother "openly opposed religious people"), but unlike the others, they were not focused on farming: "My parents did not fit that model. They belonged to intelligentsia, were interested in social justice." Further, she said:

> I think that my mother never got used to life in Israel. From the house of Wojdysławska, she grew up in a mansion and was in general a great lady. She always said she missed Europe. In Poland my parents went to Warsaw to see all the shows at Qui Pro Quo.[71] They knew all the songs by heart. In winter they went there by train twice a week! My mother was terribly deprived in Palestine. My father could not adapt either. I think that in Poland he did not really have to worry about the factory. The work went its own way, and he had responsible employees. So initially, life in Palestine was very hard. Father had to take extra care of the factory [in Palestine]. My mother also started working immediately, which was unthinkable in Poland.[72]

Tonia emphasized her parents' cultural capital and high expectations for a rich cultural life while suggesting that life in Tel Aviv had little to offer. Her recollections correspond to the opinion of Ksawery Pruszyński, a Polish journalist who visited Palestine in 1933:

> Haifa is a wonderful city. . . . But Tel Aviv . . . Someone in Poland wrote that the city is shoddy. And it is. The American journalist I met told me he didn't like this city. It is like an average, third-rate

American city. . . . He was right. . . . Tel Aviv is spoken of as a great battle, crowned with a great victory. Yes, and there it is. A country that has the only city in the world like Jerusalem, a country with a port center as marvelous as Haifa, is simply in love with a city where the asphalt of the road just freshly cracked, and the lime walls haven't dried yet. A mystery.[73]

The Bialers, accustomed to the high culture Warsaw offered, likely were disappointed with their new life in Tel Aviv.

In addition, by stating that her mother was born a Wojdysławska, Tonia emphasized her mother's good upbringing or at the very least her membership in a Polonized family of wealth and social standing. She then continued by stressing the type of work her parents did in Poland compared to the work they did in Tel Aviv. The juxtaposition is evident: life in Palestine was marked by hard work in the factory, which involved both parents, who, according to Tonia, had until then remained distant from physical labor. That was coupled with the perception that her mother had not been accustomed to work in Poland due to her gender and social standing. It is striking how readily Tonia accepted that her mother was not supposed to work and how little she may have known about the heavy burden her mother carried as a co-owner of the factory the family tried to establish in Palestine.

Tonia, Communism, and Sioma

The family arrived in Tel Aviv in May 1935. The political tension, with fascism on the rise, was mounting, which contributed to Tonia's ongoing conflict with her father:

> My father rented the first floor of the building. At the first opportunity, I told him that in the trade unions (which I hated and considered socio-fascists), they say that the workers are entitled to a half-hour breakfast break at the expense of the manufacturer, who is also supposed to provide tea, sugar, and electricity. . . . Then, when he bought machines in Italy, I claimed he was supporting Mussolini. And he had only bought where it was the cheapest.[74]

The conflict between her and her parents was a major feature of her family life. Through the lens of this conflict, Tonia's increasing involvement in the ideological debates that characterized communism becomes evident. In Palestine she was particularly preoccupied with the predominance of religion among Jews; social problems among Arabs, especially the poverty of fellaheen (Arab farmers in Palestine); and the constant tension between Jews and Arabs. She was becoming more cognizant of the social problems surrounding her.[75]

Tonia became active in a local communist group almost immediately, although how she first came in contact with the organization is unclear. The interrogation minutes from 1949 and 1950 help reconstruct her path to this illegal group of Palestinian communists. From the family that helped her family settle in Tel Aviv, she learned about the socialist newspaper *Haor*.[76] She talked to a woman who was distributing *Haor* about how to connect with communists. Thanks to her, toward the end of 1935, she joined a communist youth cell,[77] which met in small groups once a week to discuss the political situation. Her communist cell had tasks similar to those fulfilled by young communists in Poland. They wrote communist slogans on walls. With a group of her comrades, equipped with a canister full of water as a weight and a little lever on which they placed a stack of communist flyers, she climbed the flat Jaffa roofs. The flyers were dispersed into the air only when the water leaked out of the can and the lever released the leaflets. Another task required propaganda work among Zionists.[78] Tonia was asked to register for a Hebrew-language course that the Zionist Youth (HaNoar HaTzioni) organized. During the meetings, she was supposed to distribute leaflets promoting the view that the main enemy of the Jews was not Arabs but the British Empire.[79]

The British authorities of Palestine perceived communism as a threat. A memorandum from the Palestine Royal Commission, which from 1935 dealt with, among other things, anti-British and subversive propaganda, declared that the Palestinian Communist Party and its subordinate organizations aimed to "overthrow the constitutional government in the country and replace it with a Communist state."[80] Starting in 1923, the new penal code in British Palestine enabled British authorities to deport from the country those accused of communist activism.[81] In Palestine's political context, the communist threat was coupled with "interracial tensions," which, according to the document, culminated in the events of spring and summer 1935.[82] The year

1935 was a time of nationwide Arab strikes and a major Arab revolt, during which Britain employed a divide-and-conquer strategy to balance competing claims of sovereignty between Palestine's historic Arab inhabitants and newly arrived waves of Jewish immigrants. The policy backfired, not only aggravating the scale of conflict between Palestinian Arabs and Jews but also advancing anti-British sentiment among Palestine's Arabs.[83]

Tonia's fascination with communism deepened when she met Sioma Lechtman, a Russian Jew, who had received most of his education, including an ideological one, in Vienna. The exact origins of this relationship are shrouded in the mysteries of the past and various stories circulating in the family. In one of my first conversations with Vera in 2013, she told me that when Tonia first began attending Palestinian Communist Party meetings, she was told that there was a man who would be able to translate the meetings from Yiddish to German as soon as he was released from prison. In early 2020, while searching for some information on Sioma, Meryl Lavenant, my student research assistant, provided me with his *biografia de militantes*, a form of political biography included in the online Soviet archives of the Russian State Archive of Socio-Political History (RGASPI). Sioma was indeed imprisoned in Palestine four times after his arrival in 1934.[84] Tonia quite possibly first learned of Sioma while he was still imprisoned.

Eighteen-year-old Tonia and Sioma, over a year her senior, soon became a couple. They worked together by disseminating communist leaflets at night.[85] We know little about Sioma. His 1924 school diploma from Vienna states that he was born on July 1, 1916, in Dunaivtsi, Podolia (present-day Ukraine). His parents were Feiga Blatt and Israel Lechtman. The Kamenets-Podolski Archive, which should contain material from Dunaivtsi, does not have a birth certificate for 1916.[86] Since he was born in the middle of World War I in an area affected by heavy warfare, it may have disappeared in the midst of the instability. The only sign of his life in Dunaivtsi is a 1920s photo showing a group of Jewish boys, including Sioma, who were members of Hashomer Hatzair, a socialist Zionist Jewish youth group founded in Galicia in 1913.

A 1921 document issued by the British consul proves that the Lechtman family was already planning by then to go to Palestine and clarifies their travels. Sioma's family left Kiev with plans to immigrate to Palestine during the early 1920s pogroms. In 1921 they were in Warsaw, where, in the presence of the British consul, they opted for Palestinian nationality "as soon as a nationality law has come into force in that country."[87] A laissez-passer (a form of a travel document) allowed the family to travel from Warsaw to Vienna, Trieste, Alexandria, and then to Jaffa. According to the family story, after leaving Warsaw for Vienna, one of the children fell ill, so the family decided to stay in Vienna until the child recovered. It was not until over ten years later, in 1934, that the family arrived in Jaffa.[88]

A couple of photos of Sioma have survived. One is a family photo from 1927 in Vienna that shows the parents with their four children. The three girls—Luba, Chava, and Lea—wear similar white dresses, while Sioma wears a jacket. Photos of Sioma as a young man, probably from the time when he was courting or possibly already engaged to Tonia, depict a smiling young man with short hair. The family considers one photo especially precious—Tonia and Sioma together—which is perhaps the last photo taken before they left Palestine. There is much joy, love, and tenderness in their faces. There is also some determination, a sense that they are on the best path for life. Now, almost ninety years later, the only existing copy of the photo is fading.

FIGURE 2.2. Tonia and Sioma before they left Palestine in 1937. *(Private collection of Vera and Marcel Lechtman)*

In her 1950 interrogations, Tonia testified that she and Sioma decided to marry, despite her parents' disapproval. He proposed in December 1935, just a few months after the Bialer family arrived in Tel Aviv, and they married in September.[89] However, in early 1936 a series of arrests shook their communist cell. The communist leadership asked Tonia to organize a meeting on the roof of a building adjacent to her family's apartment building. Tonia was to welcome the incoming conspirators at the building's entrance and lead them to the roof. At some point, a woman came to inform them that due to recent arrests, the meeting had been canceled. The woman left. Sioma decided to get something to eat, as did Tonia. All three were arrested when leaving the building and taken to a jail in Jaffa. There, despite being guarded, they exchanged a warning not to sign a document indicating that communism was a terrorist organization. Tonia testified that interrogation officers in Palestine blackmailed her by stating that failing to denounce communism and sign the document would make it more difficult for her parents to continue being successful in their business in Palestine.[90]

Tonia was imprisoned for several months; however, similarly to her recollections of her first incarceration, her conversation with Dowgiałło and the minutes of one of her interrogations differ in regard to the length of her detention. She told Dowgiałło that she was held for eight months, while during one interrogation she testified that her imprisonment lasted six months and that she was released in August 1936.[91] She was kept in the Central Women's Prison for the Middle East in Bethlehem. I was unable to find documents from that prison in either the British National Archives or the Israel State Archives. Occasionally I came across mention of this place in memoirs, such as the life story of Leah Trachtman-Palchan, who was imprisoned there at the end of 1932. She remembered that "in the prison in Bethlehem were a large number of political prisoners. This time the room was big and our beds stood in a row. The windows were barred and so was the balcony along the inmate's rooms. . . . The prison manager was a tall Englishman with a round face and a silly smile. He seemed innocent and kind."[92] Tonia remembered this prison as a place where she had a lot of freedom. When her mother sent her some black fabric, she sewed a fashionable dress with a pleated skirt. But more important, it was her time to study Marxism:

> We had six or seven people in two rooms with a veranda. And a large table at which we could work, eat, and learn Marxism. We

were locked in, but we actually did what we wanted. We got Marxist literature, we ran ideological courses . . . they gave us everything we asked for. I borrowed the book by Lenin on free love from the prison library. I remember his definition of love, which proves that love is not like drinking a glass of water. Because thirsty people drink water. And in sexual love, to satisfy thirst, a sexual act is not enough. It takes love, friendship, attachment, and many other factors. I took it very seriously as a deep moral theory and studied diligently. I read many other interesting books there. For example, I discovered Fran Werfl—he wrote beautifully. I also read books by the German writer Emil Ludwig, the author of the biography of great people. All books came from the prison library.[93]

Tonia, Sioma, and Romek, who was imprisoned around the same time, were all released in June or July 1936.[94]

British authorities dealt with rebels by sending them back to the country they came from, Poland in Tonia's case. Romek was extradited to Poland in early 1937; hence, one of the reasons for Róża's travel to Poland in the second half of 1937 was Romek's release in July 1937. The aforementioned letters Róża kept sending from her trip show her desperate attempts to learn something about his living conditions and securing his safety after his release. In mid-1936, when both Tonia and Romek were imprisoned and Róża had not yet left for Poland, similar desperation and fear likely accompanied Tonia's parents as they struggled to find a way to postpone their children's deportation to Poland. Sioma's statelessness turned out to be a solution for Tonia. There was no country for Sioma to be sent to, so, if married, Tonia and Sioma could choose their own destination. As a communist, she opposed marriage, but practicality trumped ideology.[95] They married on September 15, 1936, in Ramat Gan, a settlement near Tel Aviv, where the marriage ceremony was cheaper.[96]

It was a religious service under a wedding canopy. Tonia was unaware of the Jewish traditions that had to accompany the event, but her mother helped her understand them and imparted religious knowledge to her. Tonia's mother also accompanied her in moments of confusion, as when they both reacted with laughter and bewilderment at some of the ceremonial requirements. The first time Tonia went to a rabbi, she was dressed inappropriately and was asked to leave. She returned properly dressed and went to a mikveh (ritual bath) to achieve the purity necessary for marriage. Further, she recollected in detail walking around the synagogue before the wedding, standing under a canopy, and laughing with her mother about the entire ceremony. It is not clear why she walked around the synagogue. It could have been to calm down and get ready for the ceremony, or perhaps Tonia confused it with the Jewish ritual of circling the canopy with the groom seven times. She described the wedding:

> My older brother could not come. He had a meeting. My parents, my sister, and my younger brother came. My brother carried a bouquet, which he lost on the bus, only paper remained . . . and my mother had prepared such beautiful roses for him! I put on a white dress with a sailor collar. At the rabbi's, it turned out that I did not have minyan.[97] So my brother went out into the street and asked passersby to come and pray under this canopy. While he gathered people, the rabbi wrote down our information. He first asked about the address of my parents, then Sioma's parents. He thought that his family was in Poland or in Russia. When the rabbi heard they lived here, he said that he would not give us a wedding without them. So we had to come again. This time, we came with the in-laws, who almost did not talk to us. . . . My mother was leading me. . . . My face was covered with a veil, and I was bursting into laughter. Mom said, "Do not laugh or I'll start cracking up—and I have to be serious." I survived it somehow. Then we took a bus home. Sioma's parents did not come because they were insulted, as always. But the sisters came. There was a grand dinner party, after which we were given bed linen wrapped in a sheet and blessed for the road. We lived in an apartment that had belonged to my older brother. We only ate at our parents' because I could not cook.[98]

According to Vera, Sioma's parents did not want to come to the wedding because they never fully reconciled with Sioma's decision to marry a Polish Jew. They perceived Russian Jewry to represent intellectual elites. The class and ethnic tension between the Bialers and the Lechtmans continued throughout the short remaining period that Sioma and Tonia lived in Palestine. Even though the Bialers certainly led a relatively modest life in Palestine, the Lechtmans' financial situation must have been even more difficult. As Tonia explained, her mother decided to plan the wedding dinner in a restaurant and not at home to avoid exposing the poor Lechtmans to their richer household.

A Dream of New Life | 67

FIGURE 2.3. Dinner with Sioma's family, 1936 or 1937. Tonia and Sioma are standing behind Sioma's mother and grandmother. *(Private collection of Vera and Marcel Lechtman)*

The Lechtmans, however, took it as a sign that they were not good enough to be invited to the Bialer home and felt offended.[99]

In her interview, Tonia noted that the occasion of the wedding merged with their departure from Tel Aviv, but in her 1949 and 1950 interrogations she recounted that soon after their wedding and just before their departure from Palestine, they attempted to lead a normal life. They rented an apartment on the outskirts of Tel Aviv and began working. In addition to helping support his own household, Sioma also financially supported his parents and siblings.[100] At first, Sioma worked as a bricklayer but soon decided to join Tonia at her father's factory. In January 1937 came the deportation order for Tonia. Her mother obtained permission for Tonia not to be deported but rather leave for France with a transit visa. Tonia received a Polish passport to Poland with a transfer visa through France, Austria, Czechoslovakia, and Romania. She did not remember exactly what passport her husband had, but he was supposed to go to Cuba or the Dominican Republic with a transit visa through France.[101]

FIGURE 2.4. A gathering of friends and family just before Tonia and Sioma's departure from Palestine, with the couple standing in the center of the back row and Julek fifth from the right. *(Private collection of Vera and Marcel Lechtman)*

While France agreed to accept communist deportees, many other countries, including Poland, refused. Many Palestinian communists were becoming increasingly frustrated with their situation in Palestine and the party's prioritization of its campaign against British and Zionist imperialism over the struggle against fascism. Many people saw deportation as a solution to their problems, or at least to their lack of financial means to travel.[102] We do not know whether these concerns were felt by Tonia and Sioma, but they may have chosen France for similar reasons.

A week before their planned departure, Sioma was arrested again and held in Jaffa. Tonia was arrested soon afterward. On the day of their departure, they were both taken to their home, where they stayed without police supervision for a few hours. The police then returned to escort them to the train station, from where they had to get to the port of Haifa. Both Tonia and Sioma were in handcuffs on the train.[103] During the interrogation, Tonia was asked repeatedly about a group photo that was supposedly taken before their departure. While looking through the family albums, Marcel and I tried to identify the photo the interrogation officers could have been referring to. A few photos could easily be linked with their departure from Palestine, including one of three people, including Tonia and Sioma, waving from a train window, and one of a group of people of different ages next to suitcases, possibly the couple's. In both photos, the atmosphere seems tranquil, people are smiling, and nothing suggests the circumstances under which they left Palestine.

III

The communist ideals that fed Tonia's sensitivities were likely born out of a variety of factors: the sharp social inequalities she observed in Łódź; the zeitgeist of the interwar period, dominated by identity questions; and her youth, which encouraged exploration. As the initial phase of Tonia's engagement with communism showed, communism was the social space where she felt accepted among similarly thinking people. It was her space to be brave, decide her own life, and become independent. It was also her answer to many questions and anxieties that she carried related to her age, gender, ethnicity, and class. It helped her build distance from her parents, who lived on the border of tradition and modernity. It helped her build distance from the Polish state and its growing antisemitism. Finally, it helped her shed some aspects of her previous identity while expanding into new areas. Yet that distance never meant separation. She was building her own space through continued conversations with her family. Communism was a means not to contradict but to expand the life she had. While pushing her to redefine her own space as a Jew, a daughter, and a woman, it was also grounding her in various relationships. Later chapters of her life further show this liminality and the rigidness with which she was growing to define herself.

3 ||| "Flies in Amber"

Paris, Spain, and the World of Letters, 1937–1942

I AM unsure when Marcel or Vera first realized that the thick folder full of documents in their possession contained their mother's letters to her family in Tel Aviv, sent from various parts of the world starting in 1937 and continuing until the early 1970s. Maybe they always knew. When I first emailed Vera in 2008 asking for access to her mother's letters, she responded that they were unavailable—hidden high in the *pawlacz,* a storage space near the ceiling above the furniture, a place for items that are considered of secondary need. Retrieving them from the pawlacz required physical and most likely also emotional labor that she was not ready for or willing to exert. When visiting Vera for the first time in 2012, I was painfully aware of their out-of-reach presence in the apartment. The big elephant in the room that I believed was the key to unlocking Tonia's story was inaccessible to me.

The movie *Tonia i jej dzieci* triggered Marcel's interest in the correspondence. After Marcel's emotional participation in its making, he realized something was missing from his own life. He reached for the letters hidden in the pawlacz and began writing a family chronicle, enriching it with excerpts from the letters. The letters told Tonia's story through her voice, or at least through what she was willing to share. Marcel also began the process of transcribing the letters, deciphering often barely legible parts or translating paragraphs that were written in French, German, or Hebrew.

The second time I visited Vera in Israel, in 2018, I was allowed to look through the vast family archive, including the trove of Tonia's letters. The process of documenting had moved up in the family hierarchy of importance from the space near the ceiling to a large closet in a room that used to be Tonia's bedroom. This time I could freely look through the materials—mostly letters and photographs but also some family documents and Tonia's newspaper clippings. Her story, or at least what she decided to share, was within my reach.

Letters

Letters, including Tonia's, are a captivating source. The paper touched decades earlier by the author promises a mystical connection. Its fragility and the script's individual nature prompt us to believe that by the very act of reading we immerse ourselves in the most intimate aspect of the author's life: the joys and sorrows they wished to share only with a few. Deciphering often barely legible writing mirrors the process of decrypting the complexities an individual life presents. The form of letters is volatile, the audience limited, the author exposed and vulnerable, all of which situates us closer to hearing the author's voice. Historical sociologist Liz Stanley calls letters "flies in amber" not only for holding the memory of the person or described events but also for representing the moment of the letters' creation.[1] Yet the voice we hear is clearly mediated. The act of writing a letter depends on the interaction between at least two people: the writer and the recipient(s). Depending on that relationship, the correspondence can take the form of a conversation, confession, monologue, or a mixture of these forms.[2] Therefore, letters are always a combination of private and public, monologue and dialogue, self-centeredness and an attempt to reconstruct a life with others and through others. Tonia's letters certainly fulfill all these epistolary functions. They helped her communicate with herself while dialoguing with others.

Letters typically are mundane and scattered, often containing "elliptical remarks" where meaning is long lost. What makes letter reading even more complicated is that they are fragmentary, never complete; they are necessarily only what remains. We do not know what fraction of Tonia's letters survived. We do not have access to the responses Tonia received; hence, it is difficult to understand what a given letter presents in the sequence of the correspondence. Nor do we know what was left out of myriad urgent quotidian matters or how much the mundane obscured the bigger picture of Tonia's life. A complex web of intertextual connections remains vague.[3]

Tonia's letters are long and filled with often vague details about her life. Their basic intent is obvious: to maintain close contact with her family. Tonia tried to be a good daughter—or perform as a good daughter—as much as she was able to, perhaps as much as she knew how to, despite the distance. While addressing her mother, she was polite and attendant to all the rules she presumably learned at home, rules she believed made her mother happy and helped her maintain a good relationship with her parents. "Do not worry about me, I am dressed well and I drink milk twice a day," she wrote in July 1937, just a few months after her departure from Palestine.[4] In the parts written to her father, she showed interest in his business, asking for updates about his textile and elastic fabric factory in Palestine and his most recent business trips to Syria or suggesting some possibilities for expanding his business to France. She also made sure he knew she and Sioma had not cut their ties to Jewish culture. "We did not isolate ourselves from Jews—we go to Jewish clubs. We remain Jewish, we are perhaps more active Jews here than you are there," she wrote shortly after arriving in France.[5] She was respectful and engaged in family matters while having slightly different correspondence with her mother and father. Tonia responded to her own perceptions of the different roles her parents played in her life.

Yet we know from her conversation with Dowgiałło that Tonia's relationship with her family was complex. Her communist engagement, expulsion from school, slow emancipation from Jewish traditions, incarcerations, and finally marriage to a man her family did not initially accept made that relationship conflict-ridden. The letters do not reflect this tension; instead, they show a loving daughter communicating with her loving family. In the letters, she often expressed a deep gratitude for their consistent support and occasionally asked for help while showing unwavering optimism and assuring them that her life was relatively stable. Tonia certainly welcomed the separation as a chance to mature and as some respite from conflict between her independent spirit and her parents' system of traditional values and authority. Over time the physical distance between her and her family may have become a space of strategic circumvention of their former problems. Her choice to present certain aspects of her life, while silencing others, was an attempt to evade their questions and worries. While performing for them, she performed for herself:

the correspondence became a mechanism to assure herself she was going to be all right. The letters were a form of double dialogue she was conducting with her family and herself.

Only occasionally does the echo of some of their former conflicts resonate on the pages of her letters. The decision to leave Palestine put her in the position of an emigrant trying to figure out her own world, a sentiment she often reiterated. In such moments, her tone, usually open and eager to share and please, was transformed into a firm voice, determined to prove to her parents that the decisions she had made were correct. But even in these moments of conflict, the letters reveal familial closeness and even intimacy. The fact that her family kept most of her letters suggests that the letters became a kind of a proxy of Tonia for them. They played a similar role in her life. "Mommy, write to us often and more. This is the only consolation for us."[6] That closeness was necessary for all of them to cope with the unexpected circumstances that began affecting them as a Jewish family with family members still residing in both Central and Western Europe. The awareness that there is "someone warm and breathing on the other side of the page," as Virginia Woolf wrote, is a necessary element of any letter writing that is predicated on an attempt to respond to the expectations of people on the other end of that exchange.[7] Even though in Tonia's case, at some point during the war, almost all she was able to do was to let them know she was still alive, that sense of nearness, even if elusive, and caring had a life-saving quality.

The letters were avenues of her self-construction with regard to who she should be in her parents' view, to the questions she heard or anticipated hearing, and to the problems she wanted to forecast or find solutions to. Through her letters—through the stories she recounted, the half-truths and half-lies she told, and the interpretations and meanings she infused her life with—she was shaping an identity for herself. The letters were her space of agency: they reflected her life experience and ultimately also created her experience.

Early Days in Paris

Tonia and Sioma left Tel Aviv in May 1937. Her first letter to her parents, dated May 6, was written on a ship just before a port of call in Alexandria, Egypt. After a twelve-hour train ride from Marseille, the couple arrived in Paris on the morning of May 12. On May 14 she wrote her second letter, in which, after providing some details of their journey, she informed her family of having found a prospect for work. "It is 5 a.m. I am sitting down and writing letters to you. Can you imagine that already on the third day after my arrival, I don't have time for anything? Today I am going to work," she wrote with a sense of satisfaction and joy.[8] Their first days in Paris were marked with the enthusiasm of a new beginning.

The paper she wrote her first letter on is thin and nearly transparent. Almost eighty years later, the handwriting is barely legible. Her script is erratic, at times careful and dense and at times messy and even sprawling as if revealing mood changes. The letters contain occasional additions in German from Sioma, a habit they continued for the next few months: Tonia wrote in Polish, while Sioma added a paragraph in German. His handwriting is careful and neat. However, his small, straight, and dense letters make reading his words a challenge. It is unclear from the letters whom Sioma's additions were directed to. Are they only for Tonia's family? As I learned from Vera, Sioma's parents were not thrilled about his relationship with Tonia, partially because Tonia was a Polish Jew and partially because they blamed her for their son's deepening communist involvement and their separation from him. After he left Palestine, he did not communicate with his family directly but only through Tonia's family. It was Tonia's younger brother, Julek, who delivered Sioma's additions to his family.[9] Marcel added an element to this story, saying that Sioma had been the Lechtman family's only breadwinner in Palestine. Marcel recounted a family anecdote according to which only Sioma was allowed to eat from the family's only plate. The rest of the family ate directly from the pots. Apart from the emotional separation, Sioma's departure meant a serious threat to the family's well-being.[10]

The first letter provides hints to the form future letters would take. They were reports of what had happened to the couple since their departure: their travels, their feelings, and the amount of their remaining dry food provisions. The mundane detail gives a glimpse into the fabric of their lives, a joy of starting a new chapter and an urge to keep Tonia's mother calm while expressing love and appreciation for Tonia's parents. Sioma's additions are laconic, devoid of the verbosity of overblown emotions that Tonia readily shared. What he provided is simple and general confirmation that he and Tonia were doing well.[11]

It is unclear what documents Tonia and Sioma had on them when they arrived in Paris. In her conversation with Dowgiałło, Tonia admitted something she did not share in the letters. They were robbed on the ship and lost some money and their marriage certificate, the only document proving that they were indeed married.[12] In one of her first letters, Tonia explained that the passport she received when she boarded the ship (supposedly from the police officer who accompanied her on the train to the ship in Palestine) was her old passport with her birth name. It contained a note from the Polish consul stating that she was "forcibly evicted."[13]

After arriving in Paris, a female German communist comrade picked them up from the station and took them to a hotel where they were welcomed by other communists who told them about the living conditions in Paris. They had transit visas—that is, only for passing through without stopping even for a day—which were to expire on June 30.[14] In the letters, however, Tonia did not exhibit any distress that she would have to live as an illegal immigrant. From Paris she wrote that the lack of permission to stay "does not matter. One can be here for a long time without being afraid of anything." The first night they devised a straightforward plan of action to receive permission to live and work in Paris. "We need to fully concentrate on Sioma's passport, because through him we hope to become legalized. Sioma needs to go see the Russian consul to get a piece of paper stating that he lost his Russian citizenship, meaning that he was born in Russia but left.... It's actually nothing," she added, "but it can bathe you in sweat to receive this scrap of paper. This scrap of paper is everything."[15] She wrote this only two days after their arrival in Paris; hence, this is clearly what they had heard but had not yet experienced. They needed some kind of proof that Sioma was born in Russia, a document Sioma's parents were supposed to provide. "Maybe Julek could go to Sioma's parents and tell them that our existence here rests on their letters to Russia. We have to have some evidence that Sioma was born in Russia. Maybe they have some documents. Anything.... Every day matters. Can they send it 'express' to Russia? Immediately," wrote Tonia.[16] In the same letter, she noted that her documents could potentially be taken care of (presumably separately from Sioma's) since her passport carried information that she had been forcibly expelled. In her case, it would be easy to prove that she was a political refugee in a dire situation.[17]

There was urgency in obtaining formal permission to stay. They had decided to immigrate to France with the expectation of beginning a new life while devoting themselves to the cause they believed in, but the political situation was unstable, and France was flooded with immigrants. As the historian Michael R. Marrus writes, "France was the most important European sanctuary from fascism" and also a place that "in comparison to North America and other Western European states . . . harbored one of the highest populations of foreign-born residents in proportion to its native citizens."[18] Paris, in particular, was a center of attraction. In 1911 foreigners made up 6.8 percent of the Parisian population, compared to 3 percent in London and 2.6 percent in Berlin.[19] In the 1920s and early 1930s, French policy toward refugees was relatively liberal. In 1933 alone France accepted 250,000 refugees, "40 percent of all refugees who fled the Third Reich."[20] But with the beginning of an economic depression, politicians began pushing for restrictions on immigrants, and public opinion turned against foreigners. In the middle of the 1930s, the question of how to treat foreigners in France became increasingly grim.[21]

With three million foreigners residing within France's borders, the conditions under which Tonia and Sioma could be granted a legal stay were being tightened. When dealing with refugees in the 1920s, the French police still intended to keep the city safe and control the labor markets, rather than expel most of the migrants they caught.[22] That began to change in the 1930s. Starting in Paris, city authorities reorganized immigration services to comb the city to verify declarations of residence. They routinely stopped people on the street who looked out of place, to check their papers and conduct background checks. This system gave authorities the means to demand good behavior from migrants, who were desperate to hold on to their jobs and remain with their families.[23] Regardless of the official policy of asylum, it was becoming increasingly more difficult to obtain work or residency permits in France. The peak of expulsions took place in 1934 and 1935 and included a significant number of refugees from Nazi Germany.[24] The next couple of years were marked by the tenure of Léon Blum, the head of the Socialist Party and the Popular Front, who eased the restrictions and created an "identity certificate" for German refugees residing in France. However, this applied only to German refugees already residing in France. There was no stipulation regarding future refugees.[25] Despite these changes, in the summer and fall of 1937, when Tonia and Sioma arrived in Paris, nearly eighteen thousand refugees from Eastern Europe—three-quarters of them Jews—entered France illegally or on tourist visas, claiming they were visiting the International Exposition of Art and Technology in Modern Life.[26] The new influx of immigrants made the situation of illegal immigrants even more dire. The arrival of Jewish migrants from Poland after 1935 exacerbated the rise of antisemitic sentiment.[27]

"In general, we do not lack a good mood here," wrote Tonia two weeks after arrival. "My dear ones, please do not worry. Everything will turn out good for us here. We have many hopes. And many promises. We just need to have some patience and to wait."[28] But even if in the first weeks after their arrival Tonia and Sioma remained optimistic, they soon must have realized how precarious the situation for people with transit visas. Without further documentation, they could not receive stable jobs with reasonable pay or a place to live. Soon after their arrival, on May 13, they rented a room in a small hotel, most likely at 4 passage Viallet.[29] The room had a built-in gas cooker, a sink with running water, and a washbowl. It cost forty-five francs per week, which was expensive, but this was their only option as illegal immigrants. "Now the prices are much higher, but what can we do? Life in Paris, in France in general, is much more expensive," she said in the letter while commenting on the changing quality of life in Paris.[30] Years later, she did not remember how they paid for their first nights in the hotel, although most likely it was with the small amount of money she received from her mother, hidden in a little sack her mother had made for her, which Tonia guarded during the entire journey to France.[31]

Tonia's initial hope that they could receive legal status in Paris relatively easily was based on an assumption that the Secours populaire (the French branch of Red Help) or the League of Human Rights (Ligue des droits de l'homme, LHR) would take "care of the paperwork immediately."[32] This piece of information appears in the letters barely a week after they arrived in Paris, so most likely it came from the German communists who assisted them during their first days in France. While trying to learn more about the scope of the assistance the groups could have offered, I followed the steps of Ivan Jablonka. He recovered the life story of his grandparents, who, soon after their arrival in Paris in 1937, went to the Secours populaire and the LHR for assistance. He found his grandparents' documents in the LHR files, from which he learned that because his grandfather had no documents, they were denied help.[33]

The LHR archive at the Bibliothèque de documentation internationale contemporaine in Paris Nanterre has no entry for "Bialer" or "Lechtman" in its individual requests index of personal files.[34] While considering various ways of obtaining legal documentation, Tonia and Sioma may not have turned to any associations in their first months in Paris despite mentioning them in their correspondence. In the letters, Tonia spoke about the different options they had, occasionally insisting that they needed some paperwork—either the certificate of Sioma's statelessness or their marriage certificate.[35] But nothing indicates that they indeed tried to receive legal help during the first couple of months after their arrival.

Despite how Tonia presented their situation, it was dire. Just a few months after their arrival, Tonia began realizing their predicament, especially in the current political climate. "All these associations that had previously accepted and worked on these kinds of matters, now can do nothing about them because of the government's exacerbations toward foreigners," she wrote in August 1937. To receive any documentation of Sioma's statelessness from the Soviet consulate in Paris, they would have to pay four hundred francs, an amount they did not have and that was impossible for them to imagine, let alone earn or borrow.[36] The more time passed, the more they realized the painfully vicious triangle of dependencies: legal stay, work, and money. At some point, she began pondering the possibility of receiving a Nansen passport, a travel document meant to grant some protection to stateless refugees. Starting in 1922, it served as a valid form of identification issued to Russian refugees who had not acquired another nationality, to enable them to travel for up to one year to a third country for work.[37] Eventually, in August, Sioma did talk to representatives for Russian immigrants and received a Russian birth certificate. With that letter he should have gone to the Paris Police Prefecture to apply for permission to stay in France, but at the time a new complication had arisen. His passport did not state that he was married, and their marriage certificate had been stolen, which meant that his efforts might not lead to providing legal documentation for Tonia as well.[38] In October 1937 they were still waiting for a replacement marriage certificate, hoping that combined with the certificate of Sioma's statelessness, it would help them both receive a Nansen passport.[39]

In her conversation with Dowgiałło, Tonia said that she and Sioma were impractical and clumsy. "We were constantly looking for help. And we were not able to find anything. Additionally, we were surrounded by Germans who had a very regulated lifestyle."[40] This may suggest that they did not officially try to receive any legal help. While waiting for documentation, which never seemed to arrive from either the Soviet Union or Palestine, they were surrounded by Germans, politically legal refugees with a right to work and access to various financial support programs. Since 1936 Germans who escaped Nazi Germany had "identification certificates" that protected them from expulsion.[41] Tonia revealed to Dowgiałło, "In our heads, they were rich. They had money for life. We did not have money to survive the next day."[42] Is it possible that the couple, while socializing with a relatively secure group despite their migrant status, had missed the real urgency of their situation?

Tonia and Sioma's position in French society was tenuous. From the first letters, Tonia expressed an urge to blend in. "One needs to dress elegantly. Sioma naturally wears a tie. I also have to be elegant," she wrote to her family. She explained further that this meant covering her head with a beret and not wearing socks.[43] At first, Tonia welcomed this with amusement and a readiness to integrate into the country they had chosen as their home. Interwar Paris experienced a shift in gender conceptions followed by a revolution of style, represented by the ubiquitous Modern Girl. It was also a model communist women adopted.[44] But it is impossible to tell what pushed Tonia to the desire to fit in. The subsequent letters emphasized the necessity of acquiring new clothes in order not to stand out, which she associated with looking like a foreigner. This meant a desperate need for money. In July she wrote that Sioma "cannot wear his old jacket, because as long as he does not have legal documents, he cannot stand out as a foreigner."[45] What led her to make that comment? Was it a remark she heard on the street or a glance she thought suggested some suspicions regarding their place in French society? Or was it an early sign of her recognizing their precarious position in France? Their situation depended on paperwork that could help them obtain jobs, rent an apartment instead of a room in an expensive hotel, and gain some safety and stability. Their mobility across social roles, ethnic stereotypes, and nations that in principle were supposed to define their experiences in Paris was seriously hampered by the borders they kept encountering. For illegal immigrants, the borders were more than the physical spaces they encountered while entering a country. These nongeographic borders differentiated those who had to wait for proper paperwork to participate and become fully respected members of that community. Theirs was a modern experience of linking their future with documentation they desperately needed.

Interestingly, while emphasizing the need for new clothes for Sioma, she downplayed her own need for new clothing: "Why are you spending money to buy me a dress?" she wrote to her mother. "I don't dress up here. We live in a working-class district. During dinner, I wear a nightgown, and I even go shopping wearing it. When we go outside the borders of our district, I wear a skirt."[46] This is an interesting statement. She needed new clothing more than Sioma because it was much easier for her to find another job if she blended in. As Tonia explained, she had found a job within a few days of their arrival; she was the one who was going out. With a group of women from Palestine, she weaved leather belts for two francs per meter. She, however, did not work there for long because the person who hired her abused the workers, most likely by not paying them. Soon after that job ended, she and Sioma received temporary manual work in a naphthalene factory, where they worked for only two days, mostly because the pay was meager. "We got twenty francs daily. Here that is terribly little, because there are sixteen-year-old girls who get forty francs. The immigrants and people who are not legal are abused here."[47] One of the consequences of the influx of migrants was a growing market of cheap labor that was unfortunately often mistreated.[48] But it was a job, which for a young couple with no money must have meant a lot. Wouldn't it then be rational to expect her to blend in with French society as much as possible, especially since she did not speak French and her clothing was the only thing that could potentially help her pass as French?

In June, after several attempts to obtain more stable employment, Tonia began thinking about starting her own business. Someone had suggested that if she had her own sewing machine, she could become a part of a larger workshop and produce shirts with the fabric the workshop provided. The quota she had to fulfill to receive more fabric for more shirts was three dozen shirts daily. Provided she reached the quota, the pay was forty-five francs daily, which felt generous. The problem was that a sewing machine was expensive: the first installment alone was two hundred francs. With the help of many people, including some family friends living in Paris and possibly also her grandmother still living in Łódź, she purchased a machine on credit. Full of hope, she wrote to her family, "When I learn how to do it, I will be able to do it in eight hours." She emphasized the comfort that came with her new life arrangements: "I sit in my room and sew. It is very comfortable because I can take care of the household and I don't have to leave. . . . Sioma helps me a lot. He overturns flaps and collars and cleans them from the threads."[49] Despite initial optimism, she was forced to give up this job a couple of weeks later. Her sewing skills were insufficient to fulfill the required quota, which resulted in inadequate earnings to pay her monthly payments for the machine.[50] In August she received a job as a live-in nanny for two small children in the household of German friends. The pay was decent: 450 francs per month, with room and board. However, the landlady did not allow Tonia and Sioma to move in together. Her rationale was that it was unacceptable for a housegirl to live with her husband, even though the room had a separate entrance. Also, the family that had agreed to hire Tonia was unaware she was an illegal immigrant. Urgently needing money, Tonia decided to take the job but lived with Sioma in the hotel.[51]

Throughout these months, Tonia worked while Sioma did not. At first, she did not talk much about how he handled his lack of employment. Only once do we hear from Sioma, who, in a letter to Tonia's grandmother in Łódź, stated, "As Tonia has already mentioned, it is possible that I will start working soon. Oh, how good, how wonderful it would be. I can't wait for this moment." The job he mentioned was to sort out furs, but it is unclear what that entailed and whether he received the position.[52] Perhaps the aforementioned excerpt from the letter where Tonia stated that Sioma needed new clothing more than she did can be linked with how she responded to the growing anxiety from his difficulty in finding a job.

On one hand, Tonia was willing to challenge traditional gender expectations and enjoy Sioma's readiness to carry out jobs traditionally prescribed for women. On the other, she worried and blamed herself for failing to fulfill domestic chores and neglecting the household. In June 1937 Tonia wrote to her mother while celebrating her release from some chores. "Sioma cooks. He learned how to cook various meals with flour dumplings (*zacierki*), and twice a day he serves them in different forms. I hardly cook. Sioma does everything. He even did a big load of laundry for me."[53] That initial change in gender roles did not prove satisfactory, especially since the opportunities for him to find work kept diminishing. In August, soon after she informed her family about her job prospects as a housegirl, she added, "Sioma has almost no prospects for work. This boy just goes crazy. He sits in the apartment for days. He does not cook."[54] The problem persisted and even intensified. In a following letter, she stated, "Sioma must cook for himself. Mommy, you can only imagine what it looks like. It hurts me terribly. Our home is neglected, and I don't have time to darn, patch, or iron, so I would like to work where I can leave work at 6 p.m. But for that I will get only three hundred francs weekly. Sioma would not be able to survive for so little. We pay forty-five for the room."⁵⁵ The letters reveal distress related to a lack of stable employment and financial hardship. However, neither in the letters nor later in the conversation with Dowgiałło did Tonia express any bitterness that she was the one fully supporting them. Only once in her conversation with Dowgiałło did she mention Sioma's difficulty accepting their poverty and his own dependence on others:

> The first period was very difficult. Sioma was impossibly ambitious and did not want to admit poverty. He might have fainted from starvation and said nothing. At the end of August, or in September, the communist newspaper *L'Humanité* organized a "propaganda meeting," a sort of fair, in the Saint-Cloud forest. There were stalls with sausages and various shows. We were invited. Feeling the smell of these miracles, I nearly fainted. They all worked; they had money. They were not wealthy, but they had enough to buy bread, to have a normal life. I told one of my friends that I was hungry. Naturally, they gave us food without any problem. They behaved very decently. But Sioma held a terrible grudge.⁵⁶

While in the letters she readily acknowledged their financial difficulties, she never admitted that they did not have enough money to buy food. At first, her parents refused to help. She reminisced years later that her mother told her that if she wanted to lead a life so different from theirs, she also had to be independent financially.⁵⁷ Nevertheless, they sent some modest monetary support almost from the very beginning. Initially, Tonia did not ask for help but occasionally emphasized that they would be happy to accept support if her parents could afford it. She was aware that her family was struggling to establish a new business in Palestine and that at this time Tonia's mother was visiting Poland in part to find ways to improve the family's financial situation.⁵⁸

Characteristically, in her letters Tonia remained optimistic, regardless of how difficult the future appeared to be. "We live frugally, but we eat well. So do not imagine that we have nothing to eat. I cook; I go to the market where I get everything cheaper. You have no reason to worry . . . and it will be even better when we get permanent jobs."⁵⁹ She emphasized her reliance on people and the belief that their problems were temporary. The support of people around them—people whom in most cases they barely knew—helped her maintain that trust:

We could not afford food. But on the ground floor in our house, as well as in every hotel in Paris, there is a concierge. He liked us a lot. He was poor himself, and he felt that I was hungry. He used to invite us for dinners. He fed us with soups of bread cut into cubes.... And I was happy. Not only did we not pay them, but he also fed us with soup. In the fall they gave us a stove. And the bedbugs came out of all the corners, they covered our bed. It was black. Something horrifying! So, although we still did not pay them, they changed the room.... Extraordinary people. They say French people are egoists, and my experience is so great.... They helped us everywhere. Everywhere.[60]

The community of German communists constituted the most important network of support for the couple. Already in the first letter, Tonia stated that the communists were "good people" who helped them within the first hours of their arrival.[61] "I am gaining faith in people, especially the German *Kameradschaft*," she stressed.[62] The group she described as comrades, or as German communists, were members of the Free German Youth (Freie Deutsche Jugend, FDJ), an organization of German communists who remained in exile in Paris and Prague. Almost immediately after 1933 and Adolf Hitler's rise to power, there was a sizable exodus of refugees from Nazi Germany. In May 1933 alone, over twenty thousand Germans arrived in France as refugees. Their goals were to maintain illegal resistance to Hitler's Third Reich and popularize the communist cause.[63]

German communists welcomed Tonia and Sioma in Paris. They helped them get their first room and Tonia her first job. They created a social and intellectual circle that the couple joined almost immediately. Tonia and Sioma were drawn to German communists partly because of their common language. German was the language Tonia and Sioma communicated in. Immersed in a German-speaking world, Tonia did not speak any French for years after arriving in Paris. After leaving Vienna, Sioma also remained in touch with his Viennese colleagues, the Austrian communists, who put him in touch with their German comrades in Paris.

Despite the precarity of their situation, Tonia and Sioma felt empowered by their communist commitment and their network of comrades, the presence of whom made them discover their mobility, even across borders. But most important perhaps, while building their life together, there was love and support between them.

Different Faces of Struggle

In November 1937 Tonia informed her mother that Sioma had enlisted to fight in the Spanish Civil War. Tonia herself had planned on attending a military course for nurses and joining Sioma in Spain in three months. "It is the most honest and most consequent decision—a fight for Spanish independence is a fight against national fascism. I don't think I need to tell you why we decided to do this—we have always been and will always be faithful to our party. I understand that you experience it as a shock, but this is our common enemy—FASCISM," she wrote.[64] The following month, probably in response to correspondence from her family about their decision, she stated, "For us, it is the way we chose a long time ago. You have to understand that our place is there. Our departure makes us very happy, and I think only there will we be able to achieve complete satisfaction." Her response was polite but decisive, with a hint of reproach. "Once again please be more level-headed and welcome the news the way we did."[65] This was the first sign of serious tension between her and her parents that emerged in the letters.

The Spanish Civil War, between the Nationalists, led by General Francisco Franco, and the Republicans, started in July 1936, hence almost one year before Sioma and Tonia left for Paris. For people motivated by leftist sympathies, it was the most important theater of the antifascist struggle. The conflict was rooted in the social, economic, and political upheaval that in 1931 gave rise to the Spanish Republic, which challenged the traditional authority of landowners, the Catholic Church, and the army.[66] In August 1936, to avoid the escalation of conflict beyond the borders of Spain, France and Britain spearheaded a nonintervention pact that included, among others, Germany and the Soviet Union. However, Hitler and Benito Mussolini almost immediately broke it by increasing their military support to the Spanish rebels. In response, Joseph Stalin began supplying the Republican side with weapons and nonlethal aid.[67] Almost from its onset, the war extended far beyond the Spanish borders; it was a dress rehearsal for the world conflict that stood around the corner. The war was turning into a conflict of fascism (the rebels) against democracy (the Republicans), a conflict of defenders of the tradition-oriented landowning elites, monarchists, and followers of the church versus those committed to social and economic reform.[68]

The Spanish Civil War was rooted in political and existential tensions that polarized the world. As a result, it spoke to writers and intellectuals as a contest for the future of humankind.[69] The official slogan of the Comintern, the organization that advocated world communism, declared that Madrid was the universal frontier separating liberty from slavery. In 1937 the *Left Review*, a journal set up by the Comintern's British section, organized a questionnaire in which many contemporary intellectuals, such as T. S. Eliot, Ezra Pound, and Samuel Beckett, were asked to share their opinions. Nancy Cunard, a poet and activist, wrote, "It is clear to many of us throughout the whole world that now, as certainly never before, we are determined or compelled to take sides. The equivocal attitude, the Ivory Tower, the paradoxical, the ironic detachment, will no longer do."[70] This conflict was presented as one between light and darkness.

Although years later Tonia claimed that she and Sioma had left Palestine with the intention of joining the Republican forces in Spain, her letters do not disclose such early plans.[71] Tonia occasionally considered Sioma joining the army as a possible solution to their conundrum of being illegal immigrants in Paris, but there is no indication that this was planned in advance and discussed with family.[72] In her interrogation of March 2, 1950, she testified that in June 1937 they learned from a friend that the International Committee for Aid to the Spanish People (Comité international d'aide au peuple espagnol) was accepting volunteers to go to Spain. They both attempted to enlist, but while Sioma was accepted, she was not: she was a woman without any unique qualifications that could help in the war effort. It was then agreed that she would join him as soon as she finished the training for nurses. However, after she began attending the course, she discovered that the Republican authorities had stopped accepting women as volunteers.[73]

They, however, may have considered going to Spain earlier, even before leaving Palestine. The Comintern announced its intentions to recruit volunteers to train and send them to Spain already in August 1936. While the Soviet Union supplied the International Brigades with the majority of its commanding officers and weapons, Paris played the role of a hub where volunteers gathered. For many people Spain represented a second chance:

"Germans and Italians who were fleeing the Nazi and Fascist regimes; Poles escaping the Pilsudski dictatorship; Romanians who were on the run from the quasi-fascist Iron Guard; or even Irish volunteers, with one civil war behind them and their society still tottering on the brink of another."[74] A significant number of volunteers were coming from Palestine, for whom economic hardship and "a strong sense of alienation from mainstream Jewish society in Palestine" pushed them to enlist.[75] For the expelled Tonia and Sioma, Spain seemed almost a natural choice. Taking their time to announce their decision to leave may suggest that they were still hesitating, or perhaps hoping, to begin a new life in Paris, but in light of the growing daily difficulties, they decided to leave. Despite how much her family knew or suspected, the decision to enlist must have come as a surprise, partly because it suggested their unwavering support for communism, which both families had difficulty accepting.

Sioma left at the beginning of December 1937.[76] While the letters from the end of November and beginning of December are chaotic and the writing hardly legible, perhaps reflecting Tonia's emotional distress due to his departure, the December 15 letter stands out: it is clear, organized, legible, and not crowded with her typical added information in the margins. Tonia announced that she would not be joining Sioma and instead was staying in Paris. The carefully written letter reflects her attempt to balance her own emotions and growing awareness that she was going to be alone in a foreign country:

> How much pain your letters caused us, how hard it was for us to decide on this step is hard to imagine. However, we could not do otherwise. For you, it is an adventure or some youthful intrusion; it is not like that, my loved ones. We have thought about it for a long time, and for us it is a great transition. We were so happy with each other, we were so good together, and such a separation in these conditions, please understand, did not come easy. Only because we both understand that it was our duty could we reconcile ourselves with this thought, and it gave us complete peace and balance and maybe more: it gave us a stimulus to continue the fight. I am proud of Sioma that he decided to do it, although, believe me, it did not come easily. He is not only fighting for Spain's independence—he is fighting against international fascism, which may threaten you tomorrow.

Later in the letter, she writes of making plans for her future in Paris. She intends to begin studying French intensely as well as radiotechnology, with the hope of getting a better job. "I still have time, and I do not want to become a maid or help in a warehouse."[77]

The tension between her and her parents must have reached its peak when, on December 19, 1937, she announced her pregnancy. She began the letter by stating that her separation from Sioma was not easy but that German comrades helped her as much as they were able to. "I did not expect so much attention and care. They are helpful morally and financially. Only now am I beginning to know the meaning of the word 'comrade,' the meaning that you are probably not able to understand." After this note of reproach, she wrote:

> I'm pregnant. This will make you worried. Yes, it won't be easy for me. I have a hard fight ahead, but it's worth it. I do not know if you understand me. I have a great obligation on my part, but at the same time I have a purpose in life for which it is worth sacrificing a lot. You may say that I am young, I could have waited, yes certainly, but not under these conditions. I do not know when I will see Sioma again, but we have to be prepared for everything (although I am sure we will be happy together again), so this is the reason why I did this. His child will be able to replace a lot for me and help me in difficult moments of my life. Our love is not an empty word or a youthful rush, no—that's why I decided to take this step, and I'm happy. Please try to understand me. I feel quite well. At the moment, I don't have a job, but with the help of my comrades I can get one in the future. In the meantime, I eat quite normally—my comrades take care of that, and my condition demands it.[78]

We do not know how exactly Tonia's mother responded, but Tonia's subsequent letters suggest that her mother was unwilling to easily accept the pregnancy. She worried about Tonia handling motherhood on her own and even suggested that Sioma had abandoned her.[79] Although Tonia alternated between "you" singular and "you" plural (and addressed all of her letters to both parents), she directed her explanations related to her pregnancy to her mother. Tonia wanted her mother to understand and probably also approve her decisions. Just before Tonia and Sioma left for France, her mother realized that Tonia was pregnant and took her to a clinic for an abortion.

Tonia never blamed her mother for that decision, but in her conversation with Dowgiałło, she strongly emphasized that it had been her mother's decision, not hers, and that Sioma regretted it. Her previous pregnancy could be a reason why Tonia felt a need to explain to her mother why she wanted this child so desperately while at the same saying that she did not expect her mother to understand.

In the letters, the future child emerges as much more than just a promise of joys of motherhood or the fruit of her love for Sioma; motherhood potentially provided Tonia with a chance to engage in a struggle that would match Sioma's. "You cannot even imagine how happy I am that I am going to become a mother. I will have somebody to fight for and somebody to worry about. This is something worth living for," she wrote in January 1938.[80] "The fact that I am expecting a child gives me a new stimulus for life, new energy, and strength to fight."[81] Where her mother saw a challenge, Tonia saw the potential to participate in Sioma's fight through her pregnancy. Where her mother saw weakness, Tonia saw an opportunity to be useful, to show her commitment to Sioma and, by extension, to the communist cause. In a letter to her brother, Julek, Tonia used the term "Spanish wives" to describe herself and other women like her—women whose husbands were engaged in the fight with fascism while they were unable to do so, either because they were not accepted as soldiers or nurses or because they had children to take care of.[82] Sioma and her child helped her interpret her life in terms of a mission. The child was her space of agency, independence, freedom, and creativity; over time it also became a space of performance in front of her mother and perhaps in front of Sioma and her comrades. The confluence between private and public helped Tonia gain agency or ways to voice some generational differences and fuller independence from her family.

Initially, after Sioma left she lived in the same hotel. Eventually, a woman from the FDJ, whose husband had also left for Spain, took her in. They shared a room with a kitchen at 55 rue Brancion, in Paris's fifteenth arrondissement. Soon after Tonia announced her pregnancy, her parents must have suggested that she move back to Łódź, but she responded, "I don't want to go at all. It's too good for me here. Secondly, here I am in much closer contact with Sioma. I get letters from him almost every other day. It is not possible in Poland. . . . Work is difficult to get there, and that would mean being dependent on Grandma; she has had enough of us."[83]

From December 1937, Tonia began living the lonely life. She had no stable employment, no money, and insufficient French language skills, but as she emphasized in her letters, she had the support of her German comrades. German was the language of their daily interactions, and Tonia occasionally complained about losing her Polish skills, almost as if indicating that the help the German comrades extended to her, the common work and commitment, made her part of their world. Tonia highlighted that she maintained trust in people because of the Kameradschaft with German communists, a trust her parents were unable to comprehend.[84] "I have comrades who do not let me put my head down for even a moment," she wrote to her mother after Vera was born.[85] She repeatedly informed her family of the assistance her comrades provided: they looked for a stroller with her, brought her fruit, and invited her for dinners. She also likely received food stamps from them for eating in a vegetarian German restaurant.[86] Their help served as an argument that her pregnancy and future child were part of the common struggle: "You write to me that I do not realize what I am doing, but I do know. I can count on the help of my comrades, and this means the world to me. This is as much their child as mine because Sioma is fighting for everybody else as much as he is for me. I want to jump for joy thinking about this child."[87] "As a single person I am nothing, in a group we are everything."[88] While emphasizing the differences between her and her mother, Tonia marked her space of freedom and agency far beyond her mother's influence.

Tonia wrote very little about what kind of work she did for the FDJ, although she mentioned social outings and public rallies. Paris does not occupy much space in her letters either. When discussing the French life they found in the letters of some volunteers from Palestine in Paris, historians Raanan Rein and Inbal Ofer note that for immigrants "Paris was a novelty. It was rich with cultural experiences that no city in Palestine could boast of. But, more importantly, it was a place where they could contemplate some of the advantages offered to the working class within a full-scale democracy."[89] None of that reflection made it into Tonia's letters; perhaps she was too consumed with daily struggles or she assumed that none of this would be of interest to her parents. It was only later, in her interview with Dowgiałło, that she spoke with a certain introspection about her life in Paris and the rich intellectual and social life she led, such as meetings with German writers and activists who had escaped Nazi Germany and tried to settle there: "In the evenings we met in one of the cafés where they recited their poems. There came Brecht, Anna Seghers, her husband—a professor of history—and many other people, mostly writers. Mostly immigrants from Germany: antifascists, Jews, and non-Jews. I was very lucky to meet them."

As she shared with Dowgiałło, there was also educational and propaganda work:

> Actually, everything was based on Marxist training. Because there were mainly Germans and Austrians among us, we learned, for example, about peasant wars. Naturally, I learned a lot less than the Germans . . . , but it really interested me. I did not know these matters from a Marxist point of view. We were taught by a true teacher of history, a German living in Paris. One of our tasks was to contact French youth and seek an agreement with young communists. It was not very successful because most of these Germans did not know French. Besides, we girls had a separate problem—in the French communist organization there was a separate faction for girls: "Jeunes filles de France." Parents would not let them meet if they knew there were boys in the organization. So, we met alone.[90]

In her interrogation of March 2, 1950, she added more details regarding the limited cooperation between French and German communists: "They had two radio stations. The intended audience for one were German girls affiliated with National Socialist organizations, the other was for all young people. We collected information for them. There was plenty of work. We received correspondence from all over Germany. Some went there [to Germany] illegally in search of information. And the main task of the radio stations was to organize anti-Nazi propaganda in Germany."[91]

Her interrogation minutes as well as the interview with Dowgiałło also revealed sentiments that she never shared in her correspondence with her family. "I felt bad in the German-Austrian Communist Party and asked the secretary to bring me to the Polish communist section," she testified in 1950. She waited two months for an answer and then was informed that the Polish section had been dissolved and that she was not allowed to have any contact with the Poles. She complied with the request.[92] Her conversation with Dowgiałło showed similar tension. On one hand, she underscored the joy of being accepted by the German communists. On the other, she realized the fragility of her participation in the movement:

> I was going to demonstrations with them. Once, on May 1, I put on a white dress with red stripes. I liked the uniform very much, so I was glad that they accepted me. And they accepted me because my husband was an Austrian. Nevertheless, they did point out to me that the Communist Party of Poland had been dissolved in 1938 by Stalin and the entire command was shot in the Soviet Union.... A special representative of a group of young communists was sent to Paris to speak with me. He said that I have no right to contact the Polish communists because maybe there is a traitor among them. And if I want to be with them [the FDJ], I must swear that I would not meet with the Polish communists. I promised. I did not know any Poles. I did not know French. I was pregnant. This was the price I had to pay so they would take care of me.[93]

Life and friendship with the German communists were much harder than she was willing to admit in her letters. She did not want to worry her parents, but she was also performing while trying to convince herself and the people around her that she was doing well. But there was perhaps more: a certain readiness of a communist to accept even the most challenging reality as part of a struggle for a better life, something she had to learn to accept and needed to believe in.

Sioma and the International Brigades

The arrival in Spain in June 1936 of the first foreigners willing to risk their lives in defense of the values the republic stood for revealed the conflict's broad appeal. The first volunteers, mostly German and Italian exiles escaping fascism, created the nucleus of the first International Brigades. Poles, Austrians, French, Hungarians, and Jews from Palestine soon began crossing the border into Spain to join the conflict as well. In many cases, the Comintern organized their travel, paid fares, provided hotel accommodations in Paris, and arranged "for the frontier crossing by hiring guides or bribing guards or a prudent combination of the two."[94] Volunteers were initially assigned to battalions reorganized into brigades formed along national and linguistic lines. Over time, five international brigades formed, with each of the brigades containing four or five battalions of six hundred men each.[95] From inception, the International Brigades thus constituted a multinational force.

Already in November 1936, the International Brigades participated in defending Madrid.[96] Their presence served to raise the morale of the Republican forces during the frequent occasions when they felt abandoned by the international community or even their own government. By April 1937 the brigades were officially incorporated into the regular Republican army.[97] Since they were used as shock troops, they suffered exceptionally heavy casualties. Some volunteers felt they were treated as cannon fodder: "We were volunteers, so in principle they would put us wherever there was a hole to fill, wherever help was needed, where there was trouble and there was a void . . . wherever people had to die," recollected one of them.[98]

Who were these people who enlisted in the war and died in great numbers? Were they indeed idealists willing to die for a cause they believed in? Or were they desperados who had run out of choices and for whom enlisting in Spain appeared as a last resort? Most historians see them in light of the process of internal exile and migration within Europe, people from the social and political margins searching for meaning in life and a place for themselves.[99] Following volunteer accounts, historian Michael Jackson divides the volunteers into four main groups: the politically exiled, the displaced (e.g., by economic dispossession), the anticipators of the world war, and the adventurers. A combination of hunger for adventure and camaraderie, a dose of idealism, and restlessness pushed them to act.[100]

Sioma left Paris for Spain in early December 1937, in the second year of the war and after the border between France and Spain was officially closed. This border closing meant that volunteers had to reach Albacete, a gathering center, illegally through the Pyrenees.[101] As an Austrian volunteer, he joined the Thälmann Battalion, comprising mostly German and Austrian (but also Scandinavian, Dutch, and Swiss) communists, which had been created in October 1936. This battalion was one of three officially included in the Eleventh International Brigade, often simply referred to as the Thälmann Brigade.[102] A plaque with Sioma's name listed as one of the Austrian communists who devoted their lives to the fight against fascism is visible to this day at the Austrian Communist Party headquarters. Historians also include Sioma among the Jewish volunteers.[103] The number of Jewish volunteers who joined the International Brigades was relatively high, ranging between four thousand and eight thousand out of a total of about thirty-five thousand volunteers from some fifty countries.[104] It is quite problematic, however, to determine who was included in the number of Jewish volunteers, especially since often it was not according to how they identified themselves but rather to how others identified them.[105] Because the volunteers most likely were assigned or chose brigades based on the language they spoke, Sioma's placement in the Thälmann Battalion is not surprising, and we do not have any indication if being a volunteer of Jewish descent meant anything to him in terms of his motivation to fight.

Taking Jackson's characterization into account, Sioma could have likely been counted among the politically exiled, a stateless Jew whose linguistic and cultural home was German—the language in which he grew up, in which he communicated with his wife, and one that drew him close to the German communists in Paris. He was a man exiled from the state where his parents chose to live—Palestine. His restlessness could be understood as a response to the ruptures that defined his and Tonia's lives and the difficulty of finding a place they could or would want to call home. Historical necessity stood behind their choices, limiting them while simultaneously providing them with a clear sense of purpose in life. "The victory will not be easy, but the Republican army has to win," wrote Tonia in January 1938 to Julek.[106] Communism was a promise to change a world that had denied many people like them a safe place they could call home; hence, "communist" was the primary identification for Sioma.

Information about the roles Sioma performed in his unit are scattered. A document compiled by Martin Sugarman, archivist at the Jewish Military Museum in London, notes that Sioma served as a mechanic, although Tonia's letters do not confirm this.[107] Unsure what that role entailed in this context, I asked for help from Michael Uhl, a German historian and the author of a book on the myth in East Germany of the Spanish volunteers. According to him, as someone with a knowledge of machinery, Sioma could have worked as an instructor in a Spanish weapons factory or on the front line maintaining trucks.[108] In January 1938, just weeks after Sioma left Paris, Tonia wrote that Sioma would not go to the front because he had a more intellectual task to fulfill.[109] In February 1938 she wrote that Sioma was being trained as a telegraphist.[110] In May 1938 he informed her that he had become a noncommissioned officer.¹¹¹ In September 1938 Tonia received information that Sioma had distinguished himself in the Battle of the Ebro (July–November 1938), one of the most difficult battles of the war. Its mortality rate among volunteers was staggering, greatly contributing to the Republicans losing the war and eventually opening a road to Madrid for Franco.¹¹² With the information of his performance at Ebro first came information that Sioma became a *Kaderkomissar* and then a *Politkomissar*.¹¹³

Following the model of the Red Army, each brigade unit had a military commander as well as a political commissar, Politkomissar, whose task it was "to permeate the rank and file with the view of the Comintern."¹¹⁴ While a Politkomissar was responsible for political consciousness in his unit, a Kaderkomissar was responsible for monitoring his unit and transferring information about soldiers to the supervisor. In other words, he was to ensure that the soldiers in his unit followed the correct version of communism—that is, the one imposed by Stalin—and were not "Trotskyites."¹¹⁵ A Kaderkomissar's responsibility was technical and focused on the organization of the troops, while a Politkomissar was responsible for more political and intellectual matters. The more ideologically important Politkomissar wore an olive-green officer's hat, with a red star within a circle, so that all the soldiers could recognize him. The Kaderkomissar, in contrast, did not have any specific insignia.

Thanks to Uhl and a researcher from Paris, Meryl Lavenant, I learned much more about Sioma when Lavenant discovered Sioma's file in the records of the International Brigades in the online RGASPI, which contains Comintern folders. Lavenant found a questionnaire, "Biografia de militantes," in which Sioma was asked to provide answers to a set of questions organized around a few categories: personal, professional, and political. As Uhl explained, these biographies have a fascinating background. In the fall of 1937 the central committee of the Spanish Communist Party began to organize a campaign focused on transferring all foreign communist members of the International Brigades from their home communist parties to the Spanish party. Each cell of the communist parties in the International Brigades provided questionnaires to its members. After filling them out, the secretary of the cell checked the facts and then sent them to a German Jewish communist, Ruth Kahn, known as Carmen, to double-check. If she approved the questionnaire, the volunteer received a red card of membership in the Spanish Communist Party. The entire process was clandestine since the Spanish minister of defense had forbidden political activities in the Republican army outside of the Popular Front.[116]

Sioma's questionnaire, filled out on May 26, 1938, provides fascinating insight into his political life and the scale of his communist engagement. It is in Spanish, but Sioma answered the questions in German, written in his characteristic narrow and almost impossible to read script. He noted that he had been jailed six times before leaving for France: twice in Vienna in 1933 and 1934 before the family left for Palestine and four times in Palestine. He had finished only elementary school but spoke and read four languages: Yiddish, Hebrew, German, and French. His favorite authors were Stalin, Lenin, Marx, and Hegel.[117] An opinion of him accompanies his questionnaire:

> Sioma Lechtman was at first a good soldier, and likewise he was very politically active and became the political commissar of a company. As a result, he showed to be very weak in difficult situations and especially in the last operation, where he was not equal to the tasks of a commissar. Politically he had good knowledge and was well trained, but he didn't understand how to combine theory with practice. He was very nervous and didn't find the right connection with the soldiers. Apart from that, though, he was a politically active comrade who worked actively in the party company. He was better suited as a party worker than as a commissar on the People's Front (*Volksfrontlinie*). He was comradely and social and averagely a good comrade.[118]

Sioma's profile was thus mixed: he was perceived as a good soldier but a weak political worker. Overall, however, his profile was not bad given that some volunteers were being arrested for weak political work and accused of divergence from Stalinism. The overall image of Sioma in these documents is one of a committed communist who invested most of his very young life to the communist struggle.

Information Tonia had on what Sioma did in Spain is fragmented. Uhl agreed with me, adding that she had only impressions of what Sioma actually did in Spain, partially because of military censorship. Sioma was not even allowed to mention to his wife the name of the town where he was.[119]

Vera

Despite the difficulties she endured during her pregnancy, Tonia remained calm and happy in her letters. She was focused on expecting the baby and avoided more complicated topics: "It is such a beautiful feeling when the little creature moves. In the first days, I was unconscious from happiness. I cannot wait."[120] A month later, she wrote, "You cannot imagine how happy I am that I will become a mother. I will have something to fight for, to take care of."[121] She mentioned the various pieces of clothing she received for the baby and herself, the baby clothes she made, the bed she planned on buying, and even a special pot for steam-cooking she requested from her mother. She assured her mother that she visited the doctor regularly and that she and the baby were healthy. "The heart is beating strongly."[122]

After some months of sharing a room with her friend Hilda Bergman from the FDJ at rue Brancion, she was forced to move to Paris Boulogne, at 102 rue du Dôme. Hilda was leaving for Spain, while another friend, Sophie Marum, had a room to rent in Paris Boulogne in an apartment she shared with her husband, Hans, and an infant. The apartment was relatively expensive (six hundred francs per quarter), but it had running water and a bathroom shared by the neighbors on the corridor. Tonia assured her family, "I am glad. Finally, I will have my own space. And here I feel happy because a park is close, and we can walk where the air is better."[123]

One of her most memorable jobs was working for Raymond-Raoul Lambert.[124] Lambert acted as secretary-general of the Refugee Assistance Committee (Comité d'assistance aux réfugiés), a humanitarian organization focused on organizing such activities as vocational training for Jewish refugees in France. The organization oscillated between dealing with antisemitism and expressing sympathy for the refugees, between "economic" fears of being flooded by poor and hungry refugees and a French tradition of fighting for refugees and humanitarian values.[125] Tonia worked at first for Lambert as his maid, but once he learned of her pregnancy, he transferred her to office work. Since she did not speak French, she helped mainly with copying and sending mail. "He always told me to take taxis and God forbid I carry anything. I did not know about office work at the time, but I wrote letters to Poland, to the Sejm members. And I was happy," she remembered.[126]

During this period, the Marums helped Tonia the most. Hans was the son of Ludwig Marum, a German politician and one of the first victims of Nazism. After launching a public attack against Hitler's policies in 1933, Ludwig was arrested and then murdered a year later. According to Hans's sister, Elizabeth, Hans was most likely warned that he might be arrested and thus escaped Germany in 1933. Sophie joined him three years later.[127] In Paris, Hans continued working on propagating communism as a member of the World Jewish Congress. Sophie had pedagogical training and worked as a babysitter, which she did mostly at home and invited Tonia to assist her with.[128]

After Sioma's departure, it was most likely Hans who helped Tonia obtain permission to stay in France. "The Germans do everything for me because I cannot get anything done through French offices," she wrote in February, months before she delivered her child.[129] Tonia revealed a bit more in a letter to Julek, at least in terms of her growing doubt about the possibility of staying in France legally. "Life in Paris is quite intense but unthinkable in the long term. Many of our comrades are thinking about returning to their homeland; where we will return, we don't know. Maybe we will live in Republican Spain."[130] A good indication of how desperate her situation was a statement that she was not considering giving up the baby for adoption.[131] Perhaps her family wanted her to consider that option or her comrades suggested it. Occasionally her parents must have suggested that she should move to Poland, but she refused: "I am receiving documents as a *poliemigrantka* (political immigrant), and as such I would lose all rights when I leave because it would mean that I could live in Poland."[132]

The year 1938 was dramatic for Europe. Antisemitism continued on the rise. In March 1938 Austria was annexed into Nazi Germany, exacerbating the problem of Austrian refugees in France. On April 10, 1938, Édouard Daladier once again became the French prime minister. His Center-Right coalition would lead France for the next two years, with a devastating effect on refugee policy. One of Daladier's first actions was a decree on May 2 that "both reversed and defended the refugee protection measures of the past by legally distinguishing the old refugees from the new." While residency rights for Russian and Armenian migrants of the 1920s were guaranteed, obtaining residency permits for any recent refugees—for example, from Germany or Spain—became increasingly difficult. With one decree, "Daladier had shifted the status of France from a refugee receiver nation to one of transit."[133] This shift was instituted while the Jewish refugee crisis was growing to unprecedented proportions. By the end of 1938 there were approximately sixty thousand Central and Eastern European Jewish refugees in France.[134]

On the surface, these policies did not affect Tonia. She had already been struggling with her illegal status. But in her letters she admitted that the matter was becoming perilous. Without legal documentation, she would not be allowed to stay in Paris. In May 1938 she wrote:

> I worry a lot about my papers. There are new challenges facing foreigners. I have to register my arrival before May 30, otherwise I am facing six months in prison and expulsion. I don't know how it will be done yet; it is very difficult for me to do anything because I have a Polish passport. Everyone reassures me that they will not expel me with a child, but you never know. I didn't write to Sioma about this at all. I can imagine how nervous he would be if I had to return to Poland.[135]

Hans Marum advised her that the best time to seek legalization in Paris was during the final month of pregnancy.[136] Tonia applied for authorization to stay in France on May 23, 1938, while very late in her pregnancy. Her application carried her birth name, date of birth, and the number on her marriage certificate, which had apparently finally arrived. Writing on the application in impeccable and elegant French, she explained that she had entered France illegally for the second time in March 1938 after an illegal stay in Liège, Belgium. Previously she had stayed in France from May to November 1937. The document states the following: "I am waiting for a baby to be born soon, and since I cannot return to Poland because of my marriage to a stateless person, I have the honor to ask your high benevolence for permission to reside in France and receive an identification card. Given my current state of affairs and the need to find myself in the next few days at a hospital, I hope for a favorable response in the shortest possible time."[137]

On May 27, only four days later, she had to be present at the prefecture to acquire an identity card. In her interrogation from March 2, 1950, she explained that the procedure lasted the entire day.[138] The document carried a photo of her right profile and a physical description, including skin tone. Her nationality was described as Polish and her religion "Israelite." She was described as a lace worker, without French references, and without a passport and possessing only a translation of her marriage certificate. Her source of support in France was a monthly allowance from her family of one thousand francs. The addresses of where she had stayed in Liège and in Paris before that were lies, and she explained that a taxi had taken her across the border. She also most likely presented a certificate confirming her advanced pregnancy, which necessitated her hospital admission.[139]

She applied for permission to stay in France almost three weeks after the infamous decree law of May 2, 1938, according to which "the police had the right to expel clandestine immigrants immediately, without granting an administrative or judicial hearing."[140] Foreigners without identity papers faced fines and prison sentences of one to twelve months, after which they were to be expelled. The bottom of her identity card stated that she had been granted a temporary residency permit but that further investigation into her case would proceed. It also included her fingerprints. Perhaps Hans Marum was correct that being pregnant worked to her advantage. In the interrogation of March 2, 1950, she explained that Hans also helped her create a story of how she came to France through Belgium.[141] Perhaps the story was also the reason why she decided not to present her passport, which carried a stamp from when she entered Paris for the first time in May 1937. She thus presented herself as a relatively recent émigré to Paris without a passport, a single mother who was supported by her family in Palestine.

A month after her visit to the prefecture, Tonia gave birth to Vera.[142] The due date had been estimated incorrectly, so for weeks Tonia lived in expectation that the child would be born any day. In order not to pay hospital fees, she went to the Medical Academy of the Boucicaut Hospital in Paris, the place where many migrant women delivered their babies. During their occasional checkups, pregnant women had to lie down in a circle, while students walked around examining them. She described this experience as humiliating.[143] She was scared of giving birth and was told to walk a lot. So, she walked. One night she went out dancing. Her contractions began that night. She woke up Sophie and Hans, who wanted to take a taxi to the hospital, but she insisted on walking. The distance between the hospital and her apartment was around four kilometers, at least an hour's walk for a woman in labor. Friends who accompanied her finally hailed a taxi once she started to vomit along the way. Like the checkups, the delivery room had beds arranged in a circle.

The doctor and a midwife observed the women from the center.[144] The hospital still has the record from Tonia's delivery. She was admitted on June 26 as Tauba Bialer, and the baby arrived without any complications the next day at 5:45 a.m. Tonia and Vera stayed in the hospital for eleven days, the average stay at the time. There are no comments for either of them on the hospital registration document. Most patients had "AS" (*assuré social*) as a comment, suggesting that the patient was registered to benefit from state financial support for health expenses.[145]

On June 27 Hans informed Tonia's family in Palestine that the baby had arrived: "On behalf of your daughter, I allow myself to inform you that yesterday she gave birth to a girl. My wife and I visited Tonia yesterday in the hospital and found both that the birth was smooth (five hours in total) and that Tonia and the child are in excellent health."[146] Tonia wrote about the arrival of Vera over two weeks later, on July 15:

> On Saturday evening, I was in the city until 10 p.m. At 11 p.m., I went to sleep. At 12:30 the pain began. We thought it was my stomach because I didn't bleed at all and because my water did not break. We went to the hospital on foot at first because I felt much better walking, then we took a taxi.... By 5:30 a.m. our beloved daughter was already in this world.
> She weighed at delivery 2,900 grams.
> She gains a great 50 grams a day.
> She now weighs 3,075.
> She cries very little.[147]

She remembered her delivery positively as a special moment of finally meeting her daughter and as a time of being taken care of. Delivery brought a sense of accomplishment:

> After the delivery, the doctor came and promised that he would fulfill my every wish because I was so good. I said, first of all, I wanted a smoke. They agreed but told me to drink a cup of strong broth before. Only after that there was coffee and a cigarette.... Everything was extraordinary. It seems to me that today even in the best clinics there are no such conditions. I spent ten days in a sixty-person room.... I felt great. There were huge spaces everywhere. And tall,

beautiful windows. . . . There was a bottle of wine under each bed. Even the doctor told me to drink it because it helps with nursing. . . . At noon they brought dinner—a cook in a tall hat came with a roast on a wooden board. Throughout my stay in France, I have not seen such a roast.[148]

The first weeks after delivery were joyous. She received guests with gifts daily. One friend washed diapers, another boiled them to get rid of any germs, and another (male) colleague cleaned the apartment.[149]

Her life, however, did change after Vera was born. Her activism in the International Committee for Aid to the Spanish People and the FDJ ended.[150] Soon after delivery, she tried to do some occasional work, such as babysitting, to earn money. Her doctor taught her how to help children with special needs and sent her to help more affluent parents. Tonia usually took Vera with her, her "muster kid," as she called her.[151] But all the jobs were temporary and did not provide enough income.[152] She had difficulty securing money to pay rent. The news coming from Spain kept proving how uncertain Sioma's return was, and the paperwork she had received was only temporary.

Most of her letters then focused on how smart and healthy little Vera was. Almost every letter ended with a statement of how people Tonia ran into—friends, nurses, doctors, even strangers on the street—told her how healthy and well taken care of her child looked.[153] Tonia performed her role as a mother extremely well. She breast-fed her infant and boasted about Vera gaining weight and the kind of solid food she was eating.[154] The fight she was fighting was a victorious one. "How much joy such a little munchkin gives. She rarely cries and is very good while eating. She eats all vegetables, salad, spinach. We are not lacking anything here. She eats everything without sugar. And such big portions. I would not be able to eat that much."[155] Vera was a child brought up in a modern way, as Tonia often emphasized in her letters. Tonia tried to love her wisely—fed her nutritious food and avoided carrying her too much to prevent her from developing unnecessary dependence. Her devotion to the child was unquestionable, but she also tried to be wise and rational.[156] Tonia's motherhood was a life mission that marked her commitment to Sioma and also perhaps to all those who believed they had a role to play in how the future unfolded.

War, Detention, and an Escape

The tone of Tonia's letters began changing in the fall of 1938. The clouds around them were getting increasingly grim. On September 30 the Munich Agreement was signed, confirming the cession of part of Czechoslovakia—the Sudetenland—to Nazi Germany. France and Britain approved the decision on October 4 at the Munich Conference. In October Tonia informed her family that she and her comrades spent most of their free time listening to the radio. News about the approaching war was entrenching them.[157] Soon after the agreement many of their German friends began escaping to America. Many left Tonia their furniture, gestures that seemingly helped her organize her own life but ultimately also must have left her in growing fear. In September she wrote to her parents:

> The situation is very serious. You may not feel it as much as we do. We sit by the radio all day. War is the topic of all conversations. Our situation as immigrants is not very pleasant. We are happy that we are in democratic France. We put all our hopes into it. Naturally, everyone here pledged to volunteer if they are mobilized.... Naturally, I'm out of the question because of the baby. However, I will not stay in Paris. Such uncertainty makes us all so nervous that it is difficult for us to maintain the peace that is so important right now. . . . France and all democratic countries cannot allow Hitler to carry out his plans with impunity because in the end he threatens the whole world. We listened to his speech last night. It is so tragic that the whole world listens to him with tension. France has made great mistakes. It's hard to dig oneself out of it now.[158]

Plus, her financial issues persisted. Initially she was still pondering a more serious job than babysitting but worried that returning to work would force her to stop breastfeeding. Whatever financial support she was receiving from the International Committee for Aid to the Spanish People ceased by the end of 1938.[159] She now relied solely on financial help from her parents, grandmother in Poland, and friends in Paris.

In September 1938 the Spanish prime minister, Juan Negrín, announced before the League of Nations his decision to withdraw foreign volunteers from Spain. They were withdrawn on September 23 from active combat.[160]

Their role was over. Tonia was hopeful but also aware that multiple political issues complicated the possibility of Sioma's quick return. In a letter, she stated that Negrín's decision "demonstrates the incredible strength of the Republican army and its peaceful pursuit." However, she added, "When will he come back? I count that it will last three months. It is not so easy because France has not yet agreed to let them all in."[161] On October 28 a farewell parade was organized in Barcelona where Dolores Ibárruri, a Republican fighter better known as La Pasionaria, made her famous speech: "Comrades of the International Brigades. You can go with pride. You are history. You are legend. You are the heroic example of the solidarity and universality of democracy."[162]

Indeed, the process of repatriation of the volunteers began toward the end of 1938. Volunteers from democratic countries, such as France and Britain, were allowed to return home, which most did.[163] But many feared returning to home countries that had been ravaged by fascism or simply had no home to return to, as was the case for the stateless Sioma. After a ceremonial inspection by President Manuel Azaña and Prime Minister Negrín, the Eleventh International Brigade was moved to Bisaura, a town on the Spanish-French border, where the men remained for months awaiting evacuation. The first group of some twenty thousand volunteers crossed the border on December 21, 1938. Six weeks later, the final group of volunteers joined them.[164]

Based on the letters she was receiving, Tonia was able to somewhat monitor where Sioma was being taken. In November 1938 she informed her family that he had been transported to a camp for the International Brigades located in Spain (perhaps Bisaura). She was growing increasingly disappointed with the situation that put both of them in limbo. It was uncertain what their next step should be:

> I didn't have a letter from him for a long time because he was so disappointed and depressed that it was impossible for him to put together a few words. I can imagine it well because I thought that in a few days we would see each other, and now the situation looks like it will last a few months. It is impossible to know at all whether they will let him into France or whether he will come only for a short time. We know nothing at all, and this uncertainty is killing us. This year was very difficult for both of us. We were hoping that would change soon, but now I do not see anything ahead of me. Naturally, Sioma is in a terrible state. He is idle there, without anything to do.

After such a long time of intense activity, the lack of anything to do does not affect him positively.[165]

At the beginning of 1939, Sioma was still in Spain and apparently unsure if he would be allowed to enter France. In February Tonia wrote:

> Sioma's situation is very difficult. France doesn't want to let them in. There is an international delegation at the border to deal with this issue. Who knows if they all will not be sent to Mexico or Cuba. Naturally, I would like Sioma to come to Paris because I do not want to think about traveling so far with our little one. In general, leaving Europe would cause me great pain. I have now applied for naturalization of Vera. I think that this way Sioma will come to Paris. Nobody knows how long it will take. In any case, Spain is interested in sending these people somewhere as soon as possible because . . . they are a burden for the government in such hard times.[166]

Tonia captured well the general French policy toward refugees, even if she did not realize the scope of the unprecedented exodus at the French-Spanish border. As historian John Sweets summarizes, "French attitudes and actions toward the Spanish refugees reflected generosity and a measure of atonement for not having aided the Spanish Republic in its hour of need; at the same time there was suspicion and not infrequent hostility to these uninvited guests whose presence was in many ways awkward for the French. . . . Veterans of the International Brigades who had found refuge in France along with the Spanish were, if anything, less welcome than the Spanish." French authorities treated them as uninvited and problematic guests who were encouraged to leave.[167]

Once the volunteers and refugees from Spain were allowed to cross the border, they were herded into several large, overcrowded camps on the shore of the Mediterranean in the French department of the Pyrénées-Orientales bordering Spain while hastily building makeshift camps for themselves. Refugees outnumbered residents by two to one. One of the places where they were confined was Argelès-sur-Mer, which became notorious for its unsanitary conditions.[168] Chaos and improvisation defined these camps, which were "spaces fenced off with barbed wire, without huts or sanitation, guarded by gendarmes, mobile guards and colonial troops. The refugees had to burrow into the sand to shelter from the winter weather. Their resistance had been lowered by months of war and long journeys on foot, and epidemics spread."[169] In her interrogation on March 4, 1950, Tonia explained that in February 1939 she found out in a letter from her husband that he was in another camp in the department, in Saint-Cyprien. She revealed that she had considered going there in early 1939, but because Sioma told her that he was trying to get back to Paris, she decided to wait.[170]

Eventually, in April 1939, Sioma was moved to a large detention camp in Gurs, located in southwestern France at the foot of the Pyrenees.[171] Established largely to house Republican refugees from the war, the camp was situated "on a plateau in south-west France covered in ferns and spiny acacia.... In summer it is a pleasant spot, with a view across to the Pyrenees, their peaks covered in snow for much of the year. But in autumn, the rains turn the ground to mud, while winter brings bitter winds and biting cold to the exposed pastures."[172] By April 22, 1939, there were already 5,558 prisoners. Others would arrive in the following weeks, bringing the total number to 6,808 by the end of May. Following a decision of the military administration, all international volunteers were grouped together in a single camp. They were to remain united in internment as they had been in fighting.[173]

Tonia's letters from this time are not dated, and only the context of each letter helps to situate them chronologically. Sioma's return to France created a new set of problems. Sioma and Tonia were in the same country but without any promise on the horizon of a reunion. One war had ended, but the danger of another was looming:

> Sioma is still in the camp and nobody knows how much longer this will last. Their situation is terrible. Initially everybody was appalled, and now people are getting used to it. There is no water; they cannot wash themselves. Hygiene is no good at all; all kinds of epidemics are threatening the entire camp. France does nothing to improve the situation. I sent him a package with some underwear, soap, and some food, but I haven't received any answers yet. You can only imagine how much I am trying to get him out. Nothing works. If I go, or send a French person, I could probably get him out, but travel costs so much that I cannot even think about this. Additionally, I don't know if I will be able to legalize myself here.[174]

The situation was deteriorating. Tonia and Sioma had fought for respect and inclusion and found themselves as outcasts. They had left Palestine for France in 1937, perhaps not of their own volition but they welcomed it as a new opportunity. Now, only two years later, in the spring of 1939, their situation had changed dramatically. While before they felt in control of their own lives, now they were dominated, perhaps even squashed, by history that allured them with options, only to challenge them by denying them choices.

In January 1939 Tonia filed another request for permission to stay (*demand d'autorisation de séjour*) to the Paris Police Prefecture. On February 1, 1939, her petition was rejected on the basis of her illegal entry to France and insufficient means of subsistence, despite "correct political attitude," "absence of criminal record," and "favorable opinion on her morality."[175] It is unclear whether she was aware that she had lost her chance to stay in Paris legally. Her letters were becoming more apprehensive. In May she informed her family that she had decided not to work, asking them if they would be willing to support her completely. She earned little and was neglecting Vera while working, and by working she risked expulsion and imprisonment. "I realize how difficult it must be for you and that perhaps this is wrong of me [presumably for asking them for help]. So please tell me honestly what you think. I hope this situation won't last long. The situation is very critical, and naturally it affects immigrants negatively. You cannot even imagine what is going on here. One could write books."[176]

Toward the end 1938, Tonia began thinking about leaving France, but where could she and Vera go? Poland was out of the question, not only because it would mean moving away from Sioma but also because her brother Romek had been arrested again in Poland.[177] She occasionally mentioned the possibility of going to Mexico or the United States but was unwilling to decide without Sioma. After Tonia's parents suggested that the couple move to Syria, she grasped that idea as a possibility. In the end, however, moving hung on Sioma's freedom.[178] Waiting was all she could do.

In those dramatic months of late 1938 and early 1939, hope was mixed with desperation. Nothing was certain, except that the heavy clouds of war were approaching. She tried to stay calm but was conflicted about what to do. She must have been aware of the expulsion awaiting her, but on May 11 she informed her family that there was no way she could leave Paris because she would not be able to pay for a place to live anywhere else.[179] However, on May 25, 1939, the Ministry of the Interior instructed the Paris Police Prefecture to notify her that she had to leave France.[180] In her conversation with Dowgiałło, she revealed the seriousness of these moments:

I was doing well in Paris, but I missed my husband terribly. And I asked an organization to be sent to him with Vera. As a wife of a member of the International Brigades, I was receiving a little bit of money, and I was able to save for the journey. In the meantime, a gendarme came to me. He told me that as an illegal immigrant I needed to leave France. I began to cry. I told him that I am leaving for Pau, near the border with Spain. He looked at me and left. But in principle I was in danger of being expelled. So, getting ahead of the fact, I went to my husband.[181]

|||

The story of Tonia in Paris is the story of a refugee driven to search for a place that would let her live according to her beliefs. It is also a story of a woman who refused to define herself as a refugee. She viewed herself as a migrant who crossed multiple real and imaginary boundaries of places she imagined as sites where she could flourish, rather than just being allowed to live. Living in Paris was her choice, as much as her life in Palestine and her departure from Poland were not. However, over time, her situation in Paris became that of a refugee whose life was tenuous and increasingly fragile. Even if it was not the so-called Jewish question that spurred her travel, it increasingly affected her life. She remained optimistic, however, because she believed in human rights as principles that had built modern France, she believed in the power of human solidarity that constituted her understanding of communism, and she did not recognize her own condition as precarious.

Despite this optimism, her loneliness must have been growing. Certainly, communism played the role of an antidote for her loneliness and the rupture she was experiencing. During those grim days, communism was a gesture of solidarity, a sense of community, which in addition to providing her with hope meant crucial material help. Her communism was a product of the social relations in which she was embedded. But the community of communists was partially imagined; she wanted to believe that they accepted her because she was a fellow human being and a communist and not only because she was Polish, pregnant, and alone. She wanted to believe that it was her humanity, not her fragility, that made her worthy of their attention and help. Communism was also important because it lent meaning to the ties she had developed, the social roles she continued, and the new roles she embraced. It gave her meaning-making agency—the ability to imbue motherhood with an important public role. Motherhood became Tonia's mission and a personal way of dealing with her arduous living circumstances. It helped her reconstruct her gender identity to make sense of her life. In her letters, she performed as a good daughter ready to calm and appease her mother. But she also used her motherhood as proof of being a good communist. Ultimately, she also performed for herself to make sense of her life and reinforce some meaning to her daily struggles with poverty, hunger, fear, and loneliness.

4 ||| Life on the Run

War and Uncertainty in France, 1939–1942

IN 1990 Tonia and her children took a trip following the path of their desperate trek through southern France in the early 1940s. On that first journey, Vera and Marcel were just toddlers—too small to remember how World War II had, almost overnight, redefined their lives and drastically limited their mother's choices. The only thing left from the second trip is a photo album that documents various moments and provides occasional captions.[1] The descriptions are limited to basic information evoking relatively happy events, lucky coincidences, or sites associated with the children's lives—the hospitals where they were born or the washroom where Tonia used to launder her son's diapers. Seen from the perspective of half a century, these sites and stories have become fully integrated aspects of the family's history. The memories the trip evoked are a gift of motherly love. Photos emphasize their life together, while the threat of the danger looming in almost every direction is absent.

One of the photos is of Tonia and Vera in front of the Paris hospital where Vera was born, and another of the house in Paris where she and Vera lived with Sophie and Hans Marum. The caption of a photo of the hospital in Pau where Marcel was born states that Tonia was unable to inform her husband of his birth, adding that a Spaniard helped her get home from Pau's city hall, where she traveled with infant Marcel to claim his birth certificate. It was raining, and the man covered her and the baby with his coat to protect them from getting drenched. He explained that he owed as much to Marcel's father for his commitment to Republican Spain.

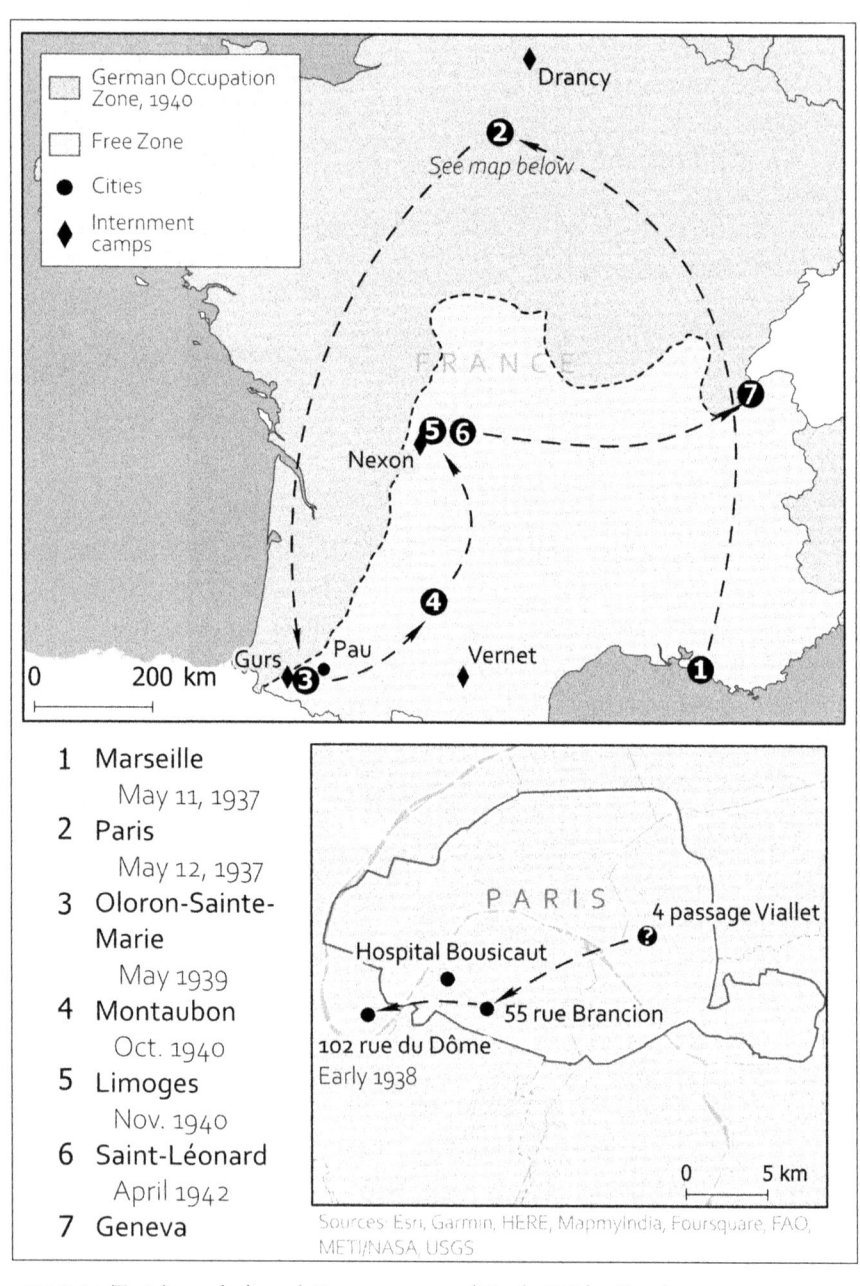

MAP 4.1. Tonia's travels through France, 1937–42. *(Map by Kaitlyn Tatro)*

Seventy-two-year-old Tonia was fragile at the time of their 1990 trip, so Marcel carried a small folding stool for her to sit on when she needed to rest.[2] In one photo, she is sitting on the stool in the middle of a big Parisian cobblestoned plaza. She had fought hard for her survival and that of her children, seemingly against the grain of the history unfolding around them. The photo reclaims her place in that history of a city that drew her in and yet never provided her with safety and comfort; she is anonymous and yet deeply entrenched in it. If we judge from the photos, the trip was certainly nostalgic: it provided Vera and Marcel with a space, however narrow, to reconnect with the sites that had affected them deeply and yet of which they have no memory, sites that marked intimate closeness to their mother, from whom they were separated for the majority of their adolescent and young adult lives.

As I strive to put in order the various events of her life—people she met, setbacks she encountered, heartbreaking disappointments she experienced—I realize that I am the one who needs chronology and causal connection to understand her life. That is my role as a historian. But perhaps my attempts are futile. Perhaps her life was not a straightforward narrative progressing toward anything, and perhaps she accepted the chaos around her and understood that danger and uncertainty had become her routine, without trying to make sense of it herself. There are many holes in her story that I will never be able to fill, since only fragments of evidence have survived. What we are left with is often chaotic and at best anecdotal, exposing the problems of combining an individual story with a master narrative, "as if the world is broken and you can find only pieces."[3] Tonia's story exposes the cracks into which an individual falls and the complex ways an individual's agency and mobility push and pull against the surge of history. It is not linear: it is convoluted, chaotic, and confusing. Tonia's story is lost in the obscurity of barely documented facts, the people she met and whose precise names she could no longer remember, and interpretations of the world around her often seen through the prism of what has happened to her since then.

With but without Sioma

Tonia left Paris suddenly in May or June 1939. The letter of expulsion from the Paris Police Prefecture could have been the final overwhelming drop of misfortune. Despite the emotions that undoubtedly accompanied her departure, sources offer competing versions of the story. In her conversation with Dowgiałło, she said that she left her Paris apartment in June 1939 in such a hurry that she forgot to collect some of her belongings, including some jewelry. She took Vera and left. She traveled by train from Paris to Pau, the capital of the Department of Pyrénées-Atlantiques in the region of Nouvelle-Aquitaine, set along the northern edge of the Pyrenees Mountains, approximately eighty kilometers from the Spanish border. The trip from Paris took a day. From Pau, she traveled to Oloron, her final destination, located sixteen kilometers from the camp in Gurs, where Sioma was being held. She said she paid for the journey with money she had saved in Paris.[4]

But her interrogation of March 4, 1950, provides a remarkably different account. In it she explained she did not have enough money for the trip, so she asked the International Committee for Aid to the Spanish People to help cover her travel expenses. Initially she was supposed to go by truck to bring some clothes to interned volunteers, but the plan changed and she traveled by train. Leaders of the FDJ asked her to serve as a liaison to the men confined in Gurs. She traveled twice: she left for the South of France for the first time in May and then ten days later returned to Paris, only to leave again for Gurs in June. As a liaison she was entrusted with a special mission: incoming and outgoing letters were censored in Gurs, so the leadership of the FDJ in Paris sent letters to Tonia to smuggle into the camp. She was inspected at the entry point, but camp security was rather superficial.[5] Visitors had only to empty their pockets when they passed through.[6] In the camp, she received letters that she then smuggled out and sent from Oloron to Paris. I was unable to confirm the existence of an outside network facilitating the correspondence. It was certainly possible, as multiple examples in history show how fast clandestine communication networks developed in and around various prisons and camps.[7] She explained that she was involved in the secret passage of letters until September 1939, the outbreak of the world war. After that, French authorities halted her freedom of movement for two months.[8] Records do not show how many times she visited the camp and Sioma prior to September. To see him, she and her one-year-old toddler walked or hitchhiked sixteen kilometers from Oloron, where she had found a place to live, to Gurs.[9]

Whatever her exact motivations and logistics, Tonia's decision to move from Paris constituted a rupture in her relatively stable life. As a single mother and migrant without a stable income, her life was precarious in Paris but had stabilized over time: she had a solid network of support, financial assistance from her parents and, most important, a place to live in a city to which she had slowly adapted. Even though she was an unwelcome migrant, she had not experienced any direct threats to her safety as a Jew at that time.[10] In the summer of 1939 Paris appeared to be a relatively safe place compared to the chaos and unpredictability the Spanish volunteers faced.

The move, however, sent her into uncharted territory. Even if her decision to serve as a liaison for the FDJ may seem problematic in her situation, it helped her to situate herself in new circumstances. By moving to the South of France, she escaped the most severe measures that soon would become the daily reality of Parisian Jews, but moving also displaced Tonia even more. This was when the war began for her. There, in the South of France, while having escaped the Paris police as an illegal migrant, she arrived in an area housing mostly communists and refugees from Spain. In a few months, the focus of persecution would shift from the communists to the Jews. But at this particular moment, she experienced the chaos and fragility of her situation more as a displaced communist than as a Jew.

After much of Catalonia was captured by Franco's Nationalists at the end of 1938 and the beginning of 1939, Oloron's mayor, the socialist Jean Mendiondou, welcomed refugees from Spain and provided them with food and medical aid. By the middle of 1939, the town had a refugee population of more than one thousand.[11] Hence, Tonia reached a town flooded with refugees. She moved in with a small group of women who were either nurses in the service of the International Brigades or had traveled to Oloron to be close to their partners. Since the group of women volunteers evacuated from Spain was not large enough to organize according to the languages they spoke, as was done with the men in demobilization camps, all of the women were grouped together, including Tonia, even though she had traveled from Paris, not Spain.[12]

During one of her interrogations, Tonia provided the names of the women she had lived with, but the transcription cannot be fully trusted: the names were most likely misremembered by Tonia and misspelled and Polonized by officers taking notes during questioning conducted under conditions of fear and violence.[13] Historian Michael Uhl, currently working on a biography of Betty Rosenfeld, a German woman who traveled to Oloron with the similar purpose of being closer to her fiancée (Sally Wittelson), who was also confined in Gurs, helped me establish some of the names of the women whom Rosenfeld met and lived with in Oloron, including Tonia. There were four German women: Auguste Guttman, Klara Hamburger, Elisabeth Kühnen, and Betty Rosenfeld. Sonia Kalna was Latvian and Czech through a fictitious marriage with a Czech. Finally, Romanian Fina Branstein was one of the finest women of the medical service of the International Brigades.[14] Tonia first stayed with this group in a hotel in Oloron. It is unclear if the hotel was a shelter-type residence or a semi-informal place for women who found themselves in Oloron either to see their loved ones or because they were forcibly being moved from Spain. After living together in the hotel, Tonia and a small group of women rented an apartment.[15]

The first letter Tonia wrote to her mother from Oloron, in June 1939, not long after her arrival, reveals the new challenges she faced: "Imagine that the same misfortune happened to me as what happened before leaving Palestine. You can imagine my anxiety. I have tried everything, but nothing has worked. There is nothing else for me but to go to Paris and settle this as soon as possible." Tonia was pregnant again. "How nervous I am; you cannot imagine at all. It costs so much money, and then I have to travel to Paris. . . . Honestly, I feel like crying when I think about it. I did not expect this because I protected myself."[16] In her conversation with Dowgiałło, she further clarified that her German comrades in Paris had given her a uterus ring to prevent her from getting pregnant, but it had malfunctioned. She tried to get rid of the fetus by carrying heavy suitcases filled with books. Nothing worked.[17]

Tonia had no money, and the journey to Paris was dangerous. In July 1939 the atmosphere was ominous. A war was imminent. Sioma was confined in an internment camp, and despite continuous hope there was no assurance of when, if ever, he would be able to reunite with her. In the following letter, she thanked her family for the money and informed them that at the moment she could not go to Paris and that even if she were able to go, she did not have anybody to leave Vera with: "Ah! I'm so unlucky. Always worries and trouble," she ended her letter.[18] In September she admitted that it was unlikely she would be able to travel to Paris. The bitter reality that foreigners were under suspicion had begun to sink in:

> It is too dangerous for foreigners. Maybe in a week or two when the situation changes, maybe I will be able to go. Do you have any news from Poland? In the first few days, I was very nervous because we were not allowed to go out. Now I am living with five other

women in one house, so life is much easier, and what is most important is that I don't feel that lonely. I am the only person [in the house] who received permission to go shopping. Maybe because I have a baby, and maybe because I am Polish. In any case, it is very convenient for us.[19]

While describing her situation in Oloron in her interrogations, Tonia used the term *résidence forcée*. She explained that women interned in the city had a right to move around but had to check in with the police occasionally.[20] But her interrogations do not illuminate whether she meant the period prior to or during the war. While searching for further explanation of résidence forcée, I exchanged a number of emails with Claude Laharie, a historian and specialist on the camp in Gurs who runs the Gurs memory center, L'Amicale du camp de Gurs.[21] He informed me that the expression does not correspond to any administrative status. In the summer of 1939, several women's shelters were opened in Oloron. Perhaps Tonia speaks of one of them. The women who stayed there were under surveillance, but not house arrest. They were free to move around, or even see a spouse in Gurs.[22] But "forced residence" became, with time, one of the weapons prefectures had at their disposal. Like internment, "assigned residence" or "forced residence" was an act of police power rather than judicial procedure and thus carried few safeguards. Forced residence was started in the Third Republic and continued in Vichy France into the 1940s. Additionally, in June 1939 the Alien Registration Act imposed tight regulations on foreigners, stipulating that they all would have to be fingerprinted and were subject to deportation for any activities perceived as violating the social order.[23] Thus, it is likely that after her move to Oloron in the summer of 1939, Tonia experienced various forms of restrictions impeding her freedom to move about and preventing her from going to Paris, where she had hoped to abort her second pregnancy. However, the worst was yet to come.

On September 3, 1939, in response to Hitler's invasion of Poland, French and British authorities declared war on Germany. In the first weeks of the French national war emergency, foreigners were swept into various camps. "Selection being impossible," as Interior Minister Albert Sarraut admitted, no foreigner was exempt.[24] The Germans and Austrians with whom Tonia lived were moved to a camp in Rieucros, located 250 kilometers east of Oloron, a camp first created for Spanish volunteers and then transformed into one for foreign women identified as a threat due to their nationality or political orientation. Transports to Rieucros foreshadowed how humans would be treated during the war. The shipment of women and children took place in cattle cars. Facilities were greatly inadequate.[25] With her husband interned at Gurs and the women she stayed with being sent to Rieucros, Tonia was witnessing the emergence of French *camps de concentration,* as French officials often called them. This is one of the darkest chapters of French policy toward Jews, beginning even before Vichy France was established.[26]

Somehow, Tonia again avoided arrest, but she was becoming more isolated. Threats to her safety were looming dangerously close. Yet Tonia remembered this period as the time not only when she was spared from arrest but also when people extended help to her, particularly her neighbors and people she saw daily in Oloron. In her letters, the war existed through gestures of kindness.[27] Later, when narrating this moment, she recognized her Polishness as protecting her. When she shopped with Vera, numerous salespeople referred to Vera as *la petite Polonaise* and gave her food items for free. The day a Warsaw train station was bombed, Tonia received a dress for Vera from a store owner.[28] These gestures of generosity came to her as a woman displaced from a country suffering a major attack. It is unclear what stirred that recognition. Did she speak Polish to Vera and was, thus, recognized as not French? Did she introduce herself as Polish? She came to Oloron as the wife of an Austrian volunteer to the Spanish Civil War and a Jew expelled from Palestine, and nonetheless the identity she emphasized was that of a Pole.[29] Perhaps she was realizing that identifying as a Jew was becoming increasingly dangerous and, hence, opted for an identity that felt safer. The war affected her directly—not yet with brutal force but with light strokes reminding her how fragile her existence was and ultimately how lucky she was to be able to find people who cared.

Faced with new challenges and surrounded by former Spanish volunteers while observing communists being detained or surveilled for their activism, Tonia hardly ever discussed communism in her letters. Only in one letter did some of her earlier enthusiasm return. In July 1939 she recounted the commemoration in Oloron of the 150th anniversary of the French Revolution:

> A few days ago, I was at a gathering of German migrants on the occasion of the 150th anniversary of the French Revolution. A professor of French history at the Sorbonne spoke. Heinrich spoke after him. Mann spoke so wonderfully and convincingly that I would

just swallow every word. This French professor in his speech compares Mann to Victor Hugo, who, as long as he lived in exile, did not have to lie about what he meant to the entire civilization. He wished everyone much success in the fight for a free, democratic Germany. You can imagine what applause he got. . . . I am still impressed by this beautiful evening. It is a pity you cannot take part in such lectures and celebrations—it adds new faith in a better tomorrow. You must admit that the whole world today is not beautiful. However, when you hear the voices of such people . . . you cannot be pessimistic. A better time is coming; it will naturally be paid for with pain and suffering. But has the old order ever been changed without a fight in history? No, the reactionary part of society is trying by all means to maintain this state. We have a strength that cannot be destroyed.[30]

This celebration appeared to expel, at least temporarily, some of her worries. It gave her a moment of spontaneous joy she had not experienced for a while. It also reminded her of the hopes she had associated with communism just a few years earlier. Uhl, with whom I shared this fragment of Tonia's letter, noticed the difference in the attitude of Tonia and Rosenfeld toward the legacy of the French Revolution. Rosenfeld also wrote to her family in Germany about the anniversary, but her tone was more critical. For her, the event was being celebrated not as a victory of the French people but as a "falsified victory of one country over another country. Only schoolchildren and the authorities took part. People were only watching for the big fireworks."[31]

Historian Adam Rayski notes that in Paris some Jewish organizations began linking the universal achievements of the French Revolution with inclusion and solidarity for Jews and Jewish refugees in France. At the same time, Jonas Geduldig, a Spanish volunteer of Jewish origins, wrote in an internment camp, "We, too, celebrated the 14th of July, the sesquicentennial anniversary of the French Revolution. Over some of the huts, the French tricolor snapped in the wind. . . . We made candles of suet and wrapped them in colored paper and lit up the insides of the barrack . . . but this made the contradiction of the situation hit us with even greater force. . . . We, the new fighters for liberty . . . were behind the barbed-wire fence." Geduldig soon escaped from the camp and joined the Jewish resistance to the Nazi occupation of France.[32] Even if Tonia and Sioma reflected occasionally on the paradoxes of their situation—freedom fighters whose existence hung by a thread—they were linking their instability with the cause they fought for, communism, and not, or at least not yet, with their Jewish identity.

Despite these occasional moments of joy, the grim reality was unforgiving. In November Tonia wrote to her parents, "I need to tell you that it has been very difficult for me recently. Life got much more expensive, and I need to feed Vera well. Besides that, I need to buy her clothes, and this is also very expensive. Because I cannot heat up our room, I need to move out to an old hotel that costs three times as much"[33] Initially, the International Committee for Aid to the Spanish People supported her. On July 4, 1939, she also received 150 francs from the Committee for Aid for the Former German and Austrian Spanish Fighters (Hilfskomitee für ehemalige deutsche und österreichische Spanienkämpfer), located in Paris.[34] Most help came from her parents, who kept sending money, food, and clothes, and later, when sending items from Palestine to France became more difficult, they sent money to their acquaintances in Paris, who then transferred it to Tonia.[35]

With time, the possibility of visiting her husband became increasingly limited. In an interrogation, Tonia explained that she saw him three times after France declared war. Her pregnancy progressed, the war was making the long walks dangerous, and the weather made it challenging to walk with a small child for sixteen kilometers.[36] In October, when Tonia visited Sioma, he sent a postcard to their family in which he wrote mostly of the joy he experienced upon Tonia's visit: "I am infinitely happy to have such a girl as a wife. Her positive energy and vitality are beyond words. Our daughter is making great progress. You can see that she is raised by a loving and caring mother. In such conditions, being such a radiant and emanating force is something that not everyone can do. I hope it won't be long until I can actively stand at her side."[37] Toward the end of the year, she informed her family that she was considering moving back to Paris due to the difficult conditions she lived in and the difficulty of seeing Sioma, but at the same time she had no money for the trip and worried about having problems with documentation in Paris.[38] Clearly, she was torn between leaving for Paris and staying in Oloron. Neither option provided her with safety and decent living conditions.

She was also profoundly aware of Sioma's terrible living conditions. Deeply distressed by what she knew and suspected as well as by the awareness that there was little she could change, Tonia wrote to her family, "Sioma is most likely very cold. I cannot see him."³⁹ The barracks built on the site of Gurs were, indeed, inadequate for cold weather. As one author explained, "Not anticipating that the refugees would stay beyond the summer, the French authorities took no pains to make the huts warm or windproof. They used planks of raw uncured timber, which quickly shrank, leaving gaps, and put in no proper windows, only wooden shutters that could just be raised a little."⁴⁰ In addition, food rations were meager. In November 1940 the German Red Cross was alarmed about the growing number of deaths from starvation in Gurs.⁴¹

Living conditions were becoming unbearable, yet at least Tonia knew where Sioma was, visiting him was within the realm of possibility, and she was still able to communicate with her parents or even occasionally receive some financial assistance from them. Looking back at her situation, I cannot help but wonder how she maintained the positive spirit that Sioma commented on in letters to the family. Despite imminent dangers lurking everywhere, she still appeared to have hope, even with the grim realities encircling her. Perhaps the secret to hope is that, unlike me, who can afford to wonder how life was even possible in these circumstances, she was deprived of this privilege. There was little she could have done to change her difficult situation. Conjuring up the possibility of moving back to Paris, she perhaps toyed more with whatever freedom of decision and movement she still had rather than actually planned on moving. Life required acknowledging and accepting difficulties as part of a reality that could not be changed.

Impossible Choices

Tonia's family has very few memories of Sioma, and even though she mentioned him in almost all of her letters, he remained a distant voice. Some photos exist of him and Tonia from Palestine. There are even photos of him, Tonia, and little Vera sitting on the grass at the Gurs camp, with barbed wire and the barracks behind them. If not for the eerie setting, they could almost be taken for a happy family on a picnic. Present in the family archives are Sioma's occasional letters written in German, a language neither of their children spoke. There is also an aluminum ash tray, a gift for Tonia's twenty-second birthday he made in Gurs out of an old pot. A letter in which Tonia mentioned Sioma's seemingly odd request for a replacement pot documents the

FIGURE 4.1. Tonia with Sioma and Vera, Gurs, France, 1937. *(Private collection of Vera and Marcel Lechtman)*

gift's history.[42] Marcel and Vera cherish every little trace of his presence in their lives but still occasionally question his decision to leave their mother in Paris while he traveled to Spain. They see it as testimony to their parents' devotion to communism, an ideology that brought them together, even if it ultimately also caused their displacement and separation.[43]

One particular element of Tonia's story is especially difficult for Vera and Marcel to comprehend: their mother's relationship, or rather its swift end, with Wiesława (Wiesia) Toruńczyk. Wiesia and Tonia met in Oloron, probably soon after Tonia arrived. Tonia grew close to Wiesia because they had a lot in common: they were Polish, they were Jewish, and Wiesia's husband, who had served as a colonel in the International Brigades, was also interned at Gurs. Wiesia loved Tonia's daughter and often took care of her. "She worked in Spain as a doctor and liked children. She told me to give up the hotel and move in with her. I totally forgot that I promised not to have contact with Polish communists, and I moved in with her."[44] Wiesia, too, was pregnant at the time, a detail Tonia neglected to reveal in her interrogation.

The friendship, however, lasted only one month, ending practically before it even began. When Sioma found out about it, he told Tonia to end it immediately. Stalin dissolved the KPP for its apparent infiltration by Polish security forces and Trotskyists, and Polish communists were perceived as untrustworthy.[45] "My husband said that if I met her again, I would not be able to come to him. He received an order. As a very disciplined person, I said 'good.' And I came back to the hotel. It was scary. 'W[iesia]' came to us, and we were cold as ice and silent," she told Dowgiałło.[46] In October 1949 Tonia's interrogation officers dedicated one entire interview to Tonia's intentions and loyalty as a communist that centered on her interactions with Wiesia. When recounting what happened, she clarified that Sioma informed her that Wiesia's husband, Henryk, was surrounded by communists who surveilled his every move. However, Wiesia, who lived outside of the camp, was not controlled, so the party did not trust her. Consequently, nobody should have any contact with her. Tonia finished her interrogation by saying, "After this conversation with my husband, I let her know that we needed to stop having any contact since the party does not trust her. Other nurses and doctors severed their contacts with her as well. She was being isolated."[47]

Under interrogation, Tonia revealed the details of that moment as a communist obliged to follow the party line rather than as a person speaking about a painful past event. While speaking with Dowgiałło, she clearly struggled with what had happened, trying to re-create the mind-set leading to her decision:

> Her husband was in the brigades as a colonel. And among the internees he was one of the most important people. Later I found out that the Soviet secret police was active in Spain, and they were creating terrible intrigues. Most likely he was on good terms with them. And she was not.... I think she knew where the boycott came from. So did I—at that time Stalin killed Leński.[48] She came from a wealthy Lwów Jewish family. Those who knew Lwów and the Lwów youth at that time told me that she and her sister were well known. She was a capable and very decent person. "W" studied in Czechoslovakia. There, she worked for the Polish ideological magazine *New Review*. When I found out she had contact with the editors of the *New Review*, I considered her a saint. Meanwhile, it turned out she was the worst enemy.[49]

On a certain level, Tonia understood why she was told to stop seeing Wiesia. Her friend was a member of a group accused of Trotskyism, understood as a deviation from the only correct version of communism as imposed by Stalin. As a Politkomissar, Sioma was responsible for controlling the political climate and protecting communist orthodoxy, which included, for example, explanations regarding the violent clashes among Republicans on the streets of Barcelona in May 1937, for which Trotskyism—a "fifth column" and agent of fascism—was blamed.[50] Following closely the only acceptable political line, Sioma could not allow his wife to become close to a potential Trotskyist. This short story of an interrupted friendship depicts well the mentality of the communists: party discipline, limitations of personal freedom, and dedication that seriously impeded personal safety. Historian Lisa Kirchenbaum notices that "communist commitments shaped personal lives, and personal relationships influenced political understandings."[51] Both Tonia and Sioma understood the need to temporarily abandon some of their social roles for their political obligations—in this case, Sioma's obligations toward his wife and his children.

Further, Sioma must have heard multiple stories coming from the Soviet Union of party members being accused and consequently punished—demoted, arrested, or killed—at the leadership's whim for apparent deviations from the main party line. Some of these stories most likely circulated as a cautionary tale of the need to stay vigilant. Sioma certainly understood that his wife's contact with a politically suspect woman was problematic for him, but he also probably suspected that this friendship was potentially dangerous for Tonia, the consequences of being accused of betrayal being impossible to predict at that particular moment. With a commitment to communism came an expectation of blind trust in its leaders. Accusations were potentially deadly, as demonstrated by purges in the Soviet Union in the late 1930s.

The question of the extent to which the International Brigades were an extension of Stalin's politics in Spain has been long discussed by historians. The Comintern's role and some of its fanatical attempts to enforce political decisions are as legendary as the International Brigades' solidarity. German communist Walter Janka recollects that the Comintern controlled the International Brigades while using Stalinist methods to purge people considered political enemies. Soviet security authorities, aided by Western European communists, arrested and/or murdered people accused of political deviations, such as Trotskyism. The communists' discipline—their unconditional following of orders and subordination to the collective mission—and their constant repression of those unwilling to obey reinforced the Stalinist political culture.⁵²

It is unclear how much reliance on and attitudes toward the Soviet Union changed after the Soviet Union and Nazi Germany signed a nonaggression treaty on August 23 and then on September 17, following Nazi aggression, the Soviet Union invaded Poland. Writer and intellectual Arthur Koestler writes in his biographical account about growing disappointment with the Soviet Union after learning about its rapprochement with Germany: "Our feelings toward Russia were rather like those of a man who has divorced a much-beloved wife; he hates her and yet it is a sort of consolation for him to know that she is still there, on the same planet, still young and alive. But now she is dead. No death is so sad and final as the death of an illusion." As Koestler further explains, *L'Humanité,* the French Communist Party's official organ, tried to justify this by explaining that the new treaty was an effort by Stalin to prevent an imperialist war.⁵³ Sioma's position on these changing attitudes toward the Soviet Union is not documented. The episode with Wiesia probably occurred before or soon after the news about the treaty was announced, therefore it is unlikely that it affected his opinion.

Despite its larger political dimension, this episode continues its own bitter life among Tonia's family members. It emerged often in my conversations with them and became an important moment in the movie *Tonia i jej dzieci,* when Marcel gives up on even trying to understand it. In one particular scene, Vera argues that being forced to choose between Wiesia and her husband, her greatest love, Tonia had to choose Sioma. The choice was simple. But Marcel goes further, asking why she was put in a situation where she had to choose: "The fact that our father said it in this manner is almost impossible to accept." "This was a hierarchy of values that we perhaps cannot understand," inserts the director of the movie. "But was he Mother's fellow (*mamy facet*) or a member of the party?" Marcel insists on asking the question that nobody sitting at the table is willing, or perhaps able, to answer. "And this is what I will never understand. I won't understand it in my life," he concludes.⁵⁴

In a conversation with me, Vera's daughter, Anna Rajf-Ligęza, said:

> My grandmother adored him [Sioma]. I don't remember her exact words, but she loved him and believed that he was the one for her. He was the most important person. She only spoke about him, especially later in life. He was the one; he was dedicated to the cause.

> But there was this one strange thing, a bit moving, a bit strange: when he was at a camp in the South of France, and he told his wife not to talk to this one Polish woman who helped her—this was an order she had received from him. They were forbidden to have any contact with Polish communists. That woman was nice and helpful, and my grandmother was not allowed to talk to her—he actually ordered it.... It made me think about my grandma's choices. She never judged him; that's how it was. It paints a very dogmatic image of what they believed in.[55]

They all see Wiesia as somebody who gave Tonia, an illegal pregnant migrant with a toddler, deeply needed friendship and support. Denying her that friendship was cruel. Soon after the episode with Wiesia, her female German and Austrian friends were arrested, and Tonia was left alone in an atmosphere of growing fear.

Her friendship with Wiesia appears to be the only contact Tonia had with Polish communists. This story is also the only window I have found into the presumably rich world of Polish female communists in Spain. A Google search for Wiesława Toruńczyk yields no results. But I have in my possession an autobiography in the form of a letter she wrote in 1988 to her son, essentially her life story. It is divided into two parts: "Retirada en Polonais" and "Généalogi."[56] I searched the document in vain for any mention of Tonia. The letter reveals Wiesia's real name: Jadwiga. Once I knew her name and her partner's name—Henryk Toruńczyk—it was easier to locate information on her. Jadwiga Kanner was a Polish Jewish doctor from Lwów. In 1997 she published her recollection of the Lwów pogroms of 1918, in which she and her mother observed the violence instigated against Jews by men from Haller's Blue Army. The violence and hatred of Polish nationalism led her to Spain.[57] Her biography from a recent publication and a partial reprint of her autobiographic letter state that she belonged to the Communist Party of Western Ukraine and not the Communist Party of Poland, as Sioma and Tonia had assumed. In 1937 she moved to Spain along with her Ukrainian husband, Jurij Welykanowich, and her brother, Zygmunt Kanner. She probably met Henryk in Spain, a Polish communist whose name she later carried and who most likely fathered her child, Jerzy Toruńczyk, born in 1940 in Oloron. Henryk (1909–66) had finished his studies in Belgium, where he belonged to the

Union of Young Socialists. After spending some time in Poland, he moved to Spain, where from 1937 he served as the head of the Thirteenth International Brigade.[58]

In Wiesia's letter, I found the names of numerous Polish women who were involved in the Spanish Civil War. For example, Dora Lorska moved from Spain to Paris, where she worked as a doctor for refugees. From there, she was transported to Auschwitz, where she produced reports of some of the medical experiments conducted on prisoners.[59] Wiesia's letter also provides many details of her life during and immediately after the war. From her descriptively rich personal narrative emerges an image of the path the *brigadistas* had to undertake after the Spanish Civil War ended, one probably similar to what Sioma experienced. Wiesia had to travel from Ador, a town in Spain near the border with France, to Perpignan in France. She wrote, "I don't know how our group got to Perpignan. Everything was a mess. Thousands, tens or maybe hundreds of thousands of refugees—it was too powerful a wave of people for the gendarmerie and the French police to focus on the border. They also dealt with and disarmed and searched the Spanish army, whose units were crossing the border more and more often." The descriptions also contain warm words about the kindness Spanish war refugees received from the local population wherever they were stationed, kindness that Tonia experienced in Oloron as well:

> There were not only policemen and gendarmes in Perpignan. There was also the French population. . . . These people began to visit us. From morning to night, people carrying food kept coming to the hall. They went from bed to bed and arranged their gifts on each one without asking—rolls and sausages, cheese, chocolate, cigarettes, cakes, and wine. What was not there?! We ate as much as we could. . . . The kindness of these people was the best.[60]

Further, the letter explained how the gendarmerie was sending people crossing the border to camps, including the one in Argelès-sur-Mer where Sioma was confined prior to being sent to Gurs. In 1940 Wiesia was interned with her son at Gurs and escaped in 1941 to Paris, where she worked in the resistance movement until 1945.[61] Remarkably, the group of Polish communists who found themselves in Spain after the KPP's dissolution became the nucleus of a special "Initiative Group" composed of International Brigades' veterans. Established in January 1939 in Paris to create a new party purged of all suspect elements, it was tasked with laying the groundwork for the transfer of several of its members from France to Poland for the purpose of starting the rebuilding process.[62] Even if Wiesia was not officially an Initiative Group member, she nevertheless returned to Poland after the war ended to rebuild the party.

Wiesia entered Tonia's story on a few other occasions after they separated. The first took place in the maternity ward at Pau on March 31, 1940, when Tonia gave premature birth to Marcel.[63] When her labor began, a friend drove her to the hospital, where she was placed in a ward for single women. At the time, this unit was intended for Spanish wives, who, in Tonia's view, were not treated with respect. Tonia recollected that the entire experience was terrible. She gave birth alone, and nobody came to help during or after the delivery. "I had the child between my legs, and I was scared of moving so as not to suffocate the child," she recalled. There were no nurses willing to help. Only on the third day did a doctor come to check on her.[64] Wiesia was in the same hospital, most likely delivering her own baby. She came by to ask Tonia if there was anything she could do to help. Tonia asked for food and something to drink. "She brought some oranges and Petit Beurres [biscuits]—I was very happy," Tonia noted. The second time both women met was in Paris in 1945, at the Polish embassy after the conclusion of the war. This time, Wiesia did not want to talk to Tonia.[65]

The irony of their short friendship is that they had both traveled to France or Spain to combat the exclusion nationalism caused. They were Jewish, but in their narratives Jewishness emerges mostly as an element of the past, as a trace of their upbringing and the families they came from, not something that actively spoke to their perception of themselves in 1940. Communism was the identity they chose in the process of reflecting on the world around them and on what caused the suffering they observed, an identity that allowed them to transcend ethnicity. And yet it was the ethnic identification, imbued with various fears, that affected their friendship.

In a noteworthy aftermath, Wiesia and Tonia met again after the war in the mid-1940s in Warsaw. Their sons attended the same school, and the teenage boys were relatively close for a few years before losing contact. Wiesia remained bitter and never tried to maintain contact with Tonia. Both women had a chance to meet again in Israel, and while Wiesia refused to talk to Tonia, she developed a close relationship with Vera.⁶⁶ In 2008, thanks to social media, Jerzy Toruńczyk renewed his contact with Marcel. A historian working on the seventieth anniversary of the creation of the Gurs camp contacted Jerzy with a question regarding a photograph of three infants on the Gurs site. Was one Marcel? In an email to Marcel, Jerzy wrote that his mother told him he was one of the babies and that it was possible Marcel was in the picture too.

Doubts about whether the photo depicts the two boys stayed with Marcel: "To be short, the probability that I am in the photo is minimal. Let's imagine that my mom went to the camp, counting on the fact that she would show me to Sioma. He was not coming, but she ran into Wiesia (with whom Sioma forbid my mom to talk), and the two ladies staged their children for a photo. No. Impossible."⁶⁷ Also, the date when the photo could have been taken implies that it is not Marcel. The infants in the photo are sitting by themselves. If we are to assume the photo is of Marcel, it must have been taken toward the end of 1940, when he was old enough to sit by himself. As Tonia testified during one of her interrogations, she saw Sioma for the last time in January 1940, two months before giving birth to Marcel.⁶⁸ Finally, Laharie from L'Amicale du camp de Gurs dispelled all doubts, saying, "The picture of the babies in Gurs is quite well known. It was taken in the spring of 1942 and shows two of the Rodriguez triplets. Exactly 50 children were born at the camp (between 1941 and 1943)."⁶⁹

There was a lot of mutual joy at renewing contact after decades of separation and identifying the famous photo. As a sign of renewed friendship, Jerzy forwarded autobiographical stories his mother had written to him in which she had recounted her Spanish experiences. Jerzy died in 2015, perhaps assuming he was one of the babies in the photo of children at Gurs. In a no less bizarre twist of history, the children of Wiesia and Tonia reinvented the story that reunited them.

Displacement

In the last letter to her family before Marcel's birth, Tonia confirmed the fear accompanying her entire pregnancy: "Recently I have been very nervous. This probably has something to do with my pregnancy, and that's why I cannot write much. Please forgive me."⁷⁰ As with Vera's birth, a friend informed her family of the birth. The friend had driven Tonia from Oloron to the hospital in Pau.[71] Three weeks after the delivery, Tonia wrote, "I gave birth three weeks early. I don't know what happened. On that day, I lifted a bucket a couple of times with Vera's washed clothes. Maybe that caused the labor. Marcel is well developed, but he did not weigh much—2.600 kilos. The delivery was easy, even easier than the one with Vera. But unfortunately, until yesterday, I have had postpartum pains that exhausted me. It was worse than the delivery. I have enough milk, and that's most important."[72] Marcel was not a child she was expecting with great joy. She felt enormous apprehension, fear, and a growing sense of the responsibility of being a mother under conditions that were impossible to control.

Having two small children made the scale of her difficulties apparent to those around her.[73] She benefited from various unexpected gestures of care and generosity, often surprising, difficult to understand, and, for a historian, challenging to contextualize. They partially conform to and partially expand on our understanding of life under conditions of war: the growing antisemitism and attacks on individual rights, the combination of personal luck and lack thereof, the presence of people who tried to help and those who remained coldly detached, and the chaos and the unknown lurking everywhere. One never knew where danger and salvation lay or how to recognize the difference between the two.

Tonia's final letter to her family from France is dated July 17, 1940. Prior to that moment, and in the period immediately following Marcel's birth, she communicated with them relatively often—two or three times per month, mostly sharing the scope of her various struggles, primarily financial. She had no money but was able somehow to obtain food for herself and Vera, all the while breastfeeding Marcel. Life was marked by fear, hunger, poverty, and loneliness as her former channels of support disintegrated. The war encircled her. Occasional pauses in correspondence from her family in Palestine or Poland concerned her.[74] As she learned about the terrifying situation in Poland from her family in Palestine, she despaired over the humiliation her grandfather living in Łódź must be experiencing at the hands of Germans. She hoped her grandparents would be able to get out of that "hell."[75] Only terrifying information seemed to be reaching her, as if intentionally challenging her with information that the world was turning into destructive chaos, while her only recourse was to remain patient and wait.[76]

FIGURE 4.2. Tonia with toddler Vera and baby Marcel, Oloron, 1940. *(Private collection of Vera and Marcel Lechtman)*

"It will somehow be" (*jakoś to będzie*) and "I will manage" (*dam sobie radę*), she kept writing, as if attempting to reassure her family as much as herself.[77] In the midst of all the worries, she remembered to send photos of her children. "I am sending you a couple photos," she wrote. "They are not too great. When I receive money, I will get better ones from a photographer."[78] She may have sent a photo of herself sitting with an infant in her arms, while tiny Vera leans against her knees and looks straight into the camera. There is a bassinet covered with white linens next to them. Tonia is wearing a light-colored apron covering her dark dress. Despite her hardships, she looks calm, almost serene.

France fell to the Nazis in May 1940, an event recognized by historians as a seismic shock.[79] As a result of the armistice of June 22, 1940, the country was divided into two zones: an occupied zone in the north and west administered by the Germans and an unoccupied zone in the south, with the spa town Vichy as its capital, that only nominally maintained its sovereignty. The demarcation line between the two zones turned into a hard frontier. Special passes were required for civilians crossing it.[80] Vichy France became a collaborative entity working to achieve Nazi goals. One of the first Vichy legislative decisions directly targeted the French Jewish population. On July 17 the government promulgated the first professional bans against Jews, denying them access to public administrative jobs. On September 27 the German military commander in France gave Jews in the occupied zone until October 20 to submit to resignation. Finally, on October 3, 1940, Vichy declared the Statut des Juifs (Status of Jews), signed by Philippe Pétain and key members of his government. On the basis of race, it assigned an inferior position to a segment of French citizens and foreigners living in France.[81]

Antisemitic policies in France were becoming increasingly more oppressive, but the documents we have do not directly reveal how much Tonia understood what was happening. Her letters suggest that rather than seeing herself as being targeted due to her Jewish identity, she believed their predicament was caused by their communism and Sioma being recognized as Austrian. On June 7, 1940, in one of the last letters to her family for the next two years, she wrote, "I have news from Sioma. He is still in the camp. Today I received a letter from him, where he writes that there is no right of asylum for Germans and Austrians, which means we won't be able to stay in France. It is not clear where we will go. Maybe to South America.... I wrote to the Red Cross asking for help. I already received an answer from them, but nothing concrete."[82]

When she wrote that letter, planning their eventual departure from France and waiting for Sioma to be released, he was no longer in Gurs. The Gurs site was emptied in the summer of 1940, and on June 5 Sioma was moved almost 250 kilometers east to a camp in Le Vernet, near Pamiers in the department of Ariège. Lina Soulan, who works in the Amicale de Vernet, helped me find traces of his presence in the camp, one of the most oppressive that the Vichy government opened in 1940. Soulan also provided a small file with documentation registering Sioma's life in the camp. One of the documents describes the color of his eyes and hair, the shape of his nose and forehead, his height, and a scar on his right forearm. The detailed information about his origin is confusing and most likely testifies to a lack of knowledge by the person collecting the information. Sioma was ignorantly recorded as having been born in Dunajewiec, Poland, department of Palestine, and being of Austrian nationality. The description may have fit French prisoners, as the reference to a department suggests, but it implies that the forms were not modified to fit foreigners. His wife's name is misspelled as Tonia Biala.[83]

Built during World War I as a camp for prisoners of war, Le Vernet was also used in 1937 and 1938 for refugees from the International Brigades, who were sheltered mostly in tents.[84] In February 1939 it was reactivated to house more refugees. Historian Helen Graham writes:

> Unlike the beach internment camps, such as Argelès, St. Cyprien and Le Barcarès, which were hastily set up to contain the Spanish refugees, Le Vernet, like Gurs and a small number of the other camps across the south-west, was expressly conceived as a punishment or disciplinary camp. So, while those refugees in the beach camps suffered appalling conditions, especially at the start, through the sheer lack of basic facilities and even shelter, in Le Vernet the inmates were subjected to an explicit prison regime.[85]

Koestler, imprisoned in Le Vernet in 1940, said that his first impression of Le Vernet was a mess of barbed wire and more barbed wire. "It ran all around the camp in a threefold fence," he writes, "and across it in various directions, with trenches running parallel," adding that "the camp was run with that mixture of ignominy, corruption, and laissez-faire so typical of the French administration." While mentioning the people contained there, he notes in a voice full of pain, "A fairly high percentage of the continent's population had become quite accustomed to the thought that they were outcasts. They could be divided into two main categories: people doomed by the biological accident of their race and people doomed for their metaphysical creed or rational conviction regarding the best way to organize human warfare."[86]

Incarcerated men were organized according to the violations they were accused of: common-law prisoners were in Unit A, and political internees and some veterans from Spain in Unit B (or, as Koestler notes, aliens with a political record). Unit C was at first devoted only to members of the International Brigades but, over time, began serving also as confinement for Jews.[87] Soulan confirms the categories for Unit A and Unit B but adds that Unit C also housed those who were locked up for reasons unknown to the prisoners themselves or the camp administration. The prefects of other departments directed foreigners to Le Vernet who seemed to them undesirable or politically suspect. Unit T was for internees in transit.[88] All sections were strictly isolated from each other. The majority of the volunteers lived in one of the poorest huts of Unit C, including Koestler. Koestler called this section the Leper Barrack, a hell that was the culmination of the crusade of the Spanish Civil War.[89] Sioma was also housed there, evidenced by a form Tonia filled out on February 19, 1942, when she registered as a Jew and provided Sioma's address: "Camp du Vernet, Quartier C."[90]

Koestler provides a good description of the camp, with prisoners confined in what he defines as hutments, each housing two hundred men:

> Its furnishings consisted of two lower and two upper platforms of planks, each two yards wide, running along the two long walls and leaving a narrow passage in the middle. The space between the lower and upper platforms was one yard, so that those on the lower planks could never stand erect. On each row slept 50 men, feet towards the passage. The rows were divided into compartments containing five men and was 105 inches wide; thus, each man disposed of a space 21 inches wide to sleep on. This meant that all five had to sleep on their sides, facing the same wall, and if one turned over, all had to turn over.[91]

That image, as well as that of the living conditions, is a striking reminder of the living arrangements in the Nazi camps situated east of France—in Germany and occupied Poland—a comparison not lost on Koestler:[92]

> The standard of comparison in the treatment of human beings having crashed to unheard-of depths, every complaint sounded frivolous and out of place.... In Liberal-Centrigrade, Vernet was the zero-point of infamy; measured in Dachau-Fahrenheit it was still 32 degrees above zero. In Vernet, beating-up was a daily occurrence; in Dachau it was prolonged until death ensued. In Vernet people were killed for lack of medical attention; in Dachau they were killed on purpose. In Vernet half of the prisoners had to sleep without blankets in 20 degrees of frost; in Dachau they were put in irons and exposed to the frost.[93]

The camp did not provide men with a separate space to eat (only over time was a canteen built); there was not even a table in the hutments and no dishes, spoons, or forks to eat with. Daily food rations were minimal: eleven ounces of bread, a cup of unsweetened black coffee, and a pint of soup at midday and in the evening, "a pale liquid containing no fat and only a few grains of chick-peas, lentils, or vermicelli. There was also a small piece of beef with midday soup, but it was so smelly that only the hungriest would eat it." The men had to rely on food parcels from families. In Koestler's estimations, only about 10 percent had access to money or food sent to them: "the contrast between the rich and poor reached the pungency of a social satire." All the other inventions of life in concentration camps was being mastered in Le Vernet as well: work under inhumane conditions, exhausting roll calls, arbitrary cruelty by the guards, and punishment for even the slightest violation of camp rules.[94]

Amicale de Vernet was created in December 1944 to preserve the camp's history and the memory of the people who passed through it. Today, it consists of one barrack, a train car used for transporting prisoners, and a cemetery for those who perished in the camp. The archive consists of photos and some documentation mostly from the local archives in Ariège and federal archives in Paris. In December 2019 I asked Marcel to search for a photo of his father among the camp photos available in the online archive. Sioma's photo was not in the folders, which included typical anthropometric camp photos of front and side views of men photographed with their camp number.[95] Marcel was disappointed. He accompanied me as much as he could in my search for any trace of his family, and he treasured any discovery about his father. He emailed me the next day, saying that he could not sleep and instead kept searching. He at last found a photo of Sioma among a group of photos that were not arranged by the camp administration. This particular collection included children, women, and men in casual situations. It is possible that the incarcerated individuals took them hoping to send them to their families. Marcel discovered Sioma in a group of four men: all four look relatively similar in age, hair color, and even hairstyle. They all stare straight at the camera with desperation, maybe indifference, perhaps even a hint of stubbornness. This is probably one of the last, if not the last, photos taken of Sioma.[96] The next day, I emailed Soulan to ask about the possibly of confirming Sioma's identity. At the same time, Marcel's son separated a photo of his grandfather from that of the other three men. A single photo of Sioma gains a different meaning. It becomes part of the family archive.

Soulan responded with another piece of curious information about the collection: in 1993 filmmaker Linda Ferrer Roca received a collection of glass plates of negatives with photos from Le Vernet found inside a box in an attic. Roca made a movie, *Photographies d'un camp* (Photographs of a camp), based

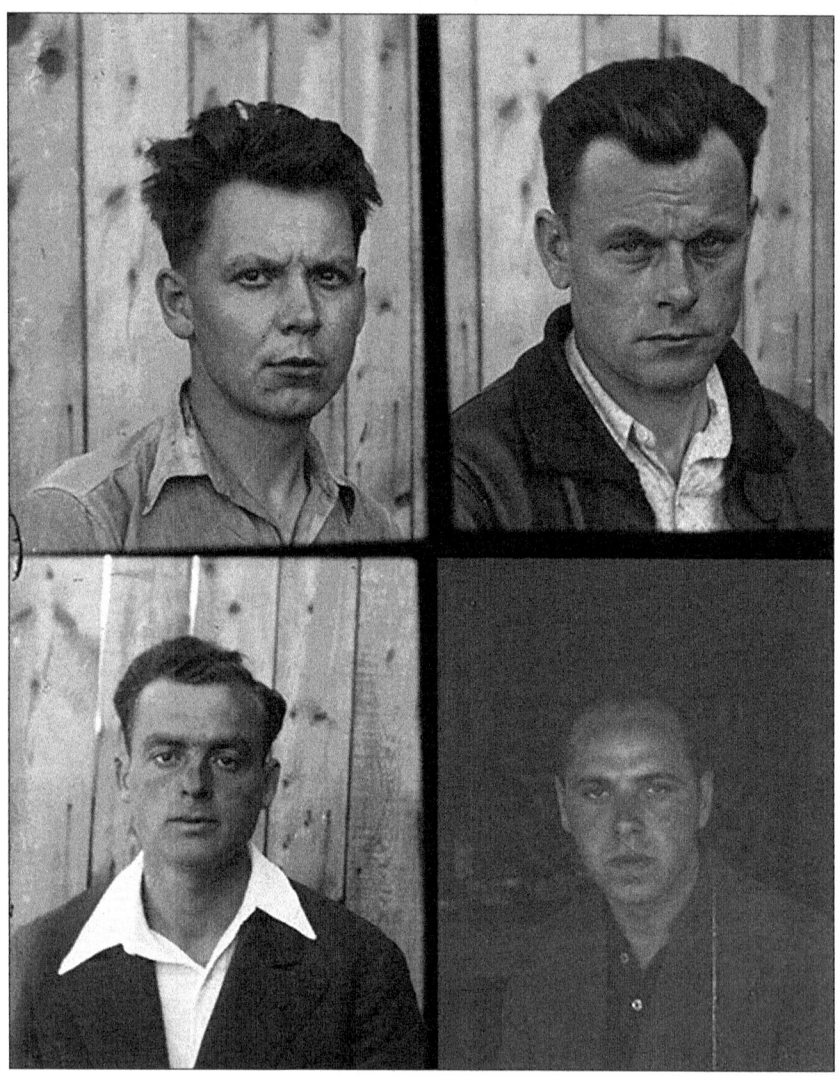

Figure 4.3. Photos of four prisoners in Vernet d'Ariège concentration camp, ca. 1941. Sioma's photo is on the bottom left. *(Collection of Amicale des anciens internés politiques et résistants du Vernet d'Ariège)*

on her reading of the photos and interviews with a select group of prisoners from Le Vernet. The movie is based on the premise that the pictures carry with them violence done to the men: the anthropometric pictures made them guilty. "Mug shots work in a double movement: the tight frame creates a proximity, but the anthropometric approach stereotypes, de facto discriminates..., distances him."[97]

Sioma's photo was not part of the anthropometric photos: as the movie explains, some men used the occasion to take photos of themselves for their families. These photos were taken outside, with some men wearing borrowed ties, some laughing as if conveying a message to their loved ones. Sioma does not wear a tie, does not laugh, but he possibly requested his photo to be taken with the intention to send it to his family. Or perhaps he was considering applying for a visa to leave France for Mexico.[98] We will never find out whether he ever sent this photo. But, in an ironic twist, it made it to his family and was trimmed by his son, who reclaimed it as part of what the family knows about their father and grandfather.

Tonia remained in touch with Sioma throughout the second half of 1939 when he was in Gurs and she in Oloron. According to her interrogations, she saw him three times after the outbreak of the French-German conflict. During September and October she was forbidden to leave her neighborhood. Once she received permission to move freely again, she visited the camp. The last time she saw him was in January 1940.[99] Soon after Marcel's birth, she lost contact with her husband.[100] There are no letters from the second half of 1940, which impedes our understanding of how well she understood her predicament and how much her moves depended on where Sioma was. In her interrogation of March 23, 1950, she revealed that in the fall of 1940 she realized Sioma had been transferred.[101] Indeed, October 1940 was a time that redefined her life. Even if life in Oloron was precarious, it was based on a recognition of who she was and whom she could reach out to for help; she was recognized as a Polish refugee and the wife of a Spanish volunteer confined temporarily by the French Third Republic. After the fall of 1940, she lived as a refugee—an enemy alien—increasingly entangled in the net of antisemitic laws of Vichy France. Jewishness doubled her vulnerability.[102]

In early October 1940 new antisemitic and exclusionary laws were introduced. A law enacted on October 4 concerning foreigners of the "Jewish race" created an even more immediate danger to many Jews as it authorized prefects to intern foreign Jews in "special camps" or assign them to live under police surveillance in remote villages. With this law, a prefect could personally decide to place a "foreigner of Jewish race" in a camp. Thirty-one camps—including a few small, temporary camps, some with only a handful of prisoners—already existed in the southern zone by the end of September 1939.[103] In October, Tonia and the majority of the women she lived with were expected to register and move to neighboring camps. Tonia most likely realized at the time that the emptied camp meant Sioma had been transferred. In her interrogation of March 4, 1950, when Tonia provided details regarding the October 1940 rounding up of people to the camps, she did not link these measures with antisemitism.[104]

Regardless, she must have felt like a hunted animal. But while the women around Tonia were being arrested, she managed to avoid arrest. Her friends advised her to escape with her children. She got in touch with some friends in Toulouse (with the International Committee for Aid to the Spanish People), who suggested that she join them. Toulouse was far away—over two hundred kilometers from Oloron but, paradoxically, only twenty-five kilometers from Le Vernet, to where her husband had been deported. She was scared to flee, so she visited a doctor to ask him to postpone her camp registration due to medical reasons. He refused but, at the same time, gave Marcel a chickenpox vaccination that gave him a fever. As a result, she received permission to register a week late. She used this delay to flee, putting Marcel's bathtub, blankets, and diapers in his baby carriage and then boarding a train to Toulouse. She had no documents because she had given them up to enter the Gurs camp in order to receive permission to visit Sioma.[105]

The story of how she escaped Oloron to avoid confinement at Gurs is only possible to comprehend through her own words. Some slight differences emerge between what she told Polish security officers in 1950 and how she narrated it to Dowgiałło. In an interrogation, she insisted that she contacted her friend Mela Ernst, who lived in Montauban and convinced her to join her.[106] In the version she presented to Dowgiałło, a couple of days after moving to Toulouse she moved to Montauban:

> Our town was full of demobilized French soldiers who did not know what to do with themselves. They helped me put the baby carriage

on the train. My French friend tried to get me to Toulouse. Every Frenchman had a *carte d'identité* and *livre de famille* in which his wife and children were registered. I was supposed to pretend to be his wife because as "me" I couldn't leave the town. On the train he seated me in a compartment with two families of gendarmes—wives and children. I was terrified. I still didn't speak French, which was obviously suspicious. Halfway there, my guardian asked me to go out into the corridor. He said they were looking for him and that he had to jump off the train on the run. He advised me to stay where I was and not speak at all. He jumped out. . . . In Toulouse, women from my compartment helped me out. I had my friends' address, but because I have no sense of direction, I do not know how—with the help of what miracle—I did not get lost. . . . I spent two nights with my friends, who then told me to leave. . . . Marcel slept in a suitcase under the bed and screamed all the time—and they could not stand that. They said that when they fled Paris they had stopped between Toulouse and Montauban on some abandoned farm and thought it was an extraordinary place. . . . One of them drove me there. . . . I was so nervous about the prospect of loneliness that I didn't even notice where I was. She left me some food stamps, some money, and assured me that they would look after me. Instead of water, there was a pond with some green algae on the farm. We were impossibly dirty and hungry. Not a living soul was around. I found some clean water, but not enough to wash in. So, I had to wash in the pond. After some time, I decided to go to the train station for diapers. I wanted to come back quickly, so I only took Verka and left Marcel in his baby carriage. And of course, I got lost. As a fugitive, I was afraid to ask for directions. But, to tell you the truth, nobody was interested in me. I got on some kind of a cart. After a while it turned out I was headed to Grenade. When I heard that, I felt weak and cried terribly. And then this little two-year-old Verka began to comfort me. I was in such a state that I couldn't even take her in my arms. In the evening, we managed to get home. Then it turned out that Marcel had disappeared. Fortunately, a six-year-old boy saw me. He explained that his mother took the screaming baby. . . . This lady turned out to be an Italian, a quiet and good woman. After all this, I was in a terrible condition, and she looked after me, brought me food—some delicious dish made on the fire. They were very poor. Compared to their situation, my life was full of luxuries they did not know at all. However, I was faced with another problem. Verka, who is allergic to everything, got a purulent rash. She was all in scabs . . . and I felt I could not cope with all this. I lasted less than a week and then called my friend in Toulouse for help.[107]

The moment when she lost her self-composure while breaking down into tears in front of Vera stands out in her conversation with Dowgiałło. But, again, as in many other stories, people she did not—perhaps could not—expect to help ended up doing so at the very last moment.

It was fall of 1940. Tonia must have reached the peak of her desperation. All contact with her husband and her family had been cut off, and for the first time since she had left Palestine her parents were unable to support her financially. The episode of almost losing Marcel most likely convinced her to leave the children at a place that appeared safe—a nursery for Jewish children in Limoges that her friends recommended. The building was discreetly located on the grounds of a beautiful villa.[108] The photos I found in Vera and Marcel's collection depict it almost as an oasis of safety. Surrounded by trees, the house gives an impression of tranquility. The dining room was spacious, and in almost every photo children are shown in the embrace of a caregiver or angelic looking nurses.

A woman named Henriette, whom Tonia knew from a medical center for refugees in Paris, admitted her to the nursery.[109] The house was run by Hanna Eisfelder Grünwald and maintained by a Jewish, communist, Swiss charity organization. Wanting to emphasize the role of communists in this endeavor, Tonia insisted in an interrogation that the house was not run by the noncommunist Children's Aid Society (Oeuvre de secours aux enfants, OSE), the largest organization in war-torn France to take care of Jewish children.[110] But the lists of children staying at the nursery in April 1942 indicate that at least at that point the facility was indeed run by the OSE.[111] The OSE was a medical-social welfare organization created in Russia by a group of young doctors in 1912 to help victims of pogroms by offering them medical aid. After being established in Russia, it opened offices in Poland in 1922, Berlin in 1923, and Paris in 1933. By 1940 it had offices in ten countries.[112] The OSE was concerned with the welfare of foreign Jews in internment camps in the South of France, ultimately evacuating Jewish children from those camps and placing them in non-Jewish homes and institutions.[113] The nursery functioned as one of their houses under the supervision of Dr. Gatson Lévy, a Jewish doctor banned from practicing by Vichy decree in 1941 and appointed medical inspector in Limoges.[114]

It is difficult to gather information about the nursery and determine when and why its leadership shifted from the hands of Grünwald to the OSE. Small pieces of this puzzle slowly began to unravel, mostly thanks to my Paris researcher, Meryl Lavenant, whose dedication to uncovering the story became unparalleled. One of her sources was the grandson of Gustave Goetschel, Pierre Goetschel, who, in an effort to recover the story of his grandfather, made a documentary illuminating the connections between Goetschel, Grünwald, and the population of Limoges.[115] This story serves as a good context to understand Tonia's decisions.

Born in 1900, Grünwald was a Jewish social worker who, from 1928 to 1931, served as the director of the Workers Social Services' Correctional Vocational School for Girls, a treatment facility for girls and young women from Hamburg and Berlin. Conflict and domestic abuse had pushed them to run away from home, and they found shelter in Grünwald's home. Grünwald approached the girls and women under her care lovingly and with a rare dose of understanding. She urged her staff to provide encouragement and teach life skills without relying on criticism or being patronizing. "Enlightenment instead of prayers, laughter instead of tears" was her motto.[116] In 1933 Grünwald left Germany for France. The same year, she traveled from Paris to Zürich twice—a trip organized by her friend Margaret Locher, who ran the nursery in Limoges—to reconnect with her husband, Marcus Grünwald, and also to appeal to Swiss political activists to assist in the humanitarian crisis she was observing in Paris. She asked for donations for a children's day-care center and a clinic for the poor. Her effort helped the Swiss Relief Organization for Emigrant Children (Schweizer Hilfswerk für emigrierte Kinder, SHEK) and its Paris branch, the Medical Assistance for Children of Refugees (Assistance médicale aux enfants de réfugiés), to open a child-care center for refugee children on the outskirts of Paris.[117]

At the outbreak of war, Grünwald moved the children from the center in Paris to Limoges in the unoccupied South of France, where her nursery was established. With the help of Gustave Goetschel, a local French Jew, she rented out a villa in Limoges at 46 rue Eugène-Varlin. Some additional money came via the League of Nations from Americans, including Eleanor Roosevelt. In total, around forty-five infants and toddlers had to be tended day and night by the assisting mothers, social workers, and paid staff. Later on, when the exodus of refugees resumed in May 1940, up to sixty small children lived there. In order to protect the children, Grünwald had to provide monthly accounting of expenses and a monthly list of children's names and national origins. Many of the youngest children and those deprived of parents were smuggled to Switzerland, where Locher was instrumental in helping them.[118]

A letter from the OSE's Dr. Levy is helpful in explaining the sudden change in the nursery's status. In July 1942 Levy informed the Limoges prefecture about a leadership change and Grünwald's departure from the nursery.[119] As German Jews, Grünwald and her family—her husband and son (born in 1938)—felt endangered. At first she tried to organize the departure of all the children under her care for the United States, but when this turned out to be impossible, she decided to leave, using a document claiming that she had an American sponsor. They fled to Marseille, an assembly point for those who were hoping to leave by ship, where they waited to be joined by Grünwald's mother.[120]

Tonia brought Vera and Marcel to the Limoges nursery in November 1940, when it was still run by Grünwald. Lists of children's names from November 1940 to April 1942 confirm their presence at the facility. Marcel's and Vera's names are marked as *recueillis du camp de Gurs*—collected from the Gurs camp.[121] They had actually avoided Gurs, thanks to their escape from Oloron, but this danger may have been the argument that spoke the loudest to Tonia when she decided to leave them at the nursery, so perhaps that is what she had told the registrant.[122] Tonia left alone for Montauban.[123] It was the first time since their birth that she was separated from her children.

Tonia left behind two different versions of what transpired next—one that she shared with Dowgiałło and another that she deposited with her interrogators. She told Dowgiałło that while she tried to settle in Montauban, she was called back to Limoges because the children had fallen ill. She stayed there as a nurse. Her name is included on a list created by Levy of unofficial staff who remained with the children.[124]

The story Tonia gave to her interrogation officers was that it was in Montauban where, in late 1940, she joined the Austrian Communist Party. Her friend Mela Ernst from the International Committee for Aid to the Spanish People introduced her to party work. In addition to learning about and discussing communism, the clandestine group of Austrian communists collected clothes and food to send to the camp in Le Vernet. Because they did not have enough money to heat their residences, they spent a lot of free time in cafés.[125] Tonia re-created an image of herself as a person deeply involved in the clandestine life of communists. "From January 1941 until August 1942, meaning until the camp in Le Vernet was moved into an unknown direction," she explained, "twice a month I was going to a camp in Le Vernet and then to Marseille," where some of the Austrian communists were hiding. From Marseille she delivered clandestine information that she passed on to her husband. In the same minutes, she described how her contact with the camp unfolded: "The departure from Limoges . . . took place in such a way that my husband received permission from the guards to see me, and he then would send the permission to me, and with it I was going to Le Vernet." What she most likely meant was that she was allowed to leave Limoges to see her husband because she had permission to visit him. These statements were part of the same interrogation minutes in which she explained that she saw Sioma for the last time in January 1940, a few months before giving birth to Marcel.[126]

Was she lying? Or did the interrogation officer misunderstand her statement regarding her conspiratorial activities in the camp? The people she spent time with in Montauban, such as Ernst, were indeed involved in the French resistance. Born in Chernivtsi in 1893, Ernst was arrested in February 1942 and was confined in Ravensbrück in April 1944.[127] Tonia, due to her connections to the communists who gathered in Montauban, was possibly close to resistance circles, but nowhere, except for the interrogation minutes, did she mention that involvement. She wrote a letter to the camp administration on June 9, 1941, asking for permission to visit her husband with her children, including Marcel, whom Sioma had not seen. She also asked for permission to see him outside of the camp.[128] The reply, dated July 5, 1941, permitted her to see him on the camp grounds.[129] However, the document clarifies that Tonia had an option to apply to the camp administration to see Sioma, demonstrating that the complicated way of contacting him she explained during her interrogation was unnecessary.

In the same interrogation, she further revealed that in Limoges she was called in by the police, where she was interrogated about the people she knew in Le Vernet. She was asked specifically about Trudi Ludke, a woman who supposedly had reported that Tonia was involved in organizing help for the interned. As a result of this interrogation and Ludke's testimony, Tonia was arrested. As Tonia further explained, Grünwald intervened in her case, arguing that she was nursing her children and hence needed to be released. Tonia further added that a local rabbi had intervened on her behalf as well, saying that she was never a communist.[130]

Determining what, if anything, is true in this story and why Tonia would reveal this only during the interrogation is difficult to know. On one hand, in the middle of 1940, Limoges was still perceived as a place where a number of Jewish institutions were managing to survive due to determination, ingenuity, and negotiation skills.[131] Goetschel's documentary depicts a thriving and helpful community with an active rabbi at its center.[132] The existence of Jewish institutions in town makes some aspects of Tonia's story viable. On the other, antisemitism was rampant in Limoges and growing, especially after June 1941. In the opinion of the regional prefect of Limoges, even French-born Jews blamed foreign Jews for antigovernment propaganda and the black market.[133] Finally, the revised Statut des Juifs promulgated a detailed census of all Jews in the unoccupied zone. Religion and ethnicity had not been part of the vital statistics in France for almost seventy years, so the decision to record all the Jews in the unoccupied zone was a step that "profoundly shocked Jewish opinion and was to have fatal consequences later when Jews were being rounded up and deported."[134]

During a 1949 interrogation, Tonia seems to have reinvented herself as a communist dedicated to the active struggle even in the midst of war and destruction. Freed from the most immediate concerns about her children, she could have devoted her energy to the antifascist resistance. In a letter she sent in 1946 to her brother after the war, however, she denied any war activism: "Well, Julek, during the war I wanted to go from Switzerland to France to take an active part in the fight against Hitler. It was not possible then."[135] Regardless of whether or not Tonia participated in the resistance, she knew a lot about the activities her comrades could have been involved with, and with that knowledge she re-created a relatively feasible story for her interrogation officers. She did it in a manner characteristic for her: she narrated it through parables, short stories with a clear moral lesson. In the midst of desperation, hope always came. It also imbued her narrative with a distinguishable feature: the evil or horror that accompanied her life did not rip through individual lives, or at least not only. It also evoked goodness that she believed remained in people, ordinary people she met.

Final Months in France

On February 18, 1942, in response to Vichy regulations calling for all Jews to register with local authorities, Tonia filled out a registration form confirming she was a Jew. She provided the date and place of her birth and information about her husband, stating he was confined at Le Vernet. Interestingly, she declared that financial support came from her parents in Palestine in the amount of one thousand francs, but she did not clarify how often she received the money. Finally, the form provides her addresses: 6 rue Eugène-Varlin (the address of the Limoges nursery) and the address of her next domicile in Saint-Léonard, which was added in pencil.[136] She was now recognized as a foreign Jew.[137] Yet during her interrogations, she underlined the predominant role her communism played: she recalled having a conversation with a local rabbi from Limoges, who tried to convince her to circumcise her son to show she was not a communist, but she refused to do so. She did not want to deny her Jewishness, since that appeared as distancing herself from victims, which she did not want do as a communist.[138]

Once she was registered, the authorities had knowledge of her whereabouts. Consequently, on March 25, 1942, the police informed Tonia that in accordance with the provisions of Ministerial Circular No. 75, she had to leave Limoges before April 10 for one of eight small towns located in the department of Haute-Vienne. Tonia signed the document, confirming she had received the prefect's mandate.[139]

The Haute-Vienne archives contain a few letters from the exchange between Tonia and the Limoges police regarding her forced move. On April 1, a week after receiving the order to leave, she requested being relocated to Bessines-sur-Gartempe, a town not listed in the May 25 notification. She explained that in Bessines-sur-Gartempe she had a friend who could help her, which would "make it easier for her to raise her children and build a home."[140] On April 20 came the answer to her earlier request, informing her that it would be impossible for her to move to Bessines-sur-Gartempe since she needed to move to one of the originally indicated by the police.[141] Continuing her conversation with the various administrative powers, she asked for a week's extension:

> Mr. Prefect,
>
> I, the undersigned Mrs. Tauba LECHTMANN, have the honor to request your kindness to grant me a week for my move to the

countryside. I have already found accommodation, but the move, the truck, the arrangement, etc. will not be possible from today to tomorrow.

I thank you in advance and ask you to accept Mr. Prefect the expression of my very respectful feelings.[142]

This exchange is startling. The order to move was one of the weapons besides internment that prefectures had in their arsenal against foreign Jews. Indeed, in the exchange between the prefecture and the police, Tonia is called a foreign Jew (*étranger israelite*).[143] Forced relocation was a less repressive form of police restriction that was used in the cases of Jews who had sufficient resources to feed and shelter themselves. They were sent to live under police surveillance in a remote place, "usually a rural area with adequate hotel and police facilities."[144] Clearly, Tonia was considered to be a person who still had resources to sustain herself and was thus granted the opportunity to continue living relatively freely. Nevertheless, the atmosphere of respect the letters maintain, as if both sides were doing each other a favor by dutifully following the rules, is mind-boggling.

Tonia had no choice but to leave Limoges. She could have left her children at the nursery there but decided against separation, mostly because the nursery had become part of the OSE, an organization she viewed critically. Leaving the nursery, she decided to take another child, Nani Glauster, a young Austrian girl who was one year older than Vera whose mother had died in labor and whose father was interned in a camp as a Spanish Civil War volunteer. While explaining this decision to Dowgiałło, she said she was told at the nursery that if she did not want this girl to be raised as a traditional Jew, she should take her. But perhaps more important was that her father was a communist and Sioma's comrade, so she felt obliged to raise her as a communist.[145] Taylorann Lenze, my research assistant, visited Nani in Vienna. Nani clearly remembered the day when Tonia decided to take her: "And she picked me up from the children's home and said, 'Where I can make it with two children, I will make it with three.'"[146]

Tonia and the three children were relocated to Saint-Léonard (twenty-five kilometers east of Limoges). "We were in this tiny village," Nani recalled, "and we lived in a room where the kitchen and bathroom were outside. It was really completely poor."[147] While in Saint-Léonard, Tonia planned to visit her husband with Marcel to give Sioma an opportunity to meet his son. Her neighbor agreed to take care of Vera and Nani while she was gone. But in the meantime, she somehow received information that Sioma was no longer in the camp and had gone without leaving an address. At the local police station, a gendarme informed her that the men in Le Vernet had been taken to a small town in Poland.[148] On August 8, Sioma was taken from Le Vernet to Chalon-sur-Saône with a convoy of *"étrangers indésirables,"* from where he was taken to Drancy and, on August 12, to Auschwitz.[149] The first deportation of Jews from Drancy had left for Auschwitz over four months earlier, on March 27. Drancy was an assembly center of transports of Jews from the unoccupied zone for deportations to Poland. The French police accompanied the deportees to the German frontier at Novéant, where the Germans took over. It took them three days to reach Auschwitz.[150]

Sioma's deportation also meant that measures against Jews had gained momentum in France. On June 11, in accordance with the Nazi plan to move all European Jews to the east, Adolf Eichmann had demanded that France's two zones supply one hundred thousand foreign and stateless Jews. Nothing appeared more necessary to French officials than to persuade Nazi officials of the effectiveness of the French administration and their police. In accordance with this demand, the Vichy administration decided to deport eastward the stateless Jews interned in the unoccupied zone and those who were already detained in Drancy. It prepared a plan to round up all foreign Jews region by region: refugee men, women, and children, making unoccupied France the only state in Europe to deliver Jews to the Nazis.[151]

In her interrogations and conversation with Dowgiałło, Tonia revealed that in August 1942 the same French gendarme who had informed her where the men from Le Vernet were taken came to her residence with an arrest order. He had only her and her two children on the list, not Nani. According to the story Tonia conveyed to Dowgiałło, she was crying and convinced him to leave them alone. He left to consult his supervisor but soon returned, intent on arresting her. Tonia had heard on an illegal radio that mothers of small children would not be arrested, which reassured her, but his reappearance now left her hysterical. She packed her meager belongings, left Nani with a neighbor, and went with the gendarme. She was taken to a camp in Nexon, where a rabbi tried to convince her to give up the children so they would be sent to a separate camp and would thus be spared deportation. She refused. She later described the ordeal to Dowgiałło:

It was the end of August, maybe September. We arrived at the camp near Limoges. There were even beds and sheets. And great food. I will never forget their spaghetti with tomato sauce, which I hadn't eaten since the outbreak of the war. Perhaps the French prepared it out of their guilty consciences.... There were several hundred people in the camp. Men separately, women separately. Not too many children. I did not see children as young as mine. A day after arriving, we were asked to come for verification. We were standing in line waiting for an official to check our files. I held Marcel in my hands, and Verka stood clinging to my skirt. He looked angry and asked what I was doing here, since my child is not yet two years old. Although Marcel was tiny, there was a card in front of him saying he was over two years old. I said nothing, and he started yelling at me. He called out to the police, "Who sent her here?" And he told me to leave immediately. A guard let me go. I wanted to go to the barrack to get my pillows. He said that in half an hour Germany will take the train cars with people and that I need to go right away. He put me in a police car. And so I went to the station. I got on the train and returned to Saint-Léonard, to my garage. Without my mom's beautiful pillows.[152]

During her interrogation, in contrast, she confessed she was already in a train car with her children, standing not far from the door, when a commandant of the camp came and released her.[153]

Documentation from Nexon confirms that Tonia was arrested on August 26 in the biggest roundup planned for the region but released the next day.[154] Nexon was one of two internment camps located nearly twenty kilometers from the region's capital: one was in Saint-Paul-d'Eyjeaux and the other in Nexon, which was supposed to play the role of gathering and verifying exemption cases and family reunifications, before the convoys of trucks or trains headed for Drancy and then the prisoners continued on by train to Auschwitz.[155] Tonia appeared to have been arrested at a moment when the Nazis did not want to bother with children. In a memorandum from June 15, 1942, Theodor Dannecker, an SS captain and associate of Eichmann, who orchestrated the Final Solution in several countries, including France, proclaimed that children should be excluded: "The essential thing is that the Jews (of both sexes) be between sixteen and forty years of age." But, apparently, the French administration insisted that children be deported as well, which Eichmann conceded to on July 20.

Serge Klarsfeld—a French-Romanian activist who as a Jewish child was saved in an OSE house and who spent his life documenting and commemorating victims of German-occupied France—estimates that 1,032 children under the age of six were sent from France to Auschwitz in 1942.[156] Vichy France was the only country where authorities deported Jews without the presence of occupying forces; yet France was also a country where a great percentage of Jews survived the war due to a dense network of resistance forces and to the help that people extended to each other, taking advantage of the leeway granted by the chaos of new orders from headquarters and the lack of German occupying forces in the south. It is not possible to more systematically answer the question of why Tonia eluded being sent away, but she indeed escaped deportation to Auschwitz.

|||

Tonia's narration of her time in France is fragmented and chaotic. France was a country where she chose to immigrate to in hope of finding a space to realize her dreams, the country that welcomed her with anticommunist suspicions and increasingly oppressive anti-Jewish regulations. Her narration centers on being able to escape repeatedly from the most unimaginable circumstances. There is nothing that predisposed her for survival, unless perhaps her long-term displacement, which started in 1937, taught her to reach out to those around her for assistance. Her story is centered on gestures of help that she received from various people, help that she did not anticipate and that came to her at unexpected moments.

The fragmented nature of her experiences in France helps us create almost two different versions of her life. On one hand, as she revealed during interrogations, she was involved in the French resistance. On the other, as she portrayed herself in her conversation with Dowgiałło, she was lucky to receive help when she needed it most. In the former, she was an active agent of her life; in the latter, she was more of a hunted animal on the run. These differences may be reflected by the nature of the documents and the conditions under which she retrieved these memories. While in the interrogations she portrayed herself as a self-assured communist ready to take matters into her own hands, in conversations from the 1990s she more often relied on references to her own vulnerability and the help that came from others. The two versions of her story provided her with a chance to present two ways her exile can be interpreted—either as a continuation or a rupture of the journey she began in 1937.

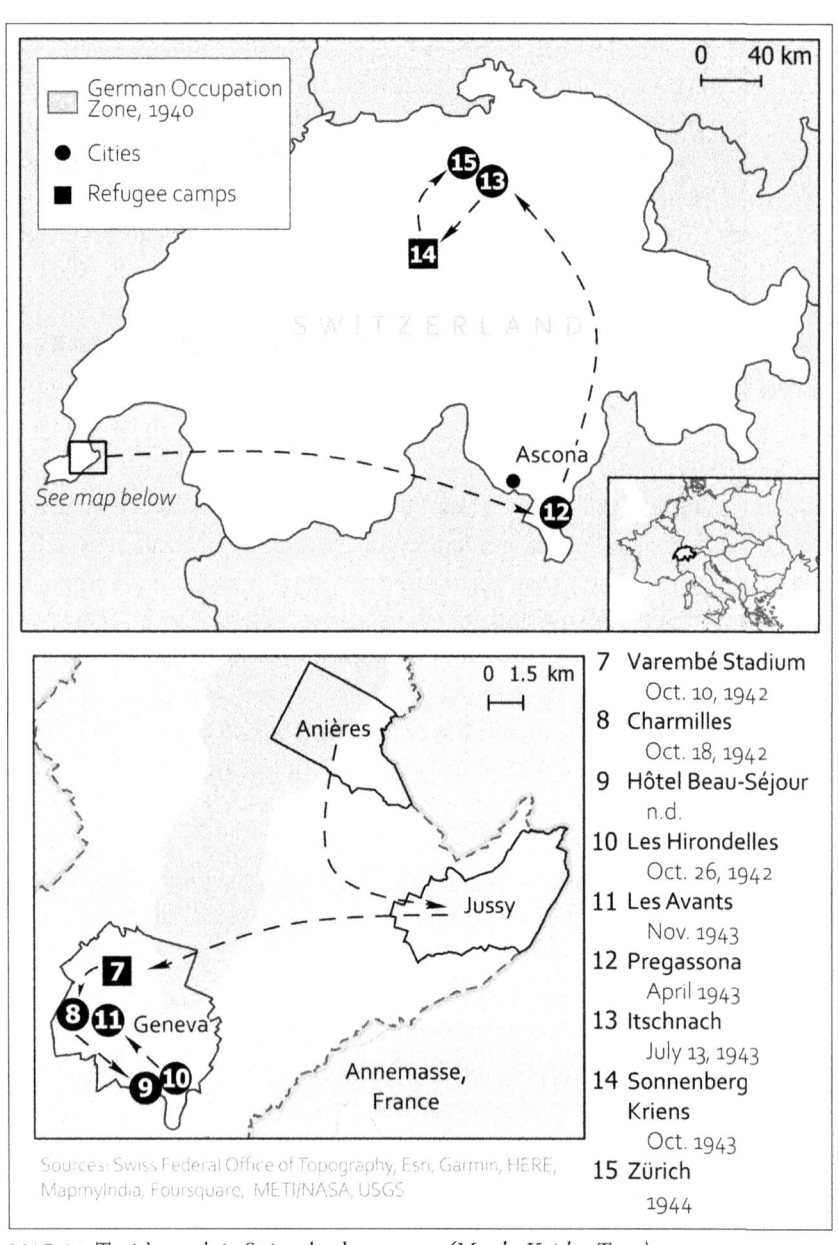

MAP 5.1. Tonia's travels in Switzerland, 1942–44. *(Map by Kaitlyn Tatro)*

5 ||| Mother, Refugee, and Social Worker
Life in Switzerland, 1942–1945

VERA'S EARLIEST memories of her childhood come from Itschnach, near Zürich in Switzerland. She was six years old, when, together with her brother, Marcel (four), and Nani, the little girl her mother cared for in Limoges, she stayed in a children's home with a group of Jewish children and a few caregivers, awaiting the war's end. Vera has fond memories of this time, like exercising with other children in front of a window on a soft carpet. In all seasons, the window remained at least partly open. This period is richly documented with beautiful photographs of children: some at play, others going on a walk to a nearby store, Vera climbing a ladder—activities she interprets as Margaret Locher, the woman who ran the children's home, pushing them to combat their fears while performing physical tasks. Vera's memories depict her early life and Marcel's as almost serene; there was no fear or hunger or absence.[1]

Marcel has no memories of this period. In 1942, when his mother crossed into Switzerland, he was only two. Vera, as the older sister, holds the key to the stories of their life when they were close to their mother, almost the only time they had together. She tells stories of him crying over breakfast or of his independent spirit. While sitting in his apartment in Stockholm and talking with me about his past, Marcel often got upset, gesticulating wildly and trying to prove that he has absolutely no memories from his childhood. Where Vera has stories, he feels only their absence. And that absence hurts him. Was his mother ever present? If so, how present was she? What does his lack of memories mean? Yet, throughout our conversations, some elements of this past began returning, such as the treat of cookies with apples he remembers that waited for him each time he saw his mother, even though he is unable to place those moments on the timeline of his life. His memories consist of isolated images that are challenging to organize into a meaningful chronology.

Crossing the Border from France to Switzerland

In October 1942 Tonia crossed the border from France to Switzerland. Although all borders are essentially imaginary lines, ones agreed upon by the state, their physical manifestations can represent life or death for the person attempting to cross. For instance, Françoise Frenkel, who tried to cross this border twice, recollected: "Thus, I made my way toward the ditch that day with a light step, walking alongside the barbed wire, just beyond which, within arm's reach lay . . . Switzerland!"[2] Tonia's documents do not reveal what prompted her to realize that she had crossed the border. But almost immediately afterward, she was arrested and taken to a border guards office in Anières, located

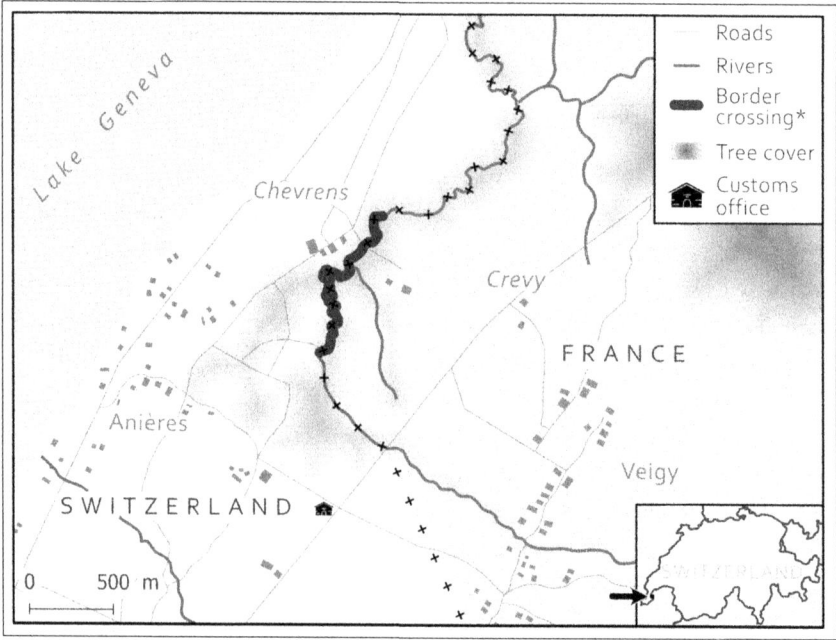

MAP 5.2. France-Switzerland border, indicating where Tonia most likely crossed into Switzerland in 1942. *(Map by Kaitlyn Tatro)*

near Lake Geneva. The Swiss state archives contain information regarding not only the place and date but also the time of her crossing: October 10, 1942, (Saturday) at 8:30 p.m.[3] Curiously, her crossing marks the period when almost every step of her life is documented in police reports and correspondence between state administration offices. An officer in Anières who served his shift from 6:30 p.m. to 11:30 p.m. prepared two reports about her crossing, both noting the arrest of four Jews trying to escape the Germans: Tonia, her children, and an older Jewish woman, Lilly Salomon-Schwarz. They also record a phone call to the police station in Jussy, located nine kilometers from Anières, urging officers to come and fetch the arrested Jews.[4]

At 10:35 p.m. a different officer at the Jussy police post filled out yet another report (an arrest report) documenting Tonia and her children's clandestine passage. (Salomon-Schwarz no longer appeared in Tonia's documents.) It noted that she carried a pair of scissors, a knife, 5,740 French francs, and a residency permit, described later in her file as a nonworking refugee residence permit (*un permis de séjour de réfugié non travailleur*).[5] In a questionnaire Tonia was asked to fill out, she stated that she had fled France for fear of being deported to Poland. She had no family members in Switzerland but a contact person, Margaret Locher, a social worker who was friends with Grünwald and ran the nursery in Limoges, where Tonia had met her. The story is straightforward: Tonia with her children and another woman had crossed the border clandestinely and were caught soon afterward.[6] After the stress of clandestinely fleeing France, she found herself in the middle of a bureaucratic muddle with someone else now in charge. But she and her children had made it. They had safely crossed the border and were admitted as refugees.

Leaving France without an exit visa was forbidden, so reaching the Swiss border unnoticed by the Vichy French border guards, gendarmes, or policemen was challenging. In the fall of 1942, Jews were arrested by the hundreds on their way to the Swiss border.[7] Yet crossing the border did not guarantee permission to stay because Swiss borders were heavily protected against people without a visa by guards and soldiers practically ignorant of Jews' predicament.[8] Around 2,850 Jews were turned away at the French-Swiss border from January 1940 to May 1945.[9]

Under interrogation in 1950, Tonia provided more details regarding her preparations and the moment of border crossing. After her release from the camp in Nexon, she decided to leave France. She did not know how to reconnect with Sioma. As her situation was becoming increasingly dangerous, there were no apparent reasons to stay in France. Interestingly, she also informed her interrogators that she had the permission of "the party," presumably the German Communist Party, to leave France.[10] She was advised to escape to neutral Switzerland, a country that had been a sanctuary for political refugees since the nineteenth century.[11]

The plan her acquaintances in Limoges proposed was for her children to stay at the nursery in Limoges while she traveled to Annemasse, a small town on the French side of the border close to Geneva, where she would go to a specific address to meet a border-crossing guide. Her hope was that after successfully crossing the border alone, she would be able to plan her children's passage. But, as she testified, to leave Limoges she had to have an exit permit. A friend from the nursery obtained an identification document with a fake name for her, a person from Alsace. Uncertainties blur the details of the remaining story. Tonia traveled to the border at Annemasse, where a few people resided who were potentially willing to serve as guides and for whom she had addresses. The first potential guide was an Italian woman who refused to help, saying that since her address was well known to French authorities, the risk of her crossing was too great. Tonia had two more addresses in Thonon-les-Bains, a town located over thirty kilometers from Annemasse. Following the suggestion of the Italian woman, she took a bus to Thonon-les-Bains, where she had more luck and was allowed to stay with one of the families. Within the first few days, she learned that Swiss authorities were only letting people with little children cross the border. The people she stayed with in Thonon-les-Bains sent a telegram back to Limoges asking that Tonia's children be sent to them.[12]

The story she presented to Dowgiałło is slightly different but is built on the same foundation of assistance received from kind strangers. People she never met before helped her contact the nursery and then traveled to Limoges to pick up her children. The story turns into a tale of rescue during which help came repeatedly from strangers at the most unexpected moments, but it also reveals interesting details regarding her escape from France:

> I got a big pendant cross from my friend to protect me, my cousin sent a package with a very elegant black costume. . . . When I got to Annemasse, I was warned not to enter the house whose address Margaret had given me because everyone knew what they were doing

and the police were monitoring the whole area. . . . I was told to escape quickly. I had two more addresses in Thonon. . . . I arrived at the [first] place after dusk. A Jew opened the door. I gave the password. Meanwhile, seeing the cross [on my chest], she started shouting, "Aren't you ashamed?" and slammed the door. Idiot! Fortunately, I had a second address. Just in case, I hid my cross. But it turned out that I had found very nice people who took great care of me. They said that separating me from my children is nonsense because the Swiss only accepted families with children. It became clear I could only save myself with the children. We started thinking about what to do. My guardians sent a telegram to the children's home in Limoges. They said that the children were to spend their holidays in Switzerland. . . . The married couple I stayed with placed me at a dentist's house. It was a family of Alsatian refugees, not Jews. The wife of this dentist went to pick up Vera and Marcel. They went on a train ride with a complete stranger—they didn't know what was happening to them at all. We spent the next month locked in a room. Our hosts behaved extremely well. Neither the mother nor grandmother could have been more kind toward my children than the wife of this dentist. They shared their very scanty food stamps with us, and this gentleman even made sure I had cigarettes . . . and I sat there waiting.[13]

In both versions, the interrogations and the interview, a stranger agreed to bring Vera and Marcel to her. And in both versions, she and her children had to hide for a while in Thonon-les-Bains, most likely between two to four weeks, waiting for someone to take them across the border.[14] In both accounts, help came from a priest active in the area coordinating smugglers who helped Jews escape from France. It was a complicated chain of events, where every move depended on the goodwill of someone else:

The son of the owner of the house where I was staying, told them [the family Tonia was staying with in Thonon] that the mother should bring the children to the priest's presbytery and that his sister and I should go to another priest, get a bike from him, and go to the village where the children were [the children being brought there by the woman Tonia stayed with]. . . . I don't remember the name of this place, but I know it was on the other side of the lake, opposite

Geneva. Following the instructions, I went with the man's sister to the indicated town.... We came to this town in the evening—it was in the first days of November 1942. The priest sent for a guide with whom we left toward the border at around 9:30 p.m. I was carrying one child, and he was carrying the other. After about half an hour of walking, the guide stopped and told me we were already on the Swiss side. At the same time, he showed me the route I should take to reach the tram stop leaving for Geneva and the border guards booth. When saying goodbye, I gave the guide a certain number of French francs, which he initially did not want to take but later accepted, declaring he would pass it on to the priest.[15]

The two accounts also point to a difference regarding the payment: in the interrogation version, she left all the money to the person who walked her across the border, whereas in her interview she stated that she paid the priest.

Ruth Fivaz-Silbermann, who has spent her professional career documenting the movement that took place during the war across the French-Swiss border, informed me that indeed there was an Abbot Jean Rosay in Douvaine, near Anières, the point where Tonia crossed, who helped dozens or more refugees cross the border. Before sending them with a guide to the border, he housed them in the presbytery or in homes of friendly families. Rosay was arrested in February 1944 and deported to Auschwitz, then Dora, and finally Bergen-Belsen, where he died. The involvement of the second priest whom Tonia mentioned is less clear. Rosay worked alone and was located close to the border, about a thirty-minute walk, which made his place ideal to facilitate border crossings.[16] Crossing the border was only possible with the help of smugglers, who never revealed their real names. Rosay's guides were local peasants, generally young men from the Catholic Rural Organization (Jeunesse agricole catholique).[17]

In her research, Fivaz-Silbermann came across Tonia as one of about fifteen thousand Jewish refugees trying to enter Switzerland from France from 1942 to 1944:

I guess Tonia was advised to bring the children to Rosay's presbytery in Douvaine, the first "town" she mentioned, which was in fact a village, and then to take a bicycle with her companion directly to the second place near the border, which could have been Veigy, another village where lots of smugglers were active. Perhaps someone else—another guide—took the children from Rosay's presbytery to Veigy where they waited for Tonia and then guided them across the border. There they were most likely channeled across the small Hermance River, where most likely there was no barbed wire at the time. On a map from the 1930s, I can see the customs office, one of two small squares at the crossing of the main road from Corsier to Douvaine and the small road coming from Anières on the left. It was not and is still not directly on the border. But this was an open field, and must have been heavily guarded.

In Fivaz-Silbermann's opinion, Tonia crossed somewhere near Chevrens in the middle of an open field.[18] Her plan was most likely to cross clandestinely and reach out to Locher. She may have been told to report to the Swiss border guards as she was assured that even if caught crossing the border illegally, she would be allowed to stay in Switzerland: her children were her guarantee she would be admitted.[19] She told Dowgiałło that the priest had informed her that after crossing the border, she should immediately take the tram to Geneva to avoid arrest. But that plan did not work: "Vera did not want to walk," Tonia explained. "I was also exhausted and falling off my feet. Then I saw the gendarme. And instead of going to the tram, I went straight to him."[20] This particular moment of meeting a Swiss guard characteristically turned into an encounter with kindness instead of fear. As she explained to Dowgiałło, she wanted to show the guard the only documents she had but could not immediately since they were hidden in her belt. She explained that she needed time to show her documents, and in response he took them home to his wife, who fed them cookies made with apples, the same ones Marcel remembers as a treat his mom baked for him. Tonia's relief, however, did not last long. Later, the guard took them to the border post at Anières and then to Jussy, where she and her children were jailed for the night.

As Fivaz-Silbermann explains, Switzerland developed two refugee policies during the war. It continued a prewar policy of limited admission based on principles not of immigration but only of transit, interpreted by some historians as a direct continuation of the anti-Jewish policy of the interwar years. According to the 1931–33 law, all refugees were supposed to "transmigrate"— that is, leave Switzerland as soon as they could arrange passage to some third country, usually overseas.[21] With the beginning of the war, visas for all foreigners became compulsory. Exceptions were made only to those who fell under the Hague Conventions of 1907: disarmed troops and prisoners of war. From a legal perspective, the country was completely closed. This policy continued even after the massive arrival of refugees from France in the summer of 1942.[22] The Swiss administration adapted a narrow definition of a political refugee: someone who was personally at risk because of political activities. But since communists were particularly undesirable in the country, Swiss federal officials used great restraint in recognizing them as political refugees. Persecution of Jews was not defined as political persecution either. This led to the recognition of only 644 political refugees from 1933 to 1945.[23]

But in the summer of 1942, at the same time Switzerland fatefully decreed its policy of strictly maintaining closed borders and turning away any illegal refugees, it also developed an emergency policy:[24]

> Under pressure from public opinion, Eduard von Steiger, head of the Federal Department of Justice and Police, officially claimed that "the [Swiss] lifeboat was full." But confidentially, he ordered a halt to the turning away of everyone at the border, at least until the protests died down. He also ordered officials to act kindly at other borders, sparing the weakest among the refugees, i.e., the elderly, the sick and children. However, the actual decision was left to the military police or the border guards.[25]

Finally, after Tonia and her children had spent almost a month at the border, where the fate of all refugees was left to chance and the border guards, Heinrich Rothmund, the head of the Federal Immigration Office, issued precise regulations on September 26 allowing people over sixty-five, pregnant women, the sick, and families with at least one child under sixteen (later restricted to under six) to cross the crowded western border. Even if this regulation was not adequate to the impending Holocaust refugee crisis, it left the Swiss door open to at least some categories of people flooding its borders.[26]

What Fivaz-Silbermann underlines in her assessment of the Swiss war policy reflects Tonia's predicament and a constant lack of assurance but also an experience that dominated her war years. Between 28,000 and 29,000 Jews were saved in Switzerland, while between 2,600 and 3,000 were turned away at the French border and approximately 300 at the Italian border. Those denied entry were then returned directly to wherever they crossed the border, which on the French border often meant being delivered straight into the hands of the Vichy police.[27] Tonia, and the woman who crossed with her, Salomon-Schwarz, were lucky. They knew that because they traveled with children, they most likely would not be turned away. Hence, Tonia had escaped at a liminal moment when the regulations against Jews began tightening in France and at the same time a small window of opportunity opened in Switzerland.

The active presence of various relief organizations (e.g., the OSE in France) and assistance from smugglers made the journey into Switzerland possible. These organizations and individuals exploited the holes in the Swiss security border. Fivaz-Silbermann sees it in the following way:

> French priests hid Jews and led them to the border, and Catholics and Protestants worked together with Jewish organizations. Increasingly, helpers falsified documents to fit Swiss regulations. To lead refugees into Switzerland, the OSE first picked out those who matched government guidelines. They then greatly falsified identities, turning young adults into teens under 16, borrowing small children from couples in order to also save other couples who had none and even "marrying" singles and giving them orphaned children to declare as their own, thereby saving both the adults and children.... Expenses of the Jewish underground were covered by the JDC [American Jewish Joint Distribution Committee]. The money reached the helpers via complicated paths, borrowing on the spot, or hidden in the luggage of "normal" travelers.... One can, therefore, say that Switzerland provided help through its mere presence as a neutral, nonbelligerent and partially-open country in the heart of Europe.[28]

State documents simplified the crossing by reducing the experience to the act of the crossing. Tonia's later interrogations and interview show that the process relied on many people: both people she knew and strangers she met along the way. They were crucial to her success at leaving France at the most dangerous moment.

Life of a Refugee

Reconstructing Tonia's experiences in Switzerland is challenging. Her memory from that period was imprecise and reflected the vulnerability of someone completely dependent on bureaucratic measures. Her letters are scattered and focus on her children; imminent in them is the need to remain positive when looking toward the future, but the enthusiastic hopefulness of the Paris days is gone. Additionally, historical research on camps and confinement for refugees in Switzerland during the war is insufficient. The rare mention of Swiss refugee camps comes mostly from Holocaust survivors' memoirs and interviews. The only concrete traces of Tonia are from the Swiss state administration. Even this rich documentation is just a silhouette of her larger story.

After being stopped at Anières and held at the police station in Jussy for interrogation, Tonia was handed over to military authorities in Geneva, where on October 15, five days after escaping France, she was once again asked to declare her status.[29] In her interview with Dowgiałło, she reflected that these multiple conversations with Swiss authorities resembled the interrogations she experienced prior to her escape to Switzerland, in Palestine, and then later in Poland. The questions were equally arbitrary and pointless.[30] Neglect fringing on cruelty was almost palpable. During sessions with the Swiss police, she had to stand while holding Marcel, while little Vera stood next to her. No one offered any help or support.[31]

Being overwhelmed by a mass of people entering the country most likely guided state representatives' behavior during these early interrogations. On the day Tonia crossed the border, October 10, 1942, sixty-eight Jewish refugees arrived in Geneva, along with about ten non-Jews. For the whole of October 1942, Geneva had to accommodate over thirteen hundred Jewish refugees, plus a smaller number of non-Jews.[32] Upon their arrival, those stopped at the border were typically first sent to a reception and then quarantine camp, which were run by military personnel, and finally to a work camp, run by the civilian office for work camps. Surprisingly little information is available about the camps. More than forty-five hundred refugees lived in Swiss camps in mid-November 1942, and in early 1943 twenty-six reception camps were still in operation.[33] Once moved to labor camps, the refugees were expected to work: men built roads and fortifications for the army and engaged in some agricultural work, as part of the government's program to increase Switzerland's food supply during the war, and women served an auxiliary role to the men by sewing, doing laundry, and preparing food in empty hotels or châteaus, turned into hostels for women refugees and their children.[34]

With its own particular twists, Tonia's story follows this pattern. She spent almost eight months without her children at a camp in Les Avants near Montreux in the mountainous Lake Geneva region, but before her transfer to Les Avants on November 21, 1942, she traveled through a system of small, isolated sites of internment that served the Swiss administration as organization points where countless documents were produced. The system ultimately assigned Tonia and her children a place in the hierarchy of the refugees that allowed them to stay in Switzerland. In October and November 1942, Tonia went through five different internment camps. After her release from Jussy, Tonia and her children were transported to the Varembé Stadium in Geneva, which had been requisitioned for a military reception camp. The federal Flüchtlingskommissar (refugee commissioner) noted that in October 1942 Varembé had enough space for 120 people, with a population constantly renewed in light of the 1,300 refugees who arrived only in October.[35] A sports stadium, Varembé offered inadequate, unheated barracks and minimal toilets.[36] It was the first place where refugees were unloaded and made to wait until assigned a place elsewhere. Tonia remembered Varembé as having awful conditions, and she estimated that between two hundred and three hundred people stayed there, mostly mothers with children. She recalled refugees receiving some blankets, but she did not get any. Her first days in the camp were "cold and rainy, but the Swiss people did not care."[37]

After a stay in the Varembé reception camp, refugees were moved to a former elementary school in Charmilles, where their paperwork was prepared. It was a small place that could accommodate up to 150 refugees, who could stay there only for a few days. They were then moved to a quarantine camp, still in Geneva, which could have been the Beau-Séjour, Les Hirondelles, Val-Fleuri, or Bout-du-Monde, former hotels, or hospitals located in the Champel neighborhood, a posh part of the city. Refugees normally stayed there for three to four weeks, waiting for Bern to approve their asylum requests.[38] This was part of their preparation for transitioning to one of the work camps.

All these sites were unwelcoming and ultimately served the same goal of confining and organizing large groups of people. Strict and often irrational discipline was imposed on the refugees. Their daily life was organized around constant inspections, roll calls, and rules. Perhaps the worst was the camp administrators' behavior, infused with antisemitism and a desire to prevent detainees from integrating into Swiss society and the labor market. In some places, to ensure refugees did not come into contact with the Swiss population, even doctors' visits were allowed only if accompanied by soldiers.[39] Being cut off from the outside world was enhanced by limitations in their correspondence; for example, they were prohibited from writing in Yiddish (in the Hebrew alphabet) and from sending mail abroad.[40]

In her conversation with Dowgiałło, Tonia was surprisingly silent about her journey through the Swiss camps, which lasted about two months after her escape to Switzerland. Despite her silence, it is the cold administrative system that offers insight into her early months in Switzerland. On December 4, 1942, in Les Hirondelles, she was asked to fill out a questionnaire prepared by the federal police that provides some details regarding her stay in Switzerland, including information about her previous paid positions, her family situation, the languages she spoke, and the potential possibility of her leaving Switzerland. One of the questions concerned her reasons for fleeing France, which she explained as being motivated not by her political views but by the persecution of Jews.[41] Les Hirondelles was a site of internment financed by the Jewish community of Geneva.[42] She may have emphasized her Jewishness because of this, or perhaps she pushed her communist activism aside due to her extreme personal vulnerability as a Jew at the time.

From October 10 to 18, she stayed in Varembé Stadium, from which she was taken for two days to Charmilles, and then on October 26 she was moved to a villa at Les Hirondelles in Champel.[43] What happened between October 18 and October 26 may not have been typical. In later interrogations in Poland, Tonia testified that while she and her children were staying in a camp, her son fell ill, and they were released to a hospital. I struggled while trying to reconcile with the documents the bits and pieces of the narrative emerging from her story. I try to believe that both—the documents and her story—carry elements of the past that somehow need to be pulled together. The lack of secondary literature to build the story's background does not make it easier. Taken out of context, the administrative documents often do not provide anything except dates, signatures, and some patchy information.

Among the various forms she filled out or signed is a document from the Hôtel Beau-Séjour titled "Engagement," which translates into "Commitment." The form describes the rules regulating refugees' stay in Switzerland. It appears in three copies in Tonia's file—one for her, one for Vera, and one for Marcel—all of which Tonia signed in pencil, possibly when she was staying at the Beau-Séjour with her children. Rules included refraining from going to bars or dance clubs, entering military zones, and going out in groups of more than five people. Refugees were also obliged to not change their residence without authorization, to stay inside between midnight and 6 a.m., observe lights-out from 10 p.m. to 5 a.m., and refrain from all activities that could be detrimental to the state, such as political activity. Further, the forms requested that she settle any expenses without delay, neither take on debt nor make unnecessary purchases, and not leave the canton of Geneva or Switzerland without a twenty-four announcement of her departure.[44] The document determined the framework of refugees' lives: refugees had to ask for permission for everything while being expected to pay for their stay. Fivaz-Silbermann explained that "their money (if they had brought any) was confiscated and deposited in the Swiss Popular Bank in order to pay for their stay at first; and even when there was something left, they could hardly obtain any of their own money to buy much-needed items, such as a coat or a pair of shoes, because the purchase had to be approved first. But charities could provide garments and small sums, for example, for buying stamps in order to be able to send letters to their families."[45]

Prewar postcards of the Hôtel Beau-Séjour show luxurious buildings designed in the architectural style of the Belle Époque, sporting turrets and tapered crowns and nestled in a charming landscape with mountains in the background. I imagine that one of its attractions was a view of Mont Blanc on a clear day. The hotel, known for its baths and hydrotherapy, experienced a progressive decline as a result of World War I, before being finally bought by the state in 1943. After having temporarily housed the headquarters of the international Red Cross, it was demolished in 1957. The avenue on which it was located is still called Beau-Séjour, but now, under at number 26, there is a large modern hospital.[46]

Tonia clearly signed the form allowing her to stay at the Hôtel Beau-Séjour, though the questionnaire does not provide any dates or details about her stay. Most likely she resided there after her release from Charmilles, as refugees were moved from overcrowded receiving facilities to some hotels functioning as camps, such as the Beau-Séjour. It is unclear whether she stayed there only with Vera while Marcel was in the hospital, or if they all stayed in the hotel and had doctors come in to check on the boy. Perhaps during this time she was able to contact the people from whom she had expected to receive help: Bertha Hohermuth from the Help to the Emigrants (Aide aux émigrés), Margaret Locher, and her parents, whom she needed to ask for money to survive.[47] On October 26 she was transferred to Les Hirondelles, where, on December 4, 1942, she filled out the aforementioned questionnaire regarding her past.[48]

These details matter for a number of reasons. First, Tonia was moved between many places within just a couple of weeks of her arrest, with the majority of the sites located in close proximity, sometimes even in the same city district. This was common practice. To deal with a large influx of refugees who had to be quickly accommodated, a relatively small city like Geneva moved them frequently between various sites. Second, in the twenty-first century, when so much historical research concentrates on trying to understand the history of Jews during the war, the relative silence regarding the refugee camps for Jews in Switzerland is puzzling. These camps of course differed from those organized by German allies, which is one reason for less interest in them. But, as my research has revealed, they are part of the history of World War II confinement and the Jewish experience and deserve to have their proper place in that history.

Tonia began writing letters again while interned at Les Hirondelles. She tried to reconnect with and get support from her parents and to reassess the changes that had taken place since August 1940, the last time she had regular correspondence with her family. The first letter is dated November 12, 1942, and carries the term *lager* (camp) next to the address of Les Hirondelles. It is written in German and addressed to "R. Lichtheim." In it, she explains how difficult life is with two small children and her inability to provide basic needs. She asks Lichtheim to inform her parents of her circumstances as she is not allowed to respond to their telegram and assure them that she and the children are well. She also asks for warm clothes, slippers, and scarves because, as she explained, "we came here without anything." "It's very beautiful that one can find people that help one so much," she ends her first letter from Switzerland.[49]

Richard Lichtheim was a Jewish activist and Zionist stationed in Geneva, considered one of the most effective and experienced Zionist diplomats, who, already in the spring of 1942, began to realize the dimension of Nazi anti-Jewish measures.[50] Due to reports of mass deportations reaching him in Geneva during the spring of 1942, Lichtheim grew convinced that the mass killings were not a coincidental by-product of the war but part of a Nazi "plan" to deal with the presence of Jews in Europe. Andrea Kirchner, a historian who has studied Lichtheim, notices: "Even though he was far from imagining that the concentration of the Jewish population meant a systematic scheme of annihilation, he was convinced that deportations equal death by July 1942 at the latest."[51] His knowledge of the suffering of the Armenian population at the hands of the Turkish regime made him realize this connection between deportation and planned mass murder. In 1915 and 1916 he passed several times through Turkey and could not overlook the mass arrests and deportations of the Armenians, which eventually culminated in genocide.[52]

The letters suggest that Lichtheim was an acquaintance of Tonia's parents. Interestingly, while writing to her parents later, Tonia commented on his apparent coldness. In both his professional and personal letters, he usually remained distant and factual, despite, or perhaps because of, his constant work in organizing relief efforts. His efforts are documented in more than fifteen hundred letters and reports to the office of the Zionist Organization in Jerusalem. His obituary points to his sense of hopelessness: "It must indeed have been an ordeal for Lichtheim to be swamped by these reports and not be able to move a stone."[53] He also tirelessly organized Palestinian certificates allowing some Jews to escape to Palestine. When he realized that copies worked as well, he began to illegally copy them.[54]

Tonia's correspondence with Lichtheim illustrates that the camps were ill-suited for children. Indeed, some sources confirm that refugees slept in large rooms or barracks on hastily arranged beds made of straw; there was no privacy, play area, school, or food suitable for children.[55] To ease the situation, the Swiss government requested that SHEK take charge of all refugee children from the ages of six to sixteen and place them in foster families or children's homes to provide them with better living conditions.[56] To quickly place children, "the government waived the requirement for residence permits from the various cantons," an administrative move that was controversial:

> There was a certain cruelty involved in asking parents who had only recently escaped with their most precious possessions—their children—to now give up these children to strangers. But the women of SHEK explained that the parents would be able to visit them and the children would be removed from the unhealthy and unpleasant atmosphere in the camps. However, the good intentions of the

SHEK women were mixed with a strong dose of paternalism. Parents had little or no control over where their children were placed. Although they were theoretically able to visit the children, SHEK deliberately placed the children far from the parents to minimize such visits, on the grounds that frequent crisis would interfere with the child's adjustment to his or her foster family. Parents received permission to spend a few days with their children only once every three months.... Although parents and children could communicate by correspondence, this too, was strictly limited.[57]

Relief organizations, the Swiss press, and some Red Cross officials widely criticized the separation of parents from children. No other country receiving refugees during this period, such as Sweden or Portugal, separated parents and children.[58] "Tearing children away from their mothers seems to me an act of inhumanity in the name of humanity," noted the Zürich-based periodical *Israelitisches Wochenblatt*. Many desperate mothers wrote to various relief organizations:

> Today, Wednesday, we will be allowed ... to see our children from 2 to 5, but the thought of the impending separation depresses us, we take walks, we hold our child in our arms like tormented souls, we press them to our breast because they will be torn from us in a moment.... My husband is in the Andelfingen camp, my son in Winterschwil (Aargau), my little daughter and I are in Langenbruck, she on the first floor, I on the third. In the night I awaken and think: Is my little one sleeping?[59]

Tonia decided to part with her children as well. From the letter that Hohermuth from Help to the Emigrants sent to a police lieutenant of the district, most likely the person responsible for refugee placement, we know Tonia allowed for her children to leave for a *home d'enfants* in Ascona, in the canton of Ticino, an Italian part of Switzerland. The handwritten note added to the document states that on November 20, 1942, the children left Geneva for Ascona.[60] The decision was voluntary yet painful. Two months later, when Tonia renewed relatively regular contact with her parents, she explained her decision:

> I let the children go to a special home because it was important for me to know that they receive a good upbringing and are in responsible

hands. This first developmental age is always the most important. I did not want them to experience a sudden change in their surroundings like what they had in Limoges. It was hard to let them go, and so I tried to make sure they are not lacking anything. I could have given them to a Swiss family, but it felt very uncertain for them to be with complete strangers, and apart from that they would most likely have been separated. It is enough that we are separated; my wish was for Marcel and Vera to feel that they belong together, that they are a small family. That's how it was. Before Marcel got used to the new environment, he did not leave Vera even for a little bit; she was his little mommy, which she promised me when saying goodbye. The headmistress of this orphanage told me many emotional scenes about their love. I hope you understand my decision and don't resent what I have done. After all, these children are everything to me now.... Even if my life is not always the easiest, I am happy the children are in good hands.[61]

The children were sent to Lili Volkart's house in Ascona, a home run in close cooperation with SHEK.[62] Apart from select photos from Ascona, we know little of the children's life there, and they were too little to remember much. Some information about Volkart helps reconstruct the environment in which they were placed, however. Volkart had not received any formal training in education or social work, but as her biographer Eveline Zeder notes, she had a "wild, defiant demeanor and a great sensitivity to any wrongdoings."[63] As a young woman, Volkart opened a hotel to help her parents financially. Already in the early 1930s, however, in the face of the wave of German and Jewish refugees, her hotel was transformed into a home for refugee children. At the beginning of the 1940s, she was taking care of around twenty children. By 1943 her children's home grew by two more houses to accommodate more. Volkart's children's home consisted of three buildings within a ten-minute walk from each other: Casa Bianca, a two-story bungalow with a greenhouse; Casa Cedro, which had a big playroom and was turned into a home for the youngest kids; and Casa Gentile, which had room for fifteen children. The majority of the children were German speakers. Altogether, she helped around 120 children during the war.[64]

Tonia visited her children in Ascona once:

> Driving through Zürich, I visited Margaret, who had an apartment there, taught gymnastics, and looked after Nani. This orphanage was intended for schoolchildren. Mine were tiny, so they got a special babysitter and their own small rooms. The head teacher was a great tutor, the author of several pedagogical books, and a very nice person. At the same time, Vera looked after Marcel extraordinarily. She was proud that she was playing with older children, but from time to time she ran to him and checked if he had dry pants. There was no mention of diapers, so she potty-trained him. She even got up at night. She thought that a peeing little brother brought shame on her family. He was a very nervous, problematic child. And she had to feel it. Her guardian tried unsuccessfully to explain that this was her [the guardian's] task. . . . My arrival disturbed their peace. Marcel recognized me immediately—he broke free from the guardian who came with them to the bus station to greet me.[65]

Her visit must have taken place when both she and Locher were preparing to move the children from Ascona to Locher's home. Interestingly, this recollection reminds us of Nani, the young girl whom Tonia took with her when she was forced to move to Saint-Léonard from Limoges in the spring of 1942, months before her escape to Switzerland. Locher got Nani from Limoges to Switzerland, where she was soon reunited with Tonia and her children. From the intense correspondence Locher engaged in with administrators of various levels soon after Tonia's arrival to Switzerland, we can reconstruct some of Locher's efforts to gain permission for Tonia and her children to move in with her and Nani.[66] In March 1943 she requested permission to have Tonia's children move in with her. In the letter she explained that instead of staying with the children for some time as she originally planned in Pregassona, near Ascona, she intended to move with them to Zürich, as her house there would be ready to accept the children sooner than she had expected.[67]

Margaret Locher, also known as Marguarite or Marga (as she preferred to be called), dominated Tonia's Switzerland story. She was most likely the one who convinced Tonia to travel to Switzerland in the first place. Hanna Eisfelder Grünwald, who ran the Limoges nursery, and Locher knew each other well. Margaret, had been a volunteer in Grünwald's prewar relief organization in Paris, the Medical Assistance for Children of Refugees (Assistance médicale aux enfants de réfugiés). The organization was later sponsored by SHEK, which took over the nursery from Grünwald before the house came under the OSE's direction.[68]

I wondered about the presence of some of these extraordinary women in Tonia's life—Grünwald, Locher, Volkart, and Hohermuth. The oldest was Grünwald (born in 1900). She worked in Germany, but already in the 1930s she had begun traveling to Zürich, where she must have met Locher, who was Swiss.[69] Most likely both women knew Volkart through SHEK. Grünwald, Locher, and Volkart insisted on remaining independent while maintaining links with organizations that coordinated similar services but on a much larger scale, such as OSE and SHEK. Tonia likely had only sporadic contact with Hohermuth, but her life and activity underlines the role female social workers played in saving children refugees, at least in the German-speaking world Tonia had already been a part of in Paris. Born in 1903 to a family of Quakers, Hohermuth attended the Zürich Women's Social School. Later she worked at the Quaker Center in Vienna (1939) and for the Social Assistance Service for Emigrants in Marseille (1940–41).[70] All four women combined social activism with a modern approach to raising children. The prewar period initiated a new way of thinking about social work as a mission that aimed at restoring an individual's sense of worth and not just offering passive help.[71] While wondering about their motivation to help, I imagine that the commitment of the women around her to the most vulnerable and their insistence on relative independence certainly must have affected how Tonia thought about service and how she began to reimagine communism.

A day after Marcel and Vera moved to Ascona, on November 20, 1942, Tonia was resettled to the civilian refugee camp in Les Avants. Some refugees of Les Avants recalled a beautiful hotel or, as described by Lore Silton, a survivor from Germany, "a lovely winter resort with fairly good accommodations."[72] Tonia, however, revealed some difficulties she encountered there:

> There were about three hundred of us now, probably one-third of us non-Jews. Lots of mothers with children, whose husbands were put in other camps. The army was in charge. We, women with small children, were to live in empty rooms. I was accommodated in a room with two French women. I was alone, but they both had

> small children.... There were military guards with rifles around the hotel. Once I went outside to hang diapers, and a soldier aimed at me—they were terrible to us! We had no milk for children, only coffee—because the army served coffee, not milk. So we gave these little, two-month-old babies coffee.... The soldiers were told that they would feed two hundred to three hundred people, and the food needed to be similar to what they have in the Swiss army.... We started to rebel, especially when it came to the babies. We wanted milk and porridge.... I used to go [to the kitchen], and if I came across a nice cook, I received a bottle of milk. But, generally speaking, I still can't believe the Swiss were such blockheads. It probably wasn't out of malice. They had just received orders to treat us like soldiers.[73]

Military discipline and Swiss soldiers with rifles ruled the camp; armed men had to accompany even a small group of women on their walks. Silton also noticed that guards changed every week to avoid fraternization with camp residents.[74] Tonia recalled problems with food supplies and Swiss guards' growing antisemitism, which led to a riot culminating in an inspection of the camp by a Jewish committee. Tonia was one of three people asked to talk to the committee as a ringleader. At the meeting she suggested organizing a kitchen to cook food for the children:

> I said I could prepare ten bottles of milk every day. It wasn't much! And cook vegetables for dinner. I knew how to do it—I had worked in an orphanage. Products were ordered in a nearby town. Every day, liver and vegetables were delivered to us. At the expense of this organization, I also ordered porridge.... Then the commandant changed. His place was taken over by a very nice elderly gentleman. He called me and suggested that we become friends. And he started bringing me Stendhal's books. He was very surprised that I did not know the book *Red and Black*. And I was afraid to say that instead of Stendhal I read reports on Trotskyist trials. This nice commander was soon dismissed. But until I left, I was very busy with this kitchen.[75]

Among the documents in the Swiss archives is a letter dated March 31, 1943, from the camp commandant (with a signature impossible to decipher) that vouches for Tonia's great work in the children's kitchen from November 1942, hence almost since the beginning of her stay there. The letter adds that she put her entire heart into this activity and was a role model for others in the camp.[76] Even if it does not corroborate her story that she conceived of the plan for the kitchen, it nevertheless confirms her engagement in that endeavor. Interestingly, Locher mentioned that as well when, on March 30, in a request to release Tonia from the camp to help run the children's home in Itschnach, she referred to Tonia's skills at organizing the children's kitchen to prove Tonia's worth as a woman needed in a children's home.[77]

Before Tonia left Les Avants, her situation improved significantly. In May 1943 she wrote a letter to Lichtheim about these changes:

> I do not know if I have already written to you, but I live alone in a small room, which is very important to me. After months of living with people, a person is happy to have a corner where one can be completely alone. This camp as a place of accommodation is perfect, and the area is beautiful. Life is acceptable. I am part of a friendly group of people; people are trying to understand each other, and in this way life in the camp takes on a completely different nature. Recently it was terrible, but you can understand it is because everyone was extremely nervous. Now you can see more smiling faces, as the anxiety is gone. This is largely influenced by the fact that we organize beautiful evenings that help us forget about our worries.[78]

She was beginning to cultivate a social life with a friendly group of people who were as vulnerable as she was. After months of uncertainty, this new life was slowly granting her the dignity of belonging to a community again.

Life in Les Avants was a significant shift for yet another reason. For the first time, she began commenting on antisemitism. Perhaps she started to recognize her own vulnerability as a Jew or for the first time her Jewishness and communism were not contradictions but rather intertwined elements of who she was. Although she no longer explicitly mentioned communism, the vignettes she provided—for example, her decision to defend a group of Jews in 1942 and to organize a kitchen for young children—are part of the same meaning-providing story she continually created, a story centered on responsibility and care for others, especially the most vulnerable. Her Jewishness and communism began to merge, even if the origins of her Jewishness were negative, being related to the sense of being prosecuted, and irrelevant to her in terms of its social and cultural dimension.

Move to Itschnach

On March 30, 1943, in a letter written in Italian to the police of the canton of Ticino, Locher requested residence permission for Tonia to stay in Pregassona, nearly forty kilometers from Ascona, and explained her future plans for Tonia and her children. Provided Tonia received permission to stay, the four of them would reside there for three months and then move together to Itschnach, where Locher intended to run a home for refugee children.[79] The level of bureaucracy they encountered in the process was quite convoluted. Locher's request had to be simultaneously sent to the police department in Bern and to the local police authority, the Dipartimento cantonale di polizia of Ticino.[80] Almost four weeks later, on April 27, 1943, Tonia received confirmation that the police department had granted her a permit to stay for three months in Pregassona. On the document someone added in pencil that since March 1943 refugees no longer needed temporary permits but could instead be interned without a limit. Tonia would be free to stay as long as Locher was willing to keep her.[81] But it was not until June 11, 1943, that Tonia was allowed to move to Pregassona. On July 13 they all moved to Itschnach.[82]

The correspondence Locher maintained with police stations in Bern, Zürich, and Lugano and also with SHEK to release Tonia from Les Avants and then change Tonia's status is in three languages—Italian, German, and French—depending on the part of Switzerland to which it was addressed. The documents carry stamps and signatures that are difficult to identify or at least organize according to the hierarchy of importance, but Bern, the capital of Switzerland, always had to agree on her move. Among the stamps, signatures, and names of various administrative levels, Tonia's voice is lost. Her last name is always misspelled, with two *n*'s at the end. What we witness are the efforts of Locher, who, while trying to bring Tonia home, engaged in a semianonymous battle with administrative powers.

On June 16, 1944, Tonia wrote one of her first letters from Switzerland to her parents, informing them about her release and reunion with her children. She asked for money to buy some clothes for Vera and Marcel. Interestingly, the letter is in German, as if she was still not completely free to write in the language of her choice, or perhaps after a long silence and growing dependency on German in daily life, it had become a more natural choice for her.[83] The letters gained some regularity: she wrote once or twice per month, generally informing her parents of her children's well-being, asking them for financial support, and describing the location of the house and views around them.

As before, she mentioned children's photos in her letters, and some of them are still in the family archive. The photos are similar to those from Limoges as they are likewise centered on the children. A beautiful sequence of photos features Vera climbing a short ladder leaning against a wall. Other photos depict children munching on corn, a girl in a tree, a boy swinging from a tree, children playing with water, and children returning from a trip. Naked, half naked, with bare feet, the children in these pictures are almost always in nature, playing, eating, or sleeping on the grass. Some feature them inside buildings focused on tasks at hand: building blocks, painting, or knitting.

No adults are featured in the images. Only in a few photos do we see traces that could remind us of their presence—a pair of feet leaned against a child's feet, for example. In two photos Locher reads a letter to the children. In one she is focused on the children, and in the other she looks straight into the camera with an awareness of the central role she plays in their lives—the calm but serious look of a woman trying to re-create a normal world for children deprived of that world. These photos are missing the wider context that is nevertheless hard to ignore. While the children in these photographs are at play, others were caught in various roundups or camps just outside of the Swiss borders and sent to die in Nazi camps.

Yet this was not the end of Tonia's encounters with the Swiss police. Soon after Tonia's arrival in Itschnach, she began going to a dentist. Her documentation includes a doctor's note informing any authorities who could have questioned her weekly or biweekly visits to Zürich that these visits were to last for about ten weeks.[84] On September 4, 1943, the police in Küsnacht, a town adjacent to Itschnach, demanded that Tonia offer an explanation of an event described in a report filed on September 1, 1943, from Zürich. In it, she admitted that on the night of August 31, she had stayed at the Hotel Krone in Zürich with a man named Simon Maringer, who was on leave from a work camp in Granges-Lens:

> On the occasion of his holiday at the beginning of this week, we arranged to meet in the city on Tuesday, August 31. We met in Zürich because I received permission from the police in Küsnacht to visit

a dentist twice a week there. In the evening I missed the train to Küsnacht. I know that after 10 p.m. there are still two trains going up the lake. But since I can't go walk around after 10 p.m., I had no choice but to stay at the hotel. Maringer rented a double bedroom. It is true that he registered in the hotel as Simon Maringer staying with his wife. The next morning, I left the hotel at 5:30 a.m. and took the train from Stadelhofen at 6:11 a.m. back to Küsnacht.[85]

The initial report compiled in Zürich on September 1 was based on an inspection at the Hotel Krone at 5:30 a.m., during which police found Maringer but not his wife. Maringer vaguely explained that she had already left, and his evasive answers appeared suspicious. The police soon realized that the woman he had stayed with was not his wife. Phone contact with the police station in Küsnacht helped establish that the woman was most likely Lechtman, the mother of two children and the wife of an interned man. The report concluded that a leave from camp "intended to satisfy sexual cravings with another married woman should not take place." After police provided Maringer with the contents of the ordinance on the control of foreign persons, he had to pay a fine.[86]

The situation was complicated. A document sent to Locher upon her request for more explanation notes that "Lechtman signed a statement on August 16 stating that she would stay between 10 p.m. and 7 a.m. in her accommodation. Tonia had permission to visit the dentist in Zürich but not to spend the night in Zürich. . . . We find it shocking that Mrs. Lechtman, as the mother of two small children, has gotten involved with a married refugee."[87] The documents quickly move from discussing the meeting of two refugees to describing a love affair, a morally deplorable act not only because it took place between two married people but also because it occurred during time allotted to refugees by a state administration for something else: leave from a work camp and a dentist visit.

Framing this contact as a love affair, the Swiss administration decided to punish Tonia by moving her to another camp.[88] On September 24, she received a letter requiring her to relocate by October 11, 1943, to a camp in Sonnenberg Kriens, located near Bern and around one hundred kilometers from Itschnach. A train ticket was included.[89]

Almost immediately after learning about Tonia's situation, Locher began writing pleas for her release. On October 10, 1943, even before Tonia's relocation, she wrote a long letter to the chief of police in Bern:

When I received a call from Dr. Bach announcing that Mrs. Lechtman had to go to a labor camp, I was extremely surprised and horrified. I responded that I did not know about the matter and that I was extremely sorry for her, but that I asked him not only to judge her by the external fact, because I know Mrs. Lechtman as a decent person and I had absolute trust in her. Mrs. Lechtman had police permission to go to Zürich because she was receiving dental treatment. I knew that afterward she met the young doctor from Les Avants camp, whom I know since he visited here with his wife and whose child I took into my home. I feel complicit in the fact that, on the telephone, I allowed Mrs. Lechtman to spend the night in Zürich only to come home on the earliest train the next day; because I knew that since she had left the camp she did not go to a cinema.

I fully understand that one has to be very strict with refugees, especially in moral terms. But just as there are few exceptional refugees, exceptions should also be made when assessing misconduct. . . .

Since July 1, besides an adopted child and the two children of Lechtman, I have taken in three other refugee children to my own house in Itschnach. These are particularly difficult children, whom the children's aid organization could not place in families or in large homes. I decided to do this only with the help of Mrs. Lechtman, as I knew that her warm, calm, quiet manner would greatly support my task. I am troubled by her departure because I cannot take anyone as a replacement and it is particularly difficult to find a skilled assistant these days.

I am convinced that you will get the impression that, despite her shortcomings, Mrs. Tonia is not an immoral woman and not a reckless girl but a valuable and reliable person.[90]

I wondered if I should share this information with Marcel and Vera. I decided to email Marcel and ask if the name Simon Maringer rang a bell. A couple of hours later, he sent me an image of two metal dog tags: one was engraved with Marcel's name and birthdate and the address of his home in 1944, which was Itschnach. The second one belonged to Georges Maringer, the son of Simon and his wife, Irene. Georges was born in France on December 1, 1941. Tonia met Irene and Simon in Les Avants, where they became friends. Simon had completed a PhD in psychology at the University of Zürich in 1936 and begun taking medical school courses in Brussels when the family was forced to flee in 1940, after the German invasion of France. They crossed the border into Switzerland in September 1942. After Tonia moved to Itschnach, the Maringers decided to place Georges at Locher's as well. Irene was sent to a women's camp until June 1944, when she spent two months working for Locher. Simon worked in various camps as a doctor and in May 1944 moved to Basel to complete his medical education. In September 1945 the rest of the family moved to Basel. Eventually they immigrated to the United States.[91]

Marcel did not know that his mother had been penalized for meeting with a friend. She never spoke about it and never discussed it with Dowgiałło. The one letter she sent during that time did not contain any alarming news: she simply informed her parents that the children were doing well and she was knitting all day long. Looking back at her letter from November, knowing that she was not with her children, her message about knitting is more telling.[92] We will never know—and do not need to know—what happened between Tonia and Simon, but her experience echoes a familiar story of blaming the most vulnerable for breaching the social contract that allowed them to enjoy the limited hospitality given to them. The terms and rules were clear, and for breaking them she met profound humiliation. That the police assumed the moral authority to condemn her and described the meeting in terms of a sexual affair is enraging, and perhaps even more infuriating is the fact that she was punished more harshly than Simon.

Tonia returned from the camp sometime in December. On December 11, she was asked to sign an explanation of the rules of conduct for those returning from camps, which once again delineated the norms of her behavior.[93]

Though she continued writing to her family, the tone of her letters began to change. Feelings of loneliness slowly began seeping into them:

> I am writing to you not to complain about my fate, because in comparison with many others I am doing great, but it is so hard for my heart today, and I think that you understand me! We live far from the city—it is great for the children—but for me it is like living in a remote area, and because of this I lose contact with friends, and you probably understand that in this situation you need friends more than ever.[94]

In addition, her relationship with Locher was becoming increasingly more tense. Apart from raving about Locher's extraordinary educational methods, Tonia was growing tired of Locher and her demands:

> You know that Locher is a vegetarian and that the children do not know what meat is at all. But they never ask and like all they eat. . . . Frau Locher is a strange person—she has many rules, which I don't necessarily agree with. She is very nice, but to be with her all day and live with her, one has to have nerves of steel. She is an old maid, so I don't think I have to tell you more.

She felt mistreated—not seen as a partner but as an assistant or "maid":

> Sometimes I am furious because I don't earn anything. I have to pay quite a lot; I have to buy everything to wear, and I am often treated like a maid. I swallow everything, say nothing and work because I want to have peace and do not want to show the children that I do not get along with Locher. They love her, and it would be a great disappointment for them. But sometimes I would like to get out of here. That is why I allow myself from time to time to go to Zürich and sit in a café and forget about everything. At the beginning of my stay in Switzerland and in France, Locher told me that we would work together—that we would take in migrant children and that we would be able to live together that way. The plan was good, but she often forgets that I am not her servant. . . . Yes, my loved ones, because she released me from the camp, I am dependent on her at every step.[95]

Her grudge against Locher grew stronger with time. Years later, she explained to Dowgiałło that Locher made her live extremely modestly: "No more than one egg a week. We had food stamps, but we didn't use them. To this day, Nani claims that Margaret was starving us. Locher actually thought that people eat too much and that it is not healthy. She measured bread with a tape measure and checked how much was gone."

Tonia cleaned, cooked, and worked in the garden:

> It was a two-story villa with six or seven rooms. And laundry. At that time, there were no washing machines. In addition, I had to collect fruit and vegetables in the garden every day, then quickly prepare

them because we only ate fresh food. It was work! Margaret only looked after the children. In principle, she did it well, but sometimes she would hit one. But she was a very interesting and good person. Maybe slightly fanatic, but . . . she wasn't mean. She thought she was saving me. Vera experienced a period of sharp revolt; she would lie on the floor and hysterically pound her legs. Margaret would lock her in for the whole day without food. But the children did not get sick. If one got a runny nose, they had to go on a diet—grated apple three times a day. So, they were afraid to get sick.[96]

Tonia experienced a mixture of emotions. On one hand, she was much safer than she had been in years, she had a place to live and a network of support, and her children were being raised in a peaceful environment. While reading her complaints about Locher, I wonder about how cognizant Tonia was of food scarcity during wartime and how fortunate she and her children were to have a safe place with even limited food. In some ways, she comes across as ungrateful.[97]

On the other, she felt humiliated and mistreated, a person with no rights who was simply expected to work. Tonia's complex and increasingly tense relationship with Locher points to those difficulties. Tonia wanted to be independent, but she still depended on Swiss authorities, and Locher, who despite her goodwill, represented those authorities as a person in a position of power. Her experience with Maringer showed this power dynamic clearly. It was Locher who was allowed to demand an explanation, it was Locher who had the right to interpret Tonia's behavior, and it was Locher's needs that were prioritized and led to Tonia's release from the camp.

Grief, worry, and hopelessness were accumulating within Tonia. Sioma rarely emerged in her letters during this time. She was clearly having difficulty writing about him, especially to his parents. "I wrote twice to Sioma's parents," she wrote to her parents in March 1944. "I cannot write about Sioma since I have not had any contact with him since August 3, 1942, and all my efforts are futile."[98] "Their letters annoyed me so much that I was not able to write. I do not feel like doing it, but I will."[99] Perhaps she had difficulty writing to them because she was unable to give them the answers they so desperately wanted about his whereabouts or perhaps they questioned her freedom and lack of contact with their son. Only occasionally did she mention that the children asked about him. "Vera said last night, 'Why doesn't a father of two children visit?' The children begin to consciously feel the lack of a father. How he would enjoy them!," she wrote in one letter. She missed him as well, as evidenced in the same letter: "I will never find a friend like Sioma. Will I still find him? Will he be the same friend after all he has experienced? These are questions that I ask myself every day and that often keep me awake at night."[100]

She was aware of the war, of course, but the letters do not reveal the extent of her knowledge. In February 1944 she wrote that she felt "sorry for leaving [France]" but that she "had to do it for the children. Maybe this terrible war will eventually end and my exile will end."[101] Her older brother, who was in Poland when war broke out, slowly disappeared from the letters. She occasionally mentioned her grandmother who was still in Łódź at the beginning of the war and who ceased being in touch. "I wrote to Grandma B. and Aunt Helcia two weeks ago. No answer," she wrote in August 1944.[102] She apparently did not know much about the terrible situation Jews were experiencing in Poland, nor was she aware that Sioma might have been deported to Poland. But the sense of loss and uncertainty must have been eating away at her. In February 1944 she wrote, "I have been very upset lately. I can't find peace, and I don't sleep at night. From time to time, I have days where I can't find peace and balance. Then I go to the children and play with them; it helps me forget everything." In the same letter, she wrote that she had hoped to be able to work soon in Poland with all returnees.[103] Clearly Poland, where she hoped to find Sioma and social work, similar to the aid she herself had received, was on her mind as a place that could help her define her future, perhaps making it less uncertain and untenable.

Working with the Unitarian Service Committee

In March 1944 Tonia was accepted to a program for social workers organized to prepare its graduates to engage in relief work in postwar Europe. She participated in the program in Zürich from May to October.[104] Tonia learned about this opportunity from leaflets that Locher, a social worker herself, kept receiving. Even though this idea was difficult for Locher to accept at first as it meant leaving Locher to take care of the small children alone, she eventually agreed. Tonia planned on spending weekday nights and weekends in Itschnach with her children.[105] Twelve refugees among a group of forty people (twenty foreigners and twenty Swiss citizens) were selected to attend the program.[106]

She shared with her family her enthusiasm for being able to engage in meaningful work:

> The program is wonderful. We are getting ready for the end of the war—Swiss and immigrants together. The atmosphere is wonderful. We have become very close over this time. . . . It will certainly not be an easy task we have undertaken, but we will take it up at the right moment with great enthusiasm. I have benefited a lot from this course. We have the best local docents. Representatives of international organizations come to us from all parts of Switzerland to familiarize us with their future plans.[107]

With a familiar enthusiasm, she immersed herself again in the world of activism. The forceful energy emanating from her letters is reminiscent of her commitment in Paris to communism and her trust in her communist community. This involvement allowed her the dignity of a person who could begin hoping for a meaningful future. "Sometimes I forget all the worries, and what's most important I forget that I am a refugee," she wrote. From the perspective of her new commitment, the world looked better. Even her relationship with Locher appeared less strained. "I feel that I am alive again," wrote Tonia.[108] She described her work to Dowgiałło:

> We had a big section devoted to hygiene and sociology. The program was the same as in a normal school. . . . In the middle of the course we had an internship. I was responsible for transporting children from France to Switzerland by train for vacation. There were three of us managing it—a married German couple and me. It was terrible because they told the children to get off, stand at attention, and count off at almost every station. In German, as in the camps—so that they did not get lost. . . . Awful. At one of the internships, I got a job in the office of an aid organization for children. I had to prepare an analysis of the children's social situation (statistics) based on social origins, age, gender. It turned out to be extremely laborious.[109]

One of the most important moments during the program was her contact with a group of Polish communists, or at least people oriented toward socialism. The details of how that interaction took place is scattered throughout her interrogation minutes. The questions her interrogators asked were general, Tonia's answers vague, and the people about whom she talked difficult to identify. She mentioned an Austrian communist, Emile Schwarz(e) (who perhaps went by the pseudonym Walter), whom she had met in Montauban and who had renewed contact with her when she was in Les Avants. She introduced him as someone who facilitated her connection with Polish communists in Switzerland. Eventually, he contacted the head of the social school she attended, who then facilitated Tonia's contact with a Polish refugee named Jan Lis.[110] Janusz Sokołowski, a Polish communist living in Switzerland, testified during his interrogations in 1949 that he met Tonia through his wife, who met her when she left their child in Itschnach.[111]

Lis, a doctor and refugee from France, Sokołowski, and Roman Przezwański, a doctoral candidate in philosophy at the University of Zürich, were among the most active Polish refugees in Switzerland. Lis and Przezwański arrived in Switzerland after the fall of France on June 22, 1940. Toward the end of 1943, Lis, Sokołowski, and Przezwański, among others, began issuing the propaganda-laden biweekly *Polska Ludowa* (People's Poland) with the goal of convincing readers that postwar Poland needed to undergo political and social changes.[112] The Democratic Alliance of Poles in Switzerland (Zjednoczenie Demokratyczne Polaków w Szwajcarii, ZDPS) distributed the periodical mostly among interned Poles.[113] The ZDPS supported the nucleus of the future KPP, which began forming in the Soviet Union in 1943 as the Union of the Polish Patriots (Związek Patriotów Polskich, ZPP), run by Wanda Wasilewska. In July 1944 the ZPP recognized the State National Council (Krajowa Rada Narodowa) as a communist-dominated Polish political representation.[114]

Lis and Przezwański helped Tonia get in touch with an American organization, the Unitarian Service Committee (USC), located in Geneva and run by Noel Field. Already in November 1944, Field began efforts to bring Tonia to Geneva: the correspondence between him and various police offices is intense. On November 29 the federal police for foreigners in Bern acknowledged that Tonia's participation in the training could lead to her working for the USC for free for the next six months.[115] On December 9 the Geneva police approved Tonia's work for the USC until the end of March 1945.[116] On December 21, 1944, Tonia once again signed a declaration to obey the rules. Every Wednesday she had to report to the police at 9 a.m. at 51 rue de Carouge.[117] On January 12, 1945, meeting place was changed from a private room to the Hôtel Beau-Séjour.[118]

This time, however, the hotel was not a place of reception for refugees but one of Field's projects: a vacation home where refugees could spend a few days.[119] On March 5 her permit was extended to May 31, 1945.[120]

Field became one of the most important people in Tonia's life for the next decade. Born in London and raised and educated in Switzerland, he was influenced by his American Quaker father. He was never a member of the Communist Party of the United States of America (CPUSA) but throughout World War II maintained the stance of a convinced communist. He was also a declared pacifist. After some work for the US Department of State, in 1937 Field and his wife, Herta, had gone to Europe in order for him to take a position in the secretariat of the League of Nations in Geneva. While in this position, he traveled to Spain where he observed International Brigades hospitals and bases. He also toured French internment camps, which is where he and his wife met Erica Glaser, a young woman who served as a nurse in Spanish hospital operating rooms along with her mother. In early 1939 the Fields helped Glaser escape Spain; later she became their foster daughter. Finally, in early 1941 Field was asked to join the USC's operations in Europe. Soon after his arrival, Field became the head of the USC in Marseille, which meant being the USC's director for all of Vichy France. He worked as a courier between Marseille and Switzerland, provided medical support, organized illegal border crossings, and secured secret accommodations for fleeing refugees.[121]

The USC was created by senior Unitarians who had witnessed the Nazi takeover of Czechoslovakia. Lisbon, the only port open for the departure of refugees due to the German takeover of France, became the USC's strategic point. The new organization's priority was to help refugees immigrate to the United States as well as provide medical care and distribute medicine, mainly for those interned in the camps of southern France. But the USC was created in an atmosphere of a growing awareness of the enormous and increasing needs in Europe. While the organizations mentioned throughout this chapter such as the USC, the Red Cross, the OSE, and the SHEK were focused on the immediate needs of refugees and people confined in internment camps, the USC also began thinking about postwar needs. The scope of the tragedies tearing Europe apart, leading to the massive number of refugees and people confined in internment camps, contributed to a new model of humanitarianism based on transnational collaborative networks "that made it possible to increase the scale of the projects undertaken."[122]

Field saw the USC as a front for a sort of "Red Aid," a procommunist organization. Through his work he defined refugees to include communists because they, in his opinion, "were getting no help from any other charitable organizations."[123] There are no records of how Field and Tonia met. Hence, it is impossible to say if Tonia's past as a communist or the unknown whereabouts of her husband, a former member of the International Brigades, helped build affinity with Field. In February 1945 Field was still very much concerned about the fate of the Spanish refugees, as his reports to the USC headquarters testify.[124] Their Spanish Civil War experiences most likely led to a strong connection between Tonia and Field, but his thinking about the future potential help that USC could offer also directly spoke to her needs. As she testified in October 1949, Lis and Przewański negotiated with Field the scale of help the USC could offer Poland after the war.[125] But when they met Tonia, they must have realized that she was best suited not only to continue that conversation with Field but also to engage in that work after the war. Tonia made the transition from her training as a social worker to her work for Field almost seamlessly:

> After finishing the course, I was offered a job in an American aid organization. Its name was the Unitarian Service Committee. This is a Protestant group that operated only in Massachusetts and New York. They are very nonreligious and liberal. They believe that Christ was not a god but a prophet. For half a year I organized on their behalf a medical team that took part in the repatriation of Poles from Germany and France. The manager who took me to the course asked me to write an indicating my motivation. I wrote that I want to get a job and to return to Poland, which is my homeland. And the manager of the Unitarian Service wanted to open branches in Poland as well as in other countries of this part of Europe—in Czechoslovakia and Hungary. They asked if I would like to take over this Polish department. I agreed. I did not return to Margaret. I went to Geneva and only occasionally visited my children.[126]

The promise of returning to Poland on a meaningful mission spoke the loudest to her. It is unclear when exactly she decided to return, but given this opportunity she most likely began thinking about it in the fall of 1944. It is also unclear what she knew about the new Poland emerging from the war, but her contact with Polish communists in Switzerland certainly gave her some insight into the country's political development.

Most of the information about their preparations for their work in the postwar world comes from Tonia's interrogations. Field began a policy of "Aid to National Groups," "whereby he dealt with a trusted representative of each Communist group, and supplied them with monthly funds in proportion to their numerical strength." As historian Tony Sharp claims, to do that Field engaged in a complex system of double bookkeeping to avoid alarming his headquarters in the United States about how he was spending money.[127] Some of Tonia's interrogation minutes confirm this fact. She revealed that to receive some money for the Polish organization, most likely ZDPS, she was told to apply for money with fictitious names and addresses.[128] From her interrogation, we learn bits and pieces of her activity—mostly building contacts with various institutions and Polish doctors and nurses who expected to return to Poland to help the country rise from the ruins left by the war.[129]

This must have been a busy time for Tonia. Beginning in 1945 she lived in Geneva, separated from her children, Locher, and perhaps also former worries about the future. Instead of waiting, she was working, preparing herself for the end of the war. She suspended writing letters to her parents. On May 25 1945, the ZDPS confirmed that due to the end of the war in Europe, Tonia was designated as an assistant to the USC medical mission. It was an official sign that the group of doctors, nurses, and social workers was getting ready to leave Switzerland and slowly began transitioning to Poland.

Back to France

In June 1945 Tonia left Switzerland for France. The war there had ended, and the USC, after some negotiations with Stefan Jędrychowski, Warsaw's delegate to France, decided to travel to internment camps in France to bring medical aid to those planning to return to Poland. After visiting camps in France and Switzerland, the small group of USC employees intended to return to Poland to continue their mission.[130] The group that left Switzerland for France consisted exclusively of Poles: at least six Polish refugees along with men from the Second Rifle Division, part of the re-created Polish Army in France, which in June 1940 had crossed into Switzerland. The group consisted of doctors, nurses, hospital orderlies, drivers, and two social workers (including Tonia).[131]

In her first letter to her parents, after many months of silence, Tonia explained in November 1945 the goal of the mission. She wrote from Épernay, a city over one hundred kilometers east of Paris where one of the camps with confined Poles was located. The group went to Paris to purchase necessary material and talk to the Polish Red Cross. It continued by driving between various camps and health services to help detainees return to Poland. She did not discuss who the returnees were or how her group determined their desire to repatriate.[132] Driving around camps located near the border with the Netherlands, the USC was in charge of deciding who was healthy enough to be able to return. It tried to send chronically ill people to French sanatoriums and healthy ones to Poland. Tonia filled out repatriation forms while doctors examined patients. "We tried to treat them right away. We got medicines for this from the French authorities. We had a truck and a passenger car from America."[133] On November 2, 1945, the first transport from Épernay left for Poland.[134] Her plans clearly signaled her desire to work with the Polish population, perhaps because Field's initiative offered her that option or because she saw this as a continuation of her commitment to communism and building a communist regime in Poland. However, some silences in her letters are striking. She worked in displaced persons (DP) camps in Germany during the peak of the Jewish refugee crisis, yet nowhere did she mention the Polish Jews who arrived at the DP camps, whom she mostly likely encountered. Neither did she mention being active in Jewish DP camps.

The only problems or concerns she had regarding this job she revealed later in her conversation with Dowgiałło. Her concerns were related to the nature of the job rather than the choices they made. "The work in Paris was chaotic. The situation was complicated by the fact that the United Nations Relief and Rehabilitation Aid [UNRRA] did not want to accept either the Polish embassy or postwar Poland."[135] She was unaware, or at least never expressed an awareness, of the conflict between the Polish government-in-exile and the representatives of the communist government being established in Poland. Also, even the issue of how to define a deported Pole was questionable: for Paris, it was those who were forcibly deported by Germans, and for Poland it included anyone who left Poland after September 1, 1939.[136] None of these doubts or questions entered her correspondence or conversations with Dowgiałło.

Around 470,000 Poles were in France at the end of the war. At first it was only the Polish Red Cross and representatives of the Polish government-in-exile who were allowed to visit the camps. With time, however, representatives of the new Warsaw authorities also gained permission.[137] Historian Aneta Nisiobęcka does not mention the USC as one of the groups involved in the process and did not come across it in her sources.[138] Tonia's occasional letters, however, show that the USC worked with the Polish Red Cross and Jędrychowski; it collaborated with the Polish government that was slowly establishing itself in postwar Poland.[139] As Nisiobęcka explains, since the Polish government-in-exile had permission to meet with Poles confined in camps, messages against returning to the new communist Poland were being spread. Perhaps, then, it was a strategic decision to invite the USC and the communists from Switzerland to counteract these efforts.[140]

In a letter to Margaret Locher in October 1945, Tonia returned to the language of her earlier engagement, when she wrote about communism during her first days in Paris in 1937 and after Sioma left. Engaging in meaningful work resulted in renewed excitement:

> Dear Margaret, thank you very much for the letters. They give me greatest pleasure. There is a lot of work here on the Belgian border. Thousands of our compatriots are going home, and we have to prepare all the transports.... Of course, we get different commands ten times a day. This doubles the work and turns all of our plans upside down. But despite it, this work is beautiful. Experiencing the return of thousands of families to their homeland is a real pleasure. People are traveling in very bad conditions: in cattle cars with little hay, with small children. Pregnant women are at risk of hunger.... I'm so glad I chose this job, even if sometimes I don't think I can stand it. We live here in very difficult conditions. The hygiene situation is of course the worst. There is no possibility of washing. We sleep only two to three hours. Despite this, I feel better here than in Switzerland. We are happy here doing really useful work.[141]

As she did before, Tonia shared her enthusiasm and readiness to work with the people closest to her, Locher and her parents. The contexts in which she wrote to her parents make her words appear as less of an attempt to calm her parents and more of a healing for herself, a return to her sense of self-worth and self-value. Her past and her present were finally merging in a vision of the future that held a place for her and her children:

> I do not lack anything, I am very happy that I am earning my living, and I will be very happy, when, in the near future, I will be able to support my children and will always be with them. . . . We work on repatriation, bringing help and consolation to people who after so many years of misery, torment, and suffering are returning in terrible transport conditions to rebuild Democratic Poland, something I have fought for my whole life and that I want to continue as long as my humble strength allows me. We now have all the possibilities, and the biggest sin would be if one of us was missing at this work. I will be there, and my children will be there as well!!![142]

The isolation from her children was a problem. "It is awful that I am so far away from them," she wrote to Locher. "Their most beautiful years are passing by, and I cannot enjoy them. I sometimes wonder why the world demands such impossible things from us mothers." She was missing the most important years of their lives but also felt that her activism was part of her motherly mission. "The world is so barbarian, we need to make it better," she wrote in the same letter where she complained about her separation from her children.[143]

Based on her letters, the beginning of 1946 was busy for Tonia. In early January she was in Paris, only to soon travel to the UNRRA headquarters in Arolsen, Germany, for a conference devoted to deportees.[144] She returned briefly to Itschnach in February but already at the beginning of March was in Paris at another conference.[145] From France she and a group of USC doctors, nurses, and social workers traveled over 350 kilometers northeast to Wermelskirchen, Germany, to a hospital where they also worked with Poles willing to be repatriated.[146] In her conversation with Dowgiałło, she commented on requisitioning a car from a German doctor and on her living conditions in Germany:

> We transported the BMW illegally thanks to our very militant American, who also obtained permission to transport medicines and other things. For example, UNRRA had a lot of warm children's clothes. And lots of stockings. Each of us got equipment—a sleeping bag, backpack, and a windbreaker for frost. We slept in military style. We

often lived in terrible conditions, which we were completely not used to. When we were traveling around the camps, we usually claimed a corner for me, an office for them, and a place to sleep. In total, we spent a year and a half together—day and night.[147]

She treated her stay in Germany as a prelude to her departure for Poland. While in Germany, the group was visited by Field who gave Tonia instructions to contact the Polish government and the representatives of UNRRA and the USC in Warsaw to establish which hospital the USC should help equip. Field's preferences were a hospital located in a working-class environment. The USC's US headquarters sent an American, Dorothea Jones, to accompany Tonia and her group of nurses and doctors to Poland. Jones's presence was supposed to increase the group's prestige and power of persuasion.

In mid-1946 Tonia traveled to Berlin to the Polish embassy to receive permission to travel to Poland. While she was taking care of the formalities that would allow her to return to Poland, she began preparing her family to accept her decision. In a letter dated December 1944, she informed her parents of her plan to leave for Poland and bring her children as soon as possible:

> When it comes to your attitude toward Poland and Poles, I am sure if you were here or in Poland you would definitely change them. Naturally antisemitism exists in Poland, and unsurprisingly the many years of Sanacja rule [and] the German occupation has further intensified it.[148] Poland is now in the process of building a new life in every respect, a true democracy that will also solve the Jewish problem. It is only a matter of time. Today the eyes of all democrats, all antifascists are turned to Poland. Poland has started great work and is working on it with enthusiasm and generosity. Just standing in the middle of this work, being in constant contact with today's Polish authorities, I can assure you that the Jewish question is at its heart and antisemitism is radically condemned everywhere. It hurts if you do not distinguish Polish traitors from the whole nation. The Polish nation did not cooperate with Germany—it gave the most beautiful, heroic evidence for this. The partisan struggle of the Polish nation will go down in the history of all peoples fighting for their freedom.[149]

|||

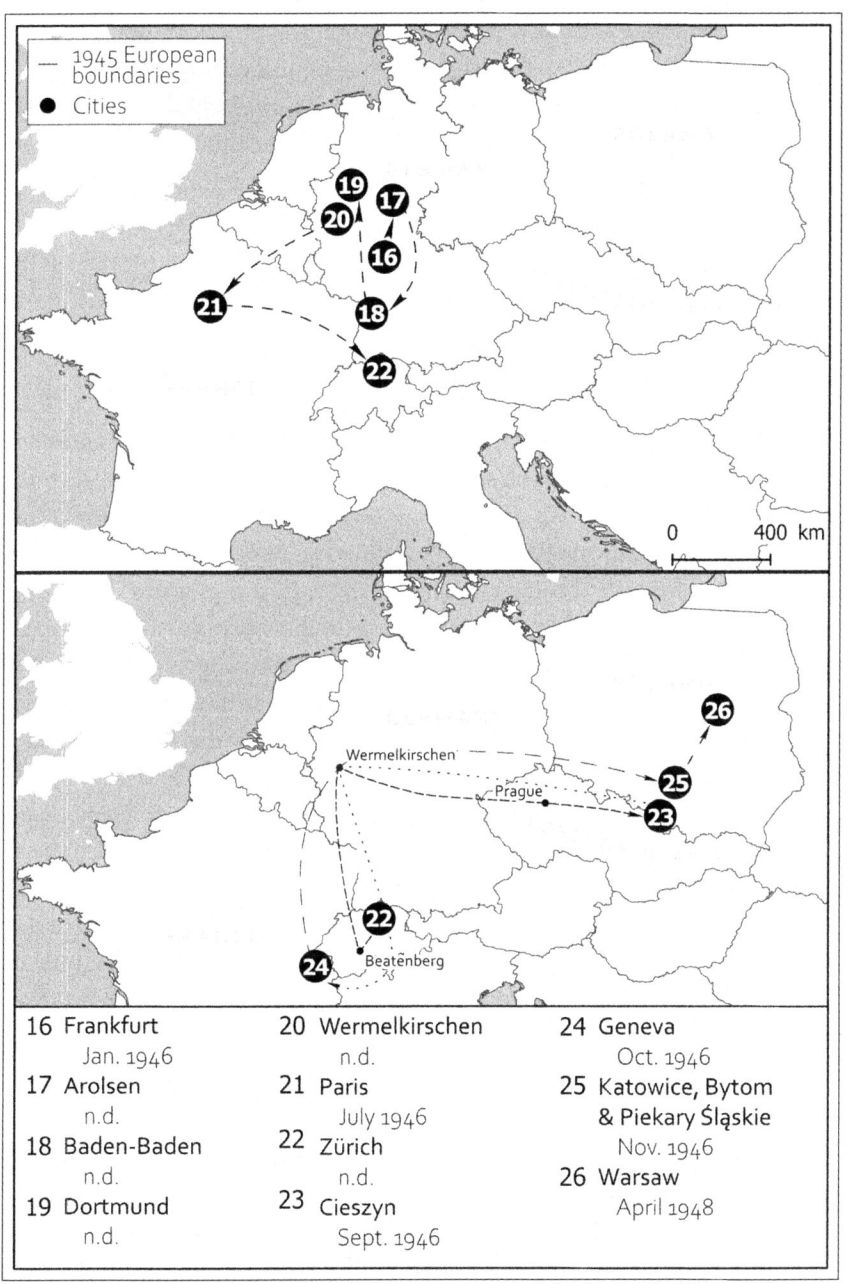

MAP 5.3. Tonia's travels in Germany and Poland, 1946–48. *(Map by Kaitlyn Tatro)*

The years of the war and the first months of the new postwar world were intense. A lot had changed in Tonia's life, and much had changed in her thinking about herself. She transformed from a migrant still partially in charge of her own decisions to a refugee dependent on the will of a state that had power over her. Her refugee position showed her the precarity of her own place and pushed her to search for ways to restore her dignity and think about the future. The documents and letters she left behind and the ones produced about her not only show that her communism remained on her moral and intellectual horizon but also that her Jewishness was entering more often into her thinking of who she was and what roles she wanted to fulfill.

Her Jewishness emerges increasingly as linked to her vulnerability. This began in France and grew in the Swiss internment camps. It perhaps pushed her to action and reinforced her communism as a commitment to a protection of the more vulnerable. It is of course unclear how much she thought of or even discussed communism in these years, but the human precarity, perhaps even vulnerability, that brought her in the 1930s to communism must have been with her all these years. The concerns of the women she met in France and Switzerland, as well as those of Noel Field and the people involved in his projects, stemmed from the same deeply humanitarian perspective of reacting to the wrongdoing they were observing. We will never know if communism, humanitarianism, or even the religious underpinnings of some of the actions she observed were ever the topics of conversations among them. Daily practices in these circumstances spoke more than words, and it was mostly these practices—practices that counterbalanced the multiple humiliations she experienced daily—that fed her involvement in communism. But her Jewishness over and over again appears as a vulnerability, not an identity, that linked her social and cultural upbringing. Her early years back in Poland—as the next chapter discusses—also reveal a lot about her progressive understanding of Polishness and the way she combined it with Jewishness and communism.

6 ||| The Return

Building Communism in Poland, 1945–1954

THE PEOPLE who came together during the filming of *Tonia i jej dzieci*—Marcel Lechtman, Vera Lechtman, and Marcel Łoziński—were friends. The two Marcels, still best friends, have a lot in common: both were born in France, spent some time in children's homes, grew up in households permeated with communism, and had mothers engaged in activism for the betterment of the world. Łoziński's mother, Eugenia, similarly to Tonia, believed that communism could guarantee a better future for her children, even if it required the suspension of her maternal role. Tonia and Eugenia met in 1945 in Paris, where Eugenia was helping to organize the Polish embassy. A member of the French Communist Party, she had lived in France since 1927. She joined the Polish Workers' Party as soon as it was created in France in January 1946.[1]

A family anecdote connects their lives. According to family lore, Tonia was arrested soon after her arrival in France in 1945 with a team of doctors from the USC. She did not have any documents confirming her nationality and asked to contact the Polish embassy. Eugenia Łozińska visited her in prison and provided her with a Polish passport that got her released.[2] Their contacts continued in the late 1950s, when they became neighbors in lower Mokotów in Warsaw. As teenagers, the two Marcels quickly developed a deep friendship.[3] In the movie, the three friends sit at a table trying to understand their own lives and the choices their mothers made.[4] Why would they temporarily suspend their maternal obligations? Was communism more important than their own children? Their conversation is calm, but Marcel Lechtman momentarily gets agitated. With a merciless camera in front of him, he is having to face questions that have plagued him for some time.

In the movie, Vera reveals how much Tonia's communism informed her motherhood. Vera recalls the lyrics of a lullaby her mother sang to her, one that Tonia learned while she was a teenager in Łódź: "Lay your head on my knees, clasp your hands, squeeze your eyes shut. The working-class child sleeps and dreams about black bread."[5] After reciting a few lines, Vera begins to sing: "There is no bread, but one has to live, a worker's tough fate. Bells ring, sad tones, somewhere you can hear the voice of a man in handcuffs."[6] The lullaby's darkness speaks to Tonia's experiences from the war: poverty, hunger, and the chaos of struggling to survive daily. But there is also hope through persistence—one has to live, as the song goes on.

Sioma

On December 21, 1945, Tonia shared with her parents the news of what happened to her husband, Sioma. Toward the end of a long letter, she began: "I was unable to write to you about this—please understand, the pain was too fresh." She explained that from Drancy, France, Sioma was transferred to a camp near the Polish town of Oświęcim (Auschwitz). He worked in a women's camp in Birkenau (also called Auschwitz II) and later in the main Auschwitz camp. Through his office work, he helped many imprisoned women. Tonia shared that she had met some women in France who informed her that Sioma had erased their names from the lists of people condemned to death. In January 1945, when the camp evacuation began, he planned to meet the incoming Soviet Army but was killed by guards during the death march on January 19. "I don't need to tell you how I received this news. I couldn't pull myself together for a long time." She ended the letter, "Isn't it terrible and cruel to survive so many years in this hell and die just before victory? Fate is merciless!"[7]

Tonia learned about Sioma's death from Auschwitz survivors in France, but there are no other details regarding his final moments. The packet of information Marcel received sometime after 2010 from the International Tracing Service at Arolsen Archives, the largest archive of victims and survivors of the Nazi regime, includes extensive documentation of his father's time in the camp. Teresa Wontor-Cichy, a researcher from the Memorial and Museum Auschwitz-Birkenau, however, contextualized the facts, helping me reconstruct his story. Spending hours on the phone with me in the midst of the COVID-19 pandemic when visits to the archives were impossible, she patiently walked me through the documents. Wontor-Cichy's contextual knowledge expanded the limited horizon the documents offered while depicting a vivid, even if deeply depressing, image of Sioma's possible experiences in the camp: his whereabouts, living conditions, and even mind-set. She emphasized the importance of responsible interpretations based on a delicate balance between official documents and the personal knowledge families have about their loved ones' experiences.[8]

Sioma departed for Auschwitz from Drancy with a convoy of what Vichy French authorities termed "undesirable strangers" on August 8, 1942.[9] Upon arrival in Auschwitz six days later, the prisoners immediately faced selection: those deemed unable to work were selected for the gas chambers, while those deemed able to work were spared immediate death. After the selection of Sioma's convoy, 233 men and 62 women were sent to work, while 712 people were killed. Sioma survived the first selection.[10] He had arrived in Auschwitz at a time when the majority of Jews were sent to Birkenau, which since March 1942 served as a concentration camp for different categories of prisoners and a center for Jewish extermination.

A Polish prisoner in Auschwitz who worked at the new arrivals registration, Edwin Bartel, recalled that on average across all the camps, the number of those selected to work was not more than 15 to 20 percent of an incoming group.[11] Jews were spared from immediate death only to be exploited for their labor. Death remained the future prospect as the prisoners lacked proper clothing, medical care, nutritious food, and decent housing. Awaiting them in the camps were hunger, merciless weather, physically grueling work, exhausting roll calls, severe punishment, and daily violence and beatings.[12]

After his arrival as a new prisoner, Sioma's *Personalbogen* was registered.[13] It is a rare document: all prisoners who left testimonies at the Memorial and Museum Auschwitz-Birkenau remember being registered, yet only a relatively small number of these documents have survived. Sioma was registered as a construction worker. He was listed as a married, stateless Jew born in Russia, with two children. Interestingly, he reported no criminal record or membership in any political organization. He arrived in Auschwitz as "a Jew of Mosaic faith" and not a communist. At the bottom of the document is Sioma's signature with his characteristic dense handwriting. The top of the form noted in red ink that he was a *Facharbeiter*—a skilled worker. The information he provided upon his arrival may tell us something about his mind-set.¹⁴ Perhaps he knew the camp was in the construction phase and hence workers were in high demand. He was young and strong, which could have saved him from immediate death. It is unclear whether he had a chance to avoid admitting being a Jew, but he could silence his communist convictions more easily.

Hermann Langbein, an Auschwitz survivor and a man Marcel perceives as his father's friend from the camp, published a short memoir in 1949 in which he mentioned Sioma. According to Langbein, Sioma was sent to Jawischowitz, one of the subcamps of the Auschwitz-Birkenau complex, where prisoners worked in the Brzeszcze coal mine, situated in two towns, Brzeszcze and Jawiszowice. Prisoners worked in twelve-hour shifts in underground tunnels that were so low they had to work on their knees, leading to phlegmon, an acute inflammation of the knees.¹⁵ Langbein reported that he managed to get Sioma from Jawischowitz to the main camp thanks to a favor that one of the SS orderlies owed him. When this orderly first learned that Sioma was a Jew, he refused. But eventually he agreed to bring Sioma to Auschwitz.¹⁶ Langbein suggested the existence of a network of mutual dependencies that provided some people with space to engage in the process of saving prisoners. He managed to move Sioma from the coal mine to the main camp in Auschwitz, where, as we learn from camp documentation, on December 16, 1942, he was admitted to the block on internal diseases at a prison hospital and released on December 21.¹⁷

The nucleus of the camp hospitals operating in Auschwitz was organized in the second half of June 1940, a few days after the first transport of Polish political prisoners was brought there. The first patients underwent an initial quarantine period and were beaten during forced heavy physical exercise, leaving them exhausted. Due to the inflow of more prisoners to the camp and a steady increase in the number of patients, the hospital system was systematically expanded. A hospital for convalescent prisoners was organized in Block 19, while Block 20 was for prisoners with infectious diseases, Block 21 was a surgical block, and Block 28 was for internal diseases.¹⁸ Władysław Fejkiel, a prisoner from the infirmary in Block 28, where Sioma was hospitalized, states that there were few patients with internal diseases "in the strict sense, because if someone suffered from, e.g., circulatory insufficiency, they were usually killed at work or died in the block, while other internal diseases that did not produce a high fever were not considered diseases by an SS doctor. Mostly in this ward there were patients lying exhausted from hunger, diarrhea, and swelling."[19]

Wondering about Sioma's illness, Wontor-Cichy speculates that he suffered from either diarrhea, a symptom of starvation caused by a lack of protein and nutrients; typhus, which most prisoners experienced; or erysipelas, a bacterial infection common in people with a compromised immune system.[20]

It was difficult to get admitted to the camp hospital. Many prisoners tried to force their way into the block. In the prevailing throng, supervising prisoners tried to bring order while beating back the sick crowd.[21] Being admitted, however, did not mean receiving appropriate treatment. Fejkiel recalls:

> Those who could move alone, dozens of times a day, crawled out of their lair and dropped to their knees in order to reach buckets that were placed between the beds. They were made of old metal cans for German marmalade.... As the disease developed, ... they were given the privilege of lying on the ground floor. Those on the lower beds did not have to get up and sit on the chipped toilet. They were allowed to do it under themselves. Of course, no one picked them up or cleaned them. The privilege of lying on the ground floor was a preparation for the last stage. This stage was a ride to the chimney.[22]

Already in the second half of 1941, SS doctors began selecting Auschwitz prisoners by putting to death those they regarded as unfit for labor.[23] SS doctors killed very sick patients by injecting phenol into their hearts or conducted medical—often lethal—experiments on them.[24] According to Franciszek Piper, one of the first historians of the camp, in 1942 along with an increased emphasis on treating prison inmates as slave laborers and the possibility of employing prisoners as doctors, camp hospitals began providing prisoners with some aid. Doctors had limited access to medicine, yet in camp hospitals exhausted prisoners had a chance to avoid slave work and long and exhausting roll calls.[25]

Sioma's six-day stay in Block 28 in December 1942 was not his last camp hospital experience. He either did not completely recover or fell sick again. On April 24, 1943, he was admitted to the surgical block (Block 21).[26] Sioma most likely had a lump in his left armpit and was operated on by Władysław Dering, a Polish prisoner-doctor and surgeon-obstetrician. Dering, a military man who had been promoted to captain two days before the outbreak of

World War II, supported National Democracy, a political party and a movement with followers situated firmly on the right, among the antisemites. In July 1940 Dering was arrested and sent to Auschwitz, where he became involved in resistance cells organized by Witold Pilecki. In the fall of the same year, he became one of the camp doctors in Block 21.[27]

Opinions about Dering are mixed. Some see him as a person who saved many lives, while others accuse him of murderous activity. In his blog, Auschwitz historian Adam Cyra quotes Władysław Bartoszewski's opinion about Dering: "He faced terrible dilemmas every day. Whom to save? The one who suffers or the one who has a chance of survival?"[28] In 1962 in England, Dering brought forward a lawsuit against Leon Uris, an American Jew who in his book *Exodus* depicted Dering as a doctor who participated in pseudomedical experiments by removing internal and external organs. The documentation of registered surgeries, including the one conducted on Sioma, was used as evidence. Dering won the suit by arguing that the organs he removed had been burned during criminal X-ray irradiation carried out by the SS doctors involved in the experiments, Carl Clauberg and Horst Shumann. The surgeries he performed were necessary to save the lives of the patients of Nazi medicine.[29]

Sioma was released from Block 21 in April or early May 1943. Langbein said that he looked weak and that additional portions of food were organized for him. "We're trying to find a good place for him. It's not so easy to find one for a Jew. Finally, Rudl took him in to the auto shop."[30] Rudl was Rudolf Friemel, and his auto shop was in the camp.[31]

Friemel's employees convinced SS men to smuggle prisoners out of the camp in a truck taking dirty laundry to Bielsko.[32] In a collection of illegal letters exchanged between Józef Cyrankiewicz of the Polish resistance movement in Auschwitz and the resistance cell outside of the camp, there is mention of a resistance group of Austrian communists who were involved in the Spanish Civil War, which included Friemel and Langbein, confirming Friemel's engagement with the resistance.[33] Before the war, Cyrankiewicz was an important member of the Polish Socialist Party, and after being deported to Auschwitz on September 4, 1942, he became one of the leaders of resistance cells. According to Langbein, Austrian communists started negotiations with the Poles and in May 1943 formed the Auschwitz Combat Group, an international resistance group under Cyrankiewicz and Langbein, among others.[34] Sioma is missing from the names of the men who participated in this group, but as Langbein states he was involved in the resistance as well.³⁵ It is thus possible that from April 1943 until May 1944, Sioma was in Auschwitz working at the auto shop and having some contact with the Polish resistance movement and possibly Cyrankiewicz. Vera believes that once in Auschwitz, her father decided to learn Polish, Tonia's first language, supposedly from Cyrankiewicz. This is most likely just family lore but suggests that while in Auschwitz, Sioma had contact with the Polish resistance. If Sioma met Cyrankiewicz, it must have been between April and November 1943 when Cyrankiewicz worked in the *Arbeitseinsatz,* and his *Kommando* was responsible for recording employed prisoners.³⁶

At some point during his imprisonment, Sioma was moved from Auschwitz's main camp to the *Desinfektion Kommando* (disinfection unit) in Birkenau. This Kommando had existed since the camp's opening as the unit in charge of disinfecting prisoner blocks to prevent the spread of diseases. While working there, Sioma helped to deliver illegal medicine to Birkenau from Auschwitz.³⁷ In May 1944 he began working for a Kommando unit in the BIIe sector of Birkenau, as confirmed by the twelve records of him receiving payment (two marks) for work he performed from May 29 to August 23, 1944, in Birkenau. The Kommando was led by a Pole, Józef Domaniecki, and consisted almost completely of Poles and Sioma, the only non-Polish speaker and the only Jew, which Wontor-Cichy thinks may indicate that Domaniecki was trying to protect Sioma as the only Jew in this Kommando.³⁸

The BIIe sector of Birkenau housed a Sinti and Roma family camp (*Zigeunerfamilienlager*), where families were held together instead of separately, as was typical in Auschwitz.³⁹ The camp existed for seventeen months from February 1943 until August 1944. On the south side it bordered a ramp, where since May 1944, SS men organized selections among deported Jews.⁴⁰ Sioma arrived in the Sinti and Roma family camp toward its end, when Kommandos were sent to prepare it for closing. He was most likely there on August 2, 1944, when the camp's liquidation began, and witnessed one of the most horrible moments in Birkenau's history. First, around two o'clock on the afternoon of August 2, trucks loaded with Roma and Sinti arrived at the camp in Birkenau. They included people who had been originally taken to the Third Reich to work. The Roma and Sinti remaining in the camp (who would soon be killed) were allowed to say goodbye to those, including loved ones, in the trucks. Later that night, after the night roll call, the remaining Roma and Sinti—over three thousand people—were driven to the gas chambers. "SS men were . . . throwing the Gypsies out of the barracks. The whiz of whips was heard, multilingual curses, crying, screaming. A revolver shot from time to time. The defenseless Gypsies resisted, fled between the blocks, hid in the barracks. . . . There were no young people among them as they had been previously transported to other camps. Most were vulnerable women, children, and the sick," recollected Józef Piwko, a Polish prisoner who witnessed the atrocity.[41]

Sioma was at BIIe when, after the Roma and Sinti camp liquidation, Jewish women from the liquidated Łódź ghetto were brought in.[42] Perhaps his continued work on the site, first as an aide and then as a warehouseman, gained him the gratitude of the women whom Tonia had heard from in Paris and then mentioned in a letter to her family.[43] Working in warehouses with clothing or food gave him some leeway to help—for example, by delivering bread and perhaps medicine and clothing to fellow prisoners. These basic items were sometimes able to prolong or even guarantee survival.

In a conversation with Dowgiałło, Tonia mentioned that at some point in Birkenau, Sioma and his friend Dawid Szmulewski worked as electricians. "They walked on roofs and photographed active gas chambers. It was Dawid's task, and my husband helped him . . . and they took these huge photos that are now hanging in Auschwitz."[44] There are indeed four large photos on display in Birkenau, although we do not know if these are the photographs referenced by Tonia. Taken by prisoners from inside of the crematorium, they document terrifying moments in the camp's history.[45]

During the summer of 1944 masses of Hungarian Jews were being sent to Birkenau—forty-two thousand from May 14 to July 9 alone.[46] The existing execution system turned out to be inefficient for murdering so many people, leading to the decision to burn corpses outside of the crematoriums.[47] "Behind the building of crematorium V, whose furnaces could not keep up with burning bodies, the Germans dug five combustion pits, each twelve meters long, six meters wide and 1.5 meters deep. Over one thousand corpses would be laid out, covered with oil, methanol, or human fat, and set on fire. Thus, the terrible spectacle began."[48] A Kommando of camp prisoners, the *Sonderkommando,* was responsible for the burning. These special units organized the people selected for death, led them to the gas chambers, moved the bodies to be burned, removed the ashes and remains of the bodies from the crematoriums, and finally crushed the remaining bits of bones and disposed of them. The first Sonderkommando was created on July 4, 1942. Later there were twelve more. Each worked for just a couple of months and was initiated by burning the preceding team's corpses.[49]

"Snatch a picture from this hell" (*Wyrwać obraz temu pieklu*) is how French philosopher and art historian Georges Didi-Huberman characterized a plan organized by camp resistance and carried out by the Sonderkommando at Birkenau to photograph this insanity and give shape to the unspeakable.[50] It is not clear exactly how the prisoners obtained a camera. After the war, some prisoners testified that they occasionally managed to get cameras from "Canada," a storage area in Birkenau where Jewish possessions were kept.[51] According to Langbein, however, a civilian camp employee snuck inside the camp with a camera containing just enough film for a few shots.[52] Most likely many men were involved in taking the photos. Szmulewski testified after the war that he stood on a roof observing the situation from above, making sure the guards who were in charge of the Sonderkommando were not watching.[53] The camera was probably hidden in a construction bucket with a double bottom and delivered to someone named Alex, an otherwise unidentified Greek Jew who worked in the gas chambers.[54] The camera was returned to Szmulewski, who smuggled the film into the main camp, from which members of the camp resistance movement delivered it to their outside resistance cell in a tube of toothpaste.[55]

Tonia heard about these actions directly from Szmulewski, who was convinced that Sioma had participated. Szmulewski may have embellished Sioma's participation to give his widow an image to hold on to. But, as Wontor-Cichy emphasizes, Sioma was in Birkenau at the site of BIIe and close to "Canada." Hence, it is quite possible that even if he was not directly involved, he was somehow helpful.[56]

Tonia stated in a letter to her family that Sioma died on January 19, 1945, just days before the Red Army liberated the camp. This was the time when the camp, in the words of Wontor-Cichy, was "already moving"; prisoners had been forced on a death march aimed at vacating the camp in response to the approaching Soviets. Wontor-Cichy assumes that Sioma was sent in the direction of Loslau (Wodzisław Śląski) in Upper Silesia, where prisoners of Auschwitz and Birkenau were sent.[57] Although

Langbein was no longer in Auschwitz at this time, he recorded that Sioma perished (*zugrunde gegangen*) but did not state what had happened.[58] In the letter, Tonia indicated that he was killed during an attempted escape. On January 19, the Red Army was in neighboring Kraków, which had been liberated two days earlier. Is it possible that after all these years in various camps, Sioma would have risked trying to join the Red Army to escape the march? According to the Memorial and Museum Auschwitz-Birkenau website, on January 19, 1945, around twenty Auschwitz prisoners were shot in the town of Brzeźce, where they were buried outside the local Catholic hospital. Was Sioma among them?[59]

Years later Tonia continued to reconsider all the possible scenarios of what might have happened to Sioma, including the possibility of him being alive:

> Even recently someone has returned, so theoretically he can still be out there. . . . But I don't think I would even like to meet him anymore. He would not be the same man anymore. However, I searched for him for a long time. A friend of my husband, whom I met later in Vienna, once told me that Sioma, along with several dozen people who still had strength, left the camp toward Kraków to meet the Red Army. They wanted to join the fight against the fascists. They were in striped uniforms. And most likely they died at the hands of Russians or Germans, maybe Polish or Ukrainian nationalists. This version seems to me the most probable. Then I learned that Sioma was in Czechoslovakia. It seemed strange to me because all his friends had landed in Paris. I thought that because he had two children with me, he would have at least wanted to talk. It was also strange that he did not contact his family, whom he loved very much. So, I just didn't believe he was alive. But I went to Prague several times—from France, Germany, Poland—and searched for him.[60]

Marcel also seeks closure. He is constantly searching the internet for new information about his father. In 2016 he contacted Peggy Steike, an artist who created a photo collage of some murdered Jews, including Sioma, on the infamous Birkenau gate. Their faces hover above lit candles. She sent Marcel a copy of the painting, now displayed in his apartment.

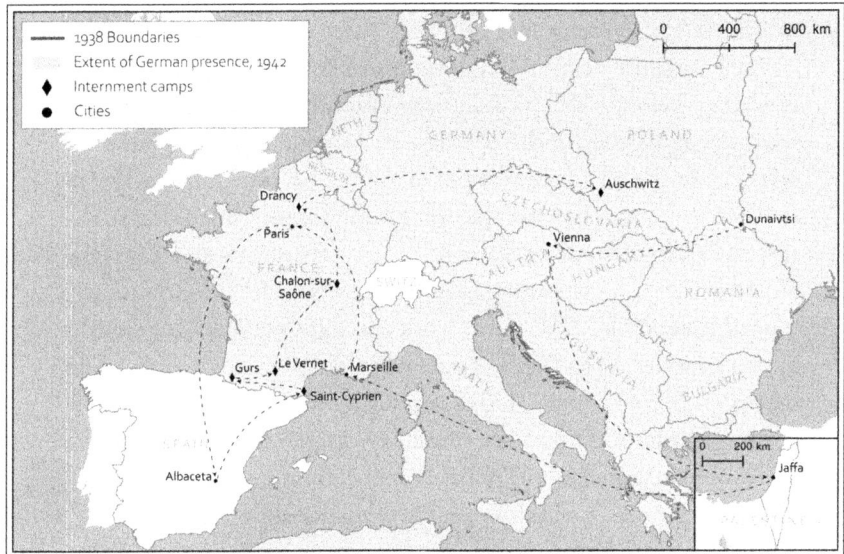

MAP 6.1. Sioma's lifetime travels, from Dunaivtsi (where he was born in 1917) to Auschwitz (where he died in 1945). *(Map by Kaitlyn Tatro)*

Reunion with Her Parents

Tonia began mentioning her desire to return to Poland in her letters as early as 1944. Sometime in mid-1946 Tonia's mother, Róża, decided to visit Tonia in Switzerland, partially with the intention of convincing her daughter to return to Palestine. Tonia's father, Aron, traveled to Denmark to undergo eye surgery, and Róża joined him as an opportunity to see her grandchildren. Not surprisingly, Róża and Aron were eager to have Tonia and her children back in Palestine. The war had ended with big losses for them. Roman, their oldest son, died in Treblinka. Aron's mother, Batia, died in Majdanek. All the family members who had remained in Łódź perished in the Holocaust.[61] Róża and Aron desperately wanted to reunite with surviving family members. But Tonia ached to return to Poland. In January 1946 she wrote a letter to her younger brother in which she sincerely revealed some of her plans:

> Well, Julek, during the war I wanted to go from Switzerland to France to take an active part in the fight against Hitler. It was not possible then, so I tried to be active in another way. I decided to go

> to Poland for a year or more to work there to rebuild the country. Today I am quite determined to return to Poland permanently; this is where I belong. My children have a future there! Obligation toward the party, toward the country, etc. won't allow me to leave for several months now [presumably to see her parents]. Naturally you in Palestine cannot feel the atmosphere in Europe. On one hand, the reaction raises its head, tries to sabotage everything by all means (the Western Bloc); on the other, democratic countries have frantically started to rebuild.... We must work and fight because danger lurks at every turn.... You know, I can't go to Switzerland for a few days with a clear conscience. That is why I had to write so categorically to our parents. You know, we think here in different categories. We know what fascism is, we experienced it severely, so we try to prevent a new danger that could threaten the whole world.

She was responding to a reproach, or maybe a letter from her brother, about her lack of time, perhaps unwillingness, to visit her family. Her letter also describes her state of mind just months before her planned return to Poland. She was driven by a desire to unite her past and present while building a better future. Working incessantly would allow her to get a grip on her life. Communism continued to be a tool to find and build life-sustaining networks, remained a source of hope for a better future, and in postwar circumstances and in light of the losses she personally had experienced also became a remedy for the tragedies that encircled her. In the same letter, she displayed her vulnerabilities, perhaps fully for the first time:

> I don't need to hide from you what I wouldn't tell anyone. I am tired. I do not have enough energy to constantly and alone decide about the fate of my children and me. You know, sometimes there is time when you would gladly put your fate in somebody's else hands. Do you understand me?!
>
> Do not think that I always have such thoughts? I am generally good, and I am satisfied with work. Maybe these are just moments of weakness no one knows about. I am glad I can write to you about it because I know you will understand me....
>
> You have read about Sioma from a letter to our parents. This poor boy had to suffer so much to die before the day of victory. Or

maybe he's still alive and can't send a message. I still hope Sioma will be found. I will never have another friend like him.... Sioma will always be my beloved, and I want to raise my children in that spirit.[62]

One of the motives driving her decision to return to Poland and her sense of mission was grief over Sioma's death. Her continued commitment to communism meant commitment to the life they were supposed to build together, and hence it meant the preservation of Sioma's presence in their lives.

Her identity as a Jew also drove her activism. That identity was built not on a sociocultural affinity for her Jewishness but on the Jewish suffering she observed during the war and learned more about after its end. In letters to her parents, she repeatedly emphasized that her and her family's experiences as Jews during the war pushed her to take a stand. "We Jews should be first in the fight against reaction," she wrote to her parents. "As honest people we cannot stand aside and observe, as the majority did while Hitler was ruling Germany. Then nobody wanted to hear about the suffering of German antifascists. Nobody wanted to believe it.... We live in times that are decisive for the entire humanity."[63] In response to her parents' questions regarding Polish antisemitism, she wrote:

> When it comes to your attitude toward Poland, I am sure this would change if you were in Poland. Naturally, antisemitism exists in Poland. It is not surprising after so many years of rule by Sanacja. Also, the German occupation only strengthened it. Poland is now at the stage of building a new life in every respect, a true democracy, which will solve the Jewish question. It is only a matter of time. Poland is being observed by all the democrats and antifascists. Poland began this great work (*wielkie dzieło*) and with enthusiasm and generosity is working on it. It hurts me that you cannot distinguish the traitors of Poland from the entire nation. The Polish nation did not collaborate with Germans—it gave the most beautiful, heroic evidence of that.[64]

In the summer of 1946, Tonia's parents left Tel Aviv for Denmark for Aron's surgery. On July 6 Róża traveled from Denmark to Itschnach to meet her grandchildren and Margaret Locher and wait for Tonia to return from Germany. She was amazed by the children and their living conditions. In her letter to Aron, Róża recounted:

> When I entered the home, Vera brought me a pair of large felt slippers. . . . I haven't seen such shiny floors. . . . Nobody enters the room in outdoor shoes. . . . Downstairs there is a dining room and a playroom lined with a rug. Each of the children has their own corner. Despite everything, the children have a lot of freedom and feel great. They don't eat meat, but they put down an admirable amount of lettuce and potatoes. They invited me to a dinner. The children ate everything, and there was no trace left on their plates. I naturally left some leftovers. Wierka [Vera] sincerely pointed out to me that you have to eat everything because if you leave it on your plate, it is difficult to wash off.[65]

At that time, Tonia was in Wermelskirchen, Germany, with a group of Polish doctors. In a letter to her mother, she admitted to being torn between joining her mother and the kids in Switzerland and going to Poland to begin her work.[66] After some deliberation, she decided to go to Switzerland for a week to meet her mother and then leave for Poland. In the letters from Germany to her mother in Switzerland, she continued mentioning her return to Poland while emphasizing that many mothers were involved in the USC mission, perhaps preparing the groundwork for the conversation she knew was coming: "Unfortunately, all of us mothers must be away—each of us stands at a different post. This is what today demands. When will this change? I'm sick of wandering and separations. I finally want to be with the children. Maybe now I can do something good in Poland."[67]

Despite Tonia's assurance that she would travel to Switzerland immediately, toward the end of July it was still uncertain when she would arrive.[68] Her passport expired on July 14. She sent it to Berlin to the Polish Military Mission to be renewed, only to find out that since the passport had been issued in Paris, it had to be renewed there.[69]

Finally, on August 9, 1946, Róża sent a letter to her husband saying that she had received a phone call that Tonia was on her way to Zürich via Beatenberg, a city located in the middle of Switzerland, around 130 kilometers from Zürich. The last time she and her daughter had seen each other was in May 1937, over nine years earlier, when Tonia and Sioma boarded a ship from Palestine to Marseille:

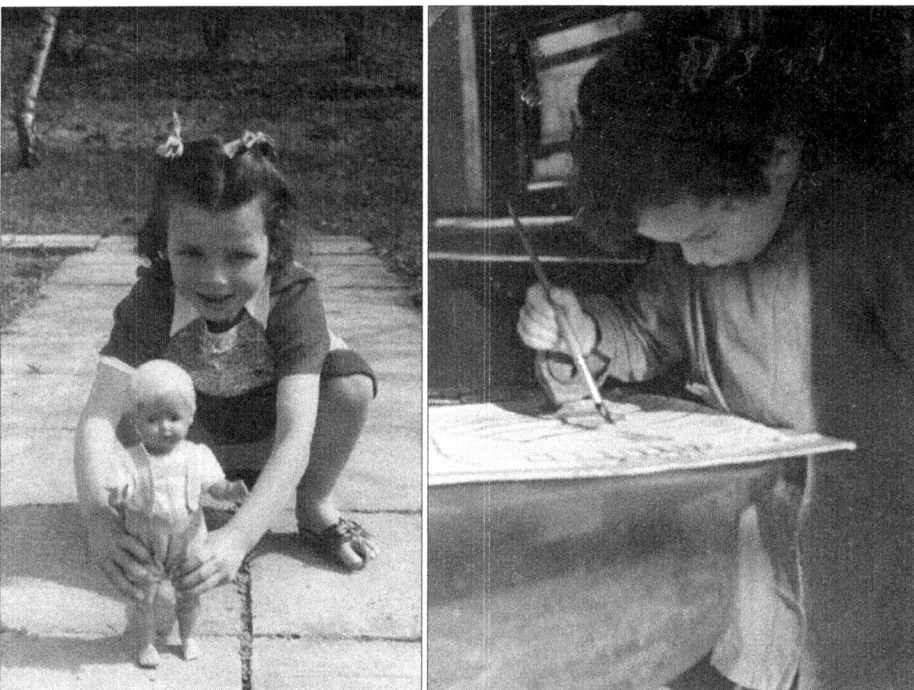

(left) FIGURE 6.1. Vera at Itschnach, ca. 1943–45. *(Private collection of Vera and Marcel Lechtman);* *(right)* FIGURE 6.2. Marcel at Itschnach, ca. 1943–45. *(Private collection of Vera and Marcel Lechtman)*

Tonia looks very bad. She is very nervous and doesn't feel quite healthy. Apparently, the doctor claims that her glands are not working normally. It is a miracle she is alive at all and looks like that.... She is a completely extraordinary person. Such a dutiful human being is rare. And that's why she is so respected and liked by all. She claims that people spoil her. But she really deserves this respect because she is a very serious and responsible person. Even doctors are afraid of her in the hospital where she works. She keeps a watchful eye on everyone. Tonia earns $180 a month plus full maintenance. She has all the money here and would like to pay for me. She is terribly proud of the money she has saved. She is collecting money to go to Poland. Perhaps she could be persuaded not to move to Poland.[70]

Tonia and her mother had only six days together before Tonia was obliged to return to Germany and then travel to Poland. The issue of returning to Palestine was most likely one of the first topics that came up. The main reason why Tonia wanted to return to Poland was not her patriotism, as Róża stated, but her aspirations to have a good job.[71] Róża defended her daughter's right to have a professional career, even if that meant not returning to Palestine. She continued writing to her husband for the next couple of days, with nonstop adoration of Tonia:

> Last night the wife of Mr. Field, the director of the Unitarian Service, came to see Tonia. If you could hear the way this woman talks about Tonia. She is the head of a hospital with two hundred beds. All doctors are afraid of her, even the chief one, and she is the youngest on the whole team. As she was also telling me that Mr. Field, who by the way is an extraordinarily enlightened man, had said that Tonia had been very lucky with people she met at various moments of her life. . . . The story of Tonia since leaving Palestine would be a suitable topic for a very interesting novel. Mrs. Field is convinced that Tonia will be successful in Poland. . . . She asked to accept her decision because Tonia can't be content with a bourgeois life.[72]

Róża noted that Tonia had had a difficult life, but she had changed, matured, and grown to be a wonderful person. An important element of this image was the opinions of Noel Field's wife and Tonia's friends. "We talked endlessly. We can be proud of our daughter. I spent one day in the company of her friends and watched as this woman has won so many friends. . . . Everyone who encounters her loves, respects, and admires her."[73] Róża wrote with deep respect for her daughter, a rebel who did not finish high school and who in her early youth had argued with her father about politics. The Bialers' initial priority—Tonia's return to Palestine—lost its urgency or was not presented as important, at least in the letters. Rather, Tonia's mother worried about ensuring that she was dressed appropriately for her work:

> I bought Tonia a beautiful English outfit, quite expensive because Tonia asked not to buy her rags, just one good thing. I also bought her an elegant nightgown and various travel trinkets she had dreamed of, and so now she only has to get a silk dress for parties at the embassy or in Poland at the ministries. Wherever she goes, she travels

as a Unitarian envoy. . . . She rides first-class and stays everywhere in first-class hotels, so she must be dressed properly. She even finds some pleasure in it.[74]

Her mother also noticed that Tonia was confident around and popular with men. "Deep down, however, she is sad and aching and lonely. She is still deluding herself that she will find Sioma."[75]

Tonia and her mother parted in mutual understanding and planned to meet again, this time with Tonia's father, in a couple of months, after Tonia's first trip to Poland. After her departure from Switzerland, Tonia wrote about the reunion with similar enthusiasm:

> I want to say that . . . the gifts make me extremely happy, but what gave me new strength was your understanding of me, your and daddy's truly boundless goodness. You know, I will tell you openly, I was afraid of our meeting. I had a terrible fear that you would not be able to understand me. . . . We have been separated for so many years, of course, so you could not get to know me as I would have liked, and I would like to know so much more about you. Particularly, I arrived in an impossible mood from the nervous tension I had lived in for weeks. Now, our team claims that . . . I have changed positively in every respect. . . . Everyone thinks I look better. . . . I will also be able to do our business in Poland with a completely different energy.[76]

Tonia's narration of this reunion for Dowgiałło, in contrast, was focused on tensions over her parent's desire for her to return to Palestine. The letters, however, reveal a transforming mother-daughter relationship and were full with discoveries about this new Tonia, a young woman who had previously caused such worry. This turned out to be a time that left them both enriched and also revealed many similarities between mother and daughter—for example, the right to have a satisfying professional life, which Róża showed with her active engagement in her husband's business and now supported for Tonia. She understood and accepted Tonia's desire to return to Poland, not so much as a continuation of her ideological engagement but more so as the possibility of occupying a position she had earned. The appeal of the new postwar Poland attracted not only Tonia but also her parents—at least her mother, who appeared eager to believe that post-1945 Poland could offer opportunities that pre-1939 Poland was unable to.[77]

On August 22 Tonia informed her mother about arriving in Wermelskirchen, where her unit was stationed. It planned to travel to Poland via Prague the next day, where it was supposed to pick up medicine sent from the United States. Her paperwork was valid until September 15, so she was hoping to be back in Zürich around the twentieth to see her parents.[78] The group arrived in Prague on August 25 from Nuremberg and planned to be in Cieszyn the next day: "Tonight I visited Prague, a beautiful city, very lively and nice. But Nuremberg, where we stayed yesterday, is completely destroyed. At least there is justice in this respect," she wrote in August from Prague.[79]

We know nothing about Tonia's initial return to Poland, where she spent close to three weeks, from the end of August until September. She reported back to Wermelskirchen on September 15, 1946. After her return to Germany, she planned on going to Geneva via Brussels to see the Fields and then to Zürich to see her parents.[80] Somewhere between September 15 and October 16, Tonia met her mother and father in Zürich, but no letters have survived from this reunion. After Tonia's departure, Róża wrote a letter to family in Palestine saying, "Tonia already left; the parting was very painful. Who knows when we will meet?"[81]

Return to Poland

Tonia spent the end of October 1946 in Wermelskirchen packing up the provisional hospital and preparing for her second trip to Poland, a mission to create a hospital that would serve the local population and facilitate the return of displaced persons from France and British-occupied Germany:[82]

> So, our work in Germany is over, for which I am very pleased. . . . We're going to Bytom and hope to bring all of our treasures. Along the way, I will be responsible for seventy-five infants. . . . It will be lots of work. I think that we will be able to arrange our stay in Bytom comfortably and that it will not last long until I can bring the children [Vera and Marcel to Poland]. You know, I have no patience anymore. Enough of this gypsy life! I can't leave Vera at Locher's for long.[83]

FIGURE 6.3. Tonia working for the Unitarian Service Committee. *(Private collection of Vera and Marcel Lechtman)*

At the beginning of November, she and her team were still in Wermelskirchen:

> The Red Cross train has not arrived yet, and we are still waiting here. Naturally not with our arms folded, as new difficulties are constantly emerging, such as passes, export permits, etc. You can imagine our impatience. I was particularly anxious about being in the country as soon as possible to be able to arrange an apartment for the children. I wanted to be in Switzerland for Christmas. Who knows if this is possible now?[84]

Finally, on November 18, almost two months after originally planned, the group arrived in Katowice, from where they traveled to Warsaw as part of a special transport that delivered hospital equipment and medicine from Germany. Her first days in Warsaw sounded like a luxurious dream. She stayed in a nice hotel with Dorothea Jones, whom she called Jonesy and who was the USC's director in Poland and over time became Tonia's friend. They planned to attend a dinner with the minister of health and go to the theater. In the next few days, Tonia planned to move to Bytom in Upper Silesia and search for an apartment. She also intended to go to Łódź to see what was left of her family's apartment.[85]

Overwhelming violence and destruction characterized the reality to which many people were returning. Polish dailies occasionally published information about the difficulties of traveling. In addition, a journalist wrote for *Życie Warszawy* in October 1945 that "disoriented crowds are roaming from city to city, camping near the train station from where they are eventually removed—they suffer hunger, cold, and poverty."[86] Roads were full of people: around 1.6 million concentration camp inmates and forced laborers were returning home. By August 1945 eight hundred thousand Poles had returned home from Germany.[87] Thousands of deported non-Jewish Poles and Jews were returning, while another two million people had lost their homes during the war and were searching for new places to live.[88]

Tonia's initial letters, though, extend no words about the desperation and poverty she must have been exposed to. Since Tonia was traveling on trains, she must have witnessed terrible scenes daily. Bytom was as destroyed as Warsaw.[89] The Red Army had advanced through it on its victorious march toward Berlin, destroying everything in its path. January 1945 marked the beginning of the Soviet entry into Upper Silesia and a terrible mass killing of the local population by Soviet soldiers.[90] None of this devastation, however, entered Tonia's correspondence. The letters are focused on the difficulties of daily life and creation of a home for her children. With a similar energy as in her letters from Paris, she attempted to convince her parents that her new life was full of joy and promise. She mostly fixated on getting her new household ready for her children, which included finding a housekeeper, still popular after the war:[91]

> I hope that at the end of next month I will be able to bring the children. . . . Of course, [the apartment] will not be completely furnished, but it may take a year or more. The main thing is to have an apartment and firewood, and in a few days we will get it. In Bytom there are a lot of families from French emigration, so soon I will find a young girl who will take care of the household and children at the same time. I really want the children to speak French at home.[92]

Years later, in her conversation with Dowgiałło, she did admit that conditions were far from ideal. For the first months, Tonia and Jonesy lived in a hotel with broken windows and frozen pipes. All their expensive items, such as jewelry, had to be kept in a lockbox. Perhaps due to the carnivalesque atmosphere of the end of the war, nonstop parties, which sometimes turned dangerous, were held on the hotel's ground floor. Tonia recalled waking up to a drunk Soviet soldier hovering above them with a gun in his hand. When they explained that they were there on an American mission, he left.[93]

Her job was to participate in rebuilding a hospital in Piekary Śląskie, five kilometers from Bytom. It was to be a surgical and trauma hospital for miners. Before the war, the hospital belonged to the Bracka Company, a Silesian insurance institution. At that point, she noted, "80 percent of patients were miners, and the rest were children from road accidents, injured by explosions . . . , etc."[94] In early 1947 a US shipment arrived with an operating room, lamps, tables, and all applicable instruments, enough equipment for two operating units. By September 1948 the total value of supplies was estimated at $89,644.[95] Along with the shipment came two employees who were to organize a blood bank and nurses who were to train Polish nurses in using the equipment. Later, a team of doctors arrived to train Polish doctors in neurological operations. Tonia summarized this hospital development: "Because we accepted people from accidents (and there were a lot of them), these two operating rooms were not enough. In fact, one of the American doctors never slept for more than two hours. And the nurses cried when he ordered surgery at two or three in the morning. . . . But from the ruins, a hospital with three hundred beds was created."[96] To this day, this hospital is informally called "the American hospital" because it emerged from American aid.[97]

In February 1947 Tonia finally traveled to Switzerland to get her children. After a temporary stay in the hospital, they moved into a big six-room apartment. They shared it with Jonesy and Frances Berges, a young American who came to help with the opening of the hospital.[98] For the next couple of years, Tonia's letters concentrated on her efforts to create a sense of home. She wrote about furniture, pots and pans, and the bedsheets and blankets Jonesy brought back from the United States. Years later she remembered this time as good and peaceful.[99] She was also proud of her newly acquired skills. She cooked and boasted to her mother about her attempts at baking. She made fruit jams. She picked mushrooms and pickled them with vegetables.[100] She even joked that the only book she read was a cookbook.[101] She maintained an image of herself as crucially concerned with the household:

> I run a household on a large scale. Every day I study French and American cookbooks. We have a pretty good cook. But what work it is to make such a household run properly and have everything in order. At first I thought I am not capable of that, but I managed. We often have official guests, we have to arrange teas, etc. You would be surprised, Mommy, how good I am. One has to think about everything: there is laundry, things need to be darned, pillows sewed, etc. And the most important thing is to choose the right people to do it all.
>
> The children make me very happy. I often go to bed and I think that everything is a dream—the children, this beautiful apartment, the life without worries.[102]

The year 1947 was the first year all three of them lived together. Vera was ten years old that summer and enjoyed school and learning folk dances as part of her extracurricular activities. Marcel was adapting more slowly. He fought with his friends and often played alone.[103] Slowly, however, they were settling down. In her letters Tonia occasionally emphasized the children's sensitivity to social issues as evidence of their socialist upbringing. For example, she

FIGURE 6.4. Tonia and her children, Switzerland, 1944 or 1945. *(Private collection of Vera and Marcel Lechtman)*

mentioned that they asked her to financially help others. "They already know our principles: first we help widows, then children and working women."[104]

After moving to Poland, Tonia also attempted to learn about the situation of her family's house in Łódź. During her first visit, she found some of its rooms in use by a Methodist church.[105] After the war, Łódź was largely abandoned. Germans escaped or were arrested, Jews were murdered or expelled, and people from all over the country arrived and often moved into empty apartments. Hence, it was not surprising that their big apartment at 85 Piotrkowska Street was inhabited. The Bialers intended to sell the house at first, but selling was not a simple endeavor. They first would have to prove they had legal rights to the property. Historian Anna Cichopek-Gajraj explains that "the 'Bierut decrees' set out legal regulations governing 'abandoned and left behind property' as early as March 1945. . . . If, after five to ten years, the property remained 'heirless,' the managing institutions or the State Treasury could acquire ownership by right of occupation."[106] Since May 1945 only the closest members of the owner—parents, siblings, children, or a spouse—were entitled to the inheritance of the deceased.[107] "The government feared that if distant relatives were allowed to make claims, citizens of other countries could become property owners in post-war Poland."[108] Aron Bialer was the only surviving owner, but he had to initiate an inheritance succession case to establish the remaining heirs, important especially in the case of houses like 85 Piotrkowska with multiple owners.[109] To start the process, in addition to finding a lawyer, they needed to obtain the death certificates for their relatives and restore their birth records.[110] Next, they had to appear in person to eliminate false kin or people interested in claiming the property. To establish the circumstances of death of prewar owners, the family members initiating the case had to have two witnesses. Only then were death certificates issued.[111] After successfully completing this cumbersome process, one could claim property and only then attempt to either rent or sell it. Even if the Bialers managed to sell, they would not have been allowed to leave the country with the money.[112] A June 20, 1945, decision of the Ministry of the Treasury forbade transferring, sending, or exporting any means of payment abroad.[113] A reference to initiating the case was the last mention of the house that appeared in Tonia's letters.

Amid all the attention to the upbringing of her children, the domestic issues, and even the attempts to find out what happened with the Łódź property, many silences stand out. Did Tonia observe any renewal of Jewish life in

Poland? Did she join any Jewish organizations that returning Jews were establishing? Was she aware of the antisemitism around her? Was she satisfied with the socialism she was helping to build? Was she finding enough balance between the attention she devoted to her children and the work she was doing for the socialist state? She briefly mentioned the January 1947 legislative elections, which historians view as fabricated: "I was also active in the elections," Tonia wrote soon afterward. "As you know, we have won. None of us expected such good results.... Now we seriously need to get to work. The whole world will admire what we are capable of!"[114] Hence, she still was full of enthusiasm for communism, perhaps viewing it, at least partially, as responsible for eradicating antisemitism. In December 1947 she stated, "As for antisemitism, I have not noticed anything, and I have not heard anyone complain about it. In my surroundings, I have met the opposite attitude—everyone is willing to help and support me. I am very glad that I came."[115] Only a year earlier, in July 1946, in Kielce—a city located about 150 kilometers from her new home in Bytom—the biggest postwar Jewish pogrom had taken place and led to the death of forty-two Jews and the injury of forty others.[116]

By the time she arrived in Poland, antisemitism was waning. The pogrom in Kielce was the last major outburst of collective anti-Jewish violence. From the standpoint of the Jewish community, 1947 was the year of "stabilization," when antisemitic violence was halted, Jewish institutions were being rebuilt, and with the help of Western Jewish funds, Polish Jewish life was being reconstructed. Cichopek-Gajraj shows that in March 1947 the director of the JDC argued, "Although it [antisemitism] still exists to a great extent, it is undeniable that much of its impetus has been lost and many antisemitic tendencies have stopped." Cichopek-Gajraj further explains that the consolidation of the communist regime in Poland brought greater repression and new laws, including those against antisemitism.[117]

Postwar Upper Silesia still had a relatively large Jewish population. Most likely if she ever planned on participating in Jewish life, she would have mentioned it to her parents. The lack of contact with the local Jewish community reveals how unimportant her Jewish cultural and social identity was for her at that time.[118] In 1947 she may have felt calm and encouraged in her optimism that communism signified some serious changes, such as the eradication of antisemitism. But if 1947 was the year of stabilization, 1948 was the beginning of the communist campaign against "cosmopolitism." The world around her was becoming more tense. Polish Stalinism was slowly settling in while shutting down political and cultural pluralism.

In the end, focusing on home and work achievements was easier and also more in line with what her parents wanted to hear. The hospital in Piekary Śląskie was the USC's biggest project in Europe. The USC's work in Poland was guaranteed in an agreement that the USC signed in May 1947 with the Social Insurance Institution (Zakład Ubezpieczeń Społecznych), a Polish state organization. The agreement stipulated that the Ministry of Work and Social Care (Ministerstwo Pracy i Opieki Społecznej) would exercise supervision over the project. American nurses and administrators, such as Jonesy, were expected to leave as soon as the USC mission was accomplished.[119] On February 22, 1948, the hospital officially opened. In a letter to Tonia's parents, Berges underlined the mission's tremendous success.[120] The hospital opened on the anniversary of George Washington's birthday and was considered the flagship American project in Poland. *Poland of Today,* a newsletter published in New York after the war, stated, "In Piekary, where tuberculosis, occupational diseases, and industrial accidents are common, Kościuszko Hospital will serve the people of the region as an outstanding example of American generosity."[121]

In March 1948 Tonia announced that she was moving to Warsaw to work in the Ministry of Industry and Trade (Ministerstwo Przemysłu i Handlu) to organize a Department for the Care of Mothers and Children (Dział Opieki nad Matką i Dzieckiem), which had, among other duties, the task of organizing orphanages, kindergartens for employees' children, and summer camps.[122] And there could have been a number of reasons why she decided to move. The 1949 interrogation of Jerzy Nowicki, one of the communists Tonia had met in Switzerland, suggests that a deteriorating relationship between Tonia and Jonesy most likely contributed to her decision to leave. There were a number of matters they did not agree on, including the salary that the Polish members of the team were receiving from Jonesy. But the same interrogation suggests perhaps more serious reasons as well. Most likely Tonia was reporting on the American to the Ministry of Public Security (Ministerstwo Bezpieczeństwa Publicznego, MBP). In the context of the nascent Cold War, Jonesy was seen as an enemy. As Nowicki emphasized in his interrogation, Jonesy, despite having an attitude critical of the American government and the treatment of African Americans, applauded the Marshall Plan, American aid that Poland did not accept.[123]

Tonia moved alone to Warsaw, leaving her children behind. In a letter to her parents, she explained:

> Unfortunately, I don't have an apartment yet. I am promised that maybe I will receive it at the beginning of next month. They are building a lot now, so I have a good chance. Only then will I be happy, because this separation from the children is terrible. I am not hysterical, but I will tell you honestly that I do not experience anything as hard as separation from those sparkles. I placed them in the Children's Home [an orphanage] near Bielsko in Jaworze Dolny. It is a beautiful neighborhood.[124]

They reunited in the fall of 1948, when the children began at their new school, affiliated with the Association of Friends of Children (Towarzystwo Przyjaciół Dzieci, TPD) in Warsaw.[125] TPD schools were driven by a desire to educate new socialist citizens according to Marxist ideas and, as a result, were models of socialist upbringing.[126] As Natalia Aleksiun suggests, TPD schools were also effectively Jewish schools; students there could avoid Catholic religion classes that were part of the typical public school curriculum at the time.[127]

In the winter of 1948, the year Tonia settled in Warsaw, the Polish United Workers Party (Polska Zjednoczona Partia Robotnicza, PZPR) was created. An era of Stalinist terror followed, which included the persecution of members of the Home Army, an anti-Nazi resistance movement loyal during the war to the Polish government-in-exile and whose units turned anticommunist afterward. She must have been aware of the terror unfolding around her. Reading her letters from the end of 1948 and early 1949 is confusing and a bit eerie. In early 1949 Władysław Gomułka—the leader of the PZPR—was demoted and replaced with a staunch Stalinist. Did it evoke in her any fears or suspicions? We do not know. The letters betray nothing, except for the difficulties and joys of running a household. In March 1948 she wrote:

> Now, Mommy, I'll tell you what my kitchen looks like. Because it is so big, I divided it into a dining part and a kitchen. I have a beautiful white gas stove; I covered the coal stove with a board covered with the cloth you once bought for me in Switzerland, and it serves as a work table. I also have a second white kitchen table and a small cupboard for dishes. . . . A shelf with the Rosenthal china is mounted

above the cabinet. Aluminum pots cleaned to a sparkle also hang on the wall. . . . I forgot to write about a beautiful white waste bin with a pedal. . . . The second part of the kitchen is separated by a screen (blue cretonne with white flowers) that came from Jonesy's kitchen in Boston. In the corner by the wall stands a table modeled on a folk style of burnt pine and three stools. A lamp with a straw hangs above the table as a good complement. To complement this, I will say that on this lovely table lies a beautiful tablecloth—a gift from Emulka [a nickname for Noemi, Tonia's sister]. Blue, cretonne curtains hang in the kitchen, which will probably fade with the onset of spring—but in the meantime, they please my eyes.

She must have realized how intensely domesticity-oriented her letters were because in the same letter, she wrote:

I can imagine what Julek would say reading this letter—the woman is crazy about her home. She cannot write about anything else from this Poland where we daily take a step forward toward socialism. Well, dear Juleczek, I think about this step toward socialism between cleaning and washing dishes and try to speed up these steps. However, I'm crazy about housing.[128]

Organizing, decorating, and making a home brought Tonia enormous pleasure. Between her work in the ministry and her efforts to organize her domestic space in the midst of postwar shortages, little time was left for anything else. In one of her letters, she noticed it was mostly Vera who took care of Marcel and even helped her clean the apartment. "I leave in the evening," Tonia wrote in May 1949, "she goes to sleep alone, cleans after dinner, and even makes my bed. . . . I don't have words. I don't know who is taking care of whom." She also mentioned the possibility of the children going to Crimea for a scouting camp, Sioma's dream a long time ago.[129] In her letters, life was calm and uneventful. Tonia remained focused on her household, as if the apartment was consuming all her energy and at the same time was protecting her from any other worries. In the letters, no apparent concerns affected her relatively idyllic life.

On July 26, 1949, Tonia was arrested by the security service of the Polish state.

Prison

Tonia's arrest came at a time when her life was falling into place. It disrupted a peaceful life and is still one of the most traumatic events in her children's memory. Vera, who was not present at the moment of the arrest, associates it with many unrelated events. In contrast, Marcel, who was present, does not remember anything, and the absence of this particular memory is a painful memory itself. Marcel's lack of recall and Vera's elaborate story of what happened emphasizes his vulnerability and her role as the depository of their mother's memory.[130]

On July 26, 1949, Tonia was at home with Marcel while Vera was at a scout summer camp. In the evening, MBP officers barged into and aggressively searched the apartment. Hours later, they announced that they were taking Tonia to a jail located on Koszykowa Street. As this was unfolding, Tonia looked at Marcel and said, "I will be home soon." Years later she still felt guilty that after giving Marcel hope she did not return for a long time. When they were leaving, MBP officer Józef Światło, infamous for his cruelty, arranged for Tonia's neighbor and friend Halina Diamant to pick Marcel up.[131] Decades later, in 1998, Diamant wrote a letter to Vera explaining that particular moment:

> On June 28, 1949, [my daughter] Oleńka was born. After a week I came home from the hospital. Tonia taught me how to bathe a baby; we were together every day. Marcel was at home, and you at the summer camp. . . . One day, Tonia did not come. I dashed to her apartment. I knocked, a man opened, said he couldn't let me in. . . . Of course, it was all extremely mysterious and disturbing. After a few hours, this man came to me and said that Tonia is under arrest, they are about to seal the apartment, and asked if I could look after Marcel. . . . It was obvious to me that I would look after her children until she returned. I understood that this was a tragic misunderstanding. I went with him to the apartment; he told me to take the children's clothes for summer and winter. I was outraged because that meant Tonia would be in jail for so long. . . . I took, as I remember, two blue blankets for you, clothes, and a photo of your father.[132]

Vera connects the moment of her mother's imprisonment with her return from summer camp. She remembers the general atmosphere as tense, and she links it with news from the Soviet Union about the imprisonment of Jewish doctors. At the end of camp, Vera had been waiting with her friend, Krysia Komar, for her mother, who did not come. Eventually Krysia's mother picked them both up. Krysia was the daughter of Wacław Komar, a man of Jewish origins who had participated in the Spanish Civil War and an important military figure in postwar Poland, working for the Polish Military Mission in France.[133] According to Vera, after arriving back in Warsaw, Krysia's mother left her outside of her apartment building, even though she knew Tonia had been arrested. She was aware of the political situation, and her husband was arrested the next day. Vera went up to her apartment, but its door was sealed. She began pounding on it, screaming for Marcel.

A neighbor opened their door and told Vera that Marcel was at the Diamants' apartment, a few blocks away. When Vera got there, Halina apologized for not picking her up. Marcel ran to Vera, embraced her, and began crying. According to Vera, he was clearly traumatized. He was the only person who had witnessed the arrest: the aggressive behavior of the officers, the searches, the humiliation. Halina did not tell Vera anything that day.[134] In another version of this story, Vera mentioned that a cleaning lady greeted her at the Diamants' door the next morning. While Halina was looking for a watch, the cleaning lady suggested that perhaps "the arrested woman's" daughter had stolen it. Halina began screaming at the woman. Marcel was terrified. Vera took him to another room to read to him to calm him down. Only in the evening did Halina reveal to Vera that her mother had been arrested.[135]

The stories Vera narrated are telling: she narrated them from the perspective of an anxious child who had a premonition of something terrible about to happen. The danger was coming from various directions: international (Stalin's plot against Jewish doctors), domestic (Komar's arrest), and also one very close to her home (the cleaning lady's accusation).

In fact, many aspects of this story cannot be true. The arrest of Jewish doctors and the antisemitic frenzy began in the Soviet Union later, in 1952.[136] Also, Komar was arrested almost three years later, in November 1952.[137] Vera conflated various events related to the arrest of either Jews or communists with the arrest of her mother. She combined communism, Jewishness, and participation in the Spanish Civil War, elements that had shaped her and became sources of fear at a relatively young age.

At first, Tonia was kept in a jail cell on Koszykowa Street and then on August 2 was moved to an MBP prison in the Mokotów district of Warsaw, where she spent the remainder of her imprisonment.[138] According to the order of temporary arrest, Tonia was accused of espionage for the United States and actions to the detriment of the Polish state, based on article 7 of the criminal code. The summary about her and her case was completed only on August 17, 1949. At that point, Tonia was also photographed, but her photo is no longer in her file.[139]

Her first interrogation took place on the day of her arrest, followed by additional questions the next day. Since Polish officers used the Soviet biographical method, compelling prisoners to tell the same story repeatedly while looking for inconsistencies, in her interrogations she was asked to return to her past many times over.[140] She reported a lot within the first days: she summarized her entire life, her communist activism, her relationship with Sioma, their hardships in France, and her escape from France. She expected to be released shortly. After her arrival in the cell, when her cellmates suggested that she should clean herself up or eat, she responded that it was unnecessary since she was going home as soon as the confusion got settled. She readily participated in the first interrogation to help establish her own innocence.[141]

Did she really not suspect that something like this might happen? She must have known that the fall of Gomułka from power meant a changing political climate. She was also most likely aware of the sudden anti-Israeli turn in the fall of 1948 that affected Jewish political and cultural pluralism and attacked Jewish communities for their connections with the West. It is also possible that due to her connections with the Poles repatriated from France, she was aware of the growing tension in Polish-French relations, which in March 1949 led to the arrests of a group of French citizens living in Warsaw accused of spying.[142] Finally, on May 11, 1949, Noel Field had been arrested in Prague, Czechoslovakia. Did she know not know this? In 1957 she shared a comment about an atmosphere saturated with seeking spies.[143] Her statement from a documentary movie about Field also suggests her awareness of his arrest.[144] But we may never know the extent to which her statements deposited in the 1990s reflect her knowledge from the late 1940s.

Tonia continued to be interrogated throughout August. She was interrogated every few days, sometimes receiving only a couple of days' break between examinations.[145] The interrogations began in the morning and lasted until midnight, with a break from four in the afternoon to eight o'clock in the evening. This routine was repeated every few days for almost a year, until May 1950, after which she was interrogated with less intensity.[146] It is doubtful she was aware of what the MBP was looking for in these interrogations. Tonia was questioned about what Field needed from her before he left Poland in 1948. She explained that during his visit to Poland in mid-1948, he had left behind a suitcase of books that he asked Tonia to send to Switzerland. She began taking care of the matter only months later, toward the end of 1948. After learning she would have to receive permission to send the suitcase, she went to Komar at the MBP to seek his assistance, but he was more interested in Field than the suitcase. The meeting ended with Komar assuring her that he would look into the matter further. In February 1949 Tonia was visited by an employee of Komar's to whom she revealed more information regarding Field and his work for the USC. She also explained that Field had sent a letter to Jakub Berman, a member of the highest echelon of the Polish communist party, through his secretary, Anna Duracz, in which Field asked Berman to confirm Field's Soviet Communist Party membership.[147] Tonia revealed that recently her conversation with Field regarding his problems with the Communist Party of the United States of America and his request to send a suitcase appeared suspicious, doubts she shared with her friend Diamant, who expressed worry that Field could be an American spy.[148] She was forced to reflect on her relationship with Field, the man who had helped her in Switzerland, and was asked about their acquaintances. She was made to recall past conversations with him and with people they both had known, while reimagining his role and identity according to questions designed to sow doubts.

All the interrogation minutes represent well-polished conversations, but this appearance is clearly misleading. As revealed in a statement Tonia gave in 1954 to the Central Commission of Party Control (Centralna Komisja Kontroli Partii), which investigated the behavior of secret police officers involved in her case, her interrogations were actually violent and chaotic. She endured a prolonged period during which she was not allowed to sleep for longer than ten minutes. She was forced to sit on the legs of an upside-down stool or stand in an uncomfortable position while interrogated. She was beaten, kicked, trampled, and humiliated. Her hair was torn out. In prison, she lost most of her teeth. For several months during her interrogations, she was forced to report being an American spy.[149] The goal of this violence and humiliation was to convince her to admit that she had collaborated as a spy with Field.[150]

Interestingly, later in life Tonia admitted a couple of times that she had believed her interrogators when they told her she was a spy.[151] Her first interrogations also suggested that she was aware there was something suspicious in Field's behavior: his insistence on staying in Eastern Europe and an unwillingness to leave for the United States. Yet, when testifying in 1957 against her interrogators, she insisted that she never admitted to having agreed to collaborate with Field because that was something she did not do.[152] At first glance, these statements appear to lack coherence. Tonia felt guilt, she believed she was a spy and that Field was a spy, and yet she refused to admit that she collaborated with Field. Some historians explain this phenomenon as being unconsciously detrimental to the party due to the loss of vigilance.[153] If Field was politically suspicious, then her inability to see through his actions made her guilty as a communist who had failed to defend the cause. Her own opinion of Field was juxtaposed with the communist secret police's knowledge of him: an American, a person particularly susceptible to Western and, hence, detrimental influences. She desperately wanted to return home, but she could also easily reinterpret her imprisonment as being larger than her personal well-being: everything she had fought for was on the line. Returning home—physically and metaphorically—meant searching and uncovering "the truth" and discovering why she was accused, what she was accused of, and who Field was if he was not who she thought him to be.[154]

A couple of months after Tonia was arrested, Jonesy tried to figure out why. The family still did not know what had happened to her or her children. In a letter to Tonia's parents, Jonesy outlined possible scenarios. Perhaps her imprisonment was due to the war years Tonia had spent in Switzerland, since as Jonesy had heard that communists who spent the war in Switzerland were being arrested. Or her arrest could have stemmed from the connection between Field and Hungarian politician László Rajk and their links to Allen Dulles, a high-ranking US government official known for his aggressive stance toward communism in the postwar years who eventually served as head of the Central Intelligence Agency (CIA). Finally, Jonesy suggested that across the Eastern Bloc arrests were taking place among members of the International

Brigades. Jonesy finished the letter by saying, "I was not as close with Noel as she [Tonia] was and I am absolutely sure that the accusations against him are not true; and even if they were true, Tonia would not have known. She would be the first to condemn the plot."[155]

Tonia was implicated in what historians call the Field affair, an event that historian Andrzej Paczkowski interprets as a repeat of the great purge of the late 1930s in the Soviet Union.[156] In a postwar Soviet reprisal against Eastern European communist politicians, Field played the role of a master spy whose story was supposed to link the different trials that were occurring in various countries at the time. His testimonies were supposed to create a rationale for Stalin's avid search for an internal enemy. As Paczkowski argues, the concept of an internal enemy was created in the 1930s in the Soviet Union but gained a new meaning in the postwar period, where the threat became someone who could easily enter an alliance with an external enemy.[157] In this particular case, Field was both.[158]

Who exactly was Noel Field? An interesting interpretation of Field's identity comes from the most recent American biography of him, by Kati Marton. Marton presents Field as both a Quaker idealist and a fanatic. In her reading, Field was a young talented man, vulnerable to the recruitment of the Soviet secret police and then betrayed by Stalin.[159] The truth is much more trivial. Much of the existing work on Field shows him as a naive idealist rather than a fanatic, a man strongly affected by his pacifist Quaker father and belief in the possibility of achieving world peace through social revolution.[160] In 1935, as a young employee of the US State Department, Field decided to collaborate with the Soviets. According to available sources, that was the only year when Field delivered any information about his State Department work to the Soviets, and there is no clarity about the quantity or quality of this material.[161] In 1936 Field resigned from the State Department, partially because he did not feel a calling for administrative office work, and left for Geneva, where, working for the League of Nations, he began humanitarian work. At the beginning of World War II, Field tried to help members of the International Brigades, scattered across the Spanish-French border in refugee camps, by providing them with food, money, documents, and medical supplies. Field and his wife, Herta, also worked in Marseille, where they organized support for the French resistance and were engaged in helping vulnerable groups of people, especially communists, escape France. In March 1942 Field helped Hans Marum, Hans's wife, Sophie, and their children escape France—the people Tonia had spent months living with prior to giving birth to Vera.[162] He saw this work—illegal border crossings, seeking secret accommodations for escaping communists, etc.—as a kind of clandestine Red Help that he carried out within the framework of the USC.[163]

The German occupation of France forced him to return to Geneva, which as a neutral country was also an outpost for the Office of Strategic Services (OSS), an American military intelligence agency that the CIA replaced after the war. It was here that Field encountered Dulles, then the OSS's director in Switzerland. The men knew each other from their work in the State Department in Washington. Their reunion in Geneva was a coincidence that turned out to be calamitous for Field. When Field left to work for the League of Nations in 1936, two Soviet spies, Ignacy Reiss and Walter Krywicki, were to contact him to ensure his further collaboration. But both soon came under suspicion and never contacted Field, Reiss being murdered by the Soviet Union's Peoples Commissariat for Internal Affairs (NKVD) and Krywicki having fled and soon afterward dying. As historian Robert Spałek points out, Field was considered suspicious but not important enough to be assassinated, and the Soviets broke all contact with him. But in 1938 Field traveled to the Soviet Union with a desire to join the Communist Party. Despite his apparent commitment, the Soviets remained suspicious of him. According to Spałek, part of the problem was most likely Field's contact with Dulles. As the USC director, Field had to pass lists of people saved in France (communists, socialists, and others) on to Dulles.[164] In the second half of the 1940s, however, Field lost his USC job because the American headquarters realized he was selectively helping communists. Deprived of work, he traveled between Geneva, Paris, Prague, and Warsaw trying to determine his next steps.[165]

Due to the beginning of the Cold War, his American upbringing, and his sympathies for communists, the atmosphere around Field was becoming increasingly intense. What perhaps turned his situation from bad to terrible was the testimony by Hede Massing, an Austrian actress, communist, and Soviet intelligence operative in Europe and the United States during the 1930s and 1940s. Having grown disillusioned with the Soviet Union, Massing became a key witness in a 1949 trial against Alger Hiss, a high American official accused of spying for the Soviet Union and who also happened to be Field's close friend.[166] During her testimony, Massing implicated Field as one of her recruits. Even before Massing's testimony, the leadership of the Czechoslovak and Hungarian security police had already received information at the beginning of 1948 of Field's involvement with Dulles and thus his participation in American espionage. With that turn of events, his situation became more dramatic: for the Soviets he was a provocateur and for the Americans a spy and traitor. Even so, at least until the spring of 1949, Field did not realize how precarious his situation had become and that the people around him were considered stigmatized and likewise suspicious.[167]

Field was arrested in Prague on May 11, 1949, as he was leaving his hotel. He had come to the city at the invitation of the head of the Czechoslovak secret police, not realizing it was a trap.[168] Soon after his arrest came orders to arrest people close to him in Czechoslovakia, Hungary, and Poland. In Poland, nine people were arrested, all who had come in contact with Field in France and Switzerland during the war, including Tonia.[169] Field's wife and foster daughter were arrested in Czechoslovakia, and his brother, Herman, was arrested in Poland when he traveled to find his missing brother.[170] For the first two weeks, Field was kept in solitary confinement and interrogated by Soviet officers. After that time, and only after that, was he turned over to the Hungarians.[171] Spałek reconstructs the vision of Field's conspiracy that the Soviet, Hungarian, and later Polish security services cocreated. According to Spałek, by financing the organizational activities of international communist groups in Switzerland during the war, Field set two goals. First, he wanted to make the leaders of these groups dependent on him. When the Red Army began to approach the Balkan countries, Czechoslovakia, and Poland, Field began realizing his second goal: under the guise of humanitarian activity, medical teams for the liberated areas were organized, and with gifts of medical equipment, medicine, and skilled staff, they infiltrated communist countries with US military personnel and OSS intelligence operatives.[172] Secret police officers from Poland, Hungary, Czechoslovakia, and the Soviet Union were convinced they were dealing with a wide range of espionage and subversive activities undertaken by American leadership.

The action against Field was preceded by a process of internal purges within a Marxist framework of class conflict with an internal enemy. One scenario of this conflict that positioned Leon Trotsky as a primary enemy had played out within the Soviet Union before the war. After the war it was the Yugoslavian leader Josip Broz Tito, who pushed for independence from Soviet leadership. Eastern European leaders, aware of the internal Soviet purges of the 1930s, were willing to blame others to protect themselves in case of purges after the war. In Poland, starting in June 1948, the communist leader Władysław Gomułka was deemed suspicious. Then Albanian and Bulgarian leaders fell. It was in Hungary where Field's work was used as an argument for collusion between Eastern European leaders and US intelligence.[173] On May 30, 1949, László Rajk was arrested. Rajk, one of the fathers of Hungarian communism and the minister of internal affairs, had served as the political commissioner for Hungarian volunteers in the Spanish Civil War. His involvement in Spain served as a clear indication of his contact with Field.[174] This fever did not end with Rajk but continued in Czechoslovakia, which in 1952 experienced a show trial against fourteen members of the Czechoslovak Communist Party, eleven of whom were sentenced to death and executed. This was the pinnacle of the show trials in Europe. Almost at the same time, in 1953 in the United States, Julius and Ethel Rosenberg were convicted and executed for spying for the Soviets.[175]

Field and consequently Tonia were clearly involved in a fabricated case. Both, as well as dozens of others, were forced to participate in the creation of a story implicating many more people. In his short overview of Field's trial in Hungary, Paczkowski compares the methods used against Field to the Bolshevik methods Arthur Koestler convincingly described in his novel 1940 *Darkness at Noon:* an old revolutionary and authoritarian party member who survived a fascist jail is arrested for treason and eventually admits to his guilt for the sake of the party. The political mechanism was based on absolute party loyalty that required one to search for and ultimately find guilt in oneself.[176] Thus, the communists not only were forced to fabricate their guilt but also had to convince themselves of their guilt. Tonia was susceptible to this mechanism as well. Evidence comes from a spy in one of Tonia's cells.

From September 1949 until early 1950, Tonia was kept in a cell with five women representing different ideological stances. Sabina Stalińska and Halina Zakrzewska had belonged to the Home Army. Ewa Piwińska was a communist. Vera Szot, arrested for her participation in the Ukrainian Insurgent Army, completed this unusual collection of women as probably the most alienated person in the cell because of Polish-Ukrainian tensions and her Ukrainian identity.[177] With the exception of Piwińska, one of these women was a cell spy.

The cell spy began writing reports in September, probably just before Piwińska joined the cell, on some of the most intimate moments of the women's cohabitation.[178] Tonia and later Piwińska were the main subjects of the reports. The reports were handwritten, rather lengthy, and signed "Postęp" (Progress). They discussed the women's interactions in the cell, focusing on the communist women's self-explorations of their relationship with communist ideology and the past. In line with that focus, Postęp noted the enormous earnestness with which Tonia responded to her interrogation officers' request to describe her contact with Field. Unlike other women in the cell, Tonia hoped that her conversations with them would help solve an issue they were working on and consequently lead to her release. "She does not even regret the months of imprisonment, but she worries about her work, apartment, and children," concluded Postęp. At the end of the first report, Postęp described Tonia in almost uncritical terms as "sincere in [her] relationships, direct, modest, straightforward, full of life, an idealist, a sincere and devoted communist, a good mother with no ambitions to gain fame or privileges. She lives the ideal that communism means happiness for future generations."[179] Imprisonment made Tonia revisit some of her former suspicions. After a number of interrogations, Tonia began to suspect that Field was a spy and even admitted she was objectively guilty, even though she was subjectively innocent. Years later, Tonia explained that she had believed "where there's smoke, there's fire." She was convinced that innocent people were not sitting in prison; those in prison were guilty.[180]

The documents Tonia either produced in prison or were produced with her cooperation show a state of confusion or perhaps an existential desire to understand her predicament and guilt. She found guilt in herself, but it was more difficult to establish what she was guilty of. She understood that her indictment meant she was suspected of collaboration, of working with the enemy, or of being naive enough to fall into traps set up by the enemy. She was accused of collaborating with an anticommunist spy, which implied betrayal of one's nation, ideology, and values. It also meant betrayal of oneself—of the commitments upon which one built one's life. In *Darkness at Noon*, Koestler portrayed a man who was innocent of the charges and yet who could not quell the suspicion that the party could never be mistaken. "The Party is the embodiment of the revolutionary idea in history. . . . She makes no mistakes. Yet, . . . the more the Party tried to build the Utopia which reason and the logic of history dictated was possible and necessary, the more repression was needed."[181] Koestler's insight helps to convey how one can be seduced by the logic of the revolution. The available documents in Tonia's case show the nuances of this process. She sought and found guilt in herself; perhaps she even found comfort in her regained agency and the fact that her submission served the communist cause. But it was not a onetime decision; she had to constantly wrench it out of herself.

In contrast to her initial imprisonment, in which had Tonia actively participated in her interrogations to understand her wrongdoing, two and a half years later in another prison cell she was placed in the position of judging someone else's attitude toward the investigation and, through it, one's guilt. In February 1952, she was moved to a cell with a woman who struggled with mental problems, Wanda Podgórska, a former secretary of Gomułka's. In 1957 Tonia testified that she was told that Podgórska was an enemy of the state who was pretending to have a mental breakdown and that Tonia should not hesitate to use violence against her if necessary. At the same time, she was supposed to be reporting on Podgórska's behavior.[182] Spałek argues that while in the cell with Podgórska, Tonia served as a cell spy called "Teresa." There were three reports from Teresa, dated February, April, and September 1953.[183]

Their cohabitation was difficult. When Tonia first entered the cell, Podgórska was in a straitjacket and was being force-fed.[184] Podgórska was violent and aggressive and refused to accept the charges against her. She called Tonia names and harassed her—for example, by rubbing a brush she shared with Tonia with a urine-soaked cloth.[185] Teresa's initial report stated:

> I have been in the same cell with Podgórska Wanda for a year. At the beginning, I was under the impression that she had a tired psyche, but after some observations from our life together, I came to the conclusion that her behavior results from a hostile attitude toward the investigative authorities. . . . She is convinced that the investigative authorities are capable of accusing an individual or even condemning someone to death for acts the person did not commit. She tells imaginary stories about abuse at the hands of prison authorities. These stories breathe such boundless hatred, these insinuations are so monstrous that they can only be spoken by a person who hates with all her soul but is therefore intentionally dishonest. Her hatred of the

authorities led her to lose her own dignity, and although she realizes this, as she has shown in various conversations with me, she does not change her behavior."[186]

Most revealing in these reports is perhaps that while describing Podgórska's behavior, Tonia must have been making comparisons to her own situation, at least to the violence and hostility she had experienced. In the reports, she clarified that Podgórska was guilty of the difficulties she found herself in, partially because she was unwilling to accept the help the interrogation officers extended to her—the help from people who represented the state Tonia desperately wanted to trust. Tonia further explained that she had tried to convince Podgórska to read books, maintain hygiene, and eat. But all in vain. She also noted that Podgórska interpreted the guard's comments that Podgórska was dirty and Tonia clean as Podgórska being guilty and Tonia innocent. Finally, she wrote, "One day we spoke about self-criticism, and Podgórska expressed the opinion that self-criticism and confession are the same things. When I protested, she tried to justify her opinion."[187]

Much of what Tonia tried to discuss with Podgórska resembles her own dilemmas. In a sense, Podgórska kept Tonia in a state of alertness about acceptance of one's guilt in light of lack of evidence or an individual's mental, but also physical, vulnerability. Recently journalist Anne Applebaum recalled what Czesław Miłosz wrote about the pleasure of conformity: "Once the intellectual has accepted that there is no other way, he eats with relish, his movements take on vigor, his color returns. Conformity grants the lightness of heart, it solves so many personal and professional dilemmas."[188] For Tonia, an acceptance of guilt brought hope that there was a way to maintain a belief in communism.

In a 1954 report to the Central Commission of Party Control written after her release from prison, Tonia admitted that "all the harassment and torture used against me during the entire period of my imprisonment were nothing compared to the conviction that I was guilty. It caused me a lot of pain to realize the blame I deserved. This conviction has not given me peace yet." Despite her dramatic experiences and breakdowns, Tonia never confessed to intentional and deliberate espionage for Field. Nor did she confirm that Field was a spy.[189] As her reports from her cohabitation with Podgórska show, she attempted to exonerate the party and defend Field while blaming herself. But the depths of despair accompanying this process are perhaps difficult to reimagine. It was not just communism on the line but also her entire life: the ideology that organized it dictated her life choices and brought Sioma to his death. In searching for ways to defend communism, she was defending her life.

The Children

In September 1949 Jonesy wrote to Tonia's parents in Israel and explained that before leaving Poland, she had tried to find out what had happened to Vera and Marcel, but the situation appeared hopeless. The one friend of Tonia's whom she contacted was too scared to reveal anything related to her imprisonment. Jonesy attempted to enter the apartment where Vera was now supposed to be living but was told that Vera was not there.[190] In December she wrote again, expressing her anxiety that nobody was able to find out much about the children's whereabouts. Interestingly, she also informed Tonia's parents that she had asked her American friend Frances Berges if she would be willing to share the name of the woman who took Vera in, but Frances decided not to because she was afraid it would be too dangerous for all parties involved.[191] In June 1950 Jonesy was still writing to the Bialers, wondering where Tonia was being confined and where the children were.[192]

Vera often shares a story of how her grandparents discovered her and Marcel's whereabouts. In this story, it was Aron Bialer's former Łódź employee, a man named Richter who ascertained in a conversation with his friend, who had been visiting his wife in a hospital in Duszniki in Silesia, that next to her in a hospital bed was a young girl sick with diphtheria who worried about her brother.[193] Richter had remained in touch with the Bialers' relatives still living in Poland and thus knew about Tonia's imprisonment and the children's disappearance. Acting with the Bialers' permission, Richter confirmed that the girl hospitalized next to his wife was indeed Vera. Further, he learned that the children were living in an orphanage in Wrocław and agreed to facilitate communication between them and their grandparents.[194] Two months later, in November 1951, the children began writing letters to the Bialers. "Grandma, we would love to be at your place because we have no one here who can really replace Mommy and Daddy, and we know that Grandma and Grandpa would replace them. But we know that this is a difficult matter, so please don't worry if it doesn't work out right away," the thirteen-year-old Vera wrote in one of the first letters.[195] Marcel was eleven.

Thanks to Richter, the children maintained contact with their grandparents, who also attempted to support them with food and clothing packages. These were sent directly to Richter, who then distributed them to the children. Almost from the very beginning, Richter understood that the most urgent matter was to have the children move to Israel. But the situation was not that simple. To begin the process, the children needed to have some documentation, including birth certificates, which they did not have. Richter wondered if the children could write to President Bolesław Bierut to ask for permission to leave for Israel; there was even a suggestion to refer to the children's father's communist past and his fight in the Spanish Civil War.[196] The children apparently did write the letter and received a response that their request had been sent to the Ministry of Security of Foreign Passports.[197] Another letter discussed the possibility of Sioma's father requesting permission for his grandchildren—the children of his only son—to travel to Israel.[198]

The history of what happened to Marcel and Vera after their mother's imprisonment is fragmented. Halina Diamant first took them in and then agreed to send them to Bierutowice, located in southwestern Poland, to a place that functioned as an orphanage for children of Spanish Civil War volunteers. From there, a year and a half later, they were moved to an orphanage in Wrocław, where Vera stayed until the end of 1954. Most likely around 1952, the children had been separated. Marcel was sent to Ząbkowice Śląskie and next to a school for training miners in Wałbrzych, both in Lower Silesia. Marcel deals with this period by blocking it out, while Vera remembers it as a period of great worry. Marcel was fighting frequently, and he had problems controlling his bladder. Vera felt humiliated when in the morning his wet underwear would be hoisted up on a mast like a flag. This is how the authorities were educating children to get a grip on themselves.

Vera maintained correspondence with her grandparents and displayed sensitivities similar to her mother's while addressing various family members by their names and sending best wishes or expressions of love. She was skillfully building relationships with a family she did not know or barely remembered. She also continued taking care of Marcel and was deeply worried about his well-being: "Grandma, we miss you terribly. Grandma, get us out of here. I don't cry anymore, but Marcel cries all night and asks when we will go to

Grandma. I understand that it is difficult to obtain a passport, but it is difficult for him to understand."[199] She informed them when it appeared that Marcel was improving: "Marcel is happier ever since we don't mention that Mommy is gone. Because when he remembers he cries and does not eat anything. At school, he is doing well, but please write to him to tell him not to fool around at school and to listen, but do not say that I wrote to you."[200]

Marcel was not the only one who struggled. In early 1952 Teresa Moździerz, a woman who worked in the children's home, initiated a conversation with the Bialers about Vera:

> The observation of Vera by the doctor and through me, however, indicates that Vera is becoming haggard not because of her stomach but because of nervousness. Especially recently, when Mr. R[ichter] could not come and did not have letters from you. It was good, therefore, that you sent her a letter to me because she received it today. Marcel doesn't get sick or nervous. He is childish still, and he doesn't experience everything as strongly as Vera does.[201]

In late 1952 Vera was sent to an orphanage in Zakopane for a short vacation. There she was welcomed by a nurse named Trudi Sokołowska, her mother's friend and the wife of Janusz Sokołowski, a man Tonia had met in Switzerland, who was also imprisoned. Trudi explained to Vera that her mother and Janusz were in Rakowiecka Prison in Warsaw. Trudi also suggested that Vera should write to her mother.[202] On January 13, 1953, Vera and Marcel received a response from their mother. "My dearest, beloved children, Wieroczek and Marceli-son! I can't find words to describe my joy and emotion while reading your beloved, wise, good letter! How I should thank you for this most beautiful New Year's Eve gift! My dearest children, I conclude from the letter that—thanks to your educators—you are growing into brave people."[203] An exchange began, allowing the children to hear from their mother and giving Tonia a chance to continue being a mother, even from behind prison bars. Tonia addressed her children with various diminutive names: Wieroczka, Marceli. She used nicknames such as *króliczku* (bunny) and *iskierki* (sparkles). Her letters are full of tenderness and love. These are the letters of a mother who understood that she needed to find something positive in their separation. She attempted to remain involved from a distance and often referred to the wishes of Sioma as if trying to reintroduce his presence in the children's lives. He had not played an important role in her conversations with her parents when she was in Switzerland, but now he returned in her words to her children as if searching for confirmation that the way she was raising them—and even the forced separation—made sense. Her communism helped her argue for their cohesion as a family and extend her and Sioma's influence into their lives, even in the unimaginable circumstances in which they found themselves:

> I am very glad you are learning well. . . . Remember that when you learn, you are now indebted to the working class, which works hard for you, you grow up to pay this debt, so . . . you must study diligently. . . . I am glad you take part in performances and dances. Your father also had the skills in this direction at school in a youth organization, and in the end he always took part in performances. Marceli, my bunny, and in which play did you play the main role? I don't know if I will have the opportunity to write before your birthday, Son, so today I am sending you my warmest wishes so that you will grow up to be the right, brave man our country needs. Remember, your father fought and died so that you could live in a People's Country, free from capitalism, that you, beloved children, could go to a school where they teach you the truth about man and the world. Remember, it cost many victims so that you could learn freely. Therefore, respect and love your school and orphanage. I kiss my sparkles—be happy![204]

Each of Tonia's four surviving letters from prison are framed by communism: as an idea that made her believe that a decent, better life for her children was possible, even in light of her absence. There is still some hope and determination from her earlier life, and there is also the power of the narrative Tonia created for her and her children, her coping mechanism:

> I love you very, very much! But these turbulent times separated us. Apparently, that's what was meant to be. Only today I realized how much our paths diverged and that there is nothing we can do about it. It's hard for me to write, but we have to face it. My beloved, I want to console you, and I know it will calm you down. I do not feel alone, abandoned on the pathless trek! I am happy and proud that my beloved children can grow up and get educated in People's Poland, that

they can enjoy what I and Sioma have been missing all my life! I don't regret for a moment that I took this path. I know it will give you comfort in this difficult situation for you. In truth, because of me, my dearest children have a difficult childhood, but how much harder it would be for you somewhere else. I will try to do everything in my power to give you at least in part what I took away from you. But here the future is open to you; you have opportunities like nowhere else. That's why I look to the future with peace.[205]

There is something deeply ironic—and painful—in her writing that their forced separation had to happen, that it was of the price she had to pay for this new and better life she had built for her children.

On the day of Tonia's release, in October 1954, a party representative took her shopping for new clothes. "I was ashamed to take off the prison clothes," she said. "I knew I stank, and my underwear was not white anymore. Everybody kept staring at me. After five years I did not know how to put on stockings," she told Dowgiałło.[206] A few months later, she was reunited with Marcel and Vera, but they had difficulty adjusting to a mother they barely knew. The mother they remembered was young and beautiful, not aging and mentally broken.

|||

A deep silence, or perhaps mystery, delineates Tonia's postwar years in Poland. Letters to her parents from the preprison and prison days show two different images of herself that she attempted to create. In correspondence with her parents, she was a proud homemaker and a mother; in correspondence from prison with her children, she was a proud mother and a committed communist. At first, she attempted to convince her parents that moving to Poland had been the right choice. Moving had provided her with an opportunity to enjoy a professional life to an extent that had not been previously possible. While in prison, she attempted to convince her children that even this tragedy did not undermine her trust in the system she had helped build and that thanks to her and Sioma's efforts they lived in a safer place. She most likely consciously silenced the doubts and observations regarding growing antisemitism, the Soviets' violent presence, and the often questionable and cruel beginning of communism in Poland. None of this makes it into the documents she left as a record of this period of her life.

At the beginning of her life in Poland, she framed this period as an obligation: the obligation of a Jew to prevent the terrible past from happening again, the obligation of a communist to build a better world, the obligation of a communist mother to build a better world for her children. While still in Wermelskirchen, she wrote in a letter to her parents, "Those poor children—they have had to have so much understanding in their lives for things they do not understand. So often they had to give up happy moments of family life. I hope that soon I will be able to give them everything back. This is one of my biggest responsibilities, isn't it?"[207] From being a homemaker for her children to acting as a homemaker in creating a new Poland, in prison she appeared to concede that communism—as a peaceful home for all—could replace her. Communism provided her with the narrative of an ideology that ordered her life, gave her life meaning, explained the loss of her husband, and offered some advice on how to continue life and raise her children alone. Even if from a certain perspective her blind belief in communism appeared as a search for hope and maybe even salvation, it most likely also meant a dramatic resignation and a loss of faith in herself. The dramatic letters she sent to her children from prison and her reports on Podgórska seem to confirm this cost. She did not trust her own judgment and instead was committed to doing everything to save her trust in communism to protect herself from a sense of overwhelming loss.

7 ||| "Life Is So Knotty"

The Final Return, 1954–1996

TONIA WAS released on October 24, 1954, after spending over five years in prison. She was informed about her release three days earlier. Due to a lack of evidence, her case had been dismissed. A note composed after her last meeting with prison officials reveals that she did not expect to be released. At that meeting, she emphasized that her personal tragedy was that she was unsuccessful in convincing her interrogators about her lack of knowledge of Noel Field's espionage activity. Before leaving prison, she asked if her release meant that the party still trusted her.[1] Her mental and physical state made the release even more challenging. She was ashamed of her tattered clothes, messy hair, missing teeth, and inability to focus. She felt old, inadequate, and incapable of dealing with the world around her. I wonder if she experienced guilt for the harm her communist beliefs caused her children but also hope that the narrative she lived by—of a committed communist—spared her that torment, at least at this moment.

Her reunion with Vera and Marcel meant facing the pain she had tried to mitigate in her letters to her children in the last years of prison.[2] The party offered her a two-week retreat in Krynica, in southern Poland, where she was supposed to reconnect with her children, but this turned out to be a disastrous idea that made them even more aware of the damage their separation had caused:

> We looked terrible—all three of us. Only I had a good coat from a department store. I told them [the people who participated in the retreat]

that we were from Paris. And a lady thought my coat came from Paris and was amazed. When we were sitting at a table, everybody was looking at us because we did not know how to use utensils—neither myself nor the children. This was terrible! I did not know how to use money—there had been a change of currency in the meantime. I did not even know what the new banknotes looked like.[3]

Probably sometime in November 1954 after this trip, seventeen-year-old Vera declared she needed to return to the orphanage to improve her grades. It was not until January 1955 that Vera agreed to move in with her mother and brother again.[4]

Vera's recollections from this period are chaotic. She has difficulty admitting that she felt uncomfortable with her mother. She acknowledges being stressed but readily skips discussing her own feelings and instead speaks about Marcel. At some point while Tonia was imprisoned, Vera and Marcel got separated. Marcel was causing many problems for his caregivers at the children's home and hence was sent to another children's home, from which he was then sent somewhere else. When leaving prison, Tonia was informed that he was in a children's home in Wałbrzych, in Lower Silesia, where she eventually found him. While there, he had been sent to a school for miners. Vera is bitter and clearly agitated when she talks about her brother, and the years of neglect hurt Marcel. Vera vacillates between attempting to capture the essence of their life in the children's homes and the question of why she and her brother were left basically alone after their mother was arrested. She hesitates to question why her mother's friends did not take care of them: "Nobody had to do anything. Did they have to? They did not. Halina had a small child and was scared." After a moment, she adds, "But they did not even get in touch with us, no one wrote to us, nobody tried to support us in any way when we were in the orphanage."[5]

Marcel remembers little. He was fourteen years old when his mother left prison. Scattered pieces of his memory are recorded in *Tonia i jej dzieci*. He begins by saying that he remembers his mother calling the children's home in Wałbrzych. After this statement, he hesitates. Vera takes over and finishes the sentence by noting that when Marcel heard he was being summoned to the phone to talk to his mother, he responded by saying that his mother was dead. Marcel confirms this and continues, stating that he saw her for the first time on a train platform in Wrocław after he had arrived from Wałbrzych. Vera was there as well. He welcomed Vera, who introduced their mother, a mother he did not recognize. Vera corrects him by saying it was their mother who first traveled to Wałbrzych to see him in the children's home; immediately after welcoming her, Marcel asked for both of them to leave. But the three of them left together immediately for Krynica, without Marcel returning to the home to collect his belongings.

Further, Marcel reads a fragment of his mother's conversation with Dowgiałło, where Tonia mentions that Marcel remembered her as being beautiful. But in 1954, after her release from prison, she looked aged and in terrible shape. Marcel stops when reading a fragment where Tonia admits that she was missing teeth; he was unable to continue reading. He admits being ashamed of her appearance. He was also ashamed when he was asked to pick his mother up from a clinic where she was being treated for mental problems with insulin shock therapy. Vera took on the responsibility of ensuring Tonia returned home safely.[6] Once again, they had to begin anew. They were older, more experienced, but tired of constantly needing to start again.

Reunited

The family story since the reunion belongs to them all: each remembers it slightly differently. It is a story of lessons in patience and rediscovery of each other. It is also a story of Tonia and her children trying to find themselves in this new world, Poland—the place their mother chose for their home and the place that welcomed them with a new meaning of displacement. In the first months after her release, Tonia received substantial help from the Communist Party, which paid for their first shopping trips and the Krynica retreat to help them reconnect. After informing her that her previous apartment had been confiscated and most of her belongings lost, party officials gave her a new apartment and modest financial assistance.[7] Almost immediately after her release, Tonia received a job at the Health Department of the State Commission for Economic Planning (Państwowa Komisja Planowania Gospodarczego, PKPG).[8] The family moved in together in January 1955 into an apartment on Stępińska Street in Warsaw. Tonia was allowed to retrieve some of her old furniture, which had been stored in the cellars of the Ministry of Industry and Trade. Only a table and a few chairs remained.[9]

FIGURE 7.1. With Dorothea Jones at Tonia's apartment on Stępińska Street in Warsaw in 1957, after Tonia's release from prison. *(Private collection of Vera and Marcel Lechtman)*

Resuming letter writing to her family was part of her return. Like how she had previously stabilized her life by recounting her days in Paris and Switzerland to her parents, Tonia again wrote about the most mundane aspects of her life. Curiously, however, she never mentioned the word "prison" in her correspondence but immediately returned to her previous habits of reporting on her good health, her children's well-being, the joy her new apartment brought her, and household responsibilities. "It is simply wonderful what great health I have," she wrote, barely two months after her release. "I am doing really well. I feel great. The kids are doing well also."[10] Only occasionally do some letters reveal the depths of her problems. "Contemporary life is so complicated, personal life is so knotty, that regardless of whether we want it or not, we experience various tragedies. But it is better to keep that at the bottom of our heart and not drag it out, as it will not change much," she wrote in May 1955.[11]

The past could not be that easily circumvented. Soon after Tonia's move to Israel, Michał Chęciński—a Polish military counterespionage officer, who in 1968 immigrated to Israel—interviewed her about her imprisonment and her interaction with her interrogators after her release. Two days after her release, she was summoned to the Communist Party's Central Committee offices to retrieve her party identification card. Franciszek Mazur and another man welcomed her and then searched for her card for a prolonged period. She remembered years later the sensation of feeling sick while waiting and being forced to answer some questions regarding her past:

> I soon realized I was not being welcomed by the two secretaries of the Central Committee to receive an ID card but rather to have statements accusing Różański, Fejgin, and Kaśkiewicz [her interrogators] extracted from me. As soon as I calmed down so they could talk to me, they got down to it. They immediately took notes. And it was exactly the same process as the prison investigation. Same method, same questions, same system. When leaving prison, I signed a pledge that I would not tell anyone anywhere what had happened in prison during the investigation. When I told the two men in the Central Committee that I had pledged not to share what happened in prison, they began laughing.[12]

The party officers who talked to her during that meeting acted as if they wanted to extract information from her but not necessarily learn what really happened. Her well-being was not a concern; rather, she felt trapped in ongoing, mind-boggling struggles of various party interests. Interestingly, however, she did not tell Chęciński the entire truth. She emphasized emotional and psychological torment but denied being beaten, which she revealed in 1957 during a trial against one of her interrogators.[13]

Around the same time, she changed her name from Tonia to the more formal Antonina. As she told Dowgiałło, one of her most violent interrogators, Jacek Różański, used the name Tonia and its diminutive version Tońcia. She did not want to hear those names in a formal setting again.[14] In a letter to her parents, she explained that she was getting too old for the rather informal name Tonia.[15] Was she attempting to regain full control over her life and distance herself from who she was forced to be under interrogation? Despite how much she tried to create this distance, the interrogations, the doubts, and the mental and physical suffering left a traumatic imprint on her, inscribing itself into her body, which spoke about her experiences even when she wanted to remain silent. Vera recalls how ingrained imprisonment was in her mother's body. She once vomited after an encounter with Różański during the 1957 trials of her interrogators. A couple of years later, while visiting her family in Israel, she dealt with the pain of a gallbladder stone attack by running in circles in a space the size of her cell. She had had her first attack in prison.[16] Imprisonment remained in her body, regardless of how intensely she wanted to expel it from her thoughts.

The process that led to her release—the saturation of Polish and Eastern European politics with abuses and imprisonments reached its limit and caused it to begin falling apart under its own weight—also created the conditions to which she returned.[17] The most immediate cause of the crisis was Joseph Stalin's death, on March 5, 1953. In December of the same year, Józef Światło, the MBP officer who had arrested Tonia, defected to the West.[18] Already in March 1954, fearing the consequences of this defection, Poland made its first attempt to confront its difficult past by punishing those they deemed responsible for its mishandlings. That same month, another MBP interrogator known for his cruelty, Różański, was fired.[19] Five months later, in September, when Tonia was still imprisoned, Światło began speaking on Radio Free Europe about the abuses of power that took place at the MBP. As historian Andrzej Paczkowski states: "His lurid tales of routine torture of political prisoners, the high life of the communist elite, its links with Moscow and a ubiquitous system of police informing, began to broadcast back to Poland from autumn 1954."[20] His stories included snippets from the minutes of Tonia's interrogations, such as information about her nervous breakdown.[21] Barely a few months after Tonia's release, in December 1954, the MBP was disbanded and replaced with the Ministry of Internal Affairs.[22]

In February 1956 came the explosive speech by Nikita Khrushchev, who in a closed meeting of the Twentieth Congress of the Communist Party denounced some of the crimes of Stalinism. This secret speech, directed at a group of party members, was soon distributed worldwide. Hence, the world Tonia was released into was anticipating change that was based on hope that publicly addressing the abuses of the past few years might create a way to reorganize public life. At the same time, there was little hope that change could be achieved with the existing institutions. Poles, especially young people, were increasingly radicalized. "Discussion clubs mushroomed—for music (including jazz), sculpture and film appreciation. Student theatre and satirical reviews appeared in Gdańsk, Łódź, Kraków, and elsewhere." The Communist Party was fractured between those who demanded change and those who strived for maintaining the status quo. In factories "mass meetings called to hear and discuss the 'secret speech' concentrated on 'cults' at their own workplaces." The biggest protests began in June 1956 in Poznań. Street protests and student and worker demonstrations were a daily occurrence. In October Soviet troops appeared near the Polish border. Soviet military advisers visited the country, ostensibly on maneuvers but clearly also as a warning signal to calm the situation.[23] Eventually, it was the appearance and promises of Władysław Gomułka, himself a recently released political prisoner (in December 1954), that stabilized the situation. As a man who had experienced Stalinist prisons firsthand, Gomułka was a symbol of renewal. In October 1956 he became the first secretary of the Community Party. On October 24 enthusiastic crowds welcomed him in Warsaw at Parade Square.[24] Despite his involvement in the establishment of communism, he became the face of change, symbolizing the end of abuse and unjust imprisonments but also only a moderate willingness to deal with past evils. He celebrated a new beginning but called for a peaceful end to the gathering and a return to work. A day earlier, on October 23, Soviet tanks had entered Hungary to quell social unrest. As a newly elected party leader, Gomułka pledged loyalty to socialism, and a similar Soviet intervention in Poland was avoided.[25]

Tonia's letters offer only a faint shadow of the ferment transforming political life in Poland, which she likely followed closely.[26] In August to October 1956, Tonia and Vera visited family in Israel.[27] Only in November, shortly after they returned, did Tonia reference in a letter to her brother Julek what must have been a world of political and personal turmoil for her:

> There are many discussions here. We have constant meetings, and for that reason I don't have time to write. The mood is great here, despite the Hungarian tragedy—we were just steps away from it. Julek, all of this is terrible. Will we ever dig ourselves out of this swamp? We can do trials—but if they fail, it's over! You know it is difficult for a person to think things through to the end.... Nevertheless, we think positively—we have a lot of enthusiasm.[28]

In those years, a pattern emerged in her communication with her family. Tonia shared the majority of her political statements with her brother Julek, who, according to Vera, shared her mother's political sympathies. She argued with him but also shared her doubts and optimism regarding political changes. In 1956 there was much to fear regarding the immediate future but equally much to hope for in terms of long-term positive changes:

> I sit by the radio and listen to a political nativity scene. It's a pity that Juleczek is not sitting next to me! But because of this, this letter is a bit chaotic, because each good joke interrupts me. Julek, things are not great here now . . . but this is how it must look right now, after the lofty days, cobwebs and dirt come out. Nevertheless, I am optimistic—but there are very hard days and months ahead of us. Can we do it? Will they let us!?[29]

These words of optimism indicate that communism as an ideology still resonated deeply with Tonia. Perhaps it is equally important to reflect on the meaning of doubts accompanying her in these months. When she left prison only two years earlier, she doubted herself more than her interrogation officers. In 1956 she continued perceiving communism as a movement shaped and strengthened via the struggle with its opponents and enemies. Different this time was that enemies were publicly exposed, offering a very tangible promise of change.

One more element pushed her to perceive this moment differently. The 1956 events forced her to face the antisemitism around her. As historian

Dariusz Stola argues, the resurgence of antisemitism was widespread: "There was a rise in the number of anti-Jewish incidents, from name-calling and bullying of Jewish children to beatings and antisemitic flyers. Amid the general upheaval and condemnation of earlier government policies, some people started blaming Jews for many, if not most, of the crimes and absurdities of the Stalin era."[30] Tonia's correspondence does not address antisemitism, perhaps out of concern for her parents, who would have been even more alarmed by the growing unrest in Poland if they knew Tonia felt unsafe. Only years later when talking to Dowgiałło did Tonia admit that antisemitism affected her household. She noted anecdotally that she used to prepare an onion salad for her children. She did not have a lot of money, but onions were cheap, and onion salad, a dish she often prepared in her prison cell, seemed like a solution to poverty. When she served it for the first time to Marcel, he refused by saying that "only rotten Jews eat that." When she explained that he was a Jew, he was appalled. "What are you telling me? In Wałbrzych, I used to beat Jews, and now you are telling me I am a Jew?" Tonia told Dowgiałło she said to her. She continued: "I did not manage to explain anything when he said that he does not want to have anything to do with the Jews. 'Listen. Your grandmother's name is Rachela, and you need to remember that.'"[31]

The year 1956 coincided with a wave of Polish immigration to the Jewish state, which Israelis dubbed "the Gomułka aliyah." In the spring and fall of 1955, the granting of permits for immigration to Israel to Polish citizens of Jewish ethnicity increased. Immigrating became much easier in the summer of 1956. The party instructed the Passport Bureau to grant visas to candidates even without relatives in Israel.[32]

This mass emigration deeply affected Tonia.[33] "I cannot stop regretting that so many people left. It's a pity that they did not stay, because the atmosphere has changed tremendously here," she wrote to her parents.[34] In addition to regret at the loss of friends and acquaintances, she felt anger at their decision to leave, a decision she did not fully comprehend. In January 1957 she wrote:

> You probably already know that a lot of people leave, mostly to you [Israel]. The Jews here are possessed by some kind of psychosis, otherwise it cannot be imagined. It is undeniable that antisemitism has recently increased in our country. In Warsaw, one feels it less, but apparently there were very unpleasant events in the provinces.

In my opinion, this period will pass quickly. As soon as the situation stabilizes, this disease [presumably antisemitism] will pass. Recently, especially in the preelection period, these elements were acting out. They damaged a lot. . . . Especially the conservative elements of the party did much harm. These are very painful matters for us here, but we are convinced that we will overcome them, like many other difficulties. There are naturally people, Jews who can't stand it nervously, who have just had enough. However, there are a lot of negative elements among the Jews in my opinion as well. They have behaved badly here all these years, and now they take their stuff under the arm and leave. You may think about it differently. These are mostly people who survived the war in the Soviet Union.[35]

Interestingly, she used language characteristic of communist propaganda—for example, by referring to people as an "element": an element among party members, an element among Jews. She never explained what she meant by Jews who "behaved badly," but her references to the Jews who arrived from the Soviet Union most likely means the Jews who participated in building communism in the first postwar phase or even Stalinism, such as Różański the interrogation officer.[36] But Jews leaving Poland bothered her, and in a letter to her brother she worried about how this readiness to leave Poland would be received. "It is a dishonor and shame," she wrote to Julek.[37]

In January 1956 Seweryn Bialer, Tonia's cousin, left Poland as well. In postwar Poland he had held a number of positions in the Communist Party, including a seat in the party steering unit, the Central Committee. Born in 1926, he grew up in Łódź in the affluent family of the brother of Tonia's grandfather. Like Tonia and her brother, he became a communist early on. He survived the war, first in the Łódź ghetto, where he witnessed the death of his father and from where in 1942 he was taken to Auschwitz. After the war, he participated in the building of the Communist Party, first as a party apparatchik and later also as a researcher in the Polish Academy of Sciences.[38] His niece, Małgorzata Górecka, recalled that he and Tonia were portrayed as family "black sheep"—people who had grown up in rich households but chose to distance themselves from the lifestyles and traditions that built those households. After the war, Bialer did not restore family relations with his mother or sister.[39] Was he close to Tonia? Their life trajectories were similar at some point, and the silence regarding him in the documents she left behind is striking. In 1956 he traveled to West Berlin, the trip during which he defected to the West. Is it possible Tonia was aware of his defection as well? If so, did it anger her as a decision to abandon the life project at the encounter of a crisis? Her silence about him may be partially due to her fear of censorship, but that in itself does not fully explain his seeming absence from her life. In West Berlin, he worked for Radio Free Europe, the same station that publicized stories by Światło. From Germany, he left for New York, where he eventually became a professor at Columbia University.[40]

Due to the intensity with which many people were fleeing Poland, Tonia's children also began considering it. They must have been communicating with Tonia's family in Israel because they all began pressuring Tonia to leave. She responded with a definitive refusal. In April 1957 she sent a long letter to her parents, similar in tone to the one she sent them after her announcement that she and Sioma had decided to engage in the Spanish Civil War. She enumerated the reasons for her refusal to leave: most important, her loyalty to Poland, her commitment to communism, and her desire to be a role model for her children:

> Can you choose your homeland at all? Yes, I feel Polish. I am emotionally and, above all, culturally bound by strong threads to Poland—I am attached to Polish comrades, to the entire nation. The party taught me that a communist is a patriot for his country—is this not valid anymore? How could I look into the eyes of the people whom I told in the previous period that for socialism, for the motherland, we must make some sacrifices, we must renounce many things, we must work. I told them that I am Polish, that for the sake of Poland I support the internal or foreign policy of the party—we all said it was the party members who love Poland the most—and now I, a party member, because it is hard or unpleasant, would look for another country to proclaim similar slogans? I suppose you will admit it would be wrong, that the place of a party member is with the working class, with the people. A party member should strive with the same zeal with which he supported the Stalinist policy in the previous period, to correct the errors resulting from this policy. It is clear that a member does not always have enough strength, that at this moment zeal cannot be revived in everyone, but that is a betrayal. . . . I have never been a great party activist, but I have always

> been faithful to the principles instilled in me by the party, principles that are also right today, because they are universal. Even if I had given up my party card, I would not have changed my opinion on this matter—after all, I did not come here on the command of the commissar to introduce communism, but I came as a Pole to fight for a better, fairer Poland. Then, in 1944, when I made the decision to return to Poland, I settled this problem and never regretted it, even in those hard years.

She had sided with those who believed in the possibility of reforming the communist system and placed herself among its zealous supporters, who remained faithful to the party while striving to correct past mistakes. "Entering the Communist Party, we joined our lives with the worker's case, and it was not abstract.... Of course, a communist can fight anywhere, but a communist leaving Poland now has an unpleasant political aftertaste," she continued.[41] A few weeks later, she wrote, "I don't doubt in the possibility of the revival of the worker's movement, a progressive movement. I don't know if I will be useful in this struggle for revival, but without the atmosphere of a struggle for the new, I don't want to and cannot live."[42]

This question of loyalty to the communist cause was directly linked to Tonia's understanding of her maternal role. In a letter, she shared her concern that she had little to offer her children: she was nervous, old in spirit, and not easy to live with. But she was able to show her children that she was not a conformist and did not choose the easy path. "What kind of person lets herself be pushed by any wind?"

> You must also understand that the children's attachment to me is not great; after all, they spent most of their lives without me. The very fact that I am a mother does not yet create bonds that are so strong that in the period when each person begins to consciously shape their life they are important. Can children be brought up here to become good people? Certainly so. Besides my children, there are millions of others who will not all grow up to be hooligans.[43]

Her loyalty was the best thing she could offer her children.

Tonia conveyed how important Poland was to her. Culturally and socially, she identified as Polish. She had grown increasingly detached from

Jewishness. She found the meaning of being Jewish in something that one of Joanna Wiszniewicz's interlocutors, who interviewed people directly affected by the 1968 events, expressed as dignity and readiness to react to antisemitic attacks.[44] Toward the end of a letter to her parents and brother, Tonia addressed her brother directly by explaining that he should not think that she had some biases against Israel. She remained a Polish Jew but was not interested in deepening or even developing her Jewish cultural identity. She treated Israel as her family's homeland, and for that reason it remained important to her. Tonia went even further, saying that if every Jew should live in Israel, then perhaps she was not a Jew, since she was much more connected to Poland. But if she were to choose a place to migrate to, she would go to a place with some revolutionary life and more Polish émigrés.[45]

Tonia noticed that even though at first her children's willingness to leave Poland hurt her, over time her emotions cooled down. "I realized the children do not have the responsibilities that I consciously took on myself a long time ago. It still pains me that the children showed a lack of attachment to the country, but this is the fault of the upbringing the Stalinist period gave them." She finished the letter by saying that she would accept her children's decision if they eventually chose Israel but noted that "a family's happiness cannot be preferred over an obligation toward one's community." She continued, "Sioma loved me very much, but he put the 'case' before me: whether the 'case' was right or not we can discuss, but it does not diminish his attitude. Sioma's children should not have an example of selfishness in me. It has to be hard sometimes."[46] She told her parents a few weeks later:

> My beloved, I would like to be clear: I really feel connected with the Polish nation with all its faults and vices. I cannot imagine my life without the problems of this country. If I was ever forced to leave the country, I would become an emigrant. Since I know the taste of such a life well, I will do everything to prevent this from happening. . . . I would like for you not to expect my arrival.[47]

She refused to leave Poland, no matter what was happening or how much she missed her family. "I have you, loving friends, the party, work—in my youthful dreams I could not have dreamed of so much happiness. The only thing that hurts me is that Sioma did not live to see this. Our happiness cost a lot, and I will defend it as much as I can."[48]

Naomi Bogusławska, a family member occasionally mentioned in the letters, offered a different perspective on why the children were eager to leave Poland. Vera was romantically involved with a man who had moved to Israel, and Marcel was having difficulty in school, so it might be easier for him to have a fresh start. In a letter to Julian, Bogusławska generalized about the larger significance of decisions to leave one's country in the context of what appears to be her own decision to stay:

> I understand your distress and your worries as I understand my father's. But the matter is not easy for us. We get really tired. Maybe the time for major decisions has not come yet; it is difficult to give up on yourself. We know well that moving means a need to evaluate our lives. Little would be left of our accomplishments. We push this awareness away from us—a bit like bankrupt people, a bit like players, and a bit like people who, despite everything, find meaning in one's life that is unique and not repeatable. Those who are torn out of here will never find themselves again. We are going through a difficult period. We thrash around like fish in an aquarium smashing their noses against glass. What to do? I do not know.[49]

Bogusławska's letter reveals a dilemma Tonia struggled with as well. Departing potentially meant a negative evaluation of her life and a resignation from the ideals that had been driving her since her youth, ideals her husband died for. Poland was experiencing turmoil, with political elites changing, new promises being offered, expectations shifting, and people giving up and leaving out of fear and/or from fatigue from promises that were never delivered. Tonia consciously chose to position herself as a person who did not give up easily and continuously believed in the validity of the communist struggle. From the letters emerges an image of a Polish citizen and a communist who, only in Poland and among those still committed to the project of creating a just and equitable world, was able to heal from the misfortunes of the previous years. Poland, the communist exemplar, even with its mistakes, was her home.

The next year opened a new chapter in that process of healing. In 1957 preparations for the trials of the main MBP officers and interrogators began. After Gomułka's return to power, those perceived as the most representative of the sins of Stalinism were to be exposed, among them the most brutal public security officers, including Roman Romkowski, Józef Różański, Józef

Dusza, Jan Kieras, and Anatol Fejgin, people responsible for the arrests and violent interrogations of many innocent individuals. In September the trials began. But due to a fear of public unrest that they might stir up, the entire process took place behind closed doors and addressed the claims of only twenty people.[50] While exposing and sacrificing people who symbolized the regime's brutality, the trials were saving the system.[51] Tonia was among those who were called to testify. In the courtroom, she had to relive the torture, humiliation, and intensity of her interrogations.[52] As she revealed in a conversation with Chęciński, some of its aspects—the moments of her encounter with her previous interrogators—were particularly upsetting:

> During the trial, Fejgin claimed that he never interrogated me. I repeated that he had reproached me for my return to Poland from Palestine. Fejgin was terribly indignant and thought that it was a mistake . . . and that as proof that these were not antisemitic statements, he said that he was a Jew. . . . Actually, Fejgin had told me during the investigation to imagine how terrible it was that my children and his children were playing in the yard together. They [Tonia's children] had infected his children with this American venom. And despite this, in court he said that he was seeing me for the first time, that he had never questioned me. This was his defense.

Further, she shared that during his trial Kaśkiewicz claimed that Sioma belonged to the Russian White Army, but a member of the Communist Planning Committee, who was present at the trial and had just managed to get some financial help to Tonia, confirmed that he had been a member of the International Brigades.[53] All of these tidbits from the trial that she remembered years later were omitted from the transcripts, but they do hint at enormous distress.[54] At one moment in a transcript, she appeared to confuse the dates of her arrest and was consequently challenged by one of the accused, her former interrogator, who argued that her mistakes suggested that her testimony was false. Anna Duracz, also a communist who was imprisoned on similar charges, openly protested against the humiliation she and Tonia were experiencing during the trials. Duracz stated that informal chats in the lobby had implied that there was a conspiracy among people accused in Field's case, like Tonia and herself.[55] That would suggest that they were still suspected of being guilty.

The trials were supposed to symbolically end a certain phase in her personal, but also professional, life. In many respects they did, regardless of the anxieties they also reopened: Światło defected to the West where he disappeared, Różański and Fejgin were imprisoned, and Field was released and reconnected with Tonia. A couple of months after the trials, at the end of 1957, Herta and Noel Field visited Tonia in Warsaw. We get snippets of this reunion in Vera's letters to her grandparents and scattered statements by Tonia, which reveal a shift in the intensity of her political engagement. From her letters we learn that she was tired of the ideological disputes that Field insisted on—of his refusal to see how his ideological choices were affecting others. Still, their fervent discussions lasted long into the night.[56] Vera wrote to her grandparents: "I got back the day before yesterday. The Fields have been with us for two weeks. Complete madness.... There are discussions from 8 a.m. to 3 a.m. They don't eat; they don't drink. Field's sister arrived yesterday. She came for only two days after ten years of not seeing her brother."[57] During one of these long nights of discussion, Field told Tonia about the torture he had endured, his desire to die, and the moaning and then shooting of László Rajk, the Hungarian communist politician implicated in Field's case.[58] Imprisonment did return to their conversations, but this tells us little about the problems that must have accompanied these conversations. Was it difficult to talk to each other after imprisonment and interrogations that brought so many doubts regarding Field in Tonia's life? How did they rebuild trust?

Much more separated them in 1957 than in the previous years. The way they reacted to their experiences created a chasm between them. Tonia described Field and his wife as fanatics who did not learn from past experiences. "I can't understand it—because Noel is a smart man. He just wants to stay true to his ideas and actually lives alone in Budapest."[59] Later when she was invited to discuss the encounters she had with Field, she admitted that when he visited Warsaw, they went for a walk, during which she showed him the scale of Polish support expressed for the victims of the Soviet invasion of Hungary in 1956. He refused to accept it and considered the Polish demonstrations of 1956 a betrayal. He remained a staunch communist, loyal to a world she considered to be faulty. When Field was released from prison and reunited with his wife, the first words he addressed to her were "Were you faithful?," according to Tonia. "What he was asking about was her faithfulness not to him but to the party." Communism remained the essence of his life, and all

FIGURE 7.2. Left to right: Tonia, Noel Field, Vera, and Marcel at a train station. *(Private collection of Vera and Marcel Lechtman)*

he still wanted, after years of being confined by communists, was to receive a Communist Party ID.[60] Tonia sensed the growing chasm between herself and the Fields and resolved never to discuss politics with him again. She saw a difference between his unwavering commitment and her commitment based on loyalty to Poland, her children, and the world she had begun building, a world framed by communism but in need of reform. She was critical of fanatic communists, potentially increasingly aware of the scope of the problems that communism caused and yet still creatively struggling to find some space for communism in her life.

A Room of Her Own

Although the end of the 1950s was a symbolic threshold for Tonia, unsurprisingly, little of this significance made it into her letters. Her continued correspondence with her family in Israel (after her father's death in 1961, the family comprised her mother and her younger brother and his family) served similar purposes as it had in the past: a platform for dialogue with the external world that aimed to normalize her life. Writing about her daily life and efforts, she was reconstructing herself again. While buffering herself from the memory and consequences of a difficult past, she relished with new confidence about what used to bring her joy: the comfort of her own home, both in the small sense (the apartment in which she lived with her children) and in the bigger sense (Poland, which was quickly changing). Thus, in her eyes communism became less of an ideology of radical social transformation and more of evidence of her loyalty that carried educational value and a lived experience of making the world a bit easier, a bit more equitable, a bit less scary.

Rather than focusing on shortages and daily struggles, she acknowledged and drew energy from the visible benefits of communism. One such moment was commenting on the multicultural, multiethnic, and multiracial groups of youth on Warsaw streets during the International Festival of Youth in July and August 1955.[61] "You don't realize what an impressive event this is. It is a Chinese circus; it is Bulgarian dances or a Ukrainian choir. Ah, it is impossible to mention it all. Vietnam, India, Africa shows us all its glory. Warsaw is teeming with laughter, games and the singing of all races and nationalities," she wrote in August 1955.[62]

On another occasion, she wrote about new opportunities:

It is easier here when it comes to children because we have many beautiful kindergartens and nurseries, where children develop beautifully. In general, our care for a child has developed to an exaggeration. The way everything is organized for these kids is amazing. We, the elders, are jealous of the little ones, and we would most gladly return to infancy. But children my age [referring to Vera and Marcel] also have so many attractions, such a beautiful life that we never dreamed of in our youth. I recently visited the Palace of Culture. It is indeed the eighth wonder of the world. The section for young people and children is a fairy tale. For older children, apart from theaters, cinemas, etc., there are rooms where they can conduct all kinds of experiments. Here there are the latest technical achievements, and children learn under the supervision of professionals. There is also a beautiful winter garden. Everything is huge, luxuriously made, with great splendor. And if you could only imagine how enormous the halls are and what the view from the thirty-seventh floor is like!63

The world looked more modern, more stable, and more equitable, and she reveled in it. She was learning to enjoy herself; she searched for and found signals of a positive change.

But the space she enjoyed most was her own apartment—her healing space that provided her opportunities for creativity and helped her rebuild her relationships with her children and, via proxy, with the world around her. In a letter to her grandparents, Vera shared her perspective about her mother: "Mom bakes a cake and changes the kitchen every day. So that these curtains were not too Zionist in color, she trimmed them with a red ribbon. Good, isn't it?"64 Tonia was trying to run a modern household: various powders and other cleaning miracles, as well as modern pots and instant soups she received from Israel, helped her gain the reputation of someone who knew how the modern kitchen should look.65 This modernism gained a new meaning, as she was transforming it from her private space to a brick in the communist project.

Not surprisingly, however, her attempts at representing herself as a perfect homemaker corresponded with a general trend of a decreased focus on female labor and productivity outside of the home in the years following the

Polish government's six-year economic plan (1950–55). On one hand, "when women's labor activism ceased to be the movement's key need, and on the other hand, the social protests raised a notion of 'relieving' women from professional work, organizing one's household gained importance in the official discourse."[66] During the little stabilization of the late 1950s and 1960s that was characterized by steady improvement in the quality of life and increase in daily consumption, women were increasingly enticed to stay at home. In light of these changes, household and family units shifted to being perceived as sites of reproduction and sites of respite where men could renew their energy for work. Female work inside the home gained meaning through its contribution to society. These changes in the conceptualization of women's labor and their commitment to domesticity were also an invitation to begin thinking about modern solutions to household problems.[67]

Tonia, with her desire to maintain a modern household and a cozy space of individual recovery, certainly reflected these trends. In her letters, she appeared to be jokingly aware of them:

> Julek, you are asking how my friends treated all my kitchen treasures. Well, they were yellow, green with jealousy, but because here we draw positive consequences from everything, I received a job at the Institute of Domestic Affairs [Instytut Gospodarstwa Domowego]. My kitchen is famous, and most likely I will be working in this institute. Juleczek, don't laugh.... But now seriously, an institute like this is created here in order to take a step forward with regard to the items of daily consumption, since we are still in the medieval period when it comes to this topic.[68]

In early 1957 Tonia officially switched jobs and began working for the Institute of Domestic Affairs, where she worked in the library's section for foreign documentation. Her brother must have expressed his doubts regarding this change because in a letter to him she said, "You don't appreciate the role of such an institute. There are institutes of this kind all over the world, and now, in connection with the slogan 'Open to the People' (*frontem do człowieka*), we want to facilitate domestic work for working women."[69]

As if in conjunction with her professional development, Tonia began transforming her apartment into a space where she could continue her communist work on a small scale. This space connected the private and public. She arranged, adorned, and made her home welcoming for gatherings of people from various social groups: her new friends; her friends from France and Switzerland; her American friends from the USC, such as Dorothea Jones (Jonesy), Frances Berges, and Noel Field; and her friends from prison, Ewa Piwińska, Halina Zakrzewska, and Krystyna Arciuch.[70] In addition to hosting many foreign guests, Tonia organized Sunday dinners for her close friends, especially her prison friends. These women, who gathered weekly for a traditional Sunday tomato soup, often returned to conversation about their prison experience. They shared their pains but also laughed about their experience. Tonia's apartment was becoming a healing space. Vera remembers being terrified and leaving conversations when the women laughed about the physical pain they had endured.[71] "It always started with some chatter, and then there were Ewa Piwińska's performances. I remember the moment when she stood on a stool while recounting how Różański entered the cell, grabbed their hair, and smacked their heads. And they would burst out laughing."[72]

Izabella (Iza) Legocka, Marcel's first wife, who lived with Tonia and Marcel from 1960 until 1969, remembers the women laughing when they recalled the surname of one of their interrogators, Józef Dusza. The word *dusza* means "soul" in Polish, and the contrast between the meaning and the person made them laugh.[73] In the early 1970s Marcel Łoziński filmed one such moment, when Ewa, Halina, and Tonia talked and laughed about their imprisonment. (Only fragments of this film have survived.) In one of the truly striking clips, Ewa, in a theatrical voice, describes a handsome and perfumed Różański entering the cell. She walks around the room while performing the way Różański behaved. We can hear Halina's voice from the background: "The Prince of Darkness. Różański in Yardley [cologne]." Ewa continues: "The investigation officer gets up at the sight of Różański entering the room. Różański says: 'Is it Piwińska? Ewa? Piwińska. Ah, Piwińska Ewa. I thought she was a decent woman. How many whores were there in the Vatican City?'" Halina begins to laugh in the background. Ewa imitates her answers from decades earlier: "In the Vatican? How were you supposed to know?" Then she plays Różański again: "'Oh well. Has she revealed the other side of the story?' The investigator says, 'No.' 'Piwińska, when will you begin talking?' 'I've already said what I had to say.' 'You fucking bitch!'"[74]

We tend to think of the division between the private (women's domain) and public (men's domain) spheres as an element of socialization in patriarchal societies. Tonia's domesticity could be perceived within a traditional and stereotypical framework, but we need to recognize these efforts also as her way to deal with the fear and vulnerability that had accumulated over decades of displacement that meant, among other things, the lack of space she could call her own and in consequence the deprivation of the sense of safety.[75] That process of creating a home certainly helped her return to normalcy after prison. It was her safe space, a space she shared with close friends where she felt empowered to reveal the most difficult moments of her imprisonment. It not only helped her bridge the private and public but also allowed her to domesticate what was painful. Within the walls of her apartment, life was returning to normalcy.

In 1959 Vera began studying medicine, was learning languages, traveled abroad, hiked in the Polish mountains, and fell in and out of love. She was living a full and happy life that brought immense joy and pride to Tonia. In 1965 Vera married and moved to Mrągowo in the Masurian Lake District, where she and her husband, Bogusław Ligęza, began their medical internships in a local hospital. The couple received a small apartment in the attic of the local children's home. In 1966 Vera gave birth to Anna Katarzyna, who became the new focus of Tonia's life.[76]

While Vera blossomed, Marcel struggled with finishing high school and finding a meaningful occupation. Tonia worried and blamed his troubles on his upbringing and early adulthood:[77]

> Everyone is amazed at Vera, and he is always overlooked. Even recently when it comes to looks, Vera overtook him. My poor son. Even when it comes to contact with you. Vera is very close to you, and he is at a distance. It certainly hurts him. It's also difficult for me. I can buy Vera different things—a scarf, brooch, or any other trinket—and with a boy, it is more difficult. He wrote two very nice letters to you, but he was stressed and tore them up. You cannot imagine how guilty I feel that I did not take him when I came to visit you. This affected him so much, and it's my fault.[78]

Eventually, in 1960, Marcel married his girlfriend, Iza, and they moved in with Tonia. Life slowly became more stable and more fulfilling for him as well.

Among visits from friends that were especially important for Tonia were additional visits from Noel Field, sometimes with his wife but more often alone. In letters Tonia occasionally emphasized that they decided not to discuss politics, which allowed their friendship to flourish. In August 1958 Tonia visited the Fields for the first time with her children in Budapest, where the Fields resided. All three were amazed by the city and the atmosphere the Fields created. "I have no poetic skills, but even I am tempted by the sights around me to write a cantata about the beauty of life, nature, and human work.... After the nervous hustle and bustle of Warsaw life, we found ourselves ... in incredible luxury and most importantly among two charming people who only think about how to make our stay pleasant."[79] What is left from that trip is a painting that Marcel did of an interior of an apartment with two green chairs and a yellow lamp in between.

Tonia and Field, who often visited without his wife, had a strong connection. They sometimes even traveled together to Zakopane for vacation.[80] These visits continued for the next almost ten years. Was this friendship more than an opportunity to recount memories from the past, or did it evolve over time into a romantic engagement? While Vera rejects the idea that there was something romantic between Tonia and Field, Marcel is convinced of a deeper connection between them. Both Vera and Marcel avoided this topic in mutual conversations. The letters Tonia sent to her mother from Bogatynia, where she briefly worked in 1963, allude to a closeness to Field. Eventually, she informed her mother that she decided to end her relationship with Field, partially due to meeting someone else. The letters provide no details as to what happened with this other man, or where she met him, or even if he existed.[81] The documents of the security police reveal a bit more about him.

Around the same time that Tonia was renewing her former contacts and learning how to enjoy her life again, the security police renewed their interest in her. The existing file, or perhaps what remained in her file from that activity, suggests that at least since 1962, Tonia and some people in her closest circles were being observed. The existing reports do not reveal anything extraordinary, just the rhythm of the daily life of a woman responsible for two growing children.[82] Eventually, the reports began paying attention to Tonia and Field's close relationship and his frequent visits to Poland. The reason for writing these reports, however, are not clear. Were they linked to the lingering distrust of Tonia or to suspicions regarding Field's work in Poland or both? Interestingly, in the report from 1963, for the first time in Tonia's documentation the name of her cousin Seweryn Bialer appears as well as that of another relative who had defected.[83] These reports also reveal the presence of Tonia's romantic interest, a German man, Walter Bloch. Apparently the secret services had intercepted their correspondence, which disclosed their intimate closeness and possibly love. Tonia ended the relationship in 1963 due to Bloch's marital status.[84] Very likely Bloch was the man she alluded to in the letter to her mother about Field.

Despite the closeness she may have developed with someone else, Field continued to be part of the family's life. When Vera gave birth to Anna, Tonia wrote to her parents that Field treated the child like his own granddaughter. "He is really touching. He brought a whole suitcase of cloth diapers he thought she could throw away after each use, convinced he had freed Vera from washing forever. He thought it would be enough for the entire period of infancy."[85] Their contact over time became less frequent but nevertheless continued to be meaningful. Field remained an important part of the family until his premature death in 1970.

The late 1960s also brought the most heartbreaking event in Tonia's life. In early 1967 Tonia's mother visited her in Warsaw, a visit that had been Tonia's longtime dream. Tonia wrote to her mother just after her return to Israel on February 18, 1967, to tell her how much joy her stay in Warsaw had evoked.[86] That same month Julian forwarded to Tonia a farewell letter that their mother had addressed to him. She had decided to commit suicide: "My Dearest. Forgive me, but I cannot do otherwise. I don't have the spiritual strength anymore. I am finished."[87]

1968

In the second half of the 1960s, Tonia lived with Marcel and Iza, while Vera lived with her family in Mrągowo. Life was calm. After her mother's death, Tonia's letters to Julek became less frequent and less detailed. Her sister, Noemi, died in 1962. Julek remained the last close family member in Israel. Their stagnant correspondence possibly reflects a decline in the prominence of political topics in Tonia's life. Tonia concerned herself mostly with her granddaughter, called Ania, and Marcel's marital problems.

The moment that shook their lives came in 1967, when the Six-Day War tore apart the Middle East. Initially, when the war broke out, official Polish media reports were cautious and not overtly critical of Israel. Soon, however, the press was filled with thunderous condemnation of the Israeli aggressors, along with expressions of solidarity with Arab nations. Following Moscow's steps, Polish authorities decided to offer military and financial support to Arab countries.[88] In public life, Polish hostility toward Jews grew. Historian Brian Porter-Szűcs says that "by 1967, the ministry of the interior claimed that 'Zionists' were engaged in 'organized, synchronized' efforts within Poland, pretending to be supportive while in reality undermining the Party's program."[89] The anti-Israeli campaign grew, reaching its pinnacle on July 19 at a meeting of the Trade Union Congress, when Gomułka warned of the dangers of Zionism in Poland and announced that every Polish citizen should have only one fatherland—the People's Poland: "But we cannot remain indifferent toward people who in the face of a threat to world peace, and thus also to the security of Poland and the peaceful work of our nation, come out in favor of the aggressor, the wreckers of peace, and imperialism. . . . We do not want a fifth column to be created in our country."[90]

The events known as the student demonstration(s) of March 1968 and their pacification by authorities were the final stage of the state actions Gomułka launched in June 1967. After the demonstrations began, an article appeared in the press emphasizing links between the disturbances and Zionists and Jewish ex-Stalinists. All of these notions of a fifth column and Zionism—which spoke to the deeply embedded antisemitism in society—served as tools to create the image of an internal threat and spin the spiral of suspicions and hate. Eventually, on March 19, 1968, Gomułka gave a speech in which he clearly called for the people of Jewish origin to leave the country. He expressed a conviction that there was a problem with self-identity among some Jews who were attached more to Israel than to Poland. Emigration was the most immediate and widespread response to these proclamations. As Stola shows, the border was opened "for those who indicated Israel as their destination and specified their ethnicity as Jewish. In 1968 a total of 3,437 people left, while only 26 were refused their passport. The following year, the number of emigres rose to 7,674."[91]

The few letters Tonia sent from this period do not exhibit any reaction to this political turmoil. None of the documents that either Vera or Tonia left behind speak of them being involved in or even reacting to the events of March 1968. Life was intensely busy and full of serious health-related family matters. Ania, two years old, was sick, and her health problems were growing more serious with every passing week. In April 1968 Tonia wrote to Julek,

"The last months were indeed terrible. This child suffered terribly. I cannot simply think about this. She is so tiny but so brave."[92] What began in February as an ear infection had turned into a brain infection that affected the child's vision and led to long months of hospitalization.

Later when asked to reflect on how the events of March 1968 affected her life, Vera recalled:

> So now it's 1968. I went to Warsaw for my three months of training. And just then, my daughter got sick. They took her to the children's hospital in Bielany. She almost lost her sight. At that time . . . parents were only allowed to visit their children in the hospital three times per week, at 3 p.m. I got a pass saying I could visit her every day, on the condition that I also see some of the other children. . . . I took a taxi to the hospital every day—not because I was so well-off but because it was March and the student protests were making it hard to get anywhere on the bus.
>
> On March 19, I was in Mrągowo.
>
> I watched Gomułka's speech in the Congress Hall on television. For me it was unbelievable. . . . And Gomułka, in that same speech, used the phrase: "two fatherlands. Choose which one you want." That really hit home with me.[93]

The context of the interview and the questions about the political significance of 1968 certainly had an impact on how Vera answered. But the reality of the family's lives in 1968, as reflected in the existing correspondence and the state documents, leaves little doubt that it was dominated by health concerns and a thickening fog of suspicion and distrust.

Vera and her husband, Bogusz, had already been under observation by the security forces since at least 1967.[94] In July 1968 security forces began an investigation into Vera's social and political stance and life in Mrągowo, in accordance with the logic of the purges of Jews from various organizations and workplaces that the anti-Zionist campaign initiated. After identifying someone as a Jew, it was easy to label them as a Zionist. It was enough to show that they sided with Israel, were critical of the anti-Zionist campaign, or maintained contacts with family in Israel.[95] In Vera's case, complaints from the hospital staff where she worked regarding her Jewish origin and ongoing contacts with Jews abroad, including Israel, Switzerland, and the United

States, spurred the investigation. Undoubtedly, the antisemitic atmosphere permeating public life at the time inspired these complaints. One of the justifications for opening the investigation was an allegation that during "Israeli aggression against the Arab states," Vera criticized the Polish government.[96] A complaint from August 1967 stated that neither Vera nor Bogusz were politically or socially engaged. Further, both were allegedly duplicitous in their public engagements and never revealed their true faces: "During the conflict with Israel, Vera publicly showed no emotions, while privately she exposed sympathies to Israel."[97] The reports were clearly vengeful, attacking Vera and her husband for their network of international and domestic support. They also describe Vera's good relationship with the head of the hospital and reflect jealousy of her accomplishments. A statement from April 1968 claimed:

> I consider it my duty to inform concerned authorities about the following facts about the director of the hospital, Długoborski, and some doctors of Jewish origins with whom he surrounded himself and favored from the moment they came to work in the area of Mrągowo.... I am thinking mainly about the Ligęza couple. They received an apartment in a children's home, where electricity, heating, a canteen, laundry facility, cleaning, etc. were almost free.... [Vera Ligęza] herself often travels abroad, constantly leaves for some educational trainings, travels to her family, is late and leaves work early, takes occasional leave at the director's consent. She compensates him by facilitating his contact with her family abroad and with the packages sent by them.... She does not even have Polish clothes. Even some of her furniture arrived from France. Her mother-in-law looks Jewish.[98]

The comment about her mother-in-law's Jewish appearance was repeated in the official note summarizing the state of the investigation into Vera and Bogusz's life.[99]

Her file includes another letter from May, which called Vera vindictive and accused her of introducing discord among hospital personnel. The problem concerned the local population, the Masurians, who inhabited the regions around Olsztyn and Mrągowo, where Vera worked. In the postwar years, many members of the local population were considered Germans and either were expelled or willingly emigrated. Apparently Vera publicly criticized one of the nurses for expressing negative opinions about Masurians. "Two employees argued—one was of Polish nationality and the other of local origins. These two women called each other Swabs [pejorative for Germans]. This matter was brought up at a staff meeting. Ligęza spoke in support of an employee, Kruk, who was also a Masurian local. Her statement was reproduced in the report, and she was reported as saying, 'We cannot tease the indigenous people, because they are at a disadvantage, when we, Poles, took these lands from them.'"[100]

As previously mentioned, emigration was the most widespread reaction to the 1968 anti-Jewish campaign. Already in April 1968 the party recommended the preparation of instructions regarding the departure of Polish citizens of Jewish origin. The borders were opened for people who specified their ethnicity as Jewish. One of the requirements for emigration was to relinquish Polish citizenship. Since these émigrés were not considered Poles, they were given not passports but instead a so-called travel document—a one-way ticket.[101]

It is hard to establish at what point the Lechtman/Ligęza family decided to leave, but emigration quickly turned into a solution for a number of their problems. In September 1968, in addition to dealing with the still recovering Ania, Vera gave birth prematurely to her second child, Piotr. It was soon discovered that he was missing an ulna in one arm, which the Polish doctors were unable to treat. They suggested going abroad to get help. Even if political matters were not on Vera's mind, solutions to her family's problems coincided with the political atmosphere.

In a conversation with Teresa Torańska, in which Vera was asked about the reasons for their departure from Poland, Vera said, "My brother, Marcel, immediately decided to emigrate from Poland. His friends convinced him to go to Sweden. He didn't know any other foreign languages; he was a nervous mess."[102] Despite how Vera remembered the various family members' decisions to leave, the situation was less straightforward. As letters indicate, Iza left Marcel suddenly in May 1968. The divorce was finalized in November of that year, leaving Marcel lost.[103] Marcel did indeed leave Poland for Sweden in early 1969, but his motivations were personal. His marriage had fallen apart, he was having problems finding direction in his life, and the move appeared as a solution to his immediate and long-term problems.[104] In February 1969 he received a visa for a three-month stay in Sweden. He arrived there in March and left for Israel twenty days later, on March 24.[105] Although her separation from Marcel was difficult for Tonia, she was not ready to make the decision to leave Poland and follow him to Israel. Both Vera and Iza assert that while others began leaving, Tonia continued to resist.[106]

There are no letters where Tonia discusses the political situation in the country; however, it is impossible to imagine that it did not affect her. As Stola emphasizes,

> antisemitic torrent of March 1968 means first and foremost a campaign of symbolic and verbal aggression that culminated in psychological terror. . . . For the Polish Jews in less than twenty years after the war, this similarity [to prewar antisemitic propaganda] was strong enough for the psychological terror to bear results. . . . This was enough for an awakening of unclear, but because of that even more painful, terror, often bordering with psychosis. Rumors about the preparation of the concentration camps for the Jews circulated; people bolted doors in fear of pogroms.[107]

Understanding of the gravity of the situation certainly depended on age and previous experiences. From stories passed down by those involved in these events, we know that generational splits within families regarding emigration decisions were common. Often the division coincided with different views on communism. While younger people were increasingly more convinced that communism was deeply harmful to individuals and societies, many older communist supporters were tragically tangled up—"people who were honest, but within something that was essentially dishonest."[108]

None of the letters Tonia sent to her brother at this time point to the generational split within her family, but that could partially be due to Tonia's fear of censorship. In the late 1960s, Dorothea Jones began corresponding with Julek in Tel Aviv. What began as an attempt to financially help Marcel travel to Israel in 1965 continued a few years later as correspondence about Tonia and her children.[109] In September 1968, after visiting Tonia in Poland, Jones sent a letter to Julek at the request of Tonia, who wanted him to know about the situation in Poland but was afraid of writing herself. "There is nothing that you can actually do at present other than be extremely careful what you write in your own letters to her, in view of the routine censorship," Jones said. She explained the ongoing crisis as well as Tonia's stance:

Student uprisings as you undoubtedly know, were blamed on the "Zionists and revisionists," which have become synonymous in current Polish political gobbledygook—and as Tonia ironically remarks, they are so naive that they think that by only using the word "Zionist" they cannot be accused of antisemitism. Many Jewish people either lost their jobs or were put in prison at the time of the student trouble, and the only difference with Stalinist times is that there have been trials of a sort, with definite prison terms given, so that some people are already coming out of the jails again. From talking to them, Tonia finds that the prison conditions are also much improved over the Stalinist period, with no real cruelty. She thinks that the current group in power or trying to get into power still do care a good deal about what the Western powers think of them, which is at least some slight limiting factors against the excesses in which they would otherwise gladly indulge.[110]

Tonia was aware of the political developments and the negative directions these developments could take. She still held on to her party ID card, but according to Jonesy she had an "extremely negative feeling" about the party and remained "in the party only for her own protection (and with the knowledge that any day she may be thrown out of it)."

She also received extensive support from people close to her:

The unpopularity of the government with the Polish people has grown to proportions much greater than what has always traditionally existed, and there is already a "backlash" from the antisemitism in that, possibly for the first time in history, an increasing sympathy for the Jews is growing. During the Six-Day War Tonia's apartment was simply filled with flowers, many of them from people she scarcely knew—she would never have believed such a thing was possible. At work and in many other situations she is finding more and more positive feelings toward the Jews expressed by people who would never have done so before, people who are incensed by what they read in the controlled press, much of which sounds like a resurrection of Hitler's press.

Tonia was also anxious and depressed "more than is normal for her." Her depression was caused by the political situation, problems between Iza and Marcel, and fear for her granddaughter. Jonesy in the United States and Margaret Locher in Switzerland communicated with each other while trying to figure out the best medical option for Vera's daughter. They also discussed Marcel's motivations for leaving Poland. Tonia slowly became resigned to his decision: she perceived Marcel's departure almost entirely as a reaction to losing Iza and for this reason was skeptical about the likelihood of Marcel finding happiness in Israel. "I think she would be a great deal more comfortable about it if it were a political decision," added Jonesy. She ended her letter with the following reflection:

> She is currently having such a painful inner struggle to come to terms with the collapse of her ideals, dreams, and beliefs that her right to her own independent thinking and decision-making becomes more important to her than ever, in terms of her own self-respect. I cannot tell you how deeply I felt this, and how much I want to urge you, despite your very understandable instincts against it, to maintain a complete "hands-off" policy, merely standing by with your love and devotion, ready to help at whatever time she is ready to ask you.[111]

The events of 1968 brought significant worries that directly affected the safety and well-being of Tonia's family. Her personal struggle to which Jonesy alluded meant not only a decision to reunite with her family in Israel but also medical options for her grandchildren. First and foremost, the decision would be an admission to a certain life failure, the end of her ideals and trust in communism. This was one aspect of her identity crisis. Based on the rich source base of memoirs and recollections of the emigrants, Stola argues that what was happening in 1968 was, first of all, a rejection of the right to be a Pole that led to a crisis of identity and a decision to leave "against Poland [*przeciwko Polsce*]."[112] Tonia confirmed her Polishness by a willing and enthusiastic return to Poland after the war. Back then her decision was questioned by her parents, but she saw it as her responsibility as a mother, a Pole, and a responsible citizen of the world. The denial of that right in 1968 was another form of expulsion that she had experienced in so many forms prior to that moment—an expulsion from Polishness as well as from the community of communists. For decades the communist networks all over Europe supported her. Despite doubts—even her imprisonment at the hands of fellow communists—she had chosen to believe. The year 1968, however, singled her out not for what she did but for who she was—not because she subconsciously made a mistake and associated with a citizen of the United States, an open enemy of socialist Poland, but because she was a Pole of Jewish origin. That attack came from those she believed were called to protect people like herself and her children against the threats of fascism.

Less than a year later, in May 1969, Tonia wrote to her brother to inform him that she and Vera would join him in Israel, the first sign of her willingness to emigrate. She inquired about what books to take and how to prepare for their impending departure.[113] The question was urgent. The future emigrants had one month from the moment they received permission to leave to pack the belongings they were allowed to take and sell the rest. To take books and artwork, permission of the Minister of Culture and the National Library was required.[114] As if in preparation for the move, in the fall of 1969, when Vera's son Piotr was ten months old, Vera moved to Warsaw, where she took a job at a children's home.[115] Vera believed that from Warsaw she would be able to arrange all the formalities for their departure within a month.[116] Vera's file contains a police analysis of her letter to her husband from July 30, 1969, in which she confirmed that she was trying to arrange their stay in Switzerland. This suggests that by July their plans were already well underway, although it is not fully clear if Switzerland was supposed to be their final destination or a stop on their way to Israel, one that was to provide the children with the medical attention they required. "If Margaret gets us jobs," she wrote, "we will receive stay visas. But this will take at least half a year, and we would have to wait in Vienna or Rome—which I don't think is possible with two children. In general, she claims that the situation of immigrants is very complicated in Switzerland now."[117] In December 1969 Margaret Locher arrived in Warsaw to bring Vera an invitation for a medical examination and treatment of her children at the University of Zurich.[118]

Even though their plans were advanced toward the end of 1969, it would take almost another two years for their departure. In July 1970 Vera's application for a permit to leave was rejected with a note claiming that she could not travel until July 1972. The justification stated that as a Zionist, she had a hostile attitude toward Poland.[119] Another document states that one of the reasons for the rejection was that Vera's husband was a Pole.[120] Vera did not wait another year and applied again in February 1971; this time her application was successful. She received permission for a temporary stay in Switzerland for medical treatment for her children.[121] She left for Switzerland a few months later and waited there for her mother. Tonia's travel document was issued on July 3, 1971; she left Poland three days later, on July 6, 1971. In 1971 the number of people leaving Poland increased again. The peak of emigrations was in 1969 when 7,674 people left; emigrations officially ended in mid-1969, so that by 1970 only another 698 people emigrated. That number, however, grew again in 1971, since this was a year when the time of suspension passed for those who had received rejections before.[122]

Vera left with her two children but without her husband, who decided to stay in Poland. At first, they had decided to apply together, but according to Vera, over time she discouraged him from leaving Poland because she knew he would have a hard time living in Israel. Tonia gave her apartment to Iza, who still lives there. She left her kitchen and trinkets in the apartment, reminding Iza of her presence for decades. Some of her habits remained as well; tomato soup is still a staple for Sunday dinner.[123]

Israel

In Israel, reunited with Vera and Marcel in 1971, Tonia encountered the loving family of her brother, who was happy to help her find a haven for the remaining years of her life. Yet, as Ania, her granddaughter, remembers, "family was her home—but Israel wasn't her choice. Poland was her place. She was here to raise the children and make amends, but she never believed in Israel."[124]

After arrival, at age fifty-three Tonia first worked as a social worker but eventually focused on taking care of Vera's household and the children. Like her early years in France and her later years in Poland, she chose to immerse herself in new responsibilities. As Ania remembers, Tonia was frugal, always trying to think economically to help Vera, who worked and was studying to earn a new medical accreditation in Israel. Ania also believes that Tonia tried to spend as little as possible to justify her living with them and not working:

She mended all her clothes and her underwear, and it was annoying for my mother, but she was fixing everything—sewing and stitching—a dead art by then. She never bought anything new for herself; she seldom sat during dinner with us. She was always moving around and not even sitting down to talk—she was very energetic, a bit anxious to see if everything was according to plan. She always walked to the farmer's market—Shuk HaCarmel—because food there was fresher and cheaper.[125]

Her cooking, mostly based on French recipes, is what many people remember her best for from this time. She required everybody to be home for dinner—nobody was allowed to eat out. Countless pages of recipes are left behind, suggesting Tonia's growing interest in cooking. Ania remembers:

She decided she was going to help raise the children; she decided to be the best homemaker: French soups, desserts. She decided to teach herself how to cook. . . . She was also very strict about it. We had to be at home at a given time for dinner, and she was upset if we did something not according to the plan. For example, I could not take an apple from the fridge if she planned on using it—she was very rigid. She had a vision in her mind of how it was supposed to be, and everybody had to be in line. It was hard for a young teenager.

She was known for a cake called Madame Lupescu, [named after] the mistress of a Romanian king. It was a chocolate cake. . . . When I was small, I would say I needed to go home because there would be Madame Lupescu. All the neighbors looked as if a real Madame Lupescu was coming. . . . She only used butter, which was unheard of in Israel, and it was a bit expensive. Most people used kosher cuisine, and they did not use butter—they used margarine. But with butter, food was much better![126]

Tonia maintained contact with many of her friends. Soon after arriving in Israel, she traveled to the United States to visit Jonesy. Some of her Polish friends, especially Ewa Piwińska and Halina Zakrzewska, visited her in Israel. Ewa, one of her closest friends, visited often, but no correspondence between them remains. In fact, very little correspondence remains from this period, as if Tonia did not continue what her parents had begun—collecting letters.

Almost no personal written sources remain to shed light on this period of her life. Though not letters, other sources have survived, including many newspaper clippings, mostly in French, regarding political developments around the world that Tonia followed.

Marcel did not stay long with Tonia and Vera. Soon after his arrival in Israel, at Ulpan, a school he attended to learn the basics of Hebrew and of Jewish culture, he met Felicja Czaplicka, and through her he met his future wife, Henryka (Henia) Czaplicka. Henia's parents had been divorced since 1956. In 1968, on the wave of the antisemitic campaign, Henia, her boyfriend, and Henia's mother decided to leave Poland. Henia and her boyfriend married to ensure that they would be able to leave together. They left on December 31, 1968, for Sweden, her mother having left for Israel a few weeks before. In 1972, while visiting her mother in Israel, Henia met Marcel. She divorced her husband and convinced Marcel to join her in Sweden. She worried that in Israel, where his mother and sister dominated his life, it would be difficult for them to begin life that belonged fully to only them.[127] The family was loving and caring but also overwhelming, with the presence of Tonia looming over their past and present. An interesting element of this story is that Józef Czaplicki, Henia's father, was a security officer of the MBP, the institution responsible for Tonia's arrest and interrogations. From my intense questioning of both Henia and Marcel, it is clear that this was never an issue for Tonia, Marcel, or Henia. Czaplicki and Tonia met once at a Christmas party that Marcel and Henia hosted in Sweden in the 1980s.[128]

The image of Tonia from these years is blurred by the strong presence of her children, their decisions and worries, and her grandchildren. In a sense, this is the most difficult part of her story to tell: the aging woman for whom a space to reinvent herself was becoming ever narrower, as if as an elderly woman she was slowly disappearing from the world's attention and perhaps also from her own attention to the world and herself. But the 1990s were also the years when, willingly or not, she was encouraged to return to her past. Ania wrote a school project on her family's history, with Tonia the main source of information, even if, as Ania admits, her grandmother was not particularly forthcoming. Historians and journalists began knocking on her door. In the 1990s Tonia gave some interviews, the longer one with Dorota Dowgiałło, the daughter of the first Polish ambassador to Israel after state socialism officially ended in Poland in 1989. She spoke little about her disappointment in communism but admitted that she had ceased believing in it.[129] Two years earlier in another interview, for Polish Radio with the Polish journalist Anna Sekudewicz, when asked what she thought about communism, she responded:

> Today I believe that I contributed to the crime committed by the entire communist movement, and I believe that I helped build a system that turned out to be mendacious. What hurts me the most is that it was all based on a terrible lie. And from this came so many tragedies and misfortunes. Millions of people died. After all, it is unthinkable that everything we fought for has become so terribly twisted. I consider myself to be complicit. In truth, I put my hand to it. And now, sitting in this country where the Jews who have suffered so much all over the world live, I cannot see how they themselves can be ruthless toward another small nation that is unable to defend itself. In a Palestinian village like this, people are about as guilty as I used to be in a Stalinist prison. And this chauvinism! Madam, I am a widow, I have been one basically all my life. And several times I had the opportunity to connect my life with someone but at the expense of another woman. And each time I thought that at the expense of another woman, I would not be happy . . . and I also think that at the expense of another nation you cannot build happiness. And this will not bring happiness to the Jews. This is truly an unsolvable matter.[130]

Communism was at the center of many of these conversations as something that imbued her life with meaning but also caused a pattern of loss she had struggled with her entire life. Were these questions she was herself interested in? Or perhaps they were opened up by the historians and journalists who explored her life story to gain insight into the topics that the fall of communism put in a new light. In the early 1990s, in light of the collapse of state socialism in Eastern Europe and slow opening of archives, these were the questions that so many were interested in. But what did she mean by admitting to participating in the crimes of communism? Was that an echo of what she did in her interrogation cell when she admitted that she was not aware of the danger her trust in Americans could cause? Did she see herself as guilty of not being vigilant enough? Perhaps, but the remaining part of that answer suggests that regardless of her guilt, she remained committed to the ideas of equity and justice that first brought her to communism.

Toward the end of her life, Tonia fell ill with emphysema and a collapsed lung. She was often out of breath and had to sit frequently. She had help in the house and kitchen from a woman who worked with her. She sat on a stool supervising the kitchen work. In the last years of her life, while bedridden, she asked Marcel to sit by her bed during his visits from Sweden, which he refused to do for long. In a conversation with me, he wondered whether his reluctance to be with her in the last days of her life was an act of resentment caused by the difficult life she had created for him and Vera when they were children. Tonia died on September 23, 1996, at seventy-eight, in the apartment in Tel Aviv, where she lived with Vera, adorned with family memorabilia, photos, and plants. She was buried in Israel, in a cemetery maintained by a nonreligious community.

Tonia and Her Children

As noted, *Tonia i jej dzieci* is the title of the movie that Marcel Łoziński produced based on a raw and honest conversation he had with the Lechtman siblings. It depicts both Vera and Marcel and their ongoing struggle to position themselves in their mother's story. Vera still lives in the apartment she occupied with her mother. In the corner of her mother's room stands a hutch with china that in one version of the story came from what remained of their Łódź household but in another was brought from the United States by Jonesy. In the same room, there is a big wardrobe where amid bedsheets and towels Vera stores family treasures: letters, documents, beautiful pieces of cloth embroidered by Tonia in prison, including little pouches that carry—with uncanny pleasure Vera points out—only Tonia's initials. The rest of the apartment is filled with family photos: children, nieces, nephews, grandchildren. This is a home where family is cherished.

Vera reigns in this space as someone who feels responsible for the integrity of her family's history. She remembers her mother's story well. In a way, she remembers it too well. The stories swirl in her head ready to be released, ready to be shared, ready to be revealed as evidence of her intimate relationship with her mother. Vera's life has been full of good and bad people, fortune and misfortune, rich memories of the distant and more distant past, all mostly revolving around her mother's life. She needs just tiny triggers—for example, an old and seemingly forgotten photo from a family album—to begin (re)constructing an anecdote. And nobody knows how much of the anecdote reflects what actually happened and how much of it is Vera's creation. She re-creates dialogues, emotions, the gestures of the protagonists in her story, even if she could not have possibly known them.[131] The stories she remembers are mostly about people—friends and acquaintances—from her mother's life. She became friends with her mother's friends; she accompanied them as much as she was able to in the last days of their lives, occasionally she becoming their only heir. She lived her mother's life more than she has lived her own. In a way, she became her own mother.

Marcel is the opposite. It is almost as if he decided not to remember. Although only two years separate him and Vera, he is treated and treats himself as someone who cannot remember the most dramatic pages of the family's history yet is the one who is heavily affected by them. This includes missing whatever was positive in these stories—for example, the possibility of meeting his father. The people who participated in his life as a young adult remember how close he and Tonia were.[132] They also remember how willingly Tonia shared stories from her past. Izabella warmly remembers morning coffee with Tonia and her stories of her family life in Łódź, the early years in Palestine, the desperate years of war.[133] Marcel Łoziński, his closest friend, remembers curious meetings of former women prisoners sharing prison stories.[134] Marcel Lechtman, however, does not recall any of these encounters. He feels excluded, or excludes himself, from this community of people privy to his mother's story. He is a charmingly warm man who, however, lives with a sense of neglect by his own mother. He is always looking for signals that he and his mother were close, that she cared for him as much as people around him believe she did. He cherishes the small similarities between him and his mother that he points out often—for example, having a permanently runny nose. In the documents and letters I have read, I see a lot of attention and love that Tonia had for both of her children. But I also see a sense of responsibility and an understanding that love and tenderness is not enough for a mother. Her communism dictated her motherhood, which perhaps appears occasionally cold from the outside. According to Łoziński, it was Henia, Marcel's second wife and the love of his life, who created that sense of belonging and worth for Marcel. She has been his foundation. She indulges his need for the connection with the past and supports him with daily tender gestures of love even when she does not seem to receive much in return: the conversations, the mental support, and finally the cookies and soups based on Tonia's recipes that she continues cooking for him.

In 2011 Marcel Łoziński invited both siblings to make a movie about their mother. The idea reached back to 1970 when he first attempted to make it. As a frequent guest in the Lechtman house, he remembered Tonia and her friends' morbid conversations about prison and their terrifying laughter. In 1970 he was a film school student in Łódź, and the scenes from Tonia's apartment appeared to be the perfect topic for a film project. At the time, he produced a seven-minute film. He tried to obtain the school's permission to grant him additional movie tape, but the material did not receive his professors' approval, and the film was confiscated and destroyed. There is no record of this material in the school archive. Decades later, having by chance found sound from the movie in Paris and fragments of the visual material in Poland, he decided to return to the project. Tonia was long gone, but her children were ready to begin talking about their mother's past.

One summer, they met for a week in Łoziński's apartment. They sat at a table with sealed envelopes full of various snippets of minutes of Tonia's interrogations. They grabbed them randomly, opened them, read tidbits, and talked about them. A lot that was disclosed in those days was new to Marcel, who did not realize the scope of his mother's communist engagement or the heavy price she paid. It also revealed a lot about Marcel and Vera's relationship. In a curious way, the conversation centered on the roles that both play within the family setting: the caregiver and the care receiver, the one who controls and the one who relinquishes control. There is one particularly painful scene in the movie where Vera claims that Marcel left Poland for Sweden without informing her and their mother and that it broke Tonia's heart. What follows is a painful moment as Vera and Marcel wonder why they are not closer. Both break down and cry. Only later, while reading family letters, does Marcel realize that Vera and Tonia both knew he was leaving. They both helped in planning his departure, so Vera's statement in the movie was not entirely true. Did Vera feel guilty for her closeness with her mother and distance from Marcel, leading to a search for the justification for such a state of affairs?

They met again with their families in Warsaw in the fall for the premiere of the movie, which Marcel had not seen. Both Łoziński and Henia insist that this was not an omission; it happened on purpose. What Marcel saw on the big screen moved him tremendously. He cried, got angry, and wanted to leave the theater. After the movie, he left Warsaw without talking to Łoziński for weeks. He felt betrayed; he felt as if his lack of memories—his weakness—was being publicly exposed. On the screen, Vera came across as mature and aware of both her mother's life difficulties and Marcel's struggles. She plays the role of Marcel's guardian—perhaps even his mother—controlling his fragile life and life narrative more than he himself is able to do. He appears lost and occasionally even accusatory toward Vera and Tonia. In my conversation with Łoziński, he sees it almost as a gift he offered his best friend, a necessary push to get him more interested in his past. Henia sees it differently, as deeply hurting her husband.[135]

It took Marcel a couple of months before he was able to talk about the movie again. He began researching his family history. He reached for the letters still hidden in the *pawlacz* and began transcribing and organizing them. He spent hours on Google trying to retrieve all lingering remains of the past and read newspapers from the 1930s, trying to fill the blanks in his memory. But when I asked him if he thought the movie pushed him to this work, he responded by neither denying nor confirming. He said he had begun asking questions regarding his family history earlier. In support of this statement, he showed me a photo of his Uncle Julek sitting behind his desk at work in the Tel Aviv factory that his grandparents had established. Behind him is a photo of the original factory. That is where it all began, a couple of years before Łoziński's film, where Marcel found interest in his family's past. It was the love and respect for his mother, but also his uncle, that motivated him. What Łoziński inspired or perhaps displayed for Marcel to see was the contrast between him and his sister, between too much memory and not enough.

Regardless of when Marcel's intense travels into the past began, when I met him he was still very much devoted to his searches. He approaches his research systematically and with great patience: he searches internet archives, reads and transcribes letters, juxtaposes various sources, and draws conclusions. He learns that empathy and context are his keys to the past. When in the summer of 2018 I met with Vera and Marcel together, Marcel was armed with information from the letters and various documents and was able to—and often did—contradict what Vera said. He employed different tools: Vera has memory; he has knowledge of documents. Thanks to this knowledge, while reclaiming the memory of his mother, he is able to retrieve his life.

Silences in our lives are painful. "What haunts are not the dead, but the gaps left within us by the secrets of others," says Phillipe Sands.[136] In February 2020 I met with Irena Grudzińska Gross to discuss the problem of silences in families shaped by the communist beliefs of its members. She is an example of someone raised in Poland by former communists, who spent most of her life in silence about her past. She thinks that mothers sometimes aggressively say too much or do not say enough; they either expose too much or they protect too much. We spoke about her mother, who had just turned one hundred and who celebrates her birthday twice. Only recently did Grudzińska Gross's family recover her mother's official birth certificate, which carries a date different from the one on which she had been celebrating.[137] But wrong facts from the past are not where the problem lies. There are more silences around her mother's engagement with communism: the details of what it means to live as a communist and what it means to live with a devotion to something larger than the family circle. In her case, family members had to embrace the fragments of the story they had heard in order to reconstruct the past for their own individual needs or continue investigating it on their own terms.

After analyzing a number of memoirs of biographies of former communists, literary scholar Agnieszka Mrozik draws a couple of conclusions. On one hand, existing work often demonizes communist women, depicting them as blood and power hungry. On the other, the silence is a mode of dealing with this past and a response to its complexity and the denigrating public discourse. "It turns out that in the Polish families," says Mrozik, "about the past one says nothing, or one says very little, half-words: some events are remembered as if through a fog." As she shows further, under the influence of the contemporary public discourse, "that past acquires the status of a 'family secret,' discovery with which the descendants and descendants of former communists and communists must 'measure' and 'learn to live.'"[138] Perhaps here is where Grudzińska Gross's case fits well, as if her mother has tried to protect her children from the past for different reasons throughout the decades.

Vera and Marcel's case is similar and yet different. Analyzing Łoziński's movie, historian Piotr Forecki creates an image of Marcel as someone who accused his mother of neglect and hence is unable to understand her communism.[139] Abigail Liebman creates an image of Vera as someone traumatized by her mother's choice of communism over motherhood.[140] In my conversation with Vera and Marcel, slightly different images emerge. Even if they were exposed to anticommunist discourse, it happened mostly indirectly and rather late in their lives. For most of their lives, they were surrounded by their mother's communist friends, who lived communism and were driven by socialist sensibilities. They instilled in both of them respect for others, equity, and the value of civic engagement. In her conversation with Liebman, Vera emphasized that her grandchildren also inherited this drive for social justice that they all carry. In one anecdote, Vera explained that her granddaughter decided not to study French in Israel because she could not understand why French and not Arabic should be taught. The population is 20 percent Arab, she pointed out, "so why is it that we don't know their language and they have to know ours?" Vera's reaction was "I listen and am bursting out of pride thinking about my mother. I am an atheist, but sometimes I believe in some continuation. And when I hear such conversations, I think that my mother sits somewhere up there and flushes with contentment while purring—yes, yes, yes!"[141]

Marcel is stricter with regard to his mother's choices but learns from the sources he collects and the history he is disentangling that history is discursive, that historical actors have to be seen against the background of the context that shaped them. Empathy and imagination, rather than bias and rejection, guide him.

I will conclude with an image borrowed from Mrozik and the book by Stefan and Witold Leder about their family and their communism, *Czerwona nić* (Red thread). There is respect for one's ancestors in the way that a heritage of civic engagement and cultivation of socialist sensibilities are celebrated as lessons of civic courage, not as a burden. Mrozik calls it the continuation of a "red thread" as a gift for future generations.[142] This is the same thread Tonia left for her children and their families.

Conclusion

AFTER HEARING me talk nonstop about Tonia and reading some of my writing about her, a good friend asked me if Tonia preferred coffee or tea. We planned a trip to France and Switzerland following her journey, and he wanted to learn more about her. Did she have any special habits? I called Marcel. Marcel liked comparing himself to his mother and over months revealed that she smoked a lot, coughed a lot, and often had a runny nose. But what did she drink? Marcel did not know. After consulting with Vera and her daughter, Anna, he called me back: "Tea, because coffee was too expensive."[1]

Tonia's story as told in this book is based on a traditional reading of the sources. I have remained transparent about their idiosyncrasies, different interpretations they offer, and silences they perpetuate. I have tried not so much to establish the most truthful version of the past as to understand what accounts for the differences various sources tell. Covering a long time span, the letters, for example, are fragmented: their regularity in certain years reflects stability, while their irregularity or even nonexistence in other periods speaks to uncertainty, conditions of war, loss, or a less intense relationship with her family. In her conversation with Dorota Dowgiałło (as well as other interviews) and in her interrogations, Tonia was pushed to reflect on her life while tailoring it to different audiences. In all these sources, she was as much in conversation with someone as with herself. Silence also tells its own story of loss and pain. For example, she rarely mentioned Sioma, but when she did, she turned him into a symbol of commitment and a role model for her children. Following philosopher Maureen Linker, intellectual empathy was my guiding principle in writing Tonia's story, especially an awareness of an intersectional nature of individual identity, a need to trust her, even if conditionally, and a desire to recognize how her but also my own vulnerabilities—the context of sources that mediate her voice and my own biases and expectations—are part of her life as well as my interpretation of it.[2]

The book hence is my interpretation of the life of a particular person, Tonia Lechtman. It is a portrait of a strong, passionate, and persistent woman who faced difficult conditions in the complicated twentieth century. I examine a particular set of identities and individual agency against historical contingencies, without defining where they begin and end. The boundaries are fluid and ever changing.

A Christmas Tree and Matzo Bread: Jewish, Polish, Jewish Polishness

Tonia was a Polish Jew who due to her Jewishness was alienated from mainstream Polish society and due to her class from mainstream Jewish society. While toward the end of her life Jewish culture and traditions were becoming important elements of her nostalgic vision of the past, she did not recognize them as essential to her identity. Her children remember that only once, in postwar Poland, she tried to introduce them to Jewish culture by attempting to find a place where they could acquire matzo.[3] She did not emphasize her Jewishness but did not deny it either. In various moments of her life, she chose or was pushed to identify as a Jew—for example, when trying to formalize her stay in France or to find a haven in either France or Switzerland. In these moments, she identified with the oppressed, the vulnerable.

Tonia was not merely a Pole nor merely a Jew, but a Polish Jew; these crossroads between the Polish and Jewish worlds best describe the forces that shaped her and the context that determined her life choices.[4] These two elements greatly contributed to how she interpreted her place in the private and public spheres, her expectations and obligations, and her imaginary horizons.[5] Jewishness was linked with the materiality of her life: it was in the food she ate or was instructed to avoid, the mezuzah marking the entrance to her family home, the rituals of her family's social calendar, and the Jewish relatives and friends whom she came to know throughout her travels in Europe. It was also in her household's internal hierarchies, with her mother and grandmother in constant tension over the balance between Jewish religious and Polish secular traditions. It was in the closeness with her Jewish schoolmates—girls representing a similar social milieu—and in the separation from many other Jews, poorer, more traditional. Polishness, in contrast, was part not only of the larger context of the sociopolitical dimension of her life but also of her immediate world: the language she used in daily interactions at home and school; the culture she was immersed in, especially through state education; and the books, including romance novels by Polish authors, she read. It was in her frequent carefree vacations on the Baltic coast or in the Polish mountains and also in the absence of non-Jewish Polish friends. Finally, it was in being free of mainstream Polish traditions, as when, for example, she served meat dishes on Christmas Eve, a traditionally meatless feast in Christian Polish culture.[6]

Her Jewishness and Polishness created a world of "sensual sensations" that delineated home—the most immediate Jewish one and the larger but equally intimate Polish one.[7] Poland was, or had the potential to become, a "room of her own."[8] Historian Katrin Steffen writes about these intersections between Polishness and Jewishness evocatively, using the term "Jewish Polishness," which she derives from the work of Jakub Appenszlak, a Jewish journalist and literary and theater critic. Steffen understands the term as a cultural and political identity of Jews who adopted the Polish language and mass culture and internalized the symbols of Polish culture while conceptualizing it romantically. Jewish Polishness is a fluid and creative synthesis.[9] Jewish Polishness was thus "an image and the result of a self-construction" in which Jews imagined their sense of belonging to the Polish nation regardless of how little reciprocation they experienced.[10]

The rebuilding of postwar Poland was hence a project that demanded Tonia's effort, involvement, and imagination. Over these years, she experienced certain aspects of her identity as vulnerabilities: first, as a Jew she experienced Polish antisemitism; then she was pushed to the margins of society as a representative of an undesirable minority in France and a minority in need of protection in Switzerland; and as a Pole and a communist, she experienced marginalization and distrust in France when she was associated with suspected Polish communists. Her absence from Poland in the second half of the 1930s and the 1940s may have made it easier to ignore Polish antisemitism and hence also reimagine Poland as a space where her vulnerabilities could be addressed, where she hoped to be healed, and where she could build a home that aligned with her and Sioma's dreams.

Eva Hoffman writes that "a culture does not exist independently of us but within us. It is inscribed in the psyche, and it gives form and focus to our mental and emotional lives. We could hardly acquire a human identity outside it. . . . In a way, we are nothing more—or less—than an encoded memory of our heritage."[11] While I struggled to fully comprehend Tonia's urge to return to Poland, Hoffman's work clarified for me the depth to which the possibility of return, of finding herself in the culture and language that shaped her, also provided the means to save herself. Her public mission was deeply embedded in her personal story: her return in 1946 symbolically meant a return to 1935. It was a symbolic return to the source, to the possibility of fulfilling her life mission that framed her adult life. But if Polishness was her project to fulfill, she understood it through her Jewish experiences—through memories of antisemitism, the sense of being hunted in France, and displacement in Switzerland.

Agents of Change: Women, Love, Communism

Historians know relatively little about the intersections of gender, class, and ethnicity and the dynamics these intersections introduced into Polish Jewish women's lives.[12] Due to the increasing visibility of women in public spaces and their household roles, we do know that their place in Jewish society positioned women as agents of change and "engines of acculturation."[13] Tonia's family reflects this pattern well. She rarely discussed women's place in her family but revealed enough to sketch the gender relations dominating it—for example, the relationship between her overbearing paternal grandmother who insisted on following Jewish traditions and her mother who engaged in small gestures of resistance against her mother-in-law. Although we do not know much about how Róża Bialer was raised or what schools she attended, we do know that she was an independent woman who married the man of her choosing, Aron Bialer, and that the family business was as much her as her husband's responsibility.[14] Later in life, it was Róża who tried to convince Aron of the importance of a professional career for their daughter and who encouraged her granddaughter to finish higher education, which Róża considered a priority before marriage. Perhaps, then, Róża, as much as Tonia, was an agent of change. Róża certainly played a key role in Tonia's life. Tonia's father is surprisingly absent; even though Tonia addressed most of her letters to both parents, she directed her letters primarily to her mother.

Tonia's identity as a Polish Jew and a woman only deepened a sense of separation or perhaps, using Marxist terms, alienation between self and various elements of her gender, social, and ethnic identity. This separation appears as the main reason for her communism. We know little about her knowledge of communist ideology. She read Stanisław Brzozowski, known for his concept of labor rooted in Marxism. She had some awareness of Rosa Luxemburg, whose portrait still hangs in her last apartment. She read some Lenin, since we know she considered his theory about love beautiful. The questionnaire Sioma filled out while fighting in the Spanish Civil War shows that he was well versed in theoretical communist literature; perhaps conversations about ideology were an important element of their relationship.

But how aware was Tonia of the activism and writing of such women as Vera Zasulich, Alexandra Kollontai, Emma Goldman, and Wanda Wasilewska? They advocated for women's full inclusion into the labor market and supported emancipation from marriages based on financial arrangements or deprived of partnership. Kollontai, for example, called for the "winged Eros": love exceeding bourgeois ideals and focusing on spiritual connection.[15] Marriage was hence not a natural choice for many communist women.[16] In contrast, marriage was meaningful for Tonia, and almost from the very beginning of her life with Sioma, she readily took up the homemaker role.

Clearly communism was a framework for her maturing, gaining independence from her parents, and overcoming the marginality of her position wherever she chose or was forced to relocate. Communism also played a role in building her social networks and organizing her life. Women, especially women either directly involved in communism or active as social workers with some communist sympathies, played a predominant role in her life: their care saved Tonia and her children and infused her communism with a sense of responsibility for others. Communism played a double role in her life, providing her with meaning that linked her past with her future and providing new roles and responsibilities, which helped her deal with trauma. Through her personal relationship with communism, we also need to read her role as a mother. Motherhood was more her public mission than a private affair. Communism was how she lived her life, how she raised her children, how she grieved. It was her space of remaking and mobility.

The question of Jewish participation in communism is often framed in terms of a unique connection between Jews and communism. Many scholars from various disciplines have asked the question of whether something specific made communism especially attractive to Jews.[17] In many interpretations, it is mixed with political phantasms, such as Judeo-Bolshevism, that justify the origins and sources of antisemitism.[18] Yet even scholars who remain consciously wary of interpretations that combine communism and Jewishness find something unique in this relationship. In historian Yuri Slezkine's interpretation, for example, (Soviet) communism was one of the promises modernity brought Jews—one of "the solutions to the 'Jewish predicament' as an attempt to gain universalist *Weltanschauung*, as an attempt by Jews to become just like everybody else."[19] Similarly, historian Paul Hanebrink notes that Jews gravitated toward Bolshevism to embrace social and cultural opportunities. Both Hanebrink and Slezkine suggest that if there was a special link between Jews and communism, it was caused by the promise communism offered and the precarity of the Jewish social and political positions that made them look for solutions that would enhance their individual and collective safety and well-being. Further, communism was not the only solution the interwar period offered.

In Polish historiography, the place of Jewish communists in Polish politics after 1945 has evoked many discussions in academic and popular history. The most contentious element of these discussions is the presence of Jewish communists within the leadership of postwar Poland. The general perception is that postwar Polish politics were dominated by Jews, who occupied key positions in the most important governmental ministries, especially the MBP, later the Ministry of Internal Affairs.[20] The question is complicated, for example, by the issue of identity: what if a Communist Party member of Jewish origins identified as Polish, and how important was their Jewish identity to their communism? Paweł Śpiewak refers to this as a problem between communist Jews and Jewish communists, a question that divided communist supporters already before the war.[21]

Despite continued discussions among historians about Jewish communists' participation in postwar Polish politics, little work has been done on women communists' involvement specifically. There exists one biography in Polish of a female Jewish communist: Julia Brystygier, an MBP director, and hence a woman occupying a key leadership position, which was rare. The book, however, focuses more on the dark legend circulating around her, presenting her as the most violent and cruel member of the Polish security forces, which sources do not confirm, according to the book's author.[22] Even less is available about the work of women communists, let alone Jewish communists, occupying mid-level party or state administration positions, which could help us sketch a better background for Tonia's work. An important attempt to fill this lacuna is a collective volume by historians who analyze the place of gender and questions of social advancement in postwar Poland, even if it does not specifically deal with Jewish women.[23]

Since her return to Poland, Tonia remained involved in public life, initially as a member of the USC and over time as an employee of various ministerial entities. She was a lower-level state official, actively participating in building communism from the bottom up. Her life story, in addition to informing us about her work commitments and responsibilities, reveals her daily engagement—on a personal and public level—in building communism: her unwavering belief that the idea is correct, despite her suffering at the hands of communist comrades; her commitment to raise her children as good communists; and her desire to showcase the household she was creating as an active space for communist networking. It is a story of a Jewish woman who had to reimagine her life repeatedly.

Camps and Prisons: Faces of (Im)mobility

Tonia's life was heavily marked by the emergence of modern ways of monitoring, categorizing, and administrating people. Her entrance into adulthood began with incarceration, first in Poland, then in Palestine. Her own narrative of her initial imprisonment in Poland is vague, but the stories she shared about her prison experiences depict a group of young people discovering their potential. We will never know of the transformation she underwent in prison, but as literature specialist Monika Rudaś-Grodzka notices, based on women's recollections and letters, "prison was a site where female subjectivity crystalized, emancipatory worldviews solidified, internal transformation and spiritual work occurred, and readiness for further political activity arose."[24] This may also have been true for Tonia: her initial imprisonments remained lessons in individual mobilization and even struggles on the local and individual scale.

Her life as a migrant began out of a desire for mobility.[25] Her movement across five countries and in two continents was the most significant feature of her life. Her early life experiences prepared her for this mobility: she learned German and traveled to Western Europe as a child and continued traveling as an adult. While these early experiences had the potential to empower her, later ones marked her life as precarious, beginning with her role as a wife visiting camps for interned members of the International Brigades, continuing with her imprisonment at Nexon to await being transferred into the unknown, and ending with displacement in Switzerland. These precarious experiences were linked to her status as an migrant, an exile, and finally a refugee.

Historian Andrea Pitzer connects the emergence of concentration camps with concerns of public health and bureaucratic efficiencies: organizing and numbering people and confining them to maintain public sanitation and disease-free communities.[26] For historian Richard Overy, such camps are products of World War I and intense popular prejudices and "expressions of national vendetta." He states that the "enemy came to be feared as the agent of social decomposition and infection" and had to be contained and isolated. Both Overy and Pitzer see the emergence of the camps in terms of the larger historical context and the time of transition from an older order of "empires and status-based societies" to a modern world of "mass political mobilization, dynamic social re-ordering and anti-imperialism."[27]

Tonia was the enemy/other, first as a communist and soon afterward as a Jew. How she was perceived shifted from a communist to someone defined and controlled because of her Jewishness. This was part of her condition in Switzerland when her life changed from the position of a hunted Jew to a Jew in need of protection—an unwanted guest seemingly needing protection also from herself. Her confinement in internment camps was marked by waiting and humiliation. She became someone so well defined by Hannah Arendt: "With us the meaning of the term 'refugee' had changed. Now 'refugees' are those of us who have been so unfortunate as to arrive in a new country without means to have to be helped by the refugee communities. . . . We lost our homes, we lost our occupations, and we lost our language."[28]

The last (and longest, 1949–54) of Tonia's imprisonments marked the heaviest of displacements, as it displaced her trust in the communism she had spent her life building. Even if she fought hard not to be reduced by hardship and continued trust in the possibility of renewing her faith in communism after being released, the years of imprisonment in Poland broke her. Earlier exiles and imprisonments had anchored her in the experience of communism that made her trust that there was a way to transform that time into something positive. Her postwar imprisonment, in contrast, furthered her displacement, exile, dislocation, and disorientation.[29] Her carceral experience shifted from bringing potential individual liberation to fear, humiliation, and eventually confusion and self-blame. The loss of trust in communism that came—even if not immediately—as the main consequence of her imprisonment in Poland meant also a loss of the story that made some sense of her previous misfortunes. As a result, it was the biggest blow.

It is worth mentioning that Tonia experienced Auschwitz only tangentially, but it nevertheless accompanied her life. First, during the war, she lived with it as a distant place where Sioma was potentially taken and where she was almost taken. Later, after the war, she lived under its shadow when she was trying to figure out what had happened to Sioma and gathering information about his possible death. Even in the early 1990s, a couple of years before her death, she still pondered whether he had indeed died.

I would like to close with a note on normalization. I began this book by arguing that Tonia was not a unique person, even though her experience appears to be extraordinary. Or, to put it differently, she was unique in her openness, trust, and perseverance, but her struggles were ordinary, even if she faced them in extraordinary times. She was a modern woman, raised with the intuition that her generation differed from the people before them. She believed in the importance of making her own decisions and the strength of individual agency with the power to transform the world. She struggled to maintain the right to her own choices in times that also brought fragmented and unstable identities that created space for individual agency but ultimately also furthered her fragility. Her condition was deeply modern, and her choices and struggles deeply human. This book is about being defined by historical conditions yet driven by ideals, dreams, and a refusal to accept what these conditions offer. It is about a life of a somewhat ordinary woman living in extraordinary times who insisted on believing that she could remain the author of her own life.

Notes

Introduction

1. Kristin Poling, "Small Acts of Storytelling: Why We Need More History," *Clio and the Contemporary*, September 26, 2020, https://clioandthecontemporary.com/2020/09/26/small-acts-of-storytelling-why-we-need-more-history/?fbclid=IwAR2UMWNRgiGfCz-3kqDfszyXMYipgdYCB8E9Gmpwq6l1rdxxy4al4sMN_vY.
2. Marci Shore, *Caviar and Ashes: A Warsaw Generation's Life and Death in Marxism, 1918–1968* (New Haven, CT: Yale University Press, 2006), 368.
3. "Choiceless choice" was coined by Lawrence L. Langer, a scholar of Holocaust literature. He used the term to describe the unprecedented situations of conflict that Jews found themselves in during the Holocaust. Lawrence L. Langer, "The Dilemma of Choice in the Deathcamps," *Centerpoint* 4, no. 1 (1980): 224.
4. This is a question that historian Mark Mazower asked in his biography of his family. Donna Ferguson, "How My Family's History in London Hid a Revolutionary Russian Secret," *The Guardian*, September 26, 2017, https://www.theguardian.com/lifeandstyle/2017/sep/26/mark-mazower-grandad-russian-secret-father-happy-london.
5. Hermione Lee, *Biography: A Very Short Introduction* (Oxford: Oxford University Press, 2018), 61, Kindle.
6. Simona Merkinaite, "The Place for Ideas in a Post-Truth World: A Conversation with Marci Shore," *Krytyka*, February 2019, https://krytyka.com/en/articles/place-ideas-post-truth-world-conversation-marci-shore, emphasis added.
7. Virginia Woolf, *Moments of Being* (San Diego: Harvest, 1985), 80.
8. Lee, *Biography*, 62.
9. Christopher Clark, *The Sleepwalkers: How Europe Went to War in 1914* (New York: Harper Perennial, 2014), introduction, Kindle.
10. I would like to thank Marci Shore for this suggestion.
11. Katrin Steffen, "'Żydowska polskość' jako koncepcja tożsamości w polsko-żydowskiej prasie okresu międzywojennego i jej dziedzictwo Naszej Trybunie w latach 1940–1952," in *Żydowski Polak, Polski Żyd: Problemy tożsamości w literaturze Polsko-Żydowskiej*, ed. Alina Molisak and Zuzanna Kołodziejska (Warsaw: Dom Wydawniczy Elipsa, 2011), 140–50.

12. Izabela Wagner, "Zdjęcie z konkursu piękności i inne dokumenty osobiste: O pracy badawczej i poszukiwaniu znaczeń 'czarnych dziur'—na przykładzie rekonstrukcji biografii Zygmunta Baumana," *Autobiografia. Literatura. Kultura. Media* 14, no. 1 (2020): 145–67.
13. I thank Natalia Aleksiun for this suggestion.
14. Aneta Ostaszewska, *Proces kształtowania kobiecej podmiotowości: Pedagogiczne studium samorozwoju bell hooks* (Warsaw: PWN, 2018), 67–68.
15. See Michal Stanislawski, *Autobiographical Jews: Essays in Jewish Self-Fashioning* (Seattle: University of Washington Press, 2004). See also a special issue of *Autobiografia. Literatura. Kultura. Media* 14, no. 1 (2020).
16. Alessandro Portelli, "What Makes Oral History Different," *The Oral History Reader*, ed. Robert Perks and Alistair Thomson (New York: Routledge, 2006), 36; Alessandro Portelli, *The Death of Luigi Trastulli and Other Stories* (New York: State University of New York Press, 1991).
17. Daniel Mendelsohn, *The Lost: The Search for Six of Six Million* (New York: Harper Perennial, 2013), 45–46.
18. About the possibility of losing an individual in the larger story, see David Nasaw, "Introduction to AHR Roundtable: Historians and Biography," *American Historical Review* 114, no. 3 (2009): 574.
19. Ivan Jablonka, *A History of the Grandparents I Never Had* (Stanford, CA: Stanford University Press, 2016), xiv.
20. Mendelsohn, *The Lost*, 569.
21. Ewa Domańska, *Mikrohistorie: Spotkania i międzyświatach* (Poznań: Wydawnictwo Poznańskie, 2005), 220. Unless otherwise noted, all translations are by author.
22. I would like to thank Colleen Moore for pointing this out. Jacques Le Goff, *The Birth of Purgatory* (Chicago: University of Chicago Press, 1986).
23. Ron Rosenbaum, "Giving Death a Face," review of *The Loss: A Search for Six of Six Million*, by Daniel Mendelshon, *New York Times*, September 24, 2006.
24. Philippe Sands, *East West Street* (London: Weidenfeld & Nicolson, 2016).
25. Katja Petrowskaja, *Maybe Esther* (New York: HarperCollins, 2018).
26. Lee, *Biography*, 59.
27. Aneta Ostaszewska, "From the Point of View of a Woman: Autobiographical Context of Feminist Studies," in *Scientific Biographies: Between the "Professional" and "Non-Professional" Dimensions of Humanistic Experiences*, ed. Marcin Kafar (Łódź: Wydawnictwo Uniwersytetu Łódzkiego, 2014), 181–82, 189.
28. I found an echo of this dilemma in Steven Zipperstein's statement "You must decide what this book means to you if you're to get it right." Steven J. Zipperstein, *Rosenfeld's Lives: Fame, Oblivion, and the Furies of Writing* (New Haven, CT: Yale University Press, 2009), 13.
29. The city carried multiple names throughout its history. I have chosen the Polish name Lwów throughout as that is what the city was called during the interwar period.

30. Phillipe Sands, "Oral History Interview with Phillipe Sands," interview by Ina Navazelskis, United States Holocaust Memorial Museum, Oral History Collection, June 7, 2016, video, 1:27:04, https://collections.ushmm.org/search/catalog/irn545776.
31. Lois Banner discusses the need for interconnections as "empathetically imagined." Lois W. Banner, "Biography as History," *American Historical Review* 114, no. 3 (2009): 582.
32. Janine Holc, "Holocaust Testimony, Autobiography, and the Effaced Self," *Autobiografia*, no. 1 (2020): 15.
33. Natalie Zemon Davis, foreword to Arlette Farge, *The Allure of the Archives* (New Haven, CT: Yale University Press, 2015), xii.
34. In my citations of the letters, I provide dates (or partial dates) and the location of the letter writer where they are available.
35. Anna Landau-Czajka, *Syn będzie Lech . . . : Asymilacja Żydów w Polsce międzywojennej* (Warsaw: Wydawnictwo Neriton, Instytut Historii PAN, 2006), 8–9.
36. I still had access to Tonia's closet through her family, but today many of these sources are housed in Polin and more easily accessible to researchers.
37. Farge, *Allure of the Archives*, 29.
38. Farge, 4.
39. Farge, 14.
40. Tomek Kitliński, "Marii Janion kontra sztuka archiwów," in *Polka: Medium, cień, wyobrażenie,* ed. Agnieszka Zawadowska, Maria Janion, Monika Grodzka, and Katarzyna Czeczot (Warsaw: Centrum Sztuki Współczesnej Fundacja Odnawiania Znaczeń, Polska Akademia, 2005), 107.
41. Farge, *Allure of the Archives*, 124.

Chapter 1: Bobbin Lace and Assimilation

1. Tonia Lechtman, interview by Dorota Dowgiałło, Tel Aviv, 1994, transcript, copy in the private collection of Vera and Marcel Lechtman.
2. Romek was born on October 21, 1913, Joel on September 15, 1919, and Noemi on May 22, 1924. Birth certificates, Akta Miasta Łodzi, Księgi Ludności Stałej, 824/ 434, Archiwum Państwowe w Łodzi, Łódź (hereafter cited as APŁ).
3. Birth certificates, Akta Miasta Łodzi, Księgi Ludności Stałej, 824/ 434, APŁ. For a document explaining how the Łódź population was registered, see Agnieszka Janik, "Ewidencja ludności przechowywana w Archiwum Państwowym w Łodzi," APŁ, 2011, http://www.lodz.ap.gov.pl/ewidencja_ludnosci.pdf.
4. Delayed registration is mentioned by Halina Rubin in her family story. Her mother's birth was registered when she was twenty-seven years old. They needed passports and hence decided to finally register the birth of an already adult daughter. The clerk made a comment on the certificate that the delay was caused

by parental negligence. Halina Rubin, *Czas odnaleziony: Podróże z moją matką* (Wołowiec: Wydawnictwo Czarne, 2018), 31–32.
5. Rubin, 31–32.
6. I would like to thank Natalia Aleksiun for this comment.
7. Anna Rajf-Ligęza, "Shorashim," manuscript (in Hebrew), 1970s, copy in the possession of the author.
8. François Guesnet, "Thinking Globally, Acting Locally: Joel Wegmeister and Modern Hasidic Politics in Warsaw," *Quest: Issues in Contemporary Jewish History*, no. 2 (October 2011): https://www.quest-cdecjournal.it/thinking-globally-acting-locally-joel-wegmeister-and-modern-hasidic-politics-in-warsaw/.
9. For more discussion on the Jewish communities living within the Kingdom of Poland, see Glenn Dynner and Marcin Wodziński, "The Kingdom of Poland and Her Jews: An Introduction," in *Polin: Studies in Polish Jewry*, vol. 27, *Jews in the Kingdom of Poland, 1815–1918*, ed. Glenn Dynner, Antony Polonsky, and Marcin Wodziński (Liverpool: Liverpool University Press, 2015), 5–7.
10. For more on this, see Agnieszka Jagodzińska, *Pomiędzy: Akulturacja Żydów Warszawy w drugiej połowie XIX wieku* (Wrocław: Wydawnictwo Uniwersytetu Wrocławskiego, 2008).
11. According to *Żydzi Dawnej Łodzi: Słownik Biograficzny*, Bialer was born in 1864. His family claims that he was born in 1865. Andrzej Kempa and Marek Szukalak, ed., *Żydzi Dawnej Łodzi: Słownik Biograficzny Żydów Łódzkich oraz z Łodzią związanych*, vol. 2, *Od A do Z* (Łódź: Oficyna Bibliofilów, 2002).
12. For an interesting example of matchmaking and marriage, see Józef Hen, *Nowolipie Street* (Bethesda, MD: DL Books, 2012), 16–18.
13. Jechiel Izajasz Trunk, "Wienerowie na pograniczu starych i nowych czasów," in *Pojln: Obrazy i wspomnienia z Łodzi*, trans. Anna Clarke (Łódź: Tygiel Kultury, 1997), 39.
14. Wiesław Puś, "The Development of the City of Łódź (1820–1939)," in *Polin: Studies in Polish Jewry*, vol. 6, *Jews in Łódź, 1820–1939*, ed. Antony Polonsky (Liverpool: Liverpool University Press, 2005), 8–12. Jews constituted Łódź's petty bourgeoisie (crafts and small trades), intelligentsia (teachers, doctors, lawyers, clerks, journalists, and artists), and industrialists, especially in the textile industry. While Germans still dominated nontextile industries, Jews were much stronger in textiles and were most pronounced among smaller industrialists—that is, in firms employing from five to fifty workers. Jerzy Tomaszewski, "Jews in Łódź in 1931 According to Statistics," in Polonsky, *Polin*, 6:182; Stanisław Liszewski, "The Role of the Jewish Community in the Organization of Urban Space in Łódź," in Polonsky, *Polin*, 6:29.
15. Stefan Pytlas, "The National Composition of Łódź Industrialists before 1914," in Polonsky, *Polin*, 6:40–41.
16. Kazimierz Badziak, "Great Capitalist Fortunes in the Polish Lands before 1939 (the Case of the Poznański Family)," in Polonsky, *Polin*, 6:61–62.

17. Puś, "Development of the City of Łódź," 8. See also Theodor R. Weeks, "Russians, Jews, and Poles: Russification and Antisemitism 1881–1914," in *Quest: Issues in Contemporary Jewish History*, no. 3 (July 2012): 149, www.quest-cdecjournal.it/focus.php?id=308.
18. Dariusz Kacprzak, "Pamięć fabrykanckiej Atlantydy/Remembering an Industrialist's Atlantis," *Herito* 8 (2012): 206.
19. Bialer Tobiasz, in Kempa and Szukalak, *Żydzi Dawnej Łodzi*, 18.
20. Local Łódź historian Waldemar Borowski tirelessly strives to reconstruct some of this story. See his website, Piotrkowska-nr, https://piotrkowska-nr.pl/owners.
21. Bialer Tobiasz, in Kempa and Szukalak, *Żydzi Dawnej Łodzi*, 18.
22. Kempa and Szukalak, *Żydzi Dawnej Łodzi*, 18.
23. The information about the number of employees comes from *Podręczny Rejestr Handlowy 1926* (Łódź: Wydawnictwo Księgi Prawomocnych Podpisów Przemysłu, Handlu i Finansów, 1926), 2:167. See also Eliezer Heller, ed., *Żydowskie przedsiębiorstwa przemysłowe w Polsce według ankiety z 1921 roku/Jewish Industrial Establishments in Poland Surveyed in 1921*, vol. 3, *Lodz City and District* (Warsaw: I. Hendler, 1923).
24. Joseph Roth, *Listy z Polski* (Kraków: Austeria, 2018), 83–85. For more on Łódź as a Polish Manchester, see Yedida Kanfer, "'Each for His Own': Economic Nationalism in Łódź, 1864–1914," in Dynner, Polonsky, and Wodziński, *Polin*, 27:153–79.
25. Kanfer, "'Each for His Own,'" 155. Rosa Luxemburg, a Marxist and revolutionary socialist, wrote about these protests: "Łódź was also the center of permanent demonstrations, strikes universal clashes with the soldiery—for five days Łódź boiled with uninterrupted fight." Quoted in Aneta Pawłowska, "A Concise History of Women Originating from the City of Lodz Acting Either as Flâneuses or Women Artists, at the Beginning of Modern Era until the End of World War II: An Attempt of Re-interpretation of the Literary and Art History Canon," *West Bohemian Historical Review* 8, no. 2 (2018): 248.
26. Kanfer, "'Each for His Own,'" 154.
27. Kanfer, 154–76.
28. Władysław Stanisław Reymont, *The Promised Land*, trans. M. H. Dziewicki (New York: Alfred A. Knopf, 1927), 2:595.
29. Wincenty Kosiakiewicz, *Bawełna* (Petersburg: Druk S. Kornatowski, 1895). Full text available at http://archive.is/qhZQE#selection-26857.0-26857.89.
30. Kacprzak, "Pamięć fabrykanckiej Atlantydy," 206.
31. E.g., "W sprawie walki z cholerą," *Rozwój*, September 13, 1910.
32. Wiesław Puś, *Żydzi w Łodzi w latach zaborów 1793–1914* (Łódź: Wydawnictwo Uniwersytetu Łódzkiego, 1988), 66. For documents mentioning Bialer, see "Do Pana Inspektora Szkolnego na m. Łódź" (a letter from Bialer regarding the exam for the teachers of the Judaic subjects, Łódź, July 13, 1917), syg. 27, and letter to Zarząd Gminy Starozakonnych, Łódź, June 21, 1917, syg. 1057/91, both in Łódzka Wyznaniowa Gmina Żydowska, 1885–1939, APŁ.

33. Letter to Zarząd Gminy Starozakonnych, Łódź, June 21, 1917, and Kopia protokołu z posiedzenia, February 20, 1916, Łódzka Wyznaniowa Gmina Żydowska, 1885–1939, syg. 1057/59, APŁ.
34. Sprawozdanie Zarządu Łódzkiej Gminy Starozakonnych za rok 1916, Sekcja pań opieki nad dziećmi pozbawionymi rodziców, Biblioteka Cyfrowa Uniwersytetu Łódzkiego, 1916, http://bcul.lib.uni.lodz.pl/dlibra/docmetadata?id=20031.
35. Michał Trębacz, *Izrael Lichtenstein: Biografia żydowskiego socjalisty* (Łódź: IPN, 2016), 38–41.
36. Y. Y. Trunk, *Poyln: Zikhroynes un bilder*, vol. 5 (New York: Medem-klub, 1944), https://www.yiddishbookcenter.org/collections/yiddish-books/spb-nybc200709/trunk-yehiel-yeshaia-poyln-zikhroynes-un-bilder-vol-1.
37. "Nota biograficzna," in Jechiel Jeszaja Trunk, *Moje życie wpisane w historię Żydów w Polsce* (Warsaw: Oficyna Naukowa, 1977), 61.
38. Delo Petrokovskogo gubernskogo pravleniia: O fabrichnykh stroeniiakh Tobiasa Bialera, v g. Lodzi, February 20, 1909, Rząd Gubernialny Piotrkowski, Wydział Administracyjny, sygn. 10389, APŁ.
39. Ezra Mendelsohn, *The Jews of East Central Europe between the World Wars* (Bloomington: Indiana University Press, 1983), 14–17; Szymon Rudnicki, "The Attitude of the Jews towards Poland's Independence," in Dynner, Polonsky, and Wodziński, *Polin*, 27:183–84. On the growing antisemitism in the decades prior to World War I, see Weeks, "Russians, Jews, and Poles," 150–51. Weeks sees 1905's events as marking a significant deterioration in Polish-Jewish relations. Weeks, 157–58.
40. Rudnicki, "Attitude of Jews," 196. This was the same place that another pogrom took place in 1946, after the war was over.
41. Eva Hoffman, *Shtetl: The Life and Death of a Small Town and the World of Polish Jews* (New York: PublicAffairs, 2007), 169.
42. Zarząd Starozakonnych m. Łodzi, September 18, 1919, Łódzka Wyznaniowa Gmina Żydowska, sygn. 1057/270, 52, APŁ.
43. The outburst of violence that took place in Łódź was not an isolated event. From June to September, an American commission visited Poland. Its goal was to investigate the situation of the Jewish population and the multiple outbursts of violence that took place in many cities in Poland. For more about the antisemitic action of the Hallerczycy, see Trębacz, *Izrael Lichtenstein*, 104–7. See also Kamil Kijek, Artur Markowski, and Konrad Zieliński, eds., *Pogromy Żydów na ziemiach polskich w XIX i XX wieku*, vol. 3, *Historiografia, polityka, recepcja społeczna (do 1939 roku)* (Warsaw: Muzeum Historii Żydów Polskich POLIN, 2019). For the most recent work on the pogroms of Jews in Lwów, see Grzegorz Gauden, *Lwów—kres iluzji: Opowieść o pogromie listopadowym 1918* (Kraków: Universitas, 2019). For the newest book about pogroms in Europe see Jeffrey Veidlinger, *In the Midst of Civilized Europe: The Pogroms of 1918–1921 and the Onset of the Holocaust* (New York: Metropolitan Books, 2021).

44. For more about the relations between Izrael and Maurycy Poznański, see the memoir of Maria Kamińska, a daughter of a Łódź industrialist: Maria Kamińska, *Ścieżkami wspomnień* (Warsaw: Książka i Wiedza, 1960), 26–28. For a more detailed description of Poznański's mausoleum, see Krzysztof Stefański, "Mauzoleum Izraela Poznańskiego na cmentarzu Żydowskim w Łodzi," in *Wielkomiejskie Cmentarze Żydowskie w Europe Środkowo-Wschodniej*, ed. Irmina Gadowska (Łódź: Uniwersytet Łódzki, 2016), 77–95.
45. Announcement in *Głos Polski*, January 18, 1925.
46. Teczka A. Bialer, Łódź, 1925, Bank Gospodarstwa Krajowego, syg. 1597, APŁ. The register of the companies from 1926 lists Aron and his brother, Icek Bialer, as proxies of his father's silk ribbon factory. *Podręczny Rejestr Handlowy 1926*, 2:167, APŁ.
47. Aron Bialer to Róża, Łódź, October 18, 1925. All letters, unless otherwise noted, are in the private collection of Vera and Marcel Lechtman.
48. Trunk, *Poyln*, 159.
49. Trunk, 160.
50. The transformation of Aron from a Hasid to a relatively secular man is striking. Perhaps it was caused by a youthful rebellion? Hasidism could be also considered a spectrum, with its followers being in different places along this spectrum at different times. Thank you, Sean Martin, for this comment.
51. Róża Bialer to Aron, n.d.
52. Marcel Lechtman, interview by author, Tel Aviv, May 2018; Vera Lechtman, interview by author, May 2012. For more on arranged marriages and their decline, see Rachel Manekin, *The Rebellion of the Daughters: Jewish Women Runaways in Habsburg Galicia* (Princeton, NJ: Princeton University Press, 2020), 33–37.
53. I thank Yedida Kanfer for helping me find and translate the story.
54. Manekin, *Rebellion of the Daughters*, 160.
55. Manekin, 160.
56. Rajf-Ligęza, "Shorashim," 5. See also Naomi Seidman, *The Marriage Plot: Or, How Jews Fell in Love with Love, and with Literature* (Stanford, CA: Stanford University Press, 2016), 92.
57. Trunk, *Poyln*, 170.
58. Trunk, 170.
59. An interesting exploration of young Jewish women from Orthodox, mostly Hasidic, homes in West Galicia and their estrangement from homes is Manekin's *Rebellion of the Daughters*.
60. Trunk, *Poyln*, chap. 18.
61. By this remark, I do not mean to suggest that Hasidism excluded interest in the Polish culture and language, as recent literature by Rachel Manekin and Naomi Seidman suggests it did not. Both authors show nuanced distinctions between Hasidism and Polish culture. See Manekin, *Rebellion of the Daughters,* and Naomi Seidman, *Sarah Schenirer and the Bais Yaahkov Movement:*

A Revolution in the Name of Tradition (London: Littman Library of Jewish Civilization, 2019).
62. Pismo wydziału hipotecznego w mieście Łodzi, in Akta Dyrekcyi Towarzystwa Kredytowego m. Łodzi tyczące się nieruchomości no 767 przy ulicy Piotrkowskiej, volumen 1 (nr repetytorium VIII. 146), 1924, sygn. 1662, 431–32, APŁ. Interestingly, as early as 1920 the former owner sued the Bialers for harm during the sale of the property and demanded the annulment of the notarial act. We do not know the details of this case, but the demands were not met. Based on notes from Łódź historian Marcin Szymański.
63. Marek Szukalak and Andrzej Kempa, *Żydzi dawnej Łodzi: Słownik biograficzny Żydów łódzkich oraz z Łodzią związanych*, volume 2 (Łódź: Oficyna Bibliofilów, 2004), and Waldek Borowski, email exchange with author, February 2018.
64. Teczka A. Bialer, 1925, Łódź, Bank Gospodarstwa Krajowego, syg. 1597, APŁ.
65. Some memoirs from Łódź also share stories of biking through big Łódź apartments on Piotrkowska—e.g., Anka Grupińska, "Zarówno dziadek, jak i ojciec uważali, że niemcy to taki naród kulturalny," in *12 opowieści żydowskich* (Wołowiec: Wydawnictwo Czarne, 2013), 39.
66. Tonia, interview by Dowgiałło.
67. Patrice Dabrowski, email exchange with author, January 2019. Based on Jotsaw [Jadwiga Sawicka], *Z Łodzi do Wschodnich Karpat* (Łódź: [czcionkami Drukarni Państwowej w Łodzi], 1927). More in Dabrowski's book *The Carpathians: Discovering the Highlands of Poland and Ukraine* (Ithaca, NY: Cornell University Press, 2021).
68. Noemi (Emi) Bialer to her parents, n.d.
69. Tonia to her mother, Zawoja, July 19, 1934.
70. Hoffman, *Shtetl*, 161.
71. Tonia, interview by Dowgiałło.
72. Tonia, interview by Dowgiałło.
73. Historian and sociologist Anna Landau-Czajka emphasizes that the Polish language was a common language for the Jewish intelligentsia of upper social strata in central Poland's cities, such as Warsaw and Łódź, and in Galician cities, such as Kraków and Lwów. It was either a language of daily use or in some cases a tool of assimilation or adaptation. Landau-Czajka, *Syn będzie Lech*, 31–34.
74. Tonia, interview by Dowgiałło.
75. Brian Porter-Szűcs, *Poland in the Modern World: Beyond Martyrdom* (Hoboken, NJ: Wiley Blackwell, 2014), 110.
76. Kamil Kijek, *Dzieci modernizmu: Świadomość, kultura i socjalizacja polityczna młodzieży żydowskiej w II Rzeczypospolitej* (Wrocław: Wydawnictwo Uniwersytetu Wrocławskiego, 2017), 16–22.
77. According to Porter-Szűcs, "only a minority went on to a secondary school, but this figure was increasing steadily." Porter-Szűcs, *Poland in the Modern World*, 110.

78. Tonia, interview by Dowgiałło. The school at first had a status of a female gymnasium, which had *niepełne prawa*—i.e., it was without the full rights of a state gymnasium. "Spis szkół wyższych, średnich, zawodowych, seminarjów nauczycielskich oraz wykaz zakładów naukowych i władz szkolnych z 1924 r.," 1924, 215. Muzeum Oświaty Ziemi Łódzkiej, part of Pedagogiczna Biblioteka Wojewódzka, Łódź; Monika Wachowicz, email exchange with author, August 2019. This status meant that the school remained under strict control and the final exam was conducted by external commissions. In 1930 it gained the status of a gymnasium with full state status. Dariusz Szlawski, *Nauczyciele łódzcy w okresie międzywojennym* (Łódź: Związek Nauczycielstwa Polskiego Zarząd Okręgu Łódzkiego, 2013), 88, 95. Tonia provided the years of her education at that school during her interrogations. Protokół przesłuchania podejrzanej, Warsaw, July 26, 1949, file 01252_8, Biuro Udostępniania i Archiwizacji Dokumentów, Instytut Pamięci Narodowej, Warsaw (hereafter cited as BU IPN).
79. Natalia Aleksiun, "Female, Jewish, Educated, and Writing Polish Jewish History," *Polin: Studies in Polish Jewry*, vol. 29, *Writing Jewish History in Eastern Europe*, ed. Natalia Aleksiun, Brian Horowitz, and Antony Polonsky (2017): 201. According to the American Jewish Joint Distribution Committee, in the academic year 1934–35, 40 percent of Jewish elementary school children attended private Jewish schools. The governmental statistics speak of only 20 percent. Kijek, *Dzieci modernizmu*, 126–27.
80. Kijek provides an interesting discussion of the meaning of "acculturation," "assimilation," and "integration" in Polish historiography. Kijek, *Dzieci modernizmu*, 233–40.
81. Kijek, 236.
82. Michael Steinlauf quoted in Gershon Bacon, "Polish-Jewish Relations in Modern Times: The Search for a Metaphor and a Historical Framework," in *New Directions in the History of the Jews in the Polish Lands*, ed. Antony Polonsky (Boston: Academic Studies Press, 2018), 69.
83. Landau-Czajka, *Syn będzie Lech*, 26, 23–24.
84. Kijek suggests that it happened rarely through baptism and the process of elimination of Jewish traditions and past from one's life. Kijek, *Dzieci modernizmu*, 235.
85. Kijek, 237.
86. Polonization was one of the possible paths, but there was also modernization through Yiddishism or Zionism. Moshe Rosman, "Hasidism as a Modern Phenomenon: The Paradox of Modernization without Secularization," *Jahrbuch des Simon-Dubnow-Instituts* 6 (2007): 215–24.
87. Seidman shows that the more traditional Jews also tried to adapt or even introduce some changes—e.g., the Bais Yaakov school for girls created as a revolution in the name of tradition. Seidman, *Sarah Schenirer*, 17–68.
88. Landau-Czajka, *Syn będzie Lech*, 45–47. For more on the crisis in the Orthodox Jewish world and the search for solutions, see Seidman, *Sarah Schenirer*.

89. Joanna Wiszniewicz, *A jednak czasem miewam sny: Historia pewnej samotności* (Wołowiec: Wydawnictwo Czarne, 2017), 13.
90. Landau-Czajka, *Syn będzie Lech*, 25, 47.
91. Landau-Czajka, 54–55. See also Kijek, *Dzieci modernizmu*, 278.
92. Pawłowska draws a similar conclusion in "Concise History of Women," 248.
93. Vera Lechtman, interview by author, May 2012.
94. The childhood memories of others also underline the importance and fairy-tale-like memories of religious Jewish life. See, e.g., Anna Lanota, "Wyjdź, Haniu, stamtąd i powiedz wszystkim, że to jest na śmierć," in *12 opowieści żydowskich*, 53–55.
95. Tonia, interview by Dowgiałło.
96. I thank Yedida Kanfer for this comment.
97. For similar recollections of Pesach from the perspective of a child, see Anka Grupińska, "Nazywam się Gizela Fudem, z domu Grünberg," in *12 opowieści żydowskich*, 165–66, and Eni Wygodzka, "Nie przyszło im do głowy, że Żydówka tak może wyglądać," in *12 opowieści żydowskich*, 207.
98. Tonia, interview by Dowgiałło. See also Grupińska, "Wyjdź, Haniu, stamtąd," 54.
99. Jewish fasting begins at sunset and ends at sunset and excludes solid food and drink. It is forbidden to wear leather shoes, wash, and bathe. The tradition of not wearing leather shoes on Yom Kippur is conducted in order to be more sacred, less human, more godlike on this most holy of days. I am grateful to Yedida Kanfer for this explanation.
100. Tonia, interview by Dowgiałło. Similarly, some of the interviewees of Anka Grupińska spoke about the importance of Yom Kippur—e.g., Anna Lanota, Grupińska, "Wyjdź, Haniu, stamtąd," 53. This tradition of swinging a live chicken—*kapparot*—was conducted in order to transfer one's sins to it.
101. Lucjan Dobroszycki and Barbara Kirschenlatt-Gimblett, eds., *Images before My Eyes: History of Jewish Life in Poland, 1864–1939* (New York: Schocken Books, 1977), and Tonia, interview by Dowgiałło.
102. Józef Hen, *Nowolipie* (Warsaw: Iskry, 1991), 26.
103. Tonia, interview by Dowgiałło.

Chapter 2: A Dream of New Life

1. Marcel Łoziński, dir., *Tonia i jej dzieci* (Warsaw: Studio Filmowe Kronika, 2011).
2. Anna Rajf-Ligęza, phone conversation with author, March 2019.
3. Protokół przesłuchania podejrzanej, Warsaw, July 5 and January 2, 1950, file 01252_8, BU IPN.
4. Jaff Schatz, *The Generation: The Rise and Fall of the Jewish Communists of Poland* (Berkeley: University of California Press, 1991), 47. See also Yuri Slezkine, *The House of Government: A Saga of the Russian Revolution* (Princeton, NJ:

Princeton University Press, 2017); Paul Hanebrink, *A Specter Haunting Europe: The Myth of Judeo-Bolshevism* (Cambridge, MA: Harvard University Press, 2018); and Paweł Śpiewak, *Żydokomuna: Interpretacje historyczne* (Warsaw: Wydawnictwo Czerwone i Czarne, 2012).

5. "Esther," in *Awaking Lives: Autobiographies of Jewish Youth in Poland before the Holocaust*, ed. Jeffrey Shandler (New Haven, CT: Yale University Press, 2002), 329. Ido Bassok argues that in those memoirs Jewish youth expressed their identity differently depending on geographical location. Ido Bassok, "Jewish Youth Movements in Poland between the Wars as Heirs of the *Kehilah*," in *Polin: Studies in Polish Jewry*, vol. 30, *Jewish Education in Eastern Europe*, ed. Aliyana R. Adler and Antony Polonsky (Liverpool: Liverpool University Press, 2018), 299–320.

6. Kamil Kijek, *Dzieci modernizmu: Świadomość, kultura i socjalizacja polityczna młodzieży żydowskiej w II Rzeczypospolitej* (Wrocław: Wydawnictwo Uniwersytetu Wrocławskiego, 2017), 21. See also Marci Shore, "Tevye's Daughters: Jews and European Modernity," *Contemporary European History* 16, no. 1 (2007): 122.

7. Kijek, *Dzieci modernizmu*, 293, 304, 325.

8. "According to Polish sources and to Western estimates, the proportion of Jews in the KPP [Communist Party of Poland, Komunistyczna Partia Polski] was never lower than 22 percent. In the larger cities, the percentage of Jews in the KPP often exceeded 50 percent and in smaller cities, frequently over 60 percent." Schatz, *Generation*, 97–98.

9. They were even more visible in youth organizations. For example, in 1930 ethnic Poles made up 19 percent of the membership of communist youth organizations and in 1933 made up 33 percent. At the same times, respectively, 51 and 31 percent of members were Jews. (Other members were Ukrainians and Belarussians.) Schatz, *Generation*, 13, 85.

10. For an interesting, relatively comprehensive discussion of various reasons that pushed Jews to communism, see Joanna Nalewajko-Kulikov, *Obywatele Jidyszlandu: Rzecz o żydowskich komunistach w Polsce* (Warsaw: Neriton, 2009), 68–71.

11. E.g., Jablonka, *Grandparents I Never Had*, 36. In a biography of her grandmother, a Jewish communist, whose past was so buried in her conspiratorial life that even her name and date of birth are uncertain, Aleksandra Domańska writes about the worldview of her communist grandmother, "A human being creates history in the darkness, and we would like to live seeing." Aleksandra Domańska, *Ulica Cioci Oli: Z dziejów jednej rewolucjonistki* (Warsaw: Krytyka Polityczna, 2013), 69. As historian Paul Hanebrink notices, it was "to slip the bonds of traditional communities, to embrace the social and cultural opportunities that modernity offered or to feel themselves part of the sweep of history." Hanebrink, *Specter Haunting Europe*, 430.

12. "A. Greyno," in Shandler, *Awaking Lives*, 83.

13. Schatz, *Generation*, 38.
14. Anna Müller, "Gender, Generational Conflict, and Communism: Tonia Lechtman's Story," in *Gender, Generations, and Communism in Central and Eastern Europe and Beyond*, ed. Anna Artwińska and Agnieszka Mrozik (New York: Routledge, 2020), 263–82.
15. Gabriele Simoncini, "Ethnic and Social Diversity in the Membership of the Communist Party of Poland: 1918–1938," *Nationalities Papers* 22, no. 1 (1994): 55–91. Simoncini compiled a list of KPP members that included Roman (Romek/Abram) Bialer. Roman is also mentioned in a memorial book of the communist prisoners of the prison in Bereza Kartuska. Leonard Borkowicz, ed., *Bereziacy* (Warsaw: Książka i Wiedza, 1965), 467.
16. Some available documents are Koło Rodziców przy Prywatnym Gimnazjum Żeńskim i Prywatnej Szkole Powszechnej Żeńskiej Marii Hochsteinowej w Łodzi, 1938, Urząd Wojewódzki Łódzki, 39/166, APŁ (Archiwum Państwowe Łódź). Izrael Lichtenstein, a Bund leader, taught at her school. See Michał Trębacz, *Izrael Lichtenstein: Biografia żydowskiego socjalisty* (Łódź: IPN, 2016), 205.
17. Protokół przesłuchania podejrzanej, Warsaw, July 26, 1949, file 01252_8, BU IPN.
18. Protokół przesłuchania podejrzanej, Warsaw, January 2, 1950, 33–35, file 01252_8, BU IPN.
19. Tonia, interview by Dowgiałło. The attitude of the Association of the Polish Scouting was diverse. Some scout instructors (mainly under the nationalist movement's influence) were reluctant to accept Jews, whereas others—for example, Aleksander Kamiński (a leading Polish scout instructor)—supported the registration of Jewish scout groups. See Aleksander Kamiński, *Analiza teoretyczna związków młodzieży do połowy XIX w.* (Warsaw: Państwowe Wydawnictwo Naukowe, 1971). I would like to thank Marek Wierzbicki for this comment.
20. Padraic Kenney, *Dance in Chains: Political Imprisonment in the Modern World* (New York: Oxford University Press, 2017), 110.
21. The MOPR demanded the release of Nicola Sacco and Bartolomeo Vanzetti, Italian migrants and anarchists convicted of murder in the United States. For a definition of the MOPR, see Krystyna Naszkowska, *My, dzieci komunistów* (Warsaw: Czerwone i Czarne, 2013), 45.
22. Schatz, *Generation*, 97.
23. Tonia, interview by Dowgiałło; and Protokół przesłuchania podejrzanej, Warsaw, January 2, 1950, 33–35, file 01252_8, BU IPN.
24. As far as I was able to determine, Wojdysławska was not related to Tonia's mother, whose birth name was also Wojdysławska. Irena Wojdysławska, "Preserving Jewish Memory: Bringing History to Life," interview by Marek Czekalski, Centropa, November 2004, https://www.centropa.org/biography/irena

-wojdyslawska; Anka Grupińska, "Z opowieści polskich Żydów," *Dwu tygodnik* 61 (July 2011), https://www.dwutygodnik.com/artykul/2450-z-opowiesci-polskich-zydow-9.html.
25. File of Komunistyczny Związek Młodzieży Polskiej, 159/Vi-10, Archiwum Akt Nowych, Warsaw (hereafter cited as AAN).
26. Wojdysławska, "Preserving Jewish Memory"; Grupińska, "Z opowieści polskich Żydów."
27. Protokół przesłuchania podejrzanej, Warsaw, January 2, 1950, 37, file 01252_8, BU IPN. Wacka was Dora Lesman, a communist and after the war an employee of the Ministry of Foreign Affairs.
28. Gershon Bacon, "Woman? Youth? Jew? The Search for Identity of Jewish Young Women in Interwar Poland," in *Gender, Place and Memory in the Modern Jewish Experience: Re-placing Ourselves,* ed. Judith Tydor Baumel and Tova Cohen (London: Vallentine Mitchell, 2003), 13; Kijek, *Dzieci modernizmu,* 328.
29. Tonia, interview by Dowgiałło.
30. File of Komunistyczny Związek Młodzieży Polskiej, October 18, 1934, 159/Vi-10, 127, 173, AAN.
31. Tonia, interview by Dowgiałło.
32. About Stanisław Brzozowski, see Sławomir Sierakowski, "Powrót zbawionego heretyka," in *Brzozowski: Przewodnik Krytyki Politycznej* (Warsaw: Wydawnictwo Krytyki Politycznej, 2001), 19. See also Lena Magnone, "Starannie edukowane dziewczęta rzucają bomby: Feminizm i socjalizm (na marginesie Płomieni)," in *Stanisław Brzozowski Powroty,* ed. Dariusz Trześniowski (Lublin: Wydawnictwo Uniwersytetu Technologiczno-Humanistycznego, 2013), 200–19.
33. Magnone, "Starannie edukowane dziewczęta rzucają bomby," 147–54.
34. In her memoirs, Maria Kamińska, a communist from Łódź, who was slightly older than Tonia, talks a lot about her fascination with Stefania Sempołowska, important Polish educator and social activist. As a woman, educator, and social activist, Sempołowska was a role model for Kamińska. The role older women played in younger women's education is clearly visible in her memoir. Maria Kamińska, *Ścieżkami wspomnień* (Warsaw: Książka i Wiedza, 1960), 230–31.
35. May 1 is International Workers' Day, while May 3 is a national Polish holiday celebrating the Polish Constitution.
36. Tonia, interview by Dowgiałło.
37. Tonia, interview by Dowgiałło.
38. Jeffrey S. Kopstein and Jason Wittenberg, *Intimate Violence: Anti-Jewish Pogrom on the Eve of the Holocaust* (Ithaca, NY: Cornell University Press, 2018), 37; Joanna Michlic-Coren, "Anti-Jewish Violence in Poland, 1918–1939 and 1945–1947," in *Polin: Studies in Polish Jewry,* vol. 13, *Focusing on the Holocaust and Its Aftermath,* ed. Antony Polonsky (Liverpool: Liverpool University Press, 2000), 34–61. This support for Piłsudski is expressed in many other Jewish

recollections. Anka Grupińska, "Śmiałam się zawsze, że żydowski piątek pachnie naftą i ciastem," in *12 opowieści żydowskich* (Wołowiec: Wydawnictwo Czarne, 2013), 97.
39. Kamińska, *Ścieżkami wspomnień*, 271, 347.
40. Protokół przesłuchania podejrzanej, Warsaw, January 2, 1950, 39, file 01252_8, BU IPN.
41. Protokół przesłuchania podejrzanej, Warsaw, July 6, 1949, 41, file 01252_8, BU IPN.
42. Protokół przesłuchania podejrzanej, Warsaw, January 2, 1950, 41, file 01252_8, BU, IPN.
43. Tonia, interview by Dowgiałło.
44. A new Polish penal law with heavy punishment for political crimes was introduced on September 1, 1932. Attempts to forcibly change the political system of the Polish state could be punished by imprisonment ranging from ten years to life. The production, distribution, and possession of written subversive materials could be punished by up to five years of imprisonment, and participation in forbidden meetings and gatherings by up to two years. In July 1934 a new decree was introduced allowing authorities to confine "persons who threaten security, peace and public order," without a court sentence, in the prison in Bereza Kartuska. Schatz, *Generation*, 129.
45. Więzienie łódzkie, 1929–1939 (1940), unit no. 197, syg. 7, APŁ.
46. According to Schatz, in the 1920s and 1930s the number of the imprisoned was significant. For example, in 1933, 11,849 were already sentenced, awaiting trial, or temporarily arrested. Schatz, *Generation*, 65.
47. Tonia, interview by Dowgiałło.
48. Jablonka, *Grandparents I Never Had*, 66.
49. Tonia, interview by Dowgiałło.
50. Protokół przesłuchania podejrzanej, Warsaw, January 2, 1950, 43, file 01252_8, BU IPN.
51. Tonia, interview by Dowgiałło; Tonia Lechtman, interview by Anna Sekudewicz, Polskie Radio Katowice, 1998, transcript, copy in the private collection of Vera and Marcel Lechtman.
52. Księga kontroli ruchu ludności (rejestr osób opuszczających gminę), Łódź, komisariat VII, nos. 4282–4531, nos. 1–4042, 96, APŁ; Piotr Zawilski, director of the APŁ, email exchange with author, February 2019.
53. Gur Alroey, *An Unpromising Land: Jewish Migration to Palestine in the Early Twentieth Century* (Stanford, CA: Stanford University Press, 2014), 53.
54. Marcin Szerle, email exchange with author, August 2018–March 2019.
55. Krzysztof Katka, "Oceaniczne perły II RP," *Wyborcza*, July 9, 2012, 19, http://wyborcza.pl/alehistoria/1,121681,12098905,Oceaniczne_perly_II_RP.html. For an interesting view on 1930s travel to Palestine, see Ksawery Pruszyński, *Palestyna po raz trzeci* (Wilno: Dom Książki Polskiej Sp. Akc., 1933).

56. Tonia, interview by Dowgiałło.
57. Mateusz Pielka, "Radykalizacja Nastrojów Antysemickich w latach trzydziestych," *Scripta Historica*, no. 21 (2015): 123–49.
58. Tonia, interview by Dowgiałło. See also Ezra Mendelson, *The Jews of East Central Europe between the Two World Wars* (Bloomington: Indiana University Press, 1987), 71, 70–80.
59. Dvora Hacohen, "British Immigration Policy to Palestine in the 1930s: Implications for Youth Aliyah," *Middle Eastern Studies* 37, no. 4 (2001): 212, 206.
60. Hacohen, "British Immigration Policy," 207.
61. Wiesław Puś, "The Development of the City of Łódź (1820–1939)," in *Polin: Studies in Polish Jewry*, vol. 6, *Jews in Łódź, 1820–1939*, ed. Antony Polonsky (Liverpool: Liverpool University Press, 2005), 15.
62. His release is discussed in letters that Tonia and Sioma kept writing to her mother from Paris. Tonia and Sioma Lechtman to her parents, July 24, 1937; Tonia and Sioma Lechtman to Róża Bialer, August 18, 1937.
63. Róża to Aron, August 15, 1937.
64. Róża to Aron, September 26, 1937.
65. Róża to Aron, August 15, 1937.
66. Róża to Julian, n.d.
67. Róża to Aron, July 15, 1937.
68. Akta Dyrekcji Towarzystwa Kredytowego m. Łodzi, tyczące się nieruchomości nr 767 przy ulicy Piotrkowskiej w mieście Łodzi położonej, vols. 1 and 2, 1661 and 1662, APŁ.
69. Bialer Aron, Application for Palestinian (Mandatory) Citizenship, 1935, Government of Palestine, Department of Immigration, 628/22, Israeli State Archives, Tel Aviv.
70. Tonia, interview by Dowgiałło.
71. Qui Pro Quo (1919–31) was a popular Warsaw theater during the interwar period that attracted the greatest actors of the Polish stage. See Tomasz Mościcki, "Qui Pro Quo," Culture.pl, June 2010, https://culture.pl/pl/tworca/qui-pro-quo.
72. Tonia, interview by Dowgiałło.
73. Pruszyński, *Palestyna po raz trzeci*, 29–30.
74. Tonia, interview by Dowgiałło.
75. Tonia, interview by Dowgiałło.
76. *Haor* (The light), a political, economic, and literary biweekly paper published in Tel Aviv, was dedicated to issues of workers without distinction by nation, people, religion, or race.
77. Protokół przesłuchania podejrzanej, Warsaw, January 2, 1950, 43; Protokół przesłuchania podejrzanej, Warsaw, July 26, 1949, both in file 01252_8, BU IPN.
78. Tonia, interview by Dowgiałło. For more on the Palestinian Communist Party's rituals, development, and attitudes toward Zionism, see Amir Locker Biletzki,

Holidays of the Revolution: Communist Identity in Israel, 1919–1965 (Albany, NY: State University of New York Press, 2020).
79. Protokół przesłuchania podejrzanej, Warsaw, January 2, 1950, 43, file 01252_8, BU IPN.
80. "Memorandum by Government of Palestine: Anti-British and Seditious Propaganda (i) Italian, (ii) Communist and System of Control (Including Control of Press)," Palestine Royal Commission, 4908/23, Israeli State Archives, Tel Aviv.
81. From 1931 to 1938, 190 communist activists were deported, and an additional 99 were listed as leaving freely. Raanan Rein and Inbal Ofer, "Becoming Brigadistas: Jewish Volunteers from Palestine in the Spanish Civil War," *European History Quarterly* 46, no. 1 (2016): 97.
82. "Memorandum," Palestine Royal Commission, 4908/23, Israeli State Archives, Tel Aviv.
83. Tonia, interview by Dowgiałło.
84. *Biografia de Militantes*, fond 545, opis 6, delo 1548, Rossiiskii gosudarstvennyi arkhiv sotsial'no-politicheskoi istorii (hereafter cited as RGASPI), Moscow.
85. Protokół przesłuchania podejrzanej, Warsaw, January 2, 1950, 47, file 01252_8, BU IPN.
86. Alexander Denisenko, Ukrainian researcher, email exchange with author, April–May 2019.
87. Laissez-passer, 1921, copy in the personal collection of Vera and Marcel Lechtman.
88. Vera, interview by author, May 2018.
89. Protokół przesłuchania podejrzanej, Warsaw, January 2, 1950, 51, file 01252_8, BU IPN.
90. Protokół przesłuchania podejrzanej, Warsaw, January 2, 1950. For more about the rituals of the Palestinian Communist Party, see Biletzki, *Holidays of the Revolution*, 27–42.
91. Protokół przesłuchania podejrzanej, Warsaw, July 26, 1949, file 01252_8, BU IPN.
92. Leah Trachtman-Palchan, *Between Tel Aviv and Moscow: A Life of Dissent and Exile in Mandate Palestine and the Soviet Union* (London: Bloomsbury, 2015), 55–56.
93. Tonia, interview by Dowgiałło.
94. Protokół przesłuchania podejrzanej, Warsaw, January 2, 1950, 55, file 01252_8, BU IPN.
95. Tonia, interview by Dowgiałło.
96. Protokół przesłuchania podejrzanej, Warsaw, January 2, 1950, 55, file 01252_8, BU IPN.
97. Minyan is the quorum of ten Jewish male adults required for certain religious ceremonies in Orthodox Judaism and usually ten adults of either sex in Conservative and Reform Judaism.
98. Tonia, interview by Dowgiałło.

99. Vera, interview by author, May 2013.
100. Marcel, interview by author, January 2020.
101. Protokół przesłuchania podejrzanej, Warsaw, January 2, 1950, 55, 57, 58, file 01252_8, BU IPN.
102. Rein and Ofer, "Becoming Brigadistas," 97.
103. Protokół przesłuchania podejrzanej, Warsaw, January 2, 1950, 58, file 01252_8, BU IPN.

Chapter 3: "Flies in Amber"

1. Stanley, quoted in Mary Jo Maynes, Jennifer L. Pierce, and Barbara Laslett, *Telling Stories: The Use of Personal Narratives in the Social Sciences and History* (Ithaca, NY: Cornell University Press, 2008), 82; Liz Stanley, "The Epistolarium: On Theorizing Letters and Correspondences," in *Auto/Biography* 12 (September 2004): 208.
2. Stefania Skwarczyńska, *Teoria Listu* (Białystok: Wydawnictwo Uniwersytetu Białegostoku, 2001), 6, 12.
3. On letters in general, see Stanley, "Epistolarium," 204, 212–13.
4. Tonia to her parents, July 15, 1937.
5. Tonia to her parents, July 1937.
6. Tonia to her parents, July 15, 1937.
7. Woolf, quoted in Anne Bower, *Epistolary Responses: The Letter in 20th Century American Fiction and Criticism* (Tuscaloosa: University of Alabama Press, 1997), 6.
8. Tonia to her parents, May 14, 1937.
9. Vera, Skype conversation with author, October 2017.
10. Vera and Marcel, interview by author, May 2018.
11. Vera, Skype conversation with author, October 2017.
12. Tonia, interview by Dowgiałło.
13. Tonia to her parents, May 14, 1937.
14. Tonia to her parents, May 14, 1937.
15. Tonia to her parents, May 14, 1937.
16. Tonia to her parents, May 27, 1937.
17. Tonia to her parents, May 14, 1937.
18. Michael R. Marrus, *The Unwanted: European Refugees from the First World War through the Cold War* (Philadelphia: Temple University Press, 2002), 145; Timothy P. Maga, "Closing the Door: The French Government and Refugee Policy, 1933–1939," *French Historical Studies* 12, no. 3 (Spring 1982): 426.
19. Clifford Rosenberg, *Policing Paris: The Origins of Modern Immigration Control between the Wars* (Ithaca, NY: Cornell University Press, 2006), 29.
20. Vicki Caron, "The Politics of Frustration: French Jewry and the Refugee Crisis in the 1930s," *Journal of Modern History* 65, no. 2 (1993): 314.

21. Marrus, *Unwanted*, 146.
22. Rosenberg, *Policing Paris*, 14. On the number of foreigners in Paris, see Maga, "Closing the Door," 426.
23. Rosenberg, *Policing Paris*, 14. See also Mary Dewhurst Lewis, "The Strangeness of Foreigners: Policing Migration and Nation in Interwar Marseille," *French Politics, Culture and Society* 20, no. 3 (2002): 68.
24. Marrus, *Unwanted*, 147.
25. Ivan Jablonka, *A History of the Grandparents I Never Had* (Stanford, CA: Stanford University Press, 2016), 94. See also Maga, "Closing the Door," 432.
26. Jablonka, *Grandparents I Never Had*, 94. Most likely Tonia and Sioma visited the exposition as well. In a letter from July, Tonia only stated, "I saw the exhibit. Something incredible." Tonia to her parents, July 15, 1937. It's possible that they visited again in August with free passes. Tonia to her parents, August 26, 1937.
27. Gerben Zaagsma, *Jewish Volunteers, the International Brigades and the Spanish Civil War* (London: Bloomsbury Academic, 2017), 29–30.
28. Tonia to her parents, May 27, 1937.
29. This is the address in the *notice d'indentification* that was filled in on May 1938 either by Tonia or based on an interview with her. Tonia Bialer's file, no. 28 351: Bialer Tauba, 19940434/340, Archives nationales, France (hereafter cited as AN).
30. Tonia, interview by Dowgiałło; Tonia to her parents, May 14, 1937.
31. Tonia, interview by Dowgiałło.
32. Tonia to her parents, May 14, 1937.
33. Jablonka, *Grandparents I Never Had*, 96–97.
34. Florence Vychtil, email exchanges with author, January–June 2019.
35. Tonia to her parents, May 27, 1937.
36. Tonia to her parents, August 5, 1937.
37. The Nansen passport was a response of the League of Nations and its newly established Office of the High Commissioner for Refugees to the refugee crisis that resulted from the Russian Revolution, the Russian Civil War, and the collapse of the Russian Empire. See Peter Gatrell, "The Nansen Passport: The Innovative Response to the Refugee Crisis That Followed the Russian Revolution," *The Conversation*, November 6, 2017. For more, see Gilbert Jaeger, "On the History of the International Protection of Refugees," *International Review of the Red Cross* 83 (September 2001): 727–38.
38. Tonia to her parents, August 15, 1937.
39. Tonia to her parents, October 12, 1937. See also Tonia to her family, October 15, 1937.
40. Tonia, interview by Dowgiałło.
41. Jablonka, *Grandparents I Never Had*, 94.
42. Tonia, interview by Dowgiałło.
43. Tonia to her parents, May 14, 1937.

44. Nick Underwood, "Dressing the Modern Jewish Communist Girl in Interwar Paris," *French Politics, Culture and Society* 34, no. 1 (2016): 88.
45. Tonia to her parents, July 15, 1937.
46. Tonia to her parents, July 15, 1937.
47. Tonia to her parents, May 27, 1937.
48. By late 1934, with over four hundred thousand unemployed in France, a French senator spoke of a hatred, muffled but ready to explode. Michael R. Marrus and Robert O. Paxton, *Vichy France and the Jews* (New York: Basic Books, 1981), 37. Additionally, the French working class was not positively predisposed to illegal immigrants. Marrus, *Unwanted*, 148.
49. Tonia to her family, June 29, 1937.
50. Tonia, interview by Dowgiałło.
51. Tonia to her family, August 5, 1937.
52. Sioma to Batia and Lotta Bialer, June 24, 1937.
53. Tonia to her family, June 9, 1937.
54. Tonia to her family, August 1937.
55. Tonia to her family, August 15, 1937.
56. Tonia, interview by Dowgiałło.
57. Tonia, interview by Dowgiałło.
58. Tonia to her mother, July 1937; another letter about financial support, Tonia to her family, October 15, 1937.
59. Tonia to her family, May 27, 1937.
60. Tonia, interview by Dowgiałło.
61. Tonia to her family, May 14, 1937.
62. Tonia to her family, July 15, 1937.
63. Maga, "Closing the Door," 428; Catherine Epstein, *The Last Revolutionaries* (Cambridge, MA: Harvard University Press, 2003), 59–60.
64. Tonia to her family, November 16, 1937.
65. Tonia to her family, December 1, 1937.
66. Lisa A. Kirchenbaum, *International Communism and the Spanish Civil War: Solidarity and Suspicion* (Cambridge: Cambridge University Press, 2015), 5.
67. For some discussion regarding the intentions and commitment of the Soviet Union toward democracy in Spain, see Kirchenbaum, 7–8.
68. Michael Jackson, *Fallen Sparrows: The International Brigades in the Spanish Civil War* (Philadelphia: American Philosophical Society Independence Square, 1994), 12.
69. Perhaps one of the most notable examples is Ernest Hemingway's 1940 novel *For Whom the Bell Tolls*.
70. "Authors Take Sides on the Spanish War," *Left Review*, 1937, London, https://www.bl.uk/collection-items/authors-take-sides-on-the-spanish-war.
71. Tonia, interview by Dowgiałło.
72. Tonia to her parents, May 27, 1937; Tonia to her parents, August 5, 1937.

73. Protokół przesłuchania podejrzanej, Warsaw, March 2, 1950, file 01252_8, BU IPN.
74. Rein and Ofer, "Becoming Brigadistas," 93.
75. Rein and Ofer, 93, 95, 98.
76. Tonia to her parents, December 3, 1937. In a letter from December 1, she informed her family that Sioma was preparing to leave.
77. Tonia to her parents, December 15, 1937.
78. Tonia to her parents, December 19, 1937.
79. Tonia to her parents, December 22, 1937.
80. Tonia to her parents, January 4, 1938.
81. Tonia to her parents, December 22, 1937.
82. Tonia to Julek, early 1938.
83. Tonia to her parents, December 22, 1937.
84. Tonia to her parents, May 14, 1937, and July 15, 1937.
85. Tonia to her parents, March 25, 1938.
86. Tonia to her parents, December 27, 1937.
87. Tonia to her parents, December 22, 1937.
88. Tonia to her parents, April 21, 1938.
89. Rein and Ofer, "Becoming Brigadistas," 99.
90. Tonia, interview by Dowgiałło.
91. Protokół przesłuchania podejrzanej, Warsaw, March 2, 1950, 58, file 01252_8, BU IPN.
92. Protokół przesłuchania podejrzanej, Warsaw, March 2, 1950, 70.
93. Tonia, interview by Dowgiałło.
94. Jackson, *Fallen Sparrows*, 3.
95. Jackson, 2.
96. Jackson, 14.
97. Arnold Krammer, "Germans against Hitler: The Thaelmann Brigade," *Journal of Contemporary History* 4, no. 2 (1969): 65–83.
98. Rein and Ofer, "Becoming Brigadistas," 102. For more on the meaning of the members of the International Brigades, see Michał Strzelczyk-Barwiński, "Kilka uwag o znaczeniu Brygad Międzynarodowych," in *No Pasaran! Polacy w Wojnie Hiszpańskiej (1936–1939)*, ed. Michał Brona (Warsaw: Wydawnictwo Ministerstwa Obrony Narodowej, 1963), 118–28.
99. Zaagsma, *Jewish Volunteers*, 20; Jackson, *Fallen Sparrows*, 52–55.
100. Jackson, *Fallen Sparrows*, 52–55.
101. Franciszek Księżarczyk, "O drogach wiodących do Hiszpanii i z powrotem do Polski," in Brona, *No Pasaran!*, 81.
102. Ernst Thälmann was Germany's leading communist and was imprisoned by the Gestapo in 1933. Krammer, "Germans against Hitler," 66–67; Jackson, *Fallen Sparrows*, 2. Some 60 to 70 percent of the battalion were members of the German Communist Party. Epstein, *Last Revolutionaries*, 63.

103. "Lechtman(n), Sioma, ÖsterreicherInnen für Spaniens Freiheit 1936–1939," Dokumentationsarchiv des österreichischen Widerstandes, accessed February 2022, https://www.doew.at/erinnern/biographien/spanienarchiv-online/spanienfreiwillige-l/lechtman-n-sioma.
104. Rein and Ofer, "Becoming Brigadistas," 93–94. According to Jackson, approximately thirty-two thousand people traveled to Spain as volunteers. Jackson, *Fallen Sparrows*, 18, 67–69. According to Zaagsma, the number of volunteers was somewhere between thirty-five thousand and forty thousand. Zaagsma, *Jewish Volunteers*, 22.
105. Zaagsma, *Jewish Volunteers*, 22.
106. Tonia to Julek, January 4, 1938.
107. Martin Sugarman, "Against Fascism: Jews Who Served in the International Brigade in the Spanish Civil War" (unpublished manuscript, last modified July 3, 2021), https://www.marxists.org/subject/jewish/spanjews.pdf.
108. Michael Uhl, email exchange with author, March 2020; Michael Uhl, *Mythos Spanien: Das Erbe der Internationalen Brigaden in der DDR* (Bonn: Verlag J. H. W. Dietz, 2004).
109. Tonia to her parents, January 15, 1938.
110. Tonia to her parents, February 12, 1938.
111. Tonia to her parents, May 7, 1938.
112. "Bitwa nad rzeką Ebro," Polskie Radio 24, November 16, 2016, https://www.polskieradio24.pl/39/156/Artykul/1288795,Bitwa-nad-rzeka-Ebro-koniec-hiszpanskiej-wojny-domowej.
113. Tonia to her parents, September 7, 1938.
114. Zaagsma, *Jewish Volunteers*, 18. For more on the work of political officers in the International Brigades, see Maciej Techniczek, "O pracy komisarzy politycznych w Republikańskiej Armii Ludowej i w Brygadach Międzynarodowych," in Brona, *No Pasaran!* 140–52.
115. Uhl, email exchange with author, January 2020.
116. Uhl, email exchanges with author, December–January 2020. The Popular Front was an alliance of leftist parties and organizations in January of 1936; it was formed partially in response to the growing influence of fascism and with intentions of winning that year's elections.
117. Lechtman profile, F 545, O6 D1548, Biografia de militantes, RGASPI.
118. Lechtman, profile, composed by Gustav, F545 OP6 D73, Biografia de militantes, RGASPI.
119. Uhl helped me understand Sioma's profile. Uhl, email exchanges with author, December–January 2020.
120. Tonia to her parents, March 3, 1938.
121. Tonia to her parents, April 1, 1938.
122. Tonia to her parents, March 10, 1938.
123. Tonia to her parents, March 10, 1938.

124. Tonia, interview by Dowgiałło.
125. Raya Cohen, "Liberty, Equality, Fraternity, but Not for All: France and the 'Alien' Jews, 1933–1942," review of *Uneasy Asylum: France and the Jewish Refugee Crisis, 1933–1942*, by Vicki Caron, in *Shoah Resource Center: The International School for Holocaust Studies* 29 (2001): 12. As Caron emphasizes, "Even the German émigré press, which was otherwise sharply critical of the committee, went out of its way to praise Lambert." Caron, "Politics of Frustration," 323.
126. Tonia, interview by Dowgiałło.
127. "Ludwig Marum," Gedenkstätte Deutscher Widerstand, accessed August 2020, https://www.gdw-berlin.de/en/recess/biographies/index_of_persons/biographie/view-bio/ludwig-marum/?no_cache=1; Andrée Fischer-Marum, "Franzosische Zustande 1933–1942: Die Marums im Franzosischen Exil—Eine Familiengeschichte," in *Fritz-Erlier-Forum: Juristin, Emigrantin, Botschafterin der Versöhnung und Erinnerung* (Baden-Württemberg, Germany: Friedrich-Ebert-Stiftung), 41–43, accessed August 2020, http://library.fes.de/pdf-files/bueros/stuttgart/09370.pdf.
128. Sophie "made an effort to look after children who fled to France with their parents—or even without them—and who had mental health problems. But she was denounced and had to stop doing this." Fischer-Marum, "Die Marums im Franzosischen Exil," 43.
129. Tonia to her parents, February 17, 1938.
130. Tonia to Julek, January 4, 1937. Her financial situation dire, she admitted in a letter that she was wearing worn-out shoes, which family friends eventually replaced for her. Tonia to her parents, January 15, 1938.
131. Tonia to her parents, February 12, 1938.
132. Tonia to her parents, January 4, 1938.
133. Maga, "Closing the Door," 435.
134. Caron, "Politics of Frustration," 327–28.
135. Tonia to her parents, May 23, 1938.
136. Tonia, interview by Dowgiałło.
137. Tonia Bialer's file, application for legal residency, 1938, 19940434/340, AN.
138. "Protokół przesłuchania podejrzanej," Warsaw, March 2, 1950, file 01252_8, BU IPN.
139. Tonia Bialer's file, application for legal residency, 1938, 19940434/340, AN.
140. Caron, "Politics of Frustration," 329.
141. Protokół przesłuchania podejrzanej, Warsaw, March 2, 1950, 136, file 01252_8, BU IPN.
142. In a letter from May 23, she informed her parents that she had signed herself up for the hospital: "It was not easy without money, but I did it." Tonia to her parents, May 23, 1938.
143. Tonia to her parents, February 12, 1938.
144. Tonia, interview by Dowgiałło.

145. Le Registre des entrées pour l'année 1938 (reference: Boucicaut 1Q 2/18), and Le Registre des naissances pour la période du 18 mai 1938 au 12 février 1939 (reference: Boucicaut 1Q 2/12), both in archive of Centre d'assistance publique Hôpitaux de Paris, Paris.
146. Hans Marum to Róża and Aron Bialer, June 27, 1938.
147. Tonia to her parents, July 1938.
148. Tonia, interview by Dowgiałło.
149. Tonia to her parents, July 1938.
150. Protokół przesłuchania podejrzanej, Warsaw, July 26, 1950, file 01252_8, BU IPN.
151. Tonia, interview by Dowgiałło.
152. Tonia to her parents, July 21, 1938.
153. Tonia to her parents, November 28, 1938.
154. Tonia to her parents, July 1938.
155. Tonia to her parents, November 28, 1938.
156. Tonia to her parents, February 25, 1938.
157. Tonia to her parents, October 27, 1938.
158. Tonia to her parents, September 27, 1938.
159. Tonia to her parents, November 7, 1938.
160. Krammer, "Germans against Hitler," 77–78.
161. Tonia to her parents, September 27, 1938.
162. Zaagsma, *Jewish Volunteers*, 109.
163. "Un groupe exceptionnel," Amicale du camp de Gurs, accessed August 2020, http://www.campgurs.com/le-camp/lhistoire-du-camp/période-espagnole-1939-brigades-internationales/un-groupe-exceptionnel/.
164. Krammer, "Germans against Hitler," 77–78. According to Geneviève Dreyfus-Armand, "in February 1939, some 275,000 Spaniards were interned." Geneviève Dreyfus-Armand, "When Spain's Refugees Turned to France," *Le Monde diplomatique,* May 2017, https://mondediplo.com/2017/05/20Spain.
165. Tonia to her parents, November 7, 1938.
166. Tonia to her parents, February 25, 1939. Jackson confirms that Mexico offered to receive veterans from the International Brigades, "but the offer provoked domestic opposition, and in the end, the Mexican government trimmed its sails." Jackson, *Fallen Sparrows*, 129–30.
167. John F. Sweets, *Choices in Vichy France: The French under Nazi Occupation* (Oxford: Oxford University Press, 1986), 112.
168. Sweets, 112–13.
169. Dreyfus-Armand, "When Spain's Refugees Turned to France."
170. Protokół przesłuchania podejrzanej, Warsaw, March 4, 1950, file 01252_8, BU IPN.
171. Protokół przesłuchania podejrzanej, Warsaw, March 4, 1950.
172. Caroline Moorehead, *Villages of Secrets: Defying the Nazis in Vichy France* (New York: HarperCollins, 2014), 35.

173. "Un groupe exceptionnel."
174. Tonia to her parents, 1939. This letter must be from after April 1939, since Sioma is already in France.
175. Tonia Bialer's file, Demand d'autorisation de sejour, 1938, 19940434/340, AN.
176. Tonia to her parents, May 11, 1939.
177. Tonia to her parents, November 7, 1938.
178. Tonia to her parents, June 15, 1939; June 22, 1939; and 1939. This last letter must be from after April 1939—possibly May or June—since Sioma was already in France.
179. Tonia to her parents, May 23, 1939, and May 11, 1939.
180. Letter from the Ministry of Interior to the police, Tonia Bialer's file, 19940434/340, AN
181. Tonia, interview by Dowgiałło.

Chapter 4: Life on the Run

1. The album is in Marcel's private collection.
2. Marcel, email exchange with author, November 2019.
3. Katja Petrowskaja, interview by Maya Caspari, "'There Are No "Other" People': A Conversation with Katja Petrowskaja," *Los Angeles Review of Books*, March 7, 2018.
4. Tonia, interview by Dowgiałło.
5. Protokół przesłuchania podejrzanej, Warsaw, March 4, 1950, file 01252_8, BU IPN.
6. Michael Uhl, Betty Rosenfeld's biographer, email exchange with author, January 2020.
7. Correspondence smuggled out of and into Auschwitz is a well-known example. E.g., see *Grypsy z Konzentrationslager Auschwitz Józefa Cyrankiewicza i Stanisława Kłodzińskiego,* ed. Irena Paczyńska (Kraków: Wydawnictwo Uniwersytetu Jagiellońskiego, 2013), and Hermann Langbein, *Against All Hope: Resistance in the Nazi Concentration Camps, 1938–1945* (New York: Paragon House, 1994), 56–60.
8. Protokół przesłuchania podejrzanej, Warsaw, July 26, 1949, file 01252_8, BU IPN.
9. Protokół przesłuchania podejrzanej, Warsaw, March 4, 1950, file 01252_8, BU IPN; Uhl, email exchange with author, January 2020.
10. Until the German occupation of France in 1940, no one really knew how many Jews lived in Paris. See Jacques Adler, *The Jews of Paris and the Final Solution: Communal Response and Internal Conflicts, 1940–1944* (Oxford: Oxford University Press, 1985), 3–7.
11. Sandra Ott, *Living with the Enemy: German Occupation, Collaboration and Justice in the Western Pyrenees, 1940–1948* (Cambridge: Cambridge University Press, 2017), 51.

12. Protokół przesłuchania podejrzanej, Warsaw, March 4, 1950, file 01252_8, BU, IPN.
13. Protokół przesłuchania podejrzanej, Warsaw, March 4, 1950.
14. Uhl, email exchange with author, January 2020.
15. Tonia, interview by Dowgiałło. See also Elizabeth Marum Lunau, "Arrival at Camps de Gurs: An Eyewitness Report," in *Between Sorrow and Strength: Women Refugees of the Nazi Period,* ed. Sibylle Quack (Washington, DC: German Historical Institute, 1995), 66.
16. Tonia to her mother, June 1939.
17. Tonia, interview by Dowgiałło.
18. Tonia to her mother, June 1939.
19. Tonia to her mother, August 3, 1939. This letter's date was added, most likely by Marcel, but it seems to be incorrect. It was probably written in September, not August.
20. Protokół przesłuchania podejrzanej, Warsaw, March 4, 1950, file 01252_8, BU IPN.
21. Laharie is an author of a book on Gurs, *Le camp de Gurs: 1939–1945: Un aspect meconnu de l'histoire du Bearn* (Pau: Infocompo, 1985).
22. Claude Laharie, email exchanges with author, October 2019.
23. Michael R. Marrus and Robert O. Paxton, *Vichy France and the Jews* (New York: Basic Books, 1981), 4, 169, 63.
24. Marrus and Paxton, 65.
25. The internment camp of Rieucros operated from January 1939 to February 1942. Julia Buck, "Suspect Women: The Politics of Exclusion in the French Camp of Rieucros, 1939–1942," *Journal of the Western Society for French History* 43 (2015), https://quod.lib.umich.edu/w/wsfh/0642292.0043.010?view=text;rgn=main; Marrus and Paxton, *Vichy France and Jews,* 66. At this time, all male émigrés aged seventeen to fifty coming from the Reich, including Austrians, were interned. Rita Thalmann, "Jewish Women Exiled in France after 1933," in Quack, *Between Sorrow and Strength,* 58.
26. Marrus and Paxton, *Vichy France and Jews,* 165.
27. Tonia to her mother, June 7, 1939, and November 14, 1939.
28. Tonia, interview by Dowgiałło.
29. Tonia to her mother, June 1939.
30. Tonia to her family, July 1939. It is likely that Tonia had a chance to listen to Heinrich Mann, who often spoke against Hitler and fascism. He spent July 1939 in Grenoble. Evelyn Juers, *House of Exile: The Lives and Times of Heinrich Mann and Nelly Kroeger-Mann* (New York: Farrar, Straus & Giroux, 2011).
31. Uhl, email exchange with author, January 2020.
32. Adam Rayski, *The Choices of the Jews under Vichy: Between Submission and Resistance* (South Bend, IN: University of Notre Dame Press, 1992), 6–7, quotation on p. 7.

33. Tonia to her family, November 28, 1939.
34. Based on documents from Bundesarchiv, Berlin, received from Uhl.
35. Tonia to her family, April 28 and May 27, 1940.
36. Protokół przesłuchania podejrzanej, Warsaw, March, 4, 1950, file 01252_8, BU IPN.
37. Sioma to Tonia's parents, October 21, 1939.
38. Tonia to her parents, November 23, 1939.
39. Tonia to her parents November 14, 1939
40. Caroline Moorehead, *Villages of Secrets: Defying the Nazis in Vichy France* (New York: HarperCollins, 2014), 35.
41. Marrus and Paxton, *Vichy France and Jews,* 172–73.
42. Tonia to her family, January 8, 1940.
43. Marcel Łoziński, dir., *Tonia i jej dzieci* (Warsaw: Studio Filmowe Kronika, 2011).
44. Tonia, interview by Dowgiałło.
45. The KPP's dissolution was part of the Great Purge of 1937. The exact number of victims is unknown. See Jaff Schatz, *The Generation: The Rise and Fall of the Jewish Communists of Poland* (Berkeley: University of California Press, 1991), 102, and Andrzej Korboński, "The Polish Communist Party 1938–1942," *Slavic Review* 26, no. 3 (1967): 430–31.
46. Tonia, interview by Dowgiałło.
47. Protokół przesłuchania podejrzanej, Warsaw, October 5, 1949, file 01252_8, BU IPN.
48. Leński was a pseudonym of Julian Leszczyński, a KPP member. In the late 1920s he supported Stalin. In 1937 he was summoned to Moscow, shortly after which he was executed. Julian Leszczyński, in *Biographical Dictionary of Central and Eastern Europe in the Twentieth Century,* ed. Wojciech Roszkowski and Jan Kofman (Oxford: Routledge, 2008), 568.
49. Tonia, interview by Dowgiałło.
50. Uhl, email exchange with author, March 2020. On the scope of political surveillance and repression in the Republican camp, see Peter Huber and Michael Uhl, "Die internationalen Brigaden: Politische Überwachung und Repression nach Sichtung der russischen und westlichen Archivakten," *Revista Internacional de la Guerra Civil, 1936–1939* 2 (2005): 11–34. See also George Orwell, *Homage to Catalonia* (London: Penguin Classic, 2013).
51. Lisa A. Kirchenbaum, *International Communism and the Spanish Civil War: Solidarity and Suspicion* (Cambridge: Cambridge University Press), 2.
52. Catherine Epstein, *The Last Revolutionaries* (Cambridge, MA: Harvard University Press, 2003), 63–65; "Ochotnicy Wolności: Dąbrowszczacy w Hiszpanii, 1936–39," *Karta* 90 (2017): 6.
53. Arthur Koestler, *Scum of the Earth* (New York: Macmillan, 1968), 31, 32.
54. Łoziński, *Tonia i jej dzieci.*
55. Anna Rajf-Ligęza, phone conversation with author, March 2018.

56. The material was passed on by Jerzy Toruńczyk to Marcel. In the letter, she mentions being seventy-six, so most likely it was written in 1987 (she was born in 1911). "Retirada en Polonais" was published in *Zeszyty Historyczne* 156 (2006): 230–55, and then, more recently, fragments were published in "Ochotnicy Wolności."
57. Jadwiga Wełykanowicz, "Lwowski Rodowód," *Zeszyty Literackie*, no. 1/97 (2007), https://www.zeszytyliterackie.pl/1495-2/. The pogroms in Lwów were described more recently in Grzegorz Gauden, *Lwów—kres iluzji: Opowieść o pogromie listopadowym 1918* (Kraków: Universitas, 2019).
58. Biography of Henryk Toruńczyk in *Karta* 90 (2017): 43, 17.
59. Dora Lorska, Medial Review Auschwitz, accessed February 2022, https://www.mp.pl/auschwitz/journal/english/253561,dr-dorota-lorska?fbclid=IwAR2tgIMrC6BYX9_lEHQn-yl7qkDyYSHzfHIBFiXU3GdeIbHNIJfdDzP1vPE. See also Manuel Requena Gallego and Rosa María, eds., *La sanidad en la Brigadas Internacionales* (Ciudad Real, Spain: Universidad de Castilla–La Mancha, 2006), 53.
60. Wiesława Toruńczyk to Jerzy Toruńczyk, "Retirada en Polonais," 1988, in the private collection of Marcel Lechtman and copy in author's possession.
61. Biography of Jadwiga Wełykanowicz in *Karta* 90 (2017): 43.
62. Shortly after the KPP's dissolution, the Comintern decided that a new party should be established. Soviet sources revealed that in a secret resolution dated May 26, 1939, the executive committee of the Comintern went officially on record as being in favor of forming the new party. Korboński, "Polish Communist Party," 430–31.
63. In Oloron she would have to pay for the birth, so she decided to travel to Pau to deliver for free at a single mothers' ward. Tonia to her family, March 27, 1940.
64. Tonia, interview by Dowgiałło. See also Tonia to her family, March 31, 1940.
65. Tonia, interview by Dowgiałło.
66. Protokół przesłuchania podejrzanej, Warsaw, October 5, 1949, file 01252_8, BU IPN; Vera, interview by author, May 2018.
67. Marcel, email exchange with author, November 2019.
68. Protokół przesłuchania podejrzanej, Warsaw, July 26, 1949, file 01252_8, BU IPN.
69. Laharie, email exchange with author, October 2019.
70. Tonia to her family, March 27, 1940.
71. Tonia, interview by Dowgiałło; Sonia to Tonia's family, April 1, 1940.
72. Tonia to her family, April 1940.
73. Tonia, interview by Dowgiałło.
74. Sioma to the family (postcard), October 21, 1939.
75. Tonia to her family, January 2 and 20, 1940.
76. Sioma to the family (postcard), October 21, 1939.
77. Tonia to her family, January 8 and 17, 1940, and February 2, 1940.
78. Tonia to her family, May 27, 1940.

79. Marrus and Paxton, *Vichy France and Jews,* 14.
80. In the west, the occupied zone included the provinces of France's entire Atlantic and English Channel coasts, Paris, and the central provinces. The demarcation line between the two zones turns northwest from the Spanish border to a point near Tours and then eastward to the Swiss frontier. Alsace and a larger part of Loraine, the northeastern border provinces, were annexed outright by Germany, returning the Franco-German frontier substantially to where it had been in 1871. Serge Klarsfeld, *History and Chronology: French Children and the Holocaust; A Memorial* (New York: New York University Press, 1996), 4–5.
81. Adam Rayski, *The Choices of the Jews under Vichy: Between Submission and Resistance* (South Bend, IN: University of Notre Dame Press, 1992), 12; Marrus and Paxton, *Vichy France and Jews,* 3–5.
82. Tonia to her family, June 7, 1940.
83. Lina Soulan, email exchange with author, March 2020. Sioma Lechtman's file (written as Lechtmann) at l'Amicale des Anciens Internés Politiques et Résistants du camp de concentration du Vernet d'Ariège.
84. Marrus and Paxton, *Vichy France and Jews,* 174.
85. Helen Graham, "A War for Our Times: The Spanish Conflict in 21st-Century Perspective," *Volunteer,* September 14, 2012, http://www.albavolunteer.org/2012/09/a-war-for-our-times-the-spanish-conflict-in-21st-century-perspective/.
86. Koestler, *Scum of the Earth,* 105, 116, 103.
87. Marrus and Paxton, *Vichy France and Jews,* 174; Koestler, *Scum of the Earth,* 105; Uhl, email exchange with author, April 2020.
88. Soulan, email exchange with author, January 2020.
89. Koestler, *Scum of the Earth,* 105, 127–29.
90. Déclaration qui doit être formulée par tout israélite établi ou réfugié en France depuis le 1er janvier 1936 (Tonia), February 1942, 985 W 485, f. 532, Archives départementales de la Haute-Vienne, Limoges, France (hereafter cited as ADHV).
91. Koestler, *Scum of the Earth,* 105.
92. Marrus and Paxton, *Vichy France and Jews,* 175.
93. Koestler, *Scum of the Earth,* 103. On November 11, 1940, the *New Republic* published an article on Le Vernet, "The French Dachau." Marrus and Paxton, *Vichy France and Jews,* 171.
94. Koestler, *The Scum of the Earth,* 106, 106–7, 119, 107.
95. "Plaques de verre," Le camp de concentration du Vernet d'Ariège 1939–1944, accessed August 2020, http://www.campduvernet.eu/album-photos/paysages/plaques-de-verre/.
96. Photo 093_03, Photos du camp, Le camp de concentration du Vernet d'Ariège 1939–1944, accessed August 2020, http://www.campduvernet.eu/album-photos/paysages/plaques-de-verre/photos-du-camp/093-03.html.

97. Linda Ferrer Roca, dir., *Photographies d'un camp* (Les Films d'ici, 1993), http://www.lesfilmsdici.fr/fr/catalogue/633-photographie-d-un-camp.html. See also Linda Ferrer-Roca and Amanda Roblès, "Histoire, mémoire et transmission," *Matériaux pour l'histoire de notre temps* 1–2, nos. 89–90 (2008): 109–14.
98. Uhl, email exchange with author, April 2020. According to Uhl, to apply for a visa to Mexico you needed ten photos.
99. Protokół przesłuchania podejrzanej, Warsaw, July 2, 1949, file 01252_8, BU IPN.
100. Tonia, interview by Dowgiałło.
101. Protokół przesłuchania podejrzanej, Warsaw, March 23, 1950, file 01252_8, BU IPN.
102. Marrus and Paxton, *Vichy France and Jews*, 67.
103. Marrus and Paxton, 4, 167, 165.
104. Protokół przesłuchania podejrzanej, Warsaw, March 4, 1950, file 01252_8, BU IPN.
105. Tonia, interview by Dowgiałło.
106. Protokół przesłuchania podejrzanej, Warsaw, March 4, 1950, file 01252_8, BU IPN.
107. Tonia, interview by Dowgiałło.
108. Jean-Marie Borzeix, *One Day in France: Tragedy and Betrayal in an Occupied Village* (New York: Bloomsbury, 2016), 77; Julie Carnis, "Limoges: Au loin, on entend la clameur d'une cour de récré...," *L'Humanité*, August 6, 2013, https://www.humanite.fr/monde/limoges-au-loin-entend-la-clameur-d-une-cour-de-re-546963.
109. Tonia, interview by Dowgiałło.
110. Protokół przesłuchania podejrzanej, Warsaw, March 6, 1950, file 01252_8, BU IPN.
111. Tonia, interview by Dowgiałło. See also Liste des enfants à la maison de Limoges, adressé à la société OSE, de la part de l'assistance médicale aux enfants de réfugiés, November 20, 1940, OSE (II) 209 (003), OSE (II) 209 (004 et 005), OSE (II) 210 (005 et 006), OSE (II) 211 (002 et 003), OSE (II) 211 (005–006), feuille 0211, OSE, Mémorial de la Shoah.
112. Catherine Richet, ed., *Organisation juive de combat: Résistance/sauvetage. France 1940–1945* (Paris: Autrement, 2006), 185–89. Sabine Zeitoun, *L'Oeuvre de Secours aux enfants (OSE) sous l'occupation en France* (Paris: L'Harmattan, 1990).
113. Patrick Henry, *We Only Know Men: The Rescue of Jews in France during the Holocaust* (Washington, DC: Catholic University of America Press, 2007), 89.
114. Tonia, interview by Dowgiałło; Gaston Lévy, *Souvenirs d'un medecin d'enfants a l'OSE en France occupée et en Suisse 1940–1954* (Paris: Témoignages de la Shoah, 2008).
115. Pierre Goetschel, dir., *L'Héritage retrouvé* (Limoges, France: Leitmotiv Production, 2014).

116. Reinhard Otto, *Wie Haste det Jemacht? Lebenslauf von Hanna Grunwald-Eisfelder* (Soltau, Germany: Mund-Schenk Verlag 1992), 9, 18, quotation on p. 19. See also Willi Engels, *Kellner, Koch, Kommunist: Erinnerungen* (Berlin: Lukas Verlag, 2016), 24.
117. Otto, *Wie Haste det Jemacht?*, 36.
118. Otto, 45.
119. Gaston Lévy to Limoges prefecture, July 12, 1942, feuille 0211, OSE, Mémorial de la Shoah.
120. Otto, *Wie Haste det Jemacht?*, 51.
121. Liste des enfants à la maison de Limoges. The Limoges nursery was suddenly closed down the day after Christmas in 1943, when the fifty or so babies and toddlers who were still there were either returned to their parents or hastily evacuated and placed in temporary refuge by the OSE. Borzeix, *One Day in France*, 77.
122. Tonia, interview by Dowgiałło.
123. Protokół przesłuchania podejrzanej, Warsaw, March 23, 1950, file 01252_8, BU IPN.
124. Tonia, interview by Dowgiałło.
125. Protokół przesłuchania podejrzanej, Warsaw, March 6, 1950, file 01252_8, BU IPN.
126. Protokół przesłuchania podejrzanej, Warsaw, July 26, 1949, file 01252_8, BU IPN.
127. Biography of Mela Ernst, ÖsterreicherInnen im KZ Ravensbrück, accessed February 2022, http://www.ravensbrueckerinnen.at/detail.php?var=1860.
128. The letter is overly polite: "ask for your high benevolence to kindly" (*solliciter de votre haute bienveillance de bien vouloir*). Tonia Lechtman to a prefect of the department of Ariege, Limoges, June 9, 1941, Amicale de Vernet, Ariège, France.
129. Prefect of the department of Ariege to Tonia Lechtman, July 5, 1941, Amicale de Vernet.
130. Protokół przesłuchania podejrzanej, Warsaw, July 26, 1949, file 01252_8, BU IPN.
131. Borzeix, *One Day in France*, 77.
132. Goetschel, *L'Héritage retrouvé*; Borzeix, *One Day in France*, 77; Pascal Plas and Simon Schwarzfuchs, eds., *Mémoires du grand rabbin deutsch: Limoges 1939–1945* (Saint-Paul, France: Lucien Souny, 2007).
133. Marrus and Paxton, *Vichy France and Jews*, 185–86.
134. Marrus and Paxton, 100.
135. Tonia to Julek, January 21, 1946.
136. Déclaration qui doit être formulée par tout israélité établi en France depuis le 1er janvier 1936, 985 W 485, f. 532, ADHV. There is an addition in pencil to the form with a new address: "Route de Clermont chez Faure à St Léonard de Noblat."
137. Tonia, interview by Dowgiałło.

138. Protokół przesłuchania podejrzanej, Warsaw, March 7, 1950, file 01252_8, BU IPN.
139. Certificate de notification, Limoges, March 25, 1942, 985 W 485, f. 803, ADHV.
140. Lechtman to the Limoges police, April 1, 1942, 985 W 485, f. 909, ADHV; Limoges police to Lechtman, April 20, 1942, 985 W 485, f. 900, ADHV.
141. Lettre de demande de s'installer à Bessines sur Gartempe, 1942, 985 W 485, f. 908, ADHV.
142. Tonia to the prefect, 1942, 985 W 485, f. 761, ADHV.
143. Note au Commissaire de Police de Limoges, sur les étrangers demandant un sursis, 1942, 985 W 485, f. 767, ADHV.
144. Marrus and Paxton, *Vichy France and Jews*, 169.
145. Protokół przesłuchania podejrzanej, Warsaw, March 7, 1950, file 01252_8, BU IPN.
146. Nani Glauster, conversation with Taylorann Lenze, Vienna, 2018.
147. Glauster, conversation with Lenze.
148. Tonia, interview by Dowgiałło.
149. Information about Sioma Lechtman's deportation, Mémorial de la Shoah, http://ressources.memorialdelashoah.org/notice.php?q=fulltext%3A%8lechtmann%29%20AND%20id_pers%3A%28%2A%29&spec_expand=1&rows=20&start=0.
150. Marrus and Paxton, *Vichy France and Jews*, 227, 259.
151. Guy Perlier, *La rafle: Août 1942; Région de Limoges* (Limoges: Editions les Monédières, 2012), 24–27.
152. Tonia, interview by Dowgiałło.
153. Protokół przesłuchania podejrzanej, Warsaw, March 7, 1950, file 01252_8, BU IPN.
154. List of prisoners from Nexon, 646 W 251, f. 401 and 402, ADHV.
155. Perlier, *La rafle*, 51; Marrus and Paxton, *Vichy France and Jews*, 432.
156. Marrus and Paxton, *Vichy France and Jews*, 263.

Chapter 5: Mother, Refugee, and Social Worker

1. Vera, interviews by author, May 2014 and May 2018.
2. Françoise Frenkel, *A Bookshop in Berlin: The Rediscovered Memoir of One Woman's Harrowing Escape from the Nazis* (New York: Atria Books, 2019), 217.
3. The time (8:30 p.m.) is confirmed in a handwritten note: Note from Jussy—du poste de la police cantonale, Anières, October 10, 1942, Justice et police Ef/2, dossier 275, Archives d'état de Genève (State Archives of Geneva), Geneva (hereafter cited as AEG).
4. Handwritten note, October 10, 1942, Anières, AEG; Tonia Lechtman's file, Aktenzeichen: N06410, no. 58, Schweizerisches Bundesarchiv (Swiss Federal Archives), Bern (hereafter cited as SB); note from Jussy—du poste de la police cantonale, October 10, 1942, Justice et police Ef/2, dossier 275, AEG.

5. Tonia Lechtman, Jussy, October 10, 1942, Justice et police Ef/2, dossier 275, AEG.
6. Tonia Lechtman questionnaire, Jussy, October 10, 1942, Justice et police Ef/2, dossier 275, AEG.
7. Ruth Fivaz-Silbermann, email exchange with author, November 2019.
8. Gregor Spuhler, *Switzerland and Refugees in the Nazi Era: Independent Commission of Experts Switzerland; Second World War* (Bern: BBL/EDMZ, 1999), 20, https://www.swissbankclaims.com/Documents/DOC_15_Bergier_Refugee.pdf.
9. Ruth Fivaz-Silbermann, "La fuite en Suisse: Migrations, stratégies, fuite, accueil, refoulement et destin des réfugiés juifs venus de France durant la Seconde Guerre mondiale" (PhD diss., University of Geneva, 2017), 38.
10. Protokół przesłuchania podejrzanej, Warsaw, March 23, 1950, file 01252_8, BU IPN.
11. Spuhler, *Switzerland and Refugees*, 13.
12. Protokół przesłuchania podejrzanej, Warsaw, July 26, 1949, file 01252_8, BU IPN.
13. Tonia, interview by Dowgiałło.
14. She told Dowgiałło it was a month, while in the interrogation she said it was two weeks. Tonia, interview by Dowgiałło; Protokół przesłuchania podejrzanej, Warsaw, March 14, 1950, 01252_8, BU IPN.
15. Protokół przesłuchania podejrzanej, Warsaw, July 24, 1950, file 01252/8, BU, IPN.
16. Fivaz-Silbermann, email exchange with author, February 2020. See also Laurent Neury, *L'Espoir au bout du pont: Histoire de la filière de Douvaine (1939–1945)* (Yens, Switzerland: Cabédita Editions, 2019).
17. Fivaz-Silbermann, email exchanges with author, November 2019 and February 2020.
18. Fivaz-Silbermann, email exchange with author, October 2019.
19. Fivaz-Silbermann, email exchange with author, November 2019.
20. Tonia, interview by Dowgiałło. See also Protokół przesłuchania podejrzanej, Warsaw, March 14, 1950, file 01252_8, BU IPN.
21. Simon Erlanger, "The Politics of 'Transmigration': Why Jewish Refugees Had to Leave Switzerland from 1944 to 1954," *Jewish Political Studies Review* 18, nos. 1–2 (2006): 1–2.
22. Ruth Fivaz-Silbermann, "Ignorance, Realpolitik and Human Rights: Switzerland between Active Refusal and Passive Help," in *Bystanders, Rescuers or Perpetrators*, ed. Corry Guttstadt, Thomas Luts, Bernd Rother, and Yessica San Roman (Berlin: Metropol Verlag and IHRA, 2016), 88–89.
23. Spuhler, *Switzerland and Refugees*, 22.
24. Fivaz-Silbermann, "Ignorance, Realpolitik and Human Rights," 91; Erlanger, "Politics of 'Transmigration,'" 1–2.

25. Fivaz-Silbermann, "Ignorance, Realpolitik and Human Rights," 92.
26. Fivaz-Silbermann, 95.
27. Fivaz-Silbermann, 96.
28. Fivaz-Silbermann, 98.
29. Geneva, October 15, 1942, Justice et police Ef/2, dossier 275, AEG.
30. Frenkel described her experience with the police similarly. See Frenkel, *Bookshop in Berlin*, 163.
31. Tonia, interview by Dowgiałło.
32. Fivaz-Silbermann, email exchange with author, April 2020.
33. The organization Help to the Emigrants (Aide aux émigrés) conducted a questionnaire with 5,490 refugees, the majority of whom were Poles—Polish Jews—who immigrated to Western Europe in the 1920s and 1930s and were subsequently forced to flee Switzerland. Bertha Hohermuth, *A Report on the Documentation of 9930 Refugees in Switzerland* (Geneva: International Migration Service [Aide aux Emigrés], 1945), 6, 14, 19.
34. Spuhler, *Switzerland and Refugees*, 156. For examples of the Polish soldiers interned in the Swiss camps and used for various work, see Adam Vetulani, *Poza płomieniami wojny: Internowani w Szwajcarii 1940–1945* (Warsaw: Ministerstwo Obrony Narodowej, 1976), 218–19.
35. Fivaz-Silbermann, email exchange with author, April 2020.
36. Fivaz-Silbermann, "La fuite en Suisse," 432.
37. Tonia, interview by Dowgiałło.
38. Spuhler, *Switzerland and Refugees*, 156; Fivaz-Silbermann, email exchange with author, April 2020.
39. Erlanger, "Politics of 'Transmigration,'" 2.
40. Spuhler, *Switzerland and Refugees*, 157.
41. Tonia Lechtman questionnaire, December 4, 1942, Geneva, Tonia Lechtman's file Aktenzeichen: N06410, Signatur: E4264#1985/196#9314*, no. 46, SB.
42. Fivaz-Silbermann, email exchanges with author, March and April 2020.
43. Tonia Lechtman questionnaire, December 4, 1942, Geneva, Tonia Lechtman's file Aktenzeichen: N06410, Signatur: E4264#1985/196#9314*, no. 46, SB.
44. Engagement (three copies), signed by Tonia Lechtman, Justice et police Ef/2, dossier 275, AEG.
45. Fivaz-Silbermann, email exchange with author, April 2020.
46. Fivaz-Silbermann, email exchange with author, March 2020. For images of the hotel, see "L'hôtel Beau-Séjour," Notre histoire, accessed 2022, https://notrehistoire.ch/entries/QqOYOmzR8EZ.
47. Protokół przesłuchania podejrzanej, Warsaw, July 26, 1949, file 01252_8, BU IPN.
48. Fivaz-Silbermann, email exchange with author, March 2020. There is less certainty about the history of Les Hirondelles. According to Fivaz-Silbermann, some indications suggest that the villa was the same place as another camp,

Bout-du-Monde, which was opened on September 25, 1942. From this time forward, both the former Les Hirondelles / Bout-du-Monde and Val-Fleuri were referred to as "camp Champel."
49. Tonia to Richard Lichtheim, November 12, 1942.
50. Andrea Kirchner, "Wie Noah auf dem Berg Ararat: Richard Lichtheim in Genf, 1939–1946," in *Der Holocaust: Neue Studien zu Tathegrängen Reaktionen und Aufarbeitungen*, ed. Jörg Osterloh and Katharina Rauschenberger (Frankfurt am Main: Fritz Bauer Institute, Jahrbuch, zur Geschichte und Wirkung des Holocaust, 2017), 42; see also Jürgen Matthäus, *Predicting the Holocaust: Jewish Organizations Report from Geneva on the Emergence of the "Final Solution," 1939–1942*, Documenting Life and Destruction: Holocaust Sources in Context (Lanham, MD: Rowman & Littlefield, 2019), 13–23.
51. Kirchner, unpublished lecture.
52. Kirchner.
53. Kirchner.
54. Kirchner, "Wie Noah auf dem Berg Ararat,"
55. Sara Kadosh, "Jewish Refugee Children in Switzerland, 1939–50," in *Remembering for the Future: The Holocaust in an Age of Genocide, Ethics and Religion*, vol. 2, ed. Margot Levy (New York: Palgrave Macmillan, 2001), 286–87.
56. SHEK emerged from the Swiss section of the Comité d'aide aux enfants des émigrés allemands in Paris. In 1935 it became the umbrella organization for an independent Swiss aid organization. See Rachel Christen, "Le Schweizer Hilfswerk für Emigrantenkinder et les enfants réfugiés pendant la Seconde Guerre mondiale," SlideShare, January 29, 2016, https://fr.slideshare.net/RahelChristen/le-schweizer-hilfswerk-fur-emigrantenkinder-et-les-enfants-refugies-pendant-la-seconde-guerre-mondiale.
57. Kadosh, "Jewish Refugee Children," 287, 289.
58. Kadosh, 289.
59. Spuhler, *Switzerland and Refugees*, 160.
60. Bertha Hohermuth of Aide aux émigrés to lieutenant of the district, November 17, 1942, Geneva, Justice et police Ef/2, dossier 275, AEG.
61. Tonia to her parents, January 23, 1943.
62. Eveline Zeder, *Ein Zuhause fur jüdische Flüchtlingskinder: Lilly Volkart und ihr Kinderheim in Ascona 1934–1947* (Zürich: Chronos Verlag, 1998), 75–76. The children also appear on the list of the children of Ascona included in a book by Rachel Chetrit-Benaudis, *Murmures d'enfants dans la nuit* (Paris: OSE, 2004), 195–97.
63. Zeder, *Ein Zugause fur judische Fluchtlingskinder,* 75.
64. Zeder, 75–76, 83–86, 88–89.
65. Tonia, interview by Dowgiałło.
66. Locher to Polizeiabteilung, Dr. Schumacher, Zürich, February 28, 1943, Tonia Lechtman's file: Aktenzeichen: N06410, Signatur: E4264#1985/196#9314*, no. 49, SB.

Notes to Pages 166–172 321

67. Locher to Mr. Canevascini, March 29, 1943, no. 52, SB.
68. Reinhard Otto, *Wie Haste det Jemacht? How Did You Do That? The Biography of Hanna Eisfelder Grunwald* (Soltau: Mund-Schenk Verlag, 1992).
69. Otto.
70. In July 1945, as a director of the Swiss branch of the International Migration Service, Hohermuth compiled a report on the 9,930 refugees in Switzerland. M. M. Chambers, *Youth-Serving Organizations: National Nongovernmental Associations* (Washington, DC: American Council on Education, 1948), 135. See also Antonia Schmidlin, "Berta Hohermuth," Historisches Lexikon der Schweiz HLS, October 20, 2014, https://hls-dhs-dss.ch/de/articles/032118/2014-10-20/.
71. Józef Łaptos, *Humanitaryzm i Polityka: Pomoc UNRRA dla Polski i polskich uchodźców w latach 1944–1947* (Kraków: Uniwersytet Pedagogiczny im. Komisji Edukacji Narodowej w Krakowie, 2018), 44.
72. Lore Silton, January 13, 1995, oral history collection, University of Southern California Shoah Foundation, Los Angeles (hereafter cited as USC Shoah Foundation). See also Lillian Fixler, October 13, 1996; Agi Hendell, May 5, 1996; Judy Jacobs, April 1, 1996; and Eva Speter, July 26, 1996, all in oral history collection, USC Shoah Foundation.
73. Tonia, interview by Dowgiałło.
74. Lore Silton, January 13, 1995, and Eva Speter, July 26, 1996, both in oral history collection, USC Shoah Foundation.
75. Tonia, interview by Dowgiałło.
76. Letter from the camp commandant, Les Avants, March 31, 1943, no. 53, SB.
77. Locher to police in Ascona, March 30, 1943, no. 51, SB. Silton mentioned the existence of a kitchen for babies, but there is no way of knowing if this was the same facility Tonia helped to organize or worked in.
78. Tonia to R. Lichtheim, May 24, 1943.
79. Locher to police of Ticino, March 30, 1943, Zollikon, no. 51, SB.
80. Locher to police of Ticino; Fivaz-Silbermann, email exchange with author, April 2020.
81. Departimento Cantonale di Polizia, April 27, 1943, no. 57; Commandement de l'Armée, May 19, 1943, Pregassona, no. 3, both in SB. On May 21 Locher wrote to the police wondering if Tonia was granted a residency permit in Pregassona. Locher to the police, May 21, 1943, no. 6, SB.
82. Locher to police in Ticino, July 14, 1943, Zürich, no 14, SB.
83. Tonia to her parents, June 16, 1944.
84. Dr. Med. Den. O. Rechenmacher, Zürich, August 26, 1943, no. 19, SB.
85. Tonia Lechtman's report at Police Department, Küsnacht, September 4, 1943, no. 21, SB.
86. Meldung: Falscher Eintrag in die Fremdenkontrolle, Zürich, September 1, 1943, no. 22, SB.

87. Der Chef der Polizeabtailung to Locher, October 16, 1943, Bern, no. 31, SB.
88. Fremdenpolizei des Kantons Zürich to Lechtman, September 10, 1943, Zürich, no. 24, SB.
89. Zentralleitung der Arbeitslager to Lechtman, Zürich, September 24, 1943, no. 27, SB.
90. Locher to der Chef der Polizeabteilung, October 10, 1943, no. 37, SB.
91. "Identification Tag with Name and Birthdate Issued to Jewish Refugee Child," Accession Number: 2008.319.2, United States Holocaust Memorial Museum, accessed February 2022, https://collections.ushmm.org/search/catalog/irn37082; Marcel, email exchange with author, April 2020.
92. Tonia to her parents, November 21, 1943.
93. Erklärung, December 11, 1943, no. 41, SB.
94. Tonia to her parents, January 16, 1944.
95. Tonia to her parents, January 16, 1944.
96. Tonia, interview by Dowgiałło.
97. I would like to thank Basia Nowak for this comment.
98. Tonia to her parents, March 27, 1944.
99. Tonia to her parents, January 16, 1944.
100. Tonia to her parents, February 6, 1944. See also Tonia to her parents, January 11, 1944.
101. Tonia to her parents, February 6, 1944.
102. Tonia to her parents, August 27, 1944. About two months later, in November 1944, she tried to contact her grandparents again, and again there was no response. Tonia to her parents, November 11, 1944.
103. Tonia to her parents, February 16, 1944.
104. Tonia to her parents, March 27, 1944.
105. Tonia, interview by Dowgiałło.
106. Fremdenpolizei, Bern, April 17, 1944, no. 42, SB.
107. Tonia to her parents, June 7, 1944.
108. Tonia to her parents, June 15, 1944.
109. Tonia, interview by Dowgiałło.
110. Protokół przesłuchania podejrzanej, Warsaw, March 23, 1950, file 01252_8, BU IPN.
111. Protokół przesłuchania podejrzanej, with Janusz Sokołowski, August, 5, 1949, file 0_1251_22, BU IPN.
112. Robert Spałek, *Komuniści przeciwko Komunistom* (Warsaw: Zysk i S-ka, IPN, 2014), 221; Vetulani, *Poza płomieniami wojny*, 108, 297. For more on the origins of *Polska Ludowa*, see the file of Janusz Sokołowski—e.g., Protokół przesłuchania podejrzanej, August 5, 1949, file 0_1251_22, BU IPN.
113. Mark Andrzejewski, "Prasa polonijna w Szwajcarii: Problemy badawcze i zarys dziejów," *Kwartalnik Historii Prasy Polskiej* 25, no. 4 (1986): 93; Spałek, *Komuniści przeciwko Komunistom*, 222.

114. Based on thousands of pages of interrogation minutes, historian Robert Spałek re-created some aspects of the history of the Polish communists in Switzerland. His book is mostly interested in the logic of the communist purges and the communist mind-set that he sees as (self-)deception and disregard for doubts, but despite the agenda by which the book is certainly driven, it does provide insight into some aspects of the world of Polish communists in Switzerland. Spałek, *Komuniści przeciwko Komunistom*, 33–51. For more on the creation of ZPP, see Marci Shore, *Caviar and Ashes: A Warsaw Generation's Life and Death in Marxism, 1918–1968* (New Haven, CT: Yale University Press, 2006), 229.
115. Chef de police, Bern, November 28, 1944, no. 61, SB.
116. Geneva police to Tonia Lechtman, December 9, 1944, no. 67, SB.
117. Declaration, December 21, 1944, no. 38, SB.
118. Department de Justice et Police, Geneva, January 12, 1945, no. 70, SB.
119. Susan Elisabeth Subak, *Rescue Flight: American Relief Workers Who Defied the Nazis* (Lincoln: University of Nebraska Press, 2010), 180.
120. Bern, March 5, 1945, no. 72, SB.
121. Tony Sharp, *Stalin's American Spy: Noel Field, Allen Dulles and the East European Show Trials* (London: Hurst, 2014), 2, 39, 68, 82, 89.
122. Aurelio Velázquez-Hernández, "The Unitarian's Service Committee Marseille Office and the American Networks to Aid Spanish Refugees (1940–1943)," *Culture and History Digital Journal* 8, no. 2 (2019), https://doi.org/10.3989/chdj.2019.021. See also Łaptos, *Humanitaryzm i Polityka*, 11.
123. Sharp, *Stalin's American Spy*, 90–91.
124. bMS 16031/2 (3), Joint Anti-Fascist Refugee Committee, Correspondence, 1944–1945.
125. Protokół przesłuchania podejrzanej, Warsaw, October 2, 1949, file 01252_8, BU IPN.
126. Tonia, interview by Dowgiałło.
127. Sharp, *Stalin's American Spy*, 104.
128. Protokół przesłuchania podejrzanej, Warsaw, October 2, 1949, file 01252_8, BU IPN.
129. Protokół przesłuchania podejrzanej, Warsaw, October 2, 1949, file 01252_8, BU IPN.
130. Aneta Nisiobęcka, *Z Lens do Wałbrzycha* (Warsaw: IPN, 2018), 100. Already at the end of December 1944, France and Poland established its diplomatic representations. In February 1945 Jędrychowski also led negotiations with the French government demanding the return of thirty-five thousand Poles to Poland, who had been deported by Germany to France. Nisiobęcka, *Z Lens do Wałbrzycha*, 105
131. Tonia, interview by Dowgiałło.
132. Tonia to her parents, November 15, 1944. See also Nisiobęcka, *Z Lens do Wałbrzycha*, 106.

133. Tonia, interview by Dowgiałło.
134. Nisiobęcka, *Z Lens do Wałbrzycha*, 113.
135. Tonia, interview by Dowgiałło. About cooperation between UNRRA and the Polish government and the various foreign organizations UNRRA supervised in Poland, see Dariusz Jarosz, "Zapomniani przyjaciele: Zagraniczna pomoc charytatywna w Polsce Ludowej w latach 1945–1949," in *Społeczeństwo, państwo, modernizacja: Studia ofiarowane Januszowi Żarnowskiemu w 70. rocznicę urodzin*, ed. Włodzimierz Mędrzecki (Warsaw: PAN, 2002), 164.
136. Nisiobęcka, *Z Lens do Wałbrzycha*, 108.
137. Nisiobęcka, 101.
138. Aneta Nisiobęcka, email exchange with author, April 2020.
139. Tonia to her parents, November 15, 1944.
140. Nisiobęcka, *Z Lens do Wałbrzycha*, 106–7.
141. Tonia to Locher, October 18, 1945.
142. Tonia to her parents, November 15, 1944.
143. Tonia to Locher, October 28, 1945.
144. Tonia to her parents, January 12 and January 20, 1946. A mapping of the travels of the USC mission to Poland was prepared as part of the project Mapping Cultural Space across Eurasia at the Harvard University's Davis Center for Russian and Eurasian Studies, accessed September 2020, http://dighist.fas.harvard.edu/projects/eurasia/exhibits/show/apu.
145. Tonia to her parents, February 12 and March 22, 1946.
146. Tonia to her parents, June 4, 1946.
147. Tonia, interview by Dowgiałło.
148. Sanacja was a political movement whose name indicated its ambition for a moral healing of Polish society. It was established in the interwar period prior to Józef Piłsudski's coup in 1926.
149. Tonia to her parents, December 21, 1944.

Chapter 6: The Return

1. Eugenia Łozińska, "Życiorys," Warsaw, October 1947, CK PZPR 10455, AAN.
2. Vera, interview by author, May 2014.
3. In a letter to her family from 1955, she spoke about this friendship. Tonia to her parents, Warsaw, September 15, 1955.
4. Marcel Łoziński made another movie based on a similar premise, a conversation while traveling with his son, Paweł, to France, the place where Łoziński was born and where his mother was buried. Not surprisingly, the movie did not sit easily with his son, who then decided to film his own version of the same trip. In both movies, they discuss parental responsibilities and the loss a child experiences when a parent is absent. Marcel Łoziński, dir., *Ojciec i syn w podróży* (Warsaw: Łoziński Production, 2013); Paweł Łoziński, dir., *Ojciec i syn* (Warsaw: Łoziński Production, 2013).

5. Tonia mentioned this song in a letter from prison in 1953. Tonia to her children, Warsaw, 1953.
6. Marcel Łoziński, dir., *Tonia i jej dzieci* (Warsaw: Studio Filmowe Kronika, 2011).
7. Tonia to her mother, Paris, December 21, 1945.
8. Teresa Wontor-Cichy, phone conversation with author, May 2020.
9. Häftlingspersonanlbogen (Männer), v. 1, 101, Archiwum Państwowego Muzeum Auschwitz-Birkenau, Auschwitz (hereafter cited as APMA-B); Sioma Lechtman in "Liste originale du convoi de deportation," Mémorial de la Shoah, accessed December 2019, http://ressources.memorialdelashoah.org/notice.php?q= fulltext%3A%28lechtmann%29%20AND%20id_pers%3A%28%2A%29&spec _expand=1&rows=20&start=0. The first transport of Jews from France took place almost six months earlier, on March 27, 1942.
10. In total, around sixty-nine thousand Jews were sent to Auschwitz from France. Franciszek Piper, *Żydzi w KL Auschwitz* (Auschwitz: Państwowe Muzeum Auschwitz-Birkenau, 2015), 15; Danuta Czech, *Kalendarz wydarzeń w KL Auschwitz* (Auschwitz: Państwowe Muzeum Auschwitz-Birkenau, 1992), 224.
11. Piper, *Żydzi w KL Auschwitz*, 90.
12. Piper, 31–33.
13. Häftlingspersonanlbogen (Männer), v. 1, 101, D-AuI-2/285, no. 345, APMA-B.
14. Wontor-Cichy, phone conversation with author, May 2020.
15. "Jawischowitz," Państwowe Muzeum Auschwitz-Birkenau, accessed August 2020, http://auschwitz.org/historia/podobozy/jawischowitz/. See also Hermann Langbein, *Die Stärkeren: Ein Bericht* (Vienna: Bund-Verlag, 1982), 127.
16. Langbein, *Die Stärkeren*, 127. Langbein claims that Wirths was influenced by the prisoners he worked with.
17. Extract from the list of prisoners entering the infirmary prison of the Auschwitz concentration camp, ABMA-B.
18. "Powstanie i rozwój szpitali," Państwowe Muzeum Auschwitz-Birkenau, accessed August 2020, http://www.auschwitz.org/historia/szpitale-obozowe/powstanie -i-rozwoj-szpitali.
19. "Auschwitz i blok 28—wspomnienia," Państwowe Muzeum Auschwitz-Birkenau, accessed August 2020, http://auschwitz.org/muzeum/o-dostepnych -danych/cytaty/blok-28/.
20. Wontor-Cichy, phone conversation with author, May 2020.
21. Fragment of Władysław Jabłecki's account in Strzelecka, *Zbrodnicza medycyna*, 28.
22. "Auschwitz i blok 28—wspomnienia."
23. "Selection in the Camp," Państwowe Muzeum Auschwitz-Birkenau, accessed February 2022, http://70.auschwitz.org/index.php?option=com_content& view=article&id=298&Itemid=179&lang=en.
24. Strzelecka, *Zbrodnicza medycyna*, 7.
25. Piper, *Żydzi w KL Auschwitz*, 36.

26. Extract from the list of prisoners entering Auschwitz concentration camp, International Tracing Service Archives, Bad Arolsen, Germany (hereafter cited as ITS).
27. Wontor-Cichy, phone conversation with author, May 2020; Adam Cyra, "Dr. Władysław Dering. Auschwitz. Brytyjskie więzienie. Niesprawiedliwe oskarżenia," *Tysol*, March 3, 2019, https://www.tysol.pl/a29886-Dr-Adam-Cyra-Dr-Wladyslaw-Dering-Auschwitz-Brytyjskie-wiezienie-Niesprawiedliwe-oskarzenia; Maria Ciesielska, "Władysław Dering i Jan Grabczyński—lekarze więźniowie w Auschwitz," *Nowa Medycyna* 2 (2019): 70–76.
28. Adam Cyra, "Dr Władysław Dering—pobyt w Auschwitz i więzieniu brytyjskim," accessed February 2022, https://www.tysol.pl/a29886-Dr-Adam-Cyra-Dr-Wladyslaw-Dering-Auschwitz-Brytyjskie-wiezienie-Niesprawiedliwe-oskarzenia.
29. Cyra, "Dr Władysław Dering."
30. Langbein, *Die Stärkeren*, 128.
31. Friemel was an Austrian communist who participated in the Spanish Civil War, where he met his future wife, Margarita Ferrer. In March 1944 he received permission to get married in Auschwitz. Margarita and their son arrived, and to the tunes of the camp orchestra they marched to the camp's Civil Registry Office to register their marriage. After the wedding reception, Wilhelm Brasse, the camp photographer, took their wedding photo. The newlyweds spent the night in the camp brothel. In October 1944 Friemel attempted to escape the camp, was caught, and was executed. Adam Cyra, "Zdjęcie ślubne z Auschwtiz," Dzieje, Portal Historyczny, October 29, 2012, https://dzieje.pl/aktualnosci/zdjecie-slubne-z-auschwitz. See also Erich Hackl, *The Wedding in Auschwitz* (London: Serpent's Tail, 2010), and Hermann Langbein, *Against All Hope: Resistance in the Nazi Concentration Camps, 1938–1945* (New York: Paragon House, 1994).
32. Hermann Langbein, *People in Auschwitz* (Chapel Hill: University of North Carolina Press, 1995), 441.
33. Irena Paczyńska, ed., *Grypsy z Konzentrationslager Auschwitz: Józefa Cyrankiewicza i Stanisława Kłodzińskiego* (Kraków: Wydawnictwo Uniwersytetu Jagiellońskiego, 2013), xxiv, 362.
34. Langbein, *People in Auschwitz*, 253; Langbein, *Against All Hope*, 83, 143.
35. Langbein, *Against All Hope*, 83; Langbein, *Die Stärkeren*, 263.
36. Paczyńska, *Grypsy z Konzentrationslager Auschwitz*, xxiv.
37. Langbein, *Die Stärkeren*, 208.
38. Extract from lists of premium payments of Auschwitz concentration camp, May 29–August 24, 1944, ITS.
39. About the construction of the *Zigeunerfamilienlager*, see Joanna Talewicz-Kwiakowska, "Romowie i Sinti w KL Auschwitz," in *Romowie w KL Auschwitz: Głosy Pamięci*, vol. 7, ed. Sławomir Kapralski, Maria Martyniak, and Joanna Talewicz-Kwiakowska (Auschwitz: Państwowe Muzeum Auschwitz-Birkenau, 2011), 17–18.

40. "Sinti and Roma (Gypsies) in Auschwitz," Państwowe Muzeum Auschwitz-Birkenau, accessed August 2020, http://auschwitz.org/en/history/categories-of-prisoners/sinti-and-roma-gypsies-in-auschwitz/.
41. Recollection of Józef Piwko, in Kapralski, Martyniak, and Talewicz-Kwiakowska, *Romowie w KL Auschwitz*, 104.
42. Wontor-Cichy, email exchange with author, March 2020. Extract from lists of premium payments of the Auschwitz concentration camp, August 15, 1944, ITS.
43. Tonia to her family, Paris, December 21, 1945.
44. Tonia, interview by Dowgiałło.
45. Piotr Kruze, "Żydowskie zdjęcia Holocaustu: Jak członkowie Sonderkommando sfotografowali Zagładę," *Wprost*, December 14, 2017, https://www.wprost.pl/kraj/10086419/3/zydowskie-zdjecia-holocaustu-jak-czlonkowie-sonderkommando-sfotografowali-zaglade.html; Georges Didi-Huberman, *Obrazy mimo wszystko* (Kraków: Universitas, 2008).
46. Wontor-Cichy, email exchange with author, March 2020.
47. Didi-Huberman, *Obrazy mimo wszystko*, 15; Wontor-Cichy, email exchange with author, March 2020.
48. Kruze, "Żydowskie zdjęcia Holocaustu."
49. Didi-Huberman, *Obrazy mimo wszystko*, 10.
50. Didi-Huberman, 18.
51. Janina Struk, *Holocaust w fotografiach: Interpretacje dowodów* (Warsaw: Prószyński i Spółka, 2007), 158–59.
52. Langbein, cited in Didi-Huberman, *Obrazy mimo wszystko*, 18.
53. Didi-Huberman, 18.
54. Didi-Huberman, 19, 148–49.
55. Kruze, "Żydowskie zdjęcia Holocaustu."
56. Tonia, interview by Dowgiałło; Wontor-Cichy, email exchange with author, March 2020.
57. Wontor-Cichy, phone conversation with author, May 2020.
58. Langbein, *Die Stärkeren*, 263.
59. "Szlakiem Marszów Śmierci," Państwowe Muzeum Auschwitz-Birkenau, accessed August 2020, http://auschwitz.org/historia/ewakuacja/szlakiem-marszow-smierci/.
60. Tonia, interview by Dowgiałło.
61. Vera, interview by author, May 2014.
62. Tonia to her brother, Julian, Arolsen, Germany, January 21, 1946.
63. Tonia to her parents, Paris, January 12, 1946.
64. Tonia to her parents, December 21, 1945.
65. Róża to Aron, Zürich, July 6, 1946.
66. Tonia to her mother, Wermelskirchen, June 6, 1946.
67. Tonia to her mother, Wermelskirchen, July 10, 1946.
68. Róża to Aron, Zürich, July 20, 1946.

69. Tonia to her mother, Wermelskirchen, July 26, 1946.
70. Róża to Aron, Beatenberg, August 9, 1946.
71. Róża to Aron, Beatenberg, August 9, 1946.
72. Róża to Aron, Zürich, August 13, 1946.
73. Róża to Aron, Itschnach-Küsnacht, August 17, 1946.
74. Róża to Aron, Zürich, August 13, 1946.
75. Róża to Aron, Itschnach-Küsnacht, August 17, 1946.
76. Tonia to her parents, Wermelskirchen, August 19, 1946.
77. I would like to thank Kamil Kijek for this suggestion.
78. Tonia to her parents, Wermelskirchen, August 22, 1946.
79. Tonia to her parents, Prague, August 25, 1946.
80. Tonia to her parents, Wermelskirchen, September 15, 1946.
81. Róża to Aron, Wermelskirchen, October 6, 1946.
82. A few letters indicate that the dates of their departure kept changing, including Tonia to her parents, Wermelskirchen, October 8 and October 26, 1946.
83. Tonia to her parents, Wermelskirchen, October 26, 1946.
84. Tonia to her parents, Wermelskirchen, November 4, 1946.
85. Tonia to her parents, Warsaw, November 25, 1946.
86. "Przed powrotem wygnańców do Ojczyzny: Kto ponosi winę za ich poniewierkę?," *Życie Warszawy,* October 9, 1945.
87. Marcin Zaremba, *Wielka Trwoga 1944–1947* (Kraków: Znak, 2012), 357.
88. "Estimates of the number of refugees in Europe at this time ranged from 9 million to 30 million. Malcolm Proudfoot, in peacetime an urban geographer from Chicago, . . . [with] his colleagues concluded that there were in fact 11,469,000 people displaced in Europe, and 7,738,000 displaced in Germany, of whom the largest groups were 2.3 million Frenchmen and -women, 1,840,000 Russians, 1,403,000 Poles, 500,000 Belgians, 402,000 Dutch, 350,000 Czechs, 328,000 Yugoslavs, 195,000 Italians, and 100,000 from the Baltic States." Ben Shephard, *Long Road Home: The Aftermath of the Second World War* (New York: Knopf, 2010), 61.
89. Tomasz Sanecki, email exchanges with author, April and July 2020. Sanecki authors a blog on the history of Bytom, *Mój historyczny blog,* www.mojhistorycznyblog.pl.
90. See Tomasz Sanecki, *Tragedia Miechowicka: 25–26 stycznia 1945* (Warsaw: Rider, 2018).
91. Anna Kordasiewicz, *(U)sługi domowe: Przemiany relacji społecznych w płatnej pracy domowej* (Toruń: Wydawnictwo Naukowe Uniwersytetu Mikołaja Kopernika, 2016).
92. Tonia to her parents, Warsaw, November 25, 1946.
93. Tonia, interview by Dowgiałło.
94. Tonia, interview by Dowgiałło.
95. For a list of supplies imported by the USC for Kościuszko Hospital with prices,

see List of supplies, November 1946–September 1949, Departament Opieki Społecznej, 1946–1949, 342, 274–75, AAN.
96. Tonia, interview by Dowgiałło.
97. Judyta Watoła, "Szpital urazowy w Piekarach Śląskich skończył 80 lat," *Wyborcza* (Katowice), June 19, 2004, https://katowice.wyborcza.pl/katowice/1 ,35063,2139013.html; Agnieszka Strzelczyk, "Urazówka w Piekarach to jeden z najlepszych szpitali w kraju," accessed August 2020, https://piekaryslaskie .naszemiasto.pl/urazowka-w-piekarach-to-jeden-z-najlepszych-szpitali-w-kraju /ga/c1-1663585/zd/4127411. See also Działalność Zagranicznych Towarzystw Charytatywnych w Polsce, Ministerstwo Pracy i Opieki Społeczne, Departament Opieki Społecznej, 1946–1949, 342, 48, AAN.
98. Tonia to her parents, Bytom, February 13, 1947.
99. Tonia, interview by Dowgiałło.
100. Tonia to her parents, Piekary Śląskie, June 20, 1946; August 4, 1946; August 29, 1947; and July 19, 1947.
101. Tonia to her parents, Piekary Śląskie, August 4, 1946.
102. Tonia to her parents, Piekary Śląskie, April 28, 1947.
103. Tonia to her parents, Piekary Śląskie, October 7, 1947.
104. Tonia to her parents, Piekary Śląskie, July 18, 1947.
105. Tonia to her parents, Bytom, January 24, 1947. See also Anna Cichopek-Gajraj, *Beyond Violence: Jewish Survivors in Poland and Slovakia, 1944–48* (Cambridge: Cambridge University Press, 2014), 70–85.
106. Cichopek-Gajraj, 72–73.
107. Łukasz Krzyżanowski, *Dom, którego nie było: Powroty ocalałych do powojennego miasta* (Wołowiec: Wydawnictwo Czarne, 2016), 275. An English version of the book was recently published as well: Łukasz Krzyżanowski, *Ghost Citizens: Jewish Return to a Postwar City*, trans. Madeline G. Levine (Cambridge, MA: Harvard University Press, 2020).
108. Cichopek-Gajraj, *Beyond Violence*, 76.
109. Tonia to her parents, Piekary Śląskie, May 10, 1947.
110. Cichopek-Gajraj, *Beyond Violence*, 81.
111. Marcin Szymański, historian of Łódź, email exchange with author, June 2020.
112. Tonia to her parents, Bytom, December 27, 1946; Piekary Śląskie, May 10, 1947. For more about the legal solution to Jewish property in the years soon after the war, see Krzyżanowski, *Dom, którego nie było*, 271–303.
113. I thank Szymański for informing me about this Ministry of the Treasury notice.
114. Tonia to her parents, Bytom, January 24, 1947. See also Krystyna Kersten, *Narodziny systemu władzy: Polska 1943–1948* (Paris: Wyd. Libella, 1986), 315–16.
115. Tonia to her parents, Piekary Śląskie, December 27, 1947.
116. See, e.g., Bożena Szaynok, *Pogrom Żydów w Kielcach 4 lipca 1946* (Warsaw: Bellona, 1992); Łukasz Kamiński and Jan Żaryn, eds., *Wokół pogrom kieleckiego* (Warsaw: IPN, 2006); and Joanna Tokarska-Bakir, *Pod klątwą: Połeczny portret*

pogrom kieleckiego (Warsaw: Czarna Owca, 2018). For more about postwar violence against Jews, see Krzyżanowski, *Dom, którego nie było*, 63–67.
117. Cichopek-Gajraj, *Beyond Violence*, 182.
118. Cichopek-Gajraj, 182.
119. Unitarian Service Committee, Ministerstwo Pracy i Opieki Społecznej, Departament Opieki Społecznej, 1946–49, 342, 142–43, AAN.
120. Frances Berges to Aron and Róza Bialer, Piekary Śląskie, March 7, 1947.
121. "Kościuszko Hospital in Piekary," *Poland of Today* 3, no. 4 (1948): 14–16. See also Tonia to her parents, Piekary Śląskie, June 20, 1947.
122. Tonia to her parents, Piekary Śląskie, March 24, 1948. See also Ministerstwo Przemysłu i Handlu, Departament Ekonomiczno-Socjalny, Wydział Społeczny, 967, AAN.
123. Protokół przesłuchania podejrzanego, Warsaw, August 22, 1949, file 1017_193_1. Tonia mentions this cooperation in the November 30 interrogation. Protokół przesłuchania podejrzanego, Warsaw, August 22, 1949, file 0_1251_8.
124. Tonia to her parents, Warsaw, July 30, 1948.
125. Tonia to her parents, Warsaw, September 10, 1948.
126. Krzysztof Kosiński, *O Nową mentalność: Życie codzienne w szkołach 1945–1956* (Warsaw: Wydawnictwo Trio, 2000), 52–53.
127. An email exchange with Natalia Aleksiun, November 2021.
128. Tonia to her parents, Warsaw, March 8, 1949.
129. Tonia to her parents, Warsaw, May 17, 1949.
130. Vera, interview by author, May 2014.
131. Tonia, interview by Dowgiałło.
132. Halina Diamant to Vera, October 29, 1998.
133. Anna Grażyna Kister, "Wacław Komar i wszystkie jego tajne misje: Zaczynał jako partyjny zabójca," Interia historia, January 2, 2015, https://nowahistoria.interia.pl/prl/news-waclaw-komar-i-wszystkie-jego-tajne-misje-zaczynal-jako-part,nId,1581972.
134. Vera, interview by author, May 2018.
135. Vera, interview by author, May 2014.
136. Jonathan Brent, *Stalin's Last Crime: The Plot against the Jewish Doctors, 1948–1953* (New York: Harper Perennial, 2004).
137. Witold Bagieński, "Wacław Komar—przyczynek do biografii (lata 1909–1945)," *Komunizm* 7 (2018): 183–225.
138. Postanowienie o tymczasowym aresztowaniu i nakaz przyjęcia, August 2, 1949, file 660_537, BU IPN.
139. Arkusz streszczenia, file 660_537, BU IPN.
140. Anna Müller, *If the Walls Could Speak: Inside a Women's Prison in Communist Poland* (Oxford: Oxford University Press, 2018).
141. Tonia, interview by Dowgiałło.

142. Dariusz Jarosz and Maria Pasztor, "Paryż-Warszawa w apogeum zimniej wojny 1948–1953," *Wiadomości Historyczne*, no. 2 (2001): 67–78.
143. Marek Jabłonowski and Włodzimierz Janowski, eds., *Proces Romana Romkowskiego, Józefa Różańskiego i Anatola Fejgina w 1957 r.* (Warsaw: Wydział Dziennikarstwa i Nauk Politycznych, 2001), 1:818.
144. Werner Schweizer, dir., *Noel Field: The Fictitious Spy* (Zürich: Dschoint Ventschr Filmproduction AG, 1996).
145. Protokół przesłuchania podejrzanej, Warsaw, August 1, 10, 12, 13, 17, 18, 24, 25, 26, 1949, file 660_537, BU IPN.
146. Jabłonowski and Janowski, *Proces Romana Romkowskiego*, 1:814–15.
147. Protokół przesłuchania podejrzanej, Warsaw, August 1 and August 2, 1949, both in file 660_537, BU IPN.
148. Protokół przesłuchania podejrzanej, Warsaw, August 10, 1949, file 660_537, BU IPN.
149. Robert Spałek, *Komuniści przeciwko Komunistom* (Warsaw: Zysk i S-ka, IPN, 2014), 248–50.
150. Jabłonowski and Janowski, *Proces Romana Romkowskiego*, 1:817.
151. Tonia, interview by Dowgiałło; Schweizer, *Noel Field*.
152. Jabłonowski and Janowski, *Proces Romana Romkowskiego*, 1:817.
153. Andrzej Paczkowski, *Trzy twarze Józefa Światło: Przyczynek do historii komunizmu w Polsce* (Warsaw: Prószyński i spółka, 2009), 107–8.
154. Tonia, interview by Dowgiałło.
155. Jonesy to the Bialers, Warsaw, September 2, 1949.
156. Andrzej Paczkowski, "Posłowie," in Herman Field and Kate Field, *Opóźniony Lot* (Warsaw: Państwowy Instytut Wydawniczy, 1997), 472.
157. Paczkowski, *Trzy twarze Józefa Światło*, 108.
158. Recently historian Robert Spałek, on the basis of interrogations of dozens of people, has re-created the intricacies of the cases of communists against communists. These interrogation transcripts show the detailed but also pointless reiterations of the accusations of communist politicians against other communists, conflicts in which Field was caught. Spałek, *Komuniści przeciwko Komunistom*.
159. Katie Marton, interview by Larissa MacFarquhar, C-Span, September 13, 2016, https://www.c-span.org/video/?414863-1/true-believer.
160. Schweizer, *Noel Field*.
161. Tony Sharp, *Stalin's American Spy: Noel Field, Allen Dulles and the East European Show Trials* (London: Hurst, 2014), 2; Kati Marton, *True Believer: Stalin's Last American Spy* (New York: Simon & Schuster, 2016). Marton also concedes that Field began collaborating around 1935. She claims that he destroyed many lives with his activity but provides little evidence for that assessment.
162. Brigitte Brändle and Gerhard Brändle, "Aus behütetem Haus in Karlsruhe in stalinistische Kerker in Ungarn," Karlsruhe, June 30, 2017, https://www.karlsruhe.de/b1/stadtgeschichte/blick_geschichte/blick115/field.de.

163. Schweizer, *Noel Field*.
164. Spałek, *Komuniści przeciwko Komunistom*, 216–18.
165. Paczkowski, "Posłowie," 481.
166. Schweizer, *Noel Field*.
167. Spałek, *Komuniści przeciwko Komunistom*, 218.
168. Sharp, *Stalin's American Spy*, 204.
169. Spałek, *Komuniści przeciwko Komunistom*, 219.
170. On August 22 his brother was arrested at the Warsaw airport while attempting to leave the city. Spałek, *Komuniści przeciwko Komunistom*, 216.
171. Schweizer, *Noel Field*.
172. Spałek, *Komuniści przeciwko Komunistom*, 223.
173. Paczkowski, "Posłowie," 477–80; Anna Sobór-Świderska, *Jakub Berman: Biografia komunisty* (Warsaw: IPN, 2009), 225.
174. Spałek, *Komuniści przeciwko Komunistom*, 224.
175. Schweizer, *Noel Field*.
176. Paczkowski, "Posłowie," 484.
177. I write more about this in Anna Müller, "Walls That Unite: Unlikely Friendship in Mokotów Prison, 1949–1956," *Rocznik Antropologii Historii* 5, no. 8 (2015): 247. The Ukrainian Insurgent Army was a Ukrainian nationalist paramilitary group; during World War II it functioned as a partisan formation.
178. Müller, "Walls That Unite," 248.
179. "Donos," August 23, 1949, file 0151_8, BU IPN.
180. Schweizer, *Noel Field*.
181. David Cesarani, *Arthur Koestler: The Homeless Mind* (New York: Free Press, 1999), 174.
182. Jabłonowski and Janowski, *Proces Romana Romkowskiego*, 1:815.
183. Raport, Do Dyrektora Departamentu X MBP, Płk. Fejgina, Warsaw, November 18, 1953, 157.
184. Jabłonowski and Janowski, *Proces Romana Romkowskiego*, 1:821.
185. December 1, 1953, file 0298_408/1, BU IPN.
186. February 8, 1953, file 0298_408/1, BU IPN.
187. December 1, 1953, file 0298_408_1, BU IPN.
188. Anne Applebaum, "History Will Judge the Complicit,?" *The Atlantic*, July/August 2020.
189. Spałek, *Komuniści przeciwko Komunistom*, 224.
190. Jonesy to the Bialers, September 22, 1949.
191. Jonesy to the Bialers, December 13, 1949.
192. Jonesy to the Bialers, June 28, 1950.
193. In another anecdote Vera repeats often, during one of her frequent hospital stays, a nun took interest in her. After finding out that Vera had no immediate family, she insisted that there must be some further family member who could help. Eventually Vera admitted that she had a grandmother in Israel and that her grandfather

had a ribbon factory. The nun hence sent a letter to her grandparents addressed to a ribbon factory. According to Vera, this worked, and the children soon gained contact with their grandparents. Vera, interviews by author, May 2014 and May 2018.
194. Richter to the Bialers, September 27, 1951.
195. Vera and Marcel to their grandparents, Wrocław, November 5, 1951.
196. Richter to the Bialers, Kłodzko, November 12, 1951.
197. Vera and Marcel to their grandparents, May 4, 1952.
198. Lechtman to the MBP, Tel Aviv, August 21, 1951.
199. Vera to her grandparents, Wrocław, January 19, 1952.
200. Vera to her grandparents, Wrocław, April 1, 1952.
201. Teresa Moździerz to the Bialers, Wrocław, February 25, 1952.
202. Vera, interview by author, May 2014.
203. Tonia to her children, Mokotów, Warsaw, January 13, 1953.
204. Tonia to her children, Mokotów, Warsaw, January 13 and March 5, 1953.
205. Tonia to her children, Mokotów, Warsaw, May 3, 1953.
206. Tonia, interview by Dowgiałło.
207. Tonia to her parents, Wermelskirchen, August 19, 1946.

Chapter 7: "Life Is So Knotty"

1. Notatka z rozmowy Tonią Lechtman i Janem Lisem, October 21, 1954, file 660_537, BU IPN.
2. On communists' return from the gulag, see Nanci Adler, *Keeping Faith with the Party: Communist Believers Return from the Gulag* (Bloomington: Indiana University Press, 2012).
3. Tonia, interview by Dowgiałło.
4. Tonia to her parents, December 13, 1954.
5. Vera, interview by author, May 2014.
6. Marcel Łoziński, dir., *Tonia i jej dzieci* (Warsaw: Studio Filmowe Kronika, 2011).
7. Tonia, interview by Dowgiałło; Notatka z rozmowy Tonią Lechtman i Janem Lisem, October 21, 1954, file 660_537, BU IPN.
8. Tonia to her parents, December 13, 1954.
9. Vera Lechtman, "'We Are Here': Jewish Narratives of Poland's March 1968 Events, as Told to Teresa Torańska," accessed January 2022, https://wearehere68.com/the-pediatrician-wera-lechtman.
10. Tonia to her parents, January 20, 1955.
11. Tonia to her parents, May 7, 1955.
12. Tonia, interview by Michał Chęciński, Israel, October 1972, copy in the private collection of Vera and Marcel Lechtman.
13. Marek Jabłonowski and Włodzimierz Janowski, eds., *Proces Romana Romkowskiego, Józefa Różańskiego i Anatola Fejgina w 1957 r.* (Warsaw: Wydział Dziennikarstwa i Nauk Politycznych, 2001), 1:814.

14. Tonia, interview by Dowgiałło.
15. Tonia to her parents, July 8, 1955.
16. Vera, interview by author, May 2014.
17. Terry Cox, "1956: Discoveries, Legacies and Memory," in *Challenging Communism in Eastern Europe: 1956 and Its Legacy,* ed. Terry Cox (New York: Routledge, 2008), 10–15.
18. For more about his escape, see Paczkowski, *Trzy twarze Józefa Światło.*
19. Paczkowski, 191.
20. Tony Kemp-Welch, "Dethroning Stalin: Poland 1956 and Its Legacy," in Cox, *Challenging Communism in Eastern Europe,* 75. See also Paczkowski, *Trzy twarze Józefa Światło.*
21. Zbigniew Błażyński, *Mówi Światło: Za kulisami bezpieki i partii 1940–1955* (Warsaw: LTW, 1985), 247.
22. Marek Jabłonowski and Włodzimierz Janowski, introduction to Jabłonowski and Janowski, *Proces Romana Romkowskiego,* 1:13; Brian Porter-Szűcs, *Poland in the Modern World: Beyond Martyrdom* (Hoboken, NJ: Wiley Blackwell, 2014), 232.
23. Kemp-Welch, "Dethroning Stalin," 75, 77, 78, 80–85.
24. Porter-Szűcs, *Poland in the Modern World,* 236; Jerzy Eisler, *Siedmiu wspaniałych* (Warsaw: Czerwone i Czarne, 2014), 80–82.
25. Porter-Szűcs, 236.
26. Vera shared her mother's communist views, at least in her early adulthood. "In Poland we experienced many difficult days, because our leader, the first party secretary—[Bolesław] Bierut—died. I am sure you read a lot about him. It was a heavy blow for all of us, and we felt it very much." Vera to her grandparents, March 27, 1956.
27. Tonia left Marcel behind. Later she explained that she worried that if she took both children, her family in Israel would have convinced them to stay. For years later she regretted it as a mistake that held Marcel back from integrating better with his Israeli family. Tonia to her parents, February 12, 1957; Vera to her grandparents, October 9, 1956.
28. Tonia to Julian, November 28, 1956.
29. Tonia to Julian, December 1956.
30. Dariusz Stola, "Jewish Emigration from Communist Poland: The Decline of Polish Jewry in the Aftermath of the Holocaust," *East European Jewish Affairs* 47, nos. 2–3 (2017): 177–78. See also Dariusz Stola, "Opening a Non-Exit State: The Passport Policy of Communist Poland, 1949–1980," *East European Politics and Societies* 29, no. 1 (2015): 96–119.
31. Tonia, interview by Dowgiałło.
32. Stola, "Jewish Emigration," 175–76.
33. Vera likewise experienced the departure of many of her friends. She wrote to her grandparents that a group of youth from the children's home was leaving. Vera to

her grandparents, February 3, 1957.
34. Tonia to her parents, November 28, 1955.
35. Tonia to her parents, January 21, 1957.
36. The late 1940s can be seen through the prism of the first conflict among the communist elites, when the communist members who spent the war in the Soviet Union pushed aside a group of Gomułka supporters, people who had spent the war in the country. Tonia seems to perceive the conflict around her in similar terms. Dariusz Stola, *Kampania antysyjonistyczna w Polsce, 1967–1968* (Warsaw: Instytut Studiów Politycznych Polskiej Akademii Nauk, 2018), 14.
37. Tonia to Julian, February 12, 1957.
38. Notatka w sprawie Bialera Seweryna, February 20, 1956, file 02012_23, BU IPN.
39. Małgorzata Górecka, email exchanges with author, January–July 2019.
40. Notatka w sprawie Bialera Seweryna, February 20, 1956, file 02012_23, BU IPN; Górecka, email exchanges with author, January–July 2019.
41. Tonia to her parents, April 9, 1957.
42. Tonia to her parents, April 21, 1957.
43. Tonia to her parents, April 9, 1957.
44. Joanna Wiszniewicz, *Życie przecięte: Opowieści pokolenia Marca* (Wołowiec: Wydawnictwo Czarne, 2008), 39.
45. Tonia to her parents and Julian, April 9, 1957.
46. Tonia to her parents and Julian, April 9, 1957.
47. Tonia to her parents, April 21, 1957.
48. Tonia to her parents, April 17, 1955.
49. Naomi Bogusławska to Julian, May 11, 1957.
50. Jabłonowski and Janowski, *Proces Romana Romkowskiego,* 1:274–75.
51. The trials ended in November 1957. Różański and Romkowski received a sentence of fifteen years in prison and Fejgin twelve. All of those imprisoned were released in October 1964 as a result of a State Council pardon. Jabłonowski and Janowski, 1:31–32, 67, 374.
52. Jabłonowski and Janowski, 1:814–26.
53. Tonia, interview by Chęciński, Tel Aviv, Israel, October 1972.
54. Vera confirms that her mother was clearly traumatized by the event, to the point that when she saw Różański, she began vomiting.
55. Jabłonowski and Janowski, *Proces Romana Romkowskiego,* 1:824, 862.
56. Tonia to her parents, August 19, 1957.
57. Vera to her grandparents, December 25, 1957.
58. Tonia to her parents, October 5, 1957; Werner Schweizer, dir., *Noel Field: The Fictitious Spy* (Zürich: Dschoint Ventschr Filmproduction AG, 1996).
59. Tonia to her parents, October 5, 1957.
60. Tonia in Schweizer, *Noel Field.*
61. Tonia to her parents, August 4, 1955; "The Fifth World Festival of Youth and Students in Warsaw," Culture.pl, accessed August 2020, https://culture.pl

/en/gallery/the-fifth-world-festival-of-youth-and-students-in-warsaw-gallery. (Tonia worked for the festival as a translator.) Tonia to her parents, July 12, 1955.
62. Tonia to her parents, August 4, 1955. For the family it was also a chance to see Nani, the girl who lived with them in Switzerland.
63. Tonia to her parents, June 13, 1955.
64. Vera to her grandparents, October 4, 1957; Tonia to her parents, January 3, 1956.
65. Tonia to her parents, June 3, 1958.
66. Katarzyna Stańczak-Wiślicz and Piotr Perkowski, "Zmiany w gospodarstwie domowym okresu PRL," in *Kobieta w gospodarstwie domowym: Ziemie polskie na tle porównawczym,* ed. Katarzyna Sierakowska (Zielona Góra: Oficyna Wydawnicza, 2012), 319.
67. Stańczak-Wiślicz and Perkowski, 330.
68. Tonia to Julian, January 21, 1957.
69. Tonia to Julian, April 21, 1957.
70. Tonia to her parents, August 5, 1958. Margaret Locher visited for the first time in June 1960. Tonia to her parents, June 20, 1960.
71. Vera, interview by author, May 2014.
72. Łoziński, *Tonia i jej dzieci.*
73. Izabella Legocka, phone interview by author, Warsaw, September 2020.
74. Łoziński, *Tonia i jej dzieci.*
75. Aneta Ostaszewska, "Własny pokój jako przestrzeń pracy twórczej," in *Współczesne przestrzenie pracy* (Warsaw: Difin, 2016), 52–53.
76. Tonia to her parents, June 19, 1958.
77. Tonia to her parents, June 19, 1958.
78. Tonia to her parents, December 5, 1957.
79. Tonia to her parents, August 16, 1958.
80. Tonia to her mother, January 29, 1959.
81. Tonia to her mother, January 17 1962; February 2, 1963.
82. Komunikat w sprawie obserwacji za kont. Ps. Mira (spr. Delta), July 19, 1962; Ustalenie, July 20, 1962; Notatka służbowa, August 19, 1962, all in file 0151_8, BU IPN.
83. Plan operacyjny przedsięwzięć dostępnych materiałów na Fielda Noela Hanibalda, December 1963, file 0151_8, BU IPN.
84. Streszcznie materiałów na Antoninę Lechtman—Bialer, December 1963, file 0151_8, BU IPN.
85. Tonia to her mother, Karpacz, March 11, 1964.
86. Tonia to her mother, February 18, 1967.
87. Róża Bialer to Julian, February 18, 1967.
88. Dariusz Stola, "Anti-Zionism as a Multipurpose Policy Instrument: The Anti-Zionist Campaign in Poland, 1967–1968," *Journal of Israeli History: Politics, Society, Culture* 25, no. 1 (2006): 175–201.
89. Porter-Szűcs, *Poland in the Modern World,* 249.

90. Quoted in Wlodzimierz Rozenbaum, "The Anti-Zionist Campaign in Poland, June–December 1967," *Intermarium* 1, no. 3, https://ciaotest.cc.columbia.edu/olj/int/int_0103b.html.
91. Stola, "Anti-Zionism as Multipurpose Policy Instrument."
92. Tonia to Julian, February 22, 1968.
93. Lechtman, "We Are Here."
94. Wyciąg doniesienie tw ps. Jastrzębski, October 23, 1967, file 1286_2495, BU IPN.
95. Stola, *Kampania antysyjonistyczna,* 179–85.
96. Dane Personalne, Ligęza—Lechtmann Wera, file 1286_2495, BU IPN.
97. Pismo do Naczelnika Wydziału III w Olsztynie, September 20, 1967, file 1286_2495, BU IPN.
98. Oświadczenie, April 24, 1968, Mrągowo, file 1286_2495, BU IPN.
99. Notatka służbowa, May 26, 1968, file 1286_2495, BU IPN.
100. Notatka służbowa, May 22, 1968, file 1286_2495, BU IPN.
101. Stola, *Kampania antysyjonistyczna,* 207–11.
102. Lechtman, "We Are Here."
103. Tonia to Julian, May 21, 1968; November 11, 1968.
104. Tonia to Julian, May 21, 1968.
105. Visa in Marcel's private collection.
106. Vera, interview by author, May 2014; Legocka, phone interview by author, September 2020.
107. Stoła, *Kampania antysyjonistyczna,* 149–50.
108. Wiszniewicz, *Życie przecięte,* 57.
109. Jonesy to Julian, November 21, 1965.
110. Jonesy to Julian, September 16, 1968.
111. Jonesy to Julian, September 16, 1968.
112. Stoła, *Kampania antysyjonistyczna,* 149–50, 229.
113. Tonia to Julian, May 7, 1968.
114. Stoła, *Kampania antysyjonistyczna,* 232.
115. Tonia to Marcel, October 11, 1969.
116. Lechtman, "We Are Here."
117. Analiza dokumentów "W," Mrągowo, August 1, 1969, 1286/2495, BU IPN.
118. Tonia to Marcel, August 20, 1969.
119. Postanowienie o zastrzeżeniu wyjazdu za granicę, July 1970, 1286/2495, BU IPN.
120. Notatka informacyjna, Warsaw, January 27, 1971, 1286/2495, BU IPN.
121. Pismo zastępcy dyrektora gabinetu Ministra Spraw Wewnętrznych, February 2, 1971, 1286/2495, BU IPN.
122. Stoła, *Kampania antysyjonistyczna,* 213, 227.
123. Legocka, phone interview by author, September 2020.
124. Ania Rajf-Ligęza, phone conversation with author, March 2019.
125. Rajf-Ligęza, phone conversation with author, March 2019.
126. Rajf-Ligęza, phone conversation with author, March 2019.

127. Henryka Lechtman, interview by Przemysław Kaniecki, March 2019, Polin Museum, Warsaw.
128. Henryka Lechtman, conversations with author, October 2018 and February 2020.
129. Tonia, interview by Dowgiałło.
130. Tonia Lechtman, interview by Anna Sekudewicz, Polish Radio, Program II, Tel Aviv, 1992.
131. Vera, interview by author, Tel Aviv, May 2014.
132. E.g., his first wife, Izabella Legocka, and his best friend, Marcel Łoziński.
133. Legocka, phone interview by author, September 2020.
134. Marcel Łoziński, Zoom interview by author, Warsaw, September 2020.
135. Łoziński, Zoom interview by author, September 2020.
136. "Humanity and Catastrophe: A Conversation with Serhii Plokhii and Phillipe Sands," Vienna, streamed live on December 9, 2019, YouTube video, 1:41:26, https://www.youtube.com/watch?v=zhoBm_aC718.
137. Irena Grudzińska Gross, conversation with author, February 2020.
138. Agnieszka Mrozik, "'Dziadek (nie) był komunistą': Między/transgeneracyjna pamięć o komunizmie w polskich (auto)biografiach rodzinnych po 1989 roku," *Teksty Drugie* no. 1 (2016): 47, 53.
139. P. Forecki, "Fantazmat Julii Brystygier," *Środkowoeuropejskie Studia Polityczne*, June 2017, 49.
140. Abigail Liebman, *Najważniejszy jest ciąg dalszy. Ziemie obiecane. Biografia Wery Lechtman* (Warsaw: Instytut Adama Mickiewicza, 2008), 105.
141. Forecki, "Fantazmat Julii Brystygier," 49–50; Liebman, *Najważniejszy*, 105.
142. Mrozik, "'Dziadek (nie) był komunistą'"; Stefan Leder and Witold Leder, *Czerwona nić: Ze wspomnień i prac rodziny Lederów* (Warsaw: Wydawnictwo Iskry, 2005).

Conclusion

1. Thank you, Tomek Zerek, for asking this question.
2. Maureen Linker, *Intellectual Empathy: Critical Thinking for Social Justice* (Ann Arbor: University of Michigan Press, 2014).
3. Vera, interview by author, May 2014.
4. In recent literature, Polish-Jewish relations are seen as developing in mutual interactions. Eugenia Prokop-Janiec, introduction to *Polacy-Żydzi: Kontakty kulturowe i literackie*, ed. Eugenia Prokop-Janiec (Kraków: Wydawnictwo Uniwersytetu Jagiellońskiego), 11. A great example of blurred boundaries between different levels of communal and individual identifications is Karen Auerbach, *The House at Ujazdowskie 16: Jewish Families in Warsaw after the Holocaust* (Bloomington: Indiana University Press, 2013).

5. Alternatively, to the perception that non-Jewish Poles and Jews lived separately, this approach is based on the assumption that in each living organism, minorities are weaved into the dominant culture and society. See, e.g., Gershon Bacon, "Polish-Jewish Relations in Modern Times: The Search for a Metaphor and a Historical Framework," in *New Directions in the History of the Jews in the Polish Lands,* ed. Antony Polonsky, Hanna Węgrzynek, and Andrzej Żbikowski (Warsaw: POLIN Museum of the History of Polish Jews, 2018), 324–37.
6. Izabella Legocka, phone interview by author, September 2020.
7. Kaja Kaźmierska describes the sentiment of home as "sensual sensations," meaning various often sensory-based memories related to how we understand and perceive home. Discussed in Wiktoria Kudela Świątek, *Odpamiętane . . . O historii mówionej na przykładzie narracji kazachstańskich Polaków o represjach na tle narodowościowym i religijnym* (Kraków: Universitas, 2013), 316.
8. Aneta Ostaszewska, "Własny pokój jako przestrzeń pracy twórczej," in *Współczesne przestrzenie pracy* (Warsaw: Difin, 2016), 46.
9. Katrin Steffen, *Żydowski Polak, Polski Żyd: Problemy tożsamości w literaturze Polsko-Żydowskiej,* ed. Alina Molisak and Zuzanna Kołodziejska (Warsaw: Dom Wydawniczy Elipsa, 2011), 140–50. I could add to the concept elaborated by Steffen the notion of hybridity that Naomi Seidman defines as "interstitial space between fixed identifications," space of ongoing construction. Naomi Seidman, *The Marriage Plot: Or, How Jews Fell in Love with Love, and with Literature* (Stanford, CA: Stanford University Press, 2016), 9.
10. William W. Hagen, review of Katrin Steffen, *Jüdische Polonität: Ethnizität und Nation im Spiegel der polnischsprachigen jüdischen Presse 1918–1939,* in *Shofar: An Interdisciplinary Journal of Jewish Studies* 25, no. 4 (2007); Katrin Steffen, "Disputed Memory: Jewish Past, Polish Remembrance," *Eurozine,* November 27, 2008, https://www.eurozine.com/disputed-memory/. Similarly, Kijek emphasizes the problem of constant and decisive influences of the non-Jewish surroundings on Jews. Kamil Kijek, *Dzieci modernizmu: Świadomość, kultura i socjalizacja polityczna młodzieży żydowskiej w II Rzeczypospolitej* (Wrocław: Wydawnictwo Uniwersytetu Wrocławskiego, 2017), 18.
11. Eva Hoffman, "The New Nomads," in *Letters of Transit: Reflections on Exile, Identity, Language, and Loss,* ed. Andre Aciman (New York: New Press, 1999), 50.
12. Natalia Aleksiun, "Female, Jewish, Educated, and Writing Polish Jewish History," in "Writing Jewish History in Eastern Europe," ed. Natalia Aleksiun, Brian Horowitz, and Antony Polonsky, *Polin: Studies in Polish Jewry* 29 (2017): 195–216; Gershon Bacon, "The Missing 52 Percent: Research on Jewish Women in Interwar Poland and Its Implications for Holocaust Studies," in *Women in the Holocaust,* ed. Dalia Ofer and Lenore J. Weitzman (New Haven, CT: Yale University Press, 1998), 55–67; Chaeran Freeze and Paula Hyman, "Introduction: A

Historiographical Survey," in *Polin: Studies in Polish Jewry*, vol. 18, *Jewish Women in Eastern Europe*, ed. Antony Polonsky (Liverpool: Liverpool University Press, 2007), 3; Monika Szabłowska-Zaremba, "Dziennikarki międzywojennej prasy polsko-żydowskiej," *Archiwum Emigracji*, nos. 1–2 (2014): 38. More recently, see a webinar with Natalia Aleksiun and Glenn Dynner, "Polish-Jewish History as Women's History," Taube Jewish Heritage Tours, August 21, 2020, YouTube video, 1:05:44, https://www.youtube.com/watch?v=u3c5Svlizhw.

13. Freeze and Hyman, "Introduction," 14. See also Dahlia S. Elazar, "'Engines of Acculturation': The Last Political Generation of Jewish Women in Interwar East Europe," *Journal of Historical Sociology* 15, no. 3 (2002): 385–87.

14. This was not a rare phenomenon for Jewish women in Eastern Europe, unlike their Western counterparts. For example, Jewish women in Germany were expected to stay at home. In Poland, according to some accounts, many Jewish women lived in stark poverty and hence were expected to work. Elazar, "'Engines of Acculturation,'" 380.

15. Alexandra Kollontai, "Make Way for the Winged Eros: A Letter to Working Youth," in *The Russia Reader*, ed. Adele Marie Baker (Durham, NC: Duke University Press, 2010), 351–61. American communist and anarchist Goldman also widely criticized marriage as an institution of paternalistic arrangements—and strongly linked to capitalism. Candance Falk, *Love, Anarchy, and Emma Goldman* (New Brunswick, NJ: Rutgers University Press, 2019).

16. Polish leftist writers and politicians perceived the institution of marriage in a similar light before World War II. Agnieszka Mrozik, "Crossing Boundaries: The Case of Wanda Wasilewska and Polish Communism," *Aspasia* 11 (2017): 33. I would like to thank Mrozik for this suggestion.

17. See, e.g., Paul Hanebrink, *A Specter Haunting Europe: The Myth of Judeo-Bolshevism* (Cambridge, MA: Harvard University Press, 2018); Paweł Śpiewak, *Żydokomuna: Interpretacje historyczne* (Warsaw: Wydawnictwo Czerwone i Czarne, 2012); and Krystyna Kersen, *Polacy. Żydzi. Komunizm. Anatomia półprawd 1939–1968* (Warsaw: Krytyka, 1992).

18. Kijek emphasizes that the concept of Judeo-Bolshevism is charged with antipathy and even anti-Jewish obsession that always "ascribes to Jews . . . hostility toward Poland and Poles or their objective harmfulness, regardless of the nature of their intentions and actions." Kijek, *Dzieci modernizmu*, 20.

19. Review of Slezkin's work in Marci Shore, "Tevye's Daughters: Jews and European Modernity," *Contemporary European History* 16, no. 1 (2007): 124–25.

20. Statistics, however, suggest that security functionaries were predominantly ethnic Polish (95 percent), with 2 percent either Ukrainian or Byelorussian. Contrary to popular belief, only 2.5 percent were Jewish. Jews typically occupied some key positions in central MBP offices, while in local offices the percentage of Jews was much lower. Ryszard Terlecki, *Miecz i tarcza komunizmu* (Warsaw: Wydawnictwo Literackie, 2013), 57; Mariusz Mazur, *W stronę antropologii*

"bezpieki," *Nieklasyczna refleksja nad aparatem bezpieczeństwa w Polsce Ludowej* (Wrocław: IPN, 2014), 271; Bożena Szaynok, "Partia wobec Żydów, Żydzi wobec partii," POLIN: Muzeum Historii Żydów Polski, December 7, 2017, YouTube video, 1:25:25, https://www.youtube.com/watch?v=r80SC-0X9Eo. According to historian Bożena Szaynok, the number of Jewish communists depends on the state administration level: more Jewish communists were in key positions in security offices. Even so, communist politicians and activists constitute marginal numbers compared to the number of Jews residing in the country.

21. Śpiewak, *Żydokomuna*, 171. See also Joanna Nalewajko-Kulikov, *A Citizen of Yiddishland: David Sfard and the Jewish Communist Milieu in Poland* (Bern: Peter Lang, 2020).
22. Patrycja Bukalska, *Krwawa Luna* (Warsaw: Wielka Litera, 2016).
23. Małgorzata Fidelis et al., *Kobiety w Polsce, 1945–1989: Nowoczesność —równouprawnienie—komunizm* (Kraków: Universitas, 2020).
24. Monika Rudaś-Grodzka, "Cela jako własny pokój: Relacje więźniarek politycznych z XIX I początku XX wieku," *Wiek XIX: Rocznik Towarzystwa Literackiego im. Adama Mickiewicza* 8, no. 50 (2015): 161.
25. Mark Mazower thinks similarly about his father's decision to emigrate. Mazower, *What You Did Not Tell: A Russian Past and the Journey Home* (New York: Other Press, 2017), 247.
26. Andrea Pitzer, *One Long Night: A Global History of Concentration Camps* (Boston: Little, Brown, 2017), 32.
27. Richard Overy, "The Concentration Camp: An International Perspective," *Eurozine*, August 25, 2011, https://www.eurozine.com/the-concentration-camp/.
28. Hannah Arendt, *The Jewish Writings*, ed. Jerome Kohn and Ron H. Feldman (New York: Schocken Books, 2007), 264.
29. Hoffman, "New Nomads," 44.

Index

activism, communist, 46, 51, 54, 61, 117, 160, 219, 245, 281, 302n81, 341n20; *masówki,* 49, 52; in Palestine, 61–62, 64; strikes, 48–49, 51–52; youth, 46–49, 52
Aide aux émigrés (Help to the Emigrants), 162, 164, 319n33
Alien Registration Act, 116
American Jewish Joint Distribution Committee (JDC), 24, 157, 213
Amicale de Vernet, 11, 130, 133
Anières, 150–51, 155, 158
Annemasse, 152
antisemitism, 51, 194, 249, 280, 282; and communism, 2, 46, 213; in France, 77, 96, 130, 135–36, 142, 145; among Hallerczycy, 28; in Łódź, prewar, 24, 27–28, 39; in Poland, 186, 201, 213, 233, 242–44, 247, 259, 261–64, 269, 279; rise of, 42, 56, 69, 97, 128, 142; and Six-Day War, 259; in Soviet Union, 218; in Swiss camps, 159, 168–69
Arab nations, 258–59, 261
Arabs: conflicts with Jews, 56, 61–62; in Israel, 276; in Palestine, 61–62
Arciuch, Krystyna, 255
Arendt, Hannah, 284
Argelès-sur-Mer, 104, 125, 131
arrests of Tonia: in France, 141–42, 145–46, 189; in Palestine, 64, 68; in Poland, interwar, 52–54; in Poland,

postwar, 216–19, 221, 236, 240, 249, 269; in Switzerland, 150–51, 162
Ascona, 164–67, 320n62
assimilation, 27, 35–37, 39, 42, 51, 294n73; of Bialer family, 30, 35, 39
Assistance médicale aux enfants de réfugiés (Medical Assistance for Children of Refugees), 139, 167
Association of Friends of Children (Towarzystwo Przyjaciół Dzieci, TPD), 215
Auschwitz, 147, 154, 195–96, 198, 244, 285; Auschwitz Combat Group, 194; children in, 147; conditions, 191; evacuation, 190, 197; extermination/executions, 191, 198, 326n31; hospitals, 192–94; prisoners, 125, 154, 191–92, 194, 325n10; resistance in, 194–95, 310n7; selections, 191, 193; Sioma in, 145, 190–95, 285; transport from Drancy to, 145–46, 190–91; women in, 190–91; work in, 190–93, 195. *See also* Birkenau
Austrian Communist Party, 92, 140
Azaña, Manuel, 103

Bartel, Edwin, 191
Battle of the Ebro, 94
Bereza Kartuska, 47, 57, 298n15, 300n44
Berges, Frances, 210, 214, 229, 255
Bergman, Hilda, 96
Berman, Jakub, 220

343

Bern, 159, 170, 172, 179
Bezpartyjny Blok Współpracy z Rządem (Non-Party Bloc for Cooperation with the Government, BBWR), 51
Bialer family: assimilation, 35, 39; economic hardships, 28, 36, 57, 82; immigration to Palestine, 54–56, 64; life in Palestine, 59–60; and non-Jewish Poles, 33; on Piotrkowska Street, 32, 58; and traditions, Jewish, 29–31, 35, 39–42, 65–67, 296nn99–100, 302n97; travel, 32, 33, 35; and Zionism, 35. *See also individual family members*
Bialer, Aron, 14, 32, 57, 229; assimilation, 29–31, 35, 293n50; birth, 20; businesses, 28–29, 51, 54–55, 57–60, 72, 274, 280, 293n46; children of, 20; death, 252; financial support of Tonia, 72, 82, 99, 102, 113, 115, 118–19, 143, 162, 171; Hasidism of, 29–31, 293n50; homeowner, 31–32, 58, 212, 294n62; marriage, 30–31, 280; meeting/engagement, Róża, 29–31; politics, 35, 51, 204; relationship with Tonia, 51, 60–61, 72–73, 84, 87, 280; relationship with Vera and Marcel, 229–30; reunion with Tonia, 200, 206
Bialer, Basia (Batia; née Wegmeister), 22, 25, 31–32, 58, 80, 177; death, 199; marriage, 30
Bialer, Fajga, 32
Bialer, Joel (Julek), 58, 74–75, 274; birth, 20, 289n2; education, 36; politics, 242; relationship with Tonia, 199–200, 216, 242, 254, 258
Bialer, Lotta, 30–32
Bialer, Noemi: 50, 66, 216; birth, 20, 289n2; death, 258; education, 36
Bialer, Roman (Romek, Abram), 20, 32, 55, 66, 177; arrest, 106; birth, 36, 289n2; as communist, 36, 46, 298n15; death, 199; education, 35–36; extradition, 65; imprisonment, 57, 65, 298n15
Bialer, Róża (Ruchla; née Wojdysławska), 21, 65, 252, 280; business engagement, 31, 57–58, 60, 82, 205, 274, 280; children of, 20; education, 31, 35, 280; financial support of Tonia, 72, 82, 99, 102, 113, 115, 118–19, 143, 162, 171; marriage, 30–31, 280; meeting, Vera and Marcel, 201–2; meeting/engagement, Aron, 29–31; politics, 35, 51; relationship with Tonia, 50–51, 53–54, 61, 72–74, 84, 87–89, 96, 204–6, 280–81; relationship with Vera and Marcel, 229–31; religion, 40–41, 59, 65–66, 278; reunion with Tonia, 199–200, 202–6; suicide, 258
Bialer, Seweryn, 244–45, 257
Bialer, Tobiasz, 14, 22–23, 30, 32; birth, 290n11; factories, 23–24, 26, 28, 293n46; homeowner, 31–32, 58, 294n62; as *Lodzermensch*, 26; marriage, 30; philanthropy, 25–26
Bialer, Zyskind, 21–22
Bierut, Bolesław, 212, 230, 334n26
Birkenau, 190–92, 195–98; Sioma in, 190, 192, 196–97
Blatt, Feiga, 62, 66, 74–75
Bloch, Walter, 258
Blue Army (Hallerczycy), 28, 124
Blum, Léon, 76
Bogusławska, Naomi, 248
Branstein, Fina, 114
Bromberg, Chaim, 23
Brystygier, Julia, 282–83
Brzozowski, Stanisław, 49–50, 54, 281
Bund, 44–46, 298n16

camps, displaced persons (DP), 183
camps, France, 103–5, 116, 118, 136, 138, 180, 182–84; Argelès-sur-Mer, 104, 125, 131; Chalon-sur-Saône, 145; children in, 116, 138, 145; conditions, 104; Drancy, 145–46, 190–91; in Épernay, 183; Nexon, 145–46, 151, 284; Rieucros, 116, 311n25; Saint-Paul-d'Eyjeaux, 146; women in, 114, 116, 136. *See also* Gurs; Le Vernet
camps, Nazi, 132, 162, 171; Dachau, 132; Jawischowitz, 192; Majdanek, 199; Ravensbrück, 141; Treblinka, 12, 199. *See also* Auschwitz; Birkenau
camps, Switzerland, 158–60, 162–63, 172–76, 182, 188; antisemitism in, 159, 168–69; in Charmilles, 159–61; children in, 158–61, 163, 167–69; conditions, 159–60, 168–69; Hôtel Beau-Séjour, 159–61, 179; Les Hirondelles, 159–60, 162, 319n48; rules, 160–62, 172, 174; in Sonnenberg Kriens, 172; Varembé Stadium, 159–60; women in, 158–59, 167, 174. *See also* Les Avants
Catholic Rural Organization (Jeunesse agricole catholique), 154
Central Commission of Party Control (Centralna Komisja Kontroli Partii), 220, 228
Central Intelligence Agency (CIA), 221, 223
Central Women's Prison for the Middle East, Bethlehem, 64
Charmilles, 159–61
Chęciński, Michał, 239–40, 249
Children's Aid Society. *See* OSE
Clauberg, Carl, 194
Comintern, 48, 85, 91, 94, 122, 313n62
Comité d'assistance aux réfugiés (Refugee Assistance Committee), 96

Comité international d'aide au people Espagnole. *See* International Committee for Aid to the Spanish People
Committee for Aid for the Former German and Austrian Spanish Fighters (Hilfskomitee für ehemalige deutsche und österreichische Spanienkämpfer), 118
communism: and antisemitism, 213; and concept of marriage, 65, 281, 340n15; doubts about, 2, 12, 43, 54, 242, 269–70, 284–85; illegality of, interwar Poland, 45–46, 53; initiation into, 44, 46–50; and Jewishness, 169, 188, 218, 282; and Jews, 44–46, 244, 282–83; and motherhood, 6, 88, 108, 189–90, 246, 272, 275, 280; and Polishness, 49, 188; reasons for engagement in, 12, 44–45; and social justice, 46–47, 50, 188, 270; and Stalinism, 94, 122; and youth, 45–49
Communist Manifesto, 49
Communist Party of Poland, 220, 237, 245–46, 252; Jews in, 182–83, 341n20; and 1956 events, 241, 243–44; and 1968 events, 262, 264. *See also* KPP; Polish United Workers Party; Polish Workers' Party
Communist Party of the Soviet Union, 45, 220, 223
Communist Party of the United States of America (CPUSA), 180, 220
communists, Austrian, 83, 90, 92, 140–41, 179, 194, 326n31. *See also* Austrian Communist Party
communists, German, 90, 93, 122; support from, 75, 77, 83, 89; tensions with Polish communists, 90–91. *See also* German Communist Party

communists, Polish, 124–25; suspicions of, 120–21, 124–25, 279; in Switzerland, 179, 182, 323n114; tensions with German communists, 90–91; and Unitarian Service Committee, 178; women, 124. *See also* Communist Party of Poland; KPP; PZPR
Communist Union of Polish Youth (Komunistyczny Związek Młodzieży Polskiej, KZMP), 48–49, 52
Cyrankiewicz, Józef, 194–95
Czaplicka, Henryka (Henia Lechtman), 13, 269, 272–74
Czaplicki, Józef, 269
Czechoslovak Communist Party, 225

Daladier, Édouard, 97
Dannecker, Theodor, 146
death march, 190, 197
Democratic Alliance of Poles in Switzerland (Zjednoczenie Demokratyczne Polaków w Szwajcarii, ZDPS), 179, 182
Department for the Care of Mothers and Children (Dział Opieki nad Matką i Dzieckiem), 214
deportation, 163, 183, 185, 208, 323n130; to Auschwitz, 145, 147, 154, 194; Jewish, 142, 145–47; mass, 162–63; from Palestine, 61, 65, 67–69, 105–6, 117, 202, 302n81; to Poland, 145, 151, 177; from Vichy France, 116, 145–47
Dering, Władysław, 193–94
Diamant, Halina, 217–18, 220, 230, 236
Domaniecki, Józef, 195
Douvaine, 154–55
Dowgiałło, Dorota, 13, 32, 269
Drancy, 145–46, 190–91
Dulles, Allen, 221, 223–24
Duracz, Anna, 220, 249

Dusza, Józef, 248–49, 255
Dział Opieki nad Matką i Dzieckiem (Department for the Care of Mothers and Children), 214

Eichmann, Adolf, 145–46
Eitington family, 57
embassy, Polish, 126, 183, 186, 189, 204
Ernst, Mela, 136, 140–41

fascism, 3, 68, 76, 103, 122, 198, 200, 266; rise of, 56, 60, 307n116; and the Spanish Civil War, 84, 86, 88, 91–92
FDJ (Freie Deutsche Jugend, Free German Youth), 83, 88–89, 91, 96, 101, 112–13
Fejgin, Anatol, 239, 249–50, 335n51
Fejkiel, Władysław, 192–93
Field, Herman, 224, 332n170
Field, Herta, 180, 204, 206, 222, 224, 250–51, 256–57
Field, Noel, 179–80, 182–83, 186, 188, 204, 222–23, 225, 249, 331n158, 331n161; arrest, 219, 224; death, 258; and Dulles, Allen, 221, 223–24; Field affair, 222–25; and Rajk, László, 221, 225, 250; release from prison, 250; as suspected spy, 220–22, 224, 226, 228, 235; and Tonia, 180–81, 186, 206, 220–22, 224–26, 228, 250–51, 256–58; trial, 225; and Unitarian Service Committee, 179–81, 204, 220, 223, 255
fifth column, 122, 259
France: antisemitism in, 77, 96, 130, 135–36, 142, 145; escape from, 1, 18, 150–55, 157–58, 160, 166, 177, 219, 222–23; expulsion from, 106–7, 111; illegal immigrants in, 16, 75, 76–79, 98, 106–7, 113, 305n48; immigrants in,

76, 89, 99, 102, 106, 117; immigration to, 1, 18, 67–68, 75–77, 87, 99, 105, 147; Nazi occupation of, 118, 129–30, 147, 223; Poles' postwar population in, 184; policies, refugee, 76, 97–99, 157; refugees in, 76, 83, 96–98, 104, 118, 125; resistance in, 112, 147; support in, 75, 77, 82–83, 101–2, 113, 147; support in escaping from, 152–55, 157. *See also* camps, France; Oloron; Paris; Vichy France
Franco, Francisco, 84, 94, 113
Free German Youth (Freie Deutsche Jugend, FDJ). *See* FDJ
French Communist Party, 123, 189
French Revolution, 117–18
Frenkel, Françoise, 150, 319n30
Friemel, Rudolf (Rudl), 194, 326n31

Geduldig, Jonas, 118
Geneva, 154–55, 158, 161–62, 179, 181–82; and Field, Noel, 179, 222–23; League of Nations in, 180, 222; and refugees, Jewish, 158, 162
German-Austrian Communist Party, 90
German Communist Party, 152, 306n102
Glaser, Erica, 180
Glauster, Nani, 144–45, 149, 166, 175, 336n62
Goetschel, Gustave, 139
Goldman, Emma, 281, 340n15
Gomułka, Władysław, 215, 219, 225, 227, 241, 243, 248, 259–60, 335n36
Górecka, Małgorzata, 244
government-in-exile, Poland, 183–84, 215
Great Depression, 28, 56
Grudzińska Gross, Irena, 275
Grünwald, Hanna Eisfelder, 138–40, 142, 151, 166–67
Grünwald, Marcus, 139–40

Gurs, 105, 112, 127, 130–31, 136, 140; children in, 125, 127; conditions, 105, 119; internees, 105, 114, 120, 125; number of prisoners, 105; Sioma in, 105, 112, 115–16, 120, 122, 124–25, 130, 135; structure, 105; visitors in, 112, 115, 120, 127, 135–36; women in, 125
Guttman, Auguste, 114

Haller, Józef, 28, 124
Hallerczycy (Blue Army), 28, 124
Hamburger, Klara, 114
HaNoar HaTzioni (Zionist Youth), 61
Haor, 61, 301n76
Hashomer Hatzair, 62
Hasidism, 29–31, 293n50, 293n61
Help to the Emigrants (Aide aux émigrés), 162, 164, 319n33
Hilfskomitee für ehemalige deutsche und österreichische Spanienkämpfer (Committee for Aid for the Former German and Austrian Spanish Fighters), 118
Hiss, Alger, 223
Hitler, Adolf, 56, 83–84, 97, 102, 116, 142, 199, 201, 264
Hohermuth, Bertha, 162, 164, 167
Holocaust, 1, 3, 6, 8–9, 15, 156, 158, 199, 287n3
Home Army, 215, 225
Hôtel Beau-Séjour, 159–61, 179
Hungary, 181, 224–25, 241–42, 250

immigrants: in France, 76, 89, 99, 102, 106, 117; illegal, in France, 16, 75–81, 85, 98–99, 107, 113, 124, 305n48; in Łódź, 22; in Palestine, 56, 59, 62; political, 97; in Switzerland, 178, 266
immigration, 262–63; to France, 1, 18, 67–68, 75–77, 87, 99, 105, 147;

immigration (*cont.*)
  to Israel, 243–45, 248, 259, 266–68, 334n33; and Mexico, 135, 205, 315n98; to Palestine, 18, 33, 36, 53–57, 62, 163; and Poland, post-1956 events, 243–45, 334n33; and Poland, post-1968 events, 259, 262–63, 267; policies, Britain, 56; policies, France, 76; policies, Poland, 56, 243, 262, 266; policies, Switzerland, 155, 319n33; to the United States, 102, 140, 174, 180, 245
imprisonment of Tonia: France, 3, 142, 189; Palestine, 3, 64–65, 68, 283; Poland, interwar, 52–53, 283
imprisonment of Tonia, postwar, 219, 225, 229, 235, 239–40, 255–56, 266, 270–71, 284–85; cell spies, 225–28; effects of the, 240, 284–85; and Field affair, 221; interrogations, 219–21, 226–27, 235, 240–41, 249, 269, 273; reasons for, 219, 221–22, 226; release, 18, 39, 228, 233, 235–37, 239–42, 285; as suspected spy, 220–21, 228; trials of interrogators, 140, 248–50
Initiative Group, 125–26
Institute of Domestic Affairs (Instytut Gospodarstwa Domowego), 254
International Brigades, 85, 120–22, 180, 221–22, 284; and communism, 94–95; Eleventh International Brigade, 92, 103; Sioma in, 92–94, 107, 181, 249; structure, 92, 94; Thälmann Battalion, 92–93, 306n102; Thirteenth International Brigade, 125; veterans, 104, 125–26, 309n166; volunteers, 85, 91–95, 225, 230, 307n104; volunteers, internment of former, 103–5, 112, 116, 131–32, 144, 309n164; volunteers, Jewish, 91, 93, 118; volunteers, withdrawal of foreign, 103; and women, 85, 114

International Committee for Aid to the Spanish People, 85, 101–2, 112, 118, 136, 140
International Exposition of Art and Technology in Modern Life, 76, 304n26
International Festival of Youth, 252, 335n61
International Organization of Help to the Revolutionaries (Międzynarodowa Organizacja Pomocy Rewolucjonistom, MOPR), 48, 298n21
Israel, 247, 267, 269, 271, 276; family in, 252, 258, 260, 265, 267, 332n193; immigration to, 230, 242–45, 247, 259, 263, 266; life in, 39, 59, 267–69, 271; and Poland, 1968 events, 259–61; and Six-Day War, 258–59
Itschnach, 149, 169–74, 177, 179, 185, 201

Jablonka, Ivan, 9–10, 53, 77
Jaffa, 55, 61, 63–64, 68
Janka, Walter, 122
JDC (American Joint Distribution Committee), 24, 157, 213
Jędrychowski, Stefan, 182, 184, 323n130
Jeunesse agricole catholique (Catholic Rural Organization), 154
Jewishness, 6, 27, 126, 135, 143, 160, 188, 201, 247, 284; and communism, 169, 188, 218, 282; and Polishness, 5, 188, 278–80
Jews, Polish, 2, 22, 36, 51, 66, 74, 183, 247, 263, 278, 281; immigration of, 56, 319n33; and Poles, ethnic, 4
Jones, Dorothea (Jonesy), 186, 209–10, 214, 216, 221–22, 229, 263–65, 268, 271; and Unitarian Service Committee, 186, 208, 214, 255
Judeo-Bolshevism, 282, 340n18

Jussy, 151, 155, 158–59

Kaderkomissar, 94
Kahn, Ruth (Carmen), 94
Kalna, Sonia, 114
Kameradschaft, 83, 89
Kamińska, Maria, 51–52, 299n34
Kanner, Jadwiga. *See* Toruńczyk, Wiesława (Wiesia)
Kaśkiewicz (interrogator), 239, 249
Khrushchev, Nikita, 241
Kieras, Jan, 249
Kingdom of Poland, 22–23, 27
Klarsfeld, Serge, 147
Koestler, Arthur, 123, 131–33, 225–27
Kollontai, Alexandra, 281
Komar, Krysia, 218
Komar, Wacław, 218, 220
Komunistyczna Partia Polski. *See* KPP
Komunistyczny Związek Młodzieży Polskiej (Communist Union of Polish Youth, KZMP), 48–49, 52
Komunistyczny Związek Młodzieży Szkolnej (Union of Communist School Youth), 48–49
Kościuszko (ship), 55
Kosiakiewicz, Wincenty, 25
KPP (Communist Party of Poland), 48–49, 91, 179; dissolution, 121, 125–26, 312n45, 313n62; members, 46, 124, 297n8, 298n15, 312n48
Krajowa Rada Narodowa (State National Council), 179
Krynica, 235, 237
Krywicki, Walter, 223
Kühnen, Elisabeth, 114
Küsnacht, 171–72
KZMP (Komunistyczny Związek Młodzieży Polskiej, Communist Union of Polish Youth), 48–49, 52

Lambert, Raymond-Raoul, 96, 308n125
Langbein, Hermann, 192, 194–95, 197–98
Lauterpacht, Hersch, 12
League of Human Rights (Ligue des droits de l'homme, LHR), 77
League of Nations, 102, 139, 180, 222–23, 304n37
Lechtman, Chava, 63, 66
Lechtman, Henia. *See* Czaplicka, Henryka
Lechtman, Israel, 62, 66, 74–75, 230
Lechtman, Lea, 63, 66
Lechtman, Luba, 63, 66
Lechtman, Marcel, 13, 15, 44, 70, 111, 127, 136, 160, 243, 334n27; arrest in Switzerland, 151, 155; birth, 109, 126–28, 135, 141, 173, 189, 313n63; in camps, Switzerland, 159–61; challenges, 210, 229–31, 236, 248, 256, 258, 262, 265, 274; in children's homes, 149, 165–67, 189, 215, 229–31, 236–37, 243; divorce, 262, 265; education, 215, 230–31, 236, 248, 256, 269; in France, 109, 128–29, 136, 144, 146; France, escape from, 152–55; and grandparents, 199, 201–2; immigration to Israel, 247, 262–63, 265, 269; in Israel, 265, 267; in Limoges, 138, 140, 144, 165; memory, struggles with, 7, 15, 43, 111, 149–50, 189–90, 217, 236, 272, 274; passage into Switzerland, 151, 158; in Poland, postwar, 189, 210, 216, 253, 258; relationship with Tonia, 43, 271–73, 275–77; relationship with Vera, 165–66, 273–74; reunion with Tonia, 170, 210, 215, 233, 235–37, 267, 274; separation from Tonia, 111, 140, 153, 159, 164–65, 174, 181–82, 209, 215, 231–33, 235, 263; separation from Vera, 230, 236;

Lechtman, Marcel (*cont.*)
and Sioma, 120, 127, 133, 141, 144, 198; in Sweden, 13, 149, 262, 269, 273; in Switzerland, 170–71, 174–77; and Tonia's arrest/imprisonment, 217–18, 221, 229–31, 236; and wife, first, 255–56, 258; and wife, second, 269, 272

Lechtman, Sioma, 1, 62–63, 67, 74, 120, 122, 125; activism, communist, 62, 64, 74, 95; birth, 62, 75, 78, 130, 191; death, 190, 197–98, 200–201, 229, 232, 248, 285; deportation from Palestine, 65, 68–69, 73; education, 62, 95; immigration to France, 1, 68, 73–74, 202; immigration to Palestine, 62–63; imprisonment, 62, 64–65, 68, 95, 195; marriage, 1, 64–67, 72, 75, 78; search for, 198, 201, 205, 285; separation from Tonia, 86–87, 105, 115, 120; statelessness, 65, 75, 78, 93, 98, 103, 191; visits with Tonia, 112, 115, 118–19, 127, 135–36, 141, 144, 284

Lechtman, Tonia (Tauba; née Bialer): abortion, 87–88; activism, communism, youth, 36, 44, 46–48; as Antonina, 240; childhood, 31–33, 39–42; death, 2, 54, 271; education, 35–36, 46, 50, 53, 204, 279, 295n78; influences, 50, 281; marriage, 1, 64–67, 72, 75, 78, 98; pregnancy with Marcel, 114–16, 119, 124, 127; pregnancy with Vera, 87–89, 91, 96, 98–99, 107

Lechtman, Vera, 13, 15, 19–20, 32, 43, 57, 70, 111, 242, 256, 271, 334n26; arrest in Switzerland, 151, 155; birth, 89, 99–101, 109, 127, 223; in camps, Switzerland, 159–61; children of, 256, 258, 260, 262, 265–67; in children's homes, 149, 165–67, 215, 229–31, 235–36; education, 210, 215, 256, 267; in France, 101, 104, 106, 109, 112, 115–20, 128–29, 136, 144–46; France, escape from, 152–55; and grandparents, 199, 201–2, 229–31, 332n193; immigration, to Israel, 247, 262–63, 266–67; in Israel, 13, 242, 267, 269, 271; in Limoges, 138, 140, 144, 165; marriage, 256; memory, 7, 111, 149, 189, 217, 255, 271–72, 274; 1968 investigation of, 259–62; passage into Switzerland, 151, 158; in Poland, postwar, 216, 231, 253, 258; relationship with Marcel, 165–66, 273–74; relationship with Tonia, 43, 236, 253, 273, 276; reunion with Tonia, 170, 210, 215, 233, 235–37, 267; separation from Marcel, 230, 236, 273–74; separation from Tonia, 111, 140, 153, 159, 164–65, 174, 181–82, 209, 215, 231–33, 235; and Sioma, 112, 120, 176; in Switzerland, 149, 170–71, 174–77; and Tonia's arrest/imprisonment, 217–18, 221, 229–31, 236, 240, 255, 332n193

Legocka, Izabella (Iza), 255–56, 258, 262–63, 265, 267, 272

Lenin, 65, 95, 281

Leński (Julian Leszczyński), 121, 312n48

Les Avants, 159, 167–70, 173, 179

Les Hirondelles, 159–60, 162, 319n48

Lesman, Dora (Wacka), 299n27

Le Vernet, 130–31, 144; background, 131; conditions, 131–35; prisoners, 133, 135; resistance in, 141; Sioma in, 11, 130, 132–33, 135–36, 143, 145; structure, 131–32

Lévy, Gatson, 139–40

L'Humanité, 82, 123

Lichtheim, Richard, 162–63, 169

Ligęza, Bogusław, 256, 260–61, 266–67

Ligęza, Piotr, 262, 266–67

Ligue des droits de l'homme (League of Human Rights, LHR), 77
Limoges (city), 141–44, 152, 166
Limoges (nursery), 138–41, 144, 149, 152–53, 165, 171, 316n121; and Grünwald, Hanna Eisfelder, 138–39, 151; and OSE, 138–40, 316n121; and Tonia in, 140, 143, 149, 152
Lis, Jan, 179, 181
Locher, Margaret (Marguarite, Marga), 151, 166–67, 177, 181–82, 184–85, 201, 265–66, 336n70; assistance by, 152, 155, 162, 166, 169–70, 172–73, 175, 321n81; care of children by, 140, 149, 170–71, 173–77, 206; and Grünwald, Hanna Eisfelder, 139, 151, 166; tensions with Tonia, 175–76, 178
Łódź, 1, 20, 23, 35, 53, 128, 212; activism, communist youth, 48, 53; antisemitism in, 24, 27–28; Bialer family in, 22–26, 28–29, 177, 199, 244, 272; Bialer house in, 31, 208, 212, 271; economic hardships in, 28–29, 56–57; ghetto, 196, 244; growth, 22–23; industrialization, 22–24, 28; *Lodzermensch*, 25–26; migration to, 22–23; pogrom, 27–28, 292n43; population, 22; population, Jewish, 22–23, 290n14; poverty, 24, 51–52; *Promised Land*, 24; worker protests, 24, 48–49, 52, 291n25
Lodzermensch, 25–26
Lorska, Dora, 125
Łozińska, Eugenia, 189
Łoziński, Marcel, 43, 123, 189, 255, 271–75, 324n4; *Tonia i jej dzieci*, 43, 70, 123, 189, 236, 271, 273–75
Ludke, Trudi, 141
Luxemburg, Rosa, 2, 281, 291n25

Majdanek, 199
Maringer, Georges, 173–74
Maringer, Irene, 172–74
Maringer, Simon, 171–74, 176
Marum, Hans, 96–100, 109, 222
Marum, Ludwig, 97
Marum, Sophie, 96–97, 99, 109, 223, 308n128
Marxism, 64–65, 90, 215, 224, 281
Massing, Hede, 223–24
Masurians, 261–62
Mazur, Franciszek, 239
MBP (Ministerstwo Bezpieczeństwa Publicznego, Ministry of Public Security), 214, 217, 219–20, 240, 248, 269, 282, 340n20; disbandment, 241
Medical Assistance for Children of Refugees (Assistance médicale aux enfants de réfugiés), 139, 167
Mendelsohn, Daniel, 8–10
Mendiondou, Jean, 113–14
Międzynarodowa Organizacja Pomocy Rewolucjonistom (International Organization of Help to the Revolutionaries, MOPR), 48, 298n21
Ministerstwo Bezpieczeństwa Publicznego. *See* MBP
Ministerstwo Pracy i Opieki Społecznej (Ministry of Work and Social Care), 214
Ministry of Industry and Trade (Ministerstwo Przemysłu i Handlu), 214, 216, 237
Ministry of Internal Affairs, 55, 241, 282
Ministry of Public Security. *See* MBP
Ministry of Work and Social Care (Ministerstwo Pracy i Opieki Społecznej), 214
Montauban, 136–37, 140–41, 179

MOPR (Międzynarodowa Organizacja Pomocy Rewolucjonistom, International Organization of Help to the Revolutionaries), 48, 298n21
Moździerz, Teresa, 231
Mrągowa, 256, 258, 260–61
Munich Agreement, 102
Mussolini, Benito, 60, 84

Nansen passport, 78, 304n37
National Democracy, 194
Nazi Germany, 97, 102, 123; refugees from, 76, 79, 83, 86, 89. *See also* camps, Nazi
Nazis, 145–47, 162, 190, 194; anti-Nazi propaganda/resistance, 90, 118, 215; and France, 18, 118, 129–30, 145, 314n80
Negrín, Juan, 102–3
Nexon, 145–46, 151, 284
Non-Party Bloc for Cooperation with the Government (Bezpartyjny Blok Współpracy z Rządem, BBWR), 51
Nowicki, Jerzy, 214

Oeuvre de secours aux enfants. *See* OSE
Office of Strategic Services (OSS), 223–24
Oloron, 112–13, 117, 119–20, 135, 313n63; assistance in, 116, 118, 128, 135; escape from, 136–37; refugees in, 114; restrictions, 115–16; women in, 114–15, 120
OSE (Oeuvre de secours aux enfants, Children's Aid Society), 138, 147, 157, 167, 180; and Limoges (nursery), 138–40, 144, 316n121
OSS (Office of Strategic Services), 223–24

Palestine, 35, 120, 200, 249; Arab-Jewish conflict, 56, 61–62; businesses of Bialer family in, 54, 57–60, 72, 82, 274; communism in, 1, 18, 61, 64, 68; deportation from, 61, 65, 67–69, 105–6, 117, 202, 302n81; immigration to, 18, 33, 36, 53–57, 62, 163; life in, 35, 58–60, 66, 74, 89; policy, British, 56, 61–62; route to/from, 55, 62–63, 67, 73, 75, 202; volunteers, Spanish Civil War, from, 86, 89, 91
Palestine Royal Commission, 61
Palestinian Communist Party, 61–62, 68
Państwowa Komisja Planowania Gospodarczego (State Commission for Economic Planning, PKPG), 237
Paris, 118, 126, 138–39, 167, 202, 236, 239; activism, communist, 89–91, 101, 178, 184; arrival in, 73–75, 77, 83; departure from, 86–87, 92, 111–12, 137; illegal status in, 75, 77–80, 85, 97–98, 105–6, 113, 119; immigrants in, 76, 89, 106, 125; and International Brigades, 85, 91; Jews in, 113, 310n10; life in, 74–75, 77, 79–82, 86–87, 89, 96–97, 107, 109, 113, 158; network, communist, 83, 89–90, 107; Paris Police Prefecture, 78, 106, 111; policies, refugee, 75–76; return to, 114–16, 119–20, 183, 185, 189; support in, 82–83, 101–2, 113; support in, from German communists, 75, 77, 83, 87–89, 91, 93, 97–99, 115; work in, 80–83, 87, 89, 96, 99, 101–2, 106
Pau, 107, 109, 112, 126, 128, 313n63
Personalbogen, 191
Pétain, Philippe, 130
Petrowskaja, Katja, 10
Pilecki, Witold, 194
Piłsudski, Józef, 51, 299n38, 324n148
Piotrkowska Street, 31–32, 39, 58, 212
Piwińska, Ewa, 225–26, 255, 268
Piwko, Józef, 196

PKPG (Państwowa Komisja Planowania Gospodarczego, State Commission for Economic Planning), 237
Płomienie (Flames), 49–50, 54
Podgórska, Wanda, 227–28, 234
pogroms, 27–28, 62, 124, 138, 213, 263, 292n40
Poland, interwar, 27; activism, Jewish youth, 45; antisemitism, 27, 39, 56, 77; assimilation, 36–37; communism, illegality of, 45–46, 53; deportations to, 65, 68, 183; education, 35–36; emigration from, 54–56. *See also* Łódź
Poland, 1956 events, 241, 250; antisemitism, 242–44; immigration, Jewish, 243–45, 247–48, 334n33
Poland, 1968 events, 247, 259–60, 264–66; antisemitism, rise of, 247, 259, 261, 263, 269; and Gomułka, Władysław, 259; immigration, Jewish, 259, 262–63, 266–67; investigation, Lechtman, Vera, 260–62
Poland, postwar: antisemitism, 186, 201, 213, 279; communism, 1, 183–84, 213, 233; communists, Jewish leaders, 282, 340n20; election, 213; government-in-exile, 183–84; property restitution, 212; purges, 222–25; rebuilding, 126, 185–86, 200–201, 234, 279; return to, 1, 126, 186, 200–202, 206, 212, 233, 246, 265, 323n130; and Unitarian Service Committee, 181–84, 186, 214, 283
Poland of Today, 214
Poles, ethnic, 4–5, 297n9, 340n20
Poles, non-Jewish, 5, 24, 27, 208, 279; and Bialer family, 33; separation from Jews, 33, 39, 339n5; tensions with Jews, 28, 39
Polishness, 2, 116, 265–66, 279; and communism, 49, 188; and Jewishness, 5, 188, 278–80

Polish Socialist Party, 194
Polish Transatlantic Ship Society (Polskie Transatlantyckie Towarzystwo Okrętowe), 55
Polish United Workers Party (Polska Zjednoczona Partia Robotnicza, PZPR), 215. *See also* Communist Party of Poland
Polish Workers' Party, 189
Politkomissar, 94, 122
Polonia (ship), 55
Polska Ludowa (People's Poland), 179, 322n112
Polska Zjednoczona Partia Robotnicza (Polish United Workers Party, PZPR), 215. *See also* Communist Party of Poland
Popular Front, 95, 307n116
Poznański, Izrael, 28
Poznański, Maurycy, 28
Pregassona, 166, 170, 321n81
Przewański, Roman, 179, 181
Puławski (ship), 55
purges, 122; Great Purge of 1937, 312n48; Poland, 1968 events, 260; postwar, 222–25
PZPR (Polska Zjednoczona Partia Robotnicza, Polish United Workers Party), 215. *See also* Communist Party of Poland

Qui Pro Quo theater, 59, 301n71

Radio Free Europe, 240, 245
Rajf-Ligęza, Anna (née Ligęza), 14, 21, 30, 256, 258–60, 262, 265–69, 277
Rajk, László, 221, 225, 250
Rakowiecka Prison, 231
Red Army, 94, 197–98, 208, 224
Red Cross, 130, 161, 164, 180, 208; Polish, 183–84

Red Help (Czerwona Pomoc), 48, 77, 223. *See also* Secours Populaire
Refugee Assistance Committee (Comité d'assistance aux réfugiés), 96
refugees, 6, 105, 131, 164, 172–73, 178, 188, 284; children, 139–40, 145, 156–57, 163, 165, 167, 170, 173; crisis, 98, 156, 183, 304n37; in France, 18, 76, 78, 83, 96–98, 104, 107, 113–14, 118, 135, 138, 145; German, 76, 78–79, 83, 97, 165; illegal, 76, 156; Jewish, 18, 76, 96, 98, 118, 154, 156, 158, 165, 319n33; Nansen passport, 78, 304n37; numbers of, 125, 158–59, 319n33, 321n70, 328n88; policies, France, 76, 97–99, 104; policies, Switzerland, 155–56, 160–61, 170, 172–73; Polish, 135, 179, 182, 319n33, 328n88; political, 75, 152, 156; Spanish, 104, 113–14, 125, 131, 181; in Switzerland, 151, 156–64, 170, 177, 180, 319n33, 321n70; and Unitarian Service Committee, 177, 180–82; women, 145, 158
Reiss, Ignacy, 223
Republican army, 92–93, 95, 103
Reymont, Władysław Stanisław, 24–26; *Promised Land*, 24–25
Richter, 229, 231
Romkowski, Roman, 248, 335n51
Rosay, Jean (abbot), 154–55
Rosenfeld, Betty, 114, 118
Rote Hilfe, 48. *See also* Red Help
Rothmund, Heinrich, 156
Różański, Józef (Jacek), 239–40, 244, 248, 250, 255, 335n51, 335n54

Saint-Léonard, 143–44, 146, 166
Salomon-Schwarz, Lilly, 151, 157
Sanacja, 186, 201, 324n148

Sands, Philippe, 10, 12, 275
Schwarz(e), Emile (Walter), 179
Schweizer Hilfswerk für emigrierte Kinder. *See* SHEK
Secours Populaire, 77
SHEK (Schweizer Hilfswerk für emigrierte Kinder, Swiss Relief Organization for Emigrant Children), 139, 163–65, 167, 170, 180, 320n56
Shumann, Horst, 194
Silberstein, Sala, 28
Silton, Lore, 167–68, 321n77
Six-Day War, 258–59, 264
six-year economic plan, 253–54
Social Insurance Institution (Zakład Ubezpieczeń Społecznych), 214
Sokołowska, Trudi, 231
Sokołowski, Janusz, 179, 231
Sonderkommando, 196–97
Soviet Union: communists during war, 244, 335n36; and International Brigades, 85; invasion of Poland, 123; and 1956 events, 241, 250; purges, 122, 222, 224–25
Spanish Civil War, 3, 132, 181; background, 84–85; Battle of the Ebro, 94; nurses in, 84–85; Republicans, 84–85, 92, 94, 122; Sioma in, 84, 117, 230, 245, 281; "Spanish wives," 88, 126; volunteers, 218–19, 225, 230, 326n31; women in, 85, 114, 125. *See also* International Brigades
Spanish Communist Party, 94–95
Spanish Republic, 4, 84, 91, 104
Stalin, Joseph, 94–95, 121–22, 312n48; death, 240; dissolution of KPP by, 91, 121; and Spanish Civil War, 84, 122–23
Stalinism, 3, 95, 214, 244–45, 247; denunciation of, 241, 243, 248; prisons

under, 241, 264, 270; terror, postwar Poland, 215, 218, 222
Stalińska, Sabina, 225
State Commission for Economic Planning (Państwowa Komisja Planowania Gospodarczego, PKPG), 237
statelessness, 4, 65, 78, 93, 98, 103, 145, 191
State National Council (Krajowa Rada Narodowa), 179
Statut de Juifs, 130, 142
Światło, Józef, 217, 240–41, 245, 250
Swiss Relief Organization for Emigrant Children. *See* SHEK
Switzerland: arrest in, 150–51; passage into, 149–52, 154–55, 157–58; policies, refugee, 155–56, 160–61, 170, 172–73; social work in, 177–78, 181–82; support in, 152–54, 162. *See also* camps, Switzerland; Itschnach
Szmulewski, Dawid, 196–97
Szot, Vera, 225

Tel Aviv, 13, 15, 263, 271, 274; arrival, 60, 64; communist activism in, 61, 301n76; death of Tonia in, 271; departure from, 67, 73; life in, 58–59, 67
Thälmann Battalion, 92–93, 306n102
Third Republic, French, 116, 135
Thonon-les-Bains, 152–53
Tito, Josip Broz, 224
Tonia. *See* Lechtman, Tonia (Tauba; née Bialer)
Tonia i jej dzieci, 43, 70, 123, 189, 236, 271, 273–75
Torunczyk, Henryk, 121, 124
Torunczyk, Jerzy, 124, 126–27
Torunczyk, Wiesława (Wiesia) (Jadwiga Kanner), 120–21, 123–27
Toulouse, 136–38

Towarzystwo Przyjaciół Dzieci (Association of Friends of Children, TPD), 215
Trachtman-Palchan, Leah, 64
trials: of interrogators, 240, 248–50; interwar, 53; and 1968 events, 264; postwar, 222; show, 225
Trotsky, Leon, 224
Trotskyism, 94, 121–22, 168
Trunk, Jechiel Jeszaja (Izajasz), 22, 26, 29–31
Twentieth Congress of the Communist Party, 241

Union of Communist School Youth (Komunistyczny Związek Młodzieży Szkolnej), 48–49
Union of School Youth (Związek Młodzieży Szkolnej), 48
Union of the Polish Patriots (Związek Patriotów Polskich, ZPP), 179
Unitarian Service Committee (USC), 179–86, 202, 214, 328n95; background, 180; and communism, 181, 184; and Field, Noel, 179–81, 186, 204, 220, 223, 255; and Jones, Dorothea, 186, 208; Kościuszko Hospital, 214; and Tonia, 179, 181–83, 186, 189, 204–6, 208–10, 255, 283
UNRRA (United Nations Relief and Rehabilitation Aid), 183, 185–86
Uris, Leon, 194
USC. *See* Unitarian Service Committee

Varembé Stadium, 159–60
Vichy France, 116, 129, 151, 157, 180; antisemitic policies of, 130, 135–36, 139, 143, 147; deportations, 145, 147, 191
Vienna, 1, 62–63, 83, 95
Volkart, Lili, 165–67

Warsaw, 116, 250, 258, 260, 266, 273–74; antisemitism in, 243; family, Bialer and Wegmeister, in, 21, 22, 29; family, Sioma's, in, 62–63; high culture in, 26, 35, 59–60, 301n71; population, Jewish, 22; postwar, 39, 126, 189, 208, 219, 252, 257; prisons, 219, 231; settlement in, postwar, 214–15, 237; and Unitarian Service Committee, 184, 186, 208
Wasilewska, Wanda, 179, 281
Wegmeister, Joel, 21–22
Wermelskirchen, 185, 202, 206, 208, 234
Wiszniewicz, Joanna, 37, 247
Wojdysławska, Irena, 48–49, 294n24
Wojdysławski, Yosef, 31
women: in camps, 116, 133, 136, 146, 158, 168, 174, 190–91, 196; communist, 5, 75, 79, 124, 226, 275, 281–83; domesticity, 209–10, 215–16, 239, 253–55, 279–80, 283; gender conceptions, 30, 50, 60, 79, 81; and marriage as concept, 281; in Orthodox families, 31, 293n59; Polish Jewish, 280, 283, 340n14; prisoners, 47, 64, 225–26, 255, 272, 283; role models, 50, 54, 167, 299n34; in SHEK, 163–64, 167; as social workers, 6, 139–40, 151, 167, 177, 181–82, 185, 267, 281; in Spanish Civil War, 85, 114, 125; "Spanish wives," 88, 126; as support network, 6–7, 124, 137–38, 167, 281; and traditions, Jewish, 21, 30
Woolf, Virginia, 4–5, 73

Workers Social Services' Correctional Vocational School for Girls, 139
World War I, 5, 20, 62, 131, 161, 284
World War II, 3, 109, 113, 162, 332n177; approach of, 102, 105–6, 115; declaration of war, 116, 119; end of, 126, 178, 181–82, 184, 199, 209; invasion of Poland, 116; outbreak of, 36, 58, 112, 139, 177

Yiddishism, 44, 295n86

Zakład Ubezpieczeń Społecznych (Social Insurance Institution), 214
Zakrzewska, Halina, 225, 255, 268
Zasulich, Vera, 281
ZDPS (Zjednoczenie Demokratyczne Polaków w Szwajcarii, Democratic Alliance of Poles in Switzerland), 179, 182
Zionism, 31, 35, 44–45, 56, 61–62, 68, 162, 253, 259–60, 267, 295n86
Zionist Organization in Jerusalem, 163
Zionist Youth (HaNoar HaTzioni), 61
Zjednoczenie Demokratyczne Polaków w Szwajcarii (Democratic Alliance of Poles in Switzerland, ZDPS), 179, 182
Zürich, 166–67, 171–73, 175, 177, 202, 206
Związek Młodzieży Szkolnej (Union of School Youth), 48
Związek Patriotów Polskich (Union of the Polish Patriots, ZPP), 179